Creative Documentary

Creative
Documentary
Theory and
Practice

Wilma de Jong

Erik Knudsen

Jerry Rothwell

Source: New Orleans star of 'Age of stupid', Al Duvernay, riding his motorbike with
Director Franny Armstrong filming. Copyright Spanner Films/Chris Graythen

Routledge
Taylor & Francis Group

LONDON AND NEW YORK

First published 2012 by Pearson Education Limited

Published 2013 by Routledge
2 Park Square, Milton Park, Abingdon, Oxon OX14 4RN
711 Third Avenue, New York, NY 10017, USA

Routledge is an imprint of the Taylor & Francis Group, an informa business

ISBN: 978-1-4058-7422-9 (pbk)

British Library Cataloguing in Publication Data
A CIP catalogue record for this book can be obtained from the British Library

Library of Congress Cataloging in Publication Data
A CIP catalog record for this book can be obtained from the Library of Congress

Set in 9/12pt Giovanni Book by 35

Contents

CONTENTS

About the authors

Wilma de Jong

Wilma is a part-time lecturer at the University of Sussex and an award-winning film producer/filmmaker. She teaches Documentary Theory and Practice on the MA Digital Documentary course and on subjects related to media and politics. She owned an independent film company for 14 years, and produced and directed films for broadcasters, NGOs and corporate industry. In 2008 she co-edited with Dr Thomas Austin *Rethinking Documentary: New Perspectives, New Practices* (Open University Press), and was recently involved in the Interactive Documentary Project *Against the Tide* (www.tide.org.uk). Her research for this book has been made possible by an AHRC grant.

Erik Knudsen

Erik is a filmmaker and Professor of Film Practice at the University of Salford, Manchester, UK. Currently the Head of the School of Media, Music and Performance, earlier roles have included programme-leading the MA in Fiction Film Production, the MA in Television Documentary Production and the MA in Wildlife Documentary Production. He is also visiting professor, and the former Head of the Editing Department, at the Escuela Internacional de Cine y Televisión in Cuba. Among a number of broader academic duties, he is an Arts and Humanities Research Council Peer Review College member and sits on the editorial board of the *Journal of Media Practice*. He also runs his own film production company, One Day Films Limited, and his films include: *Heart of Gold* (40 minutes, documentary, 2006), *Sea of Madness* (86 minutes, fiction, 2006), *Brannigan's March* (99 minutes, fiction, 2004), *Bed of Flowers* (50 minutes, documentary, 2001), *Signs of Life* (70 minutes, fiction, 1999), *Reunion* (50 minutes, documentary, 1995) and *One Day Tafo* (70 minutes, documentary, 1991). His recent work includes *Veil* (for Horse and Bamboo Theatre Company's touring show, 2008), *Vanilla Chip* (17 minutes, documentary, 2009) and his latest feature film, *The Silent Accomplice* (84 minutes, fiction, 2010).

Jerry Rothwell

Jerry is a documentary filmmaker whose work includes the feature documentaries *Heavy Load* (IFC/ITVS/BBC), about a group of people with learning disabilities who form a punk band, *Donor Unknown* (More 4/Arte/VPRO) about a sperm donor and his offspring, and *Deep Water* (Pathe/FilmFour/UK Film Council co-directed with Louise Osmond), about Donald Crowhurst's ill-fated voyage in the 1968 round-the-world yacht race. Another strand of Jerry's work has been participatory and community filmmaking, working with people to tell their own stories on film. He played a lead role in developing Hi8us Projects' improvised dramas with young people for Channel 4, in establishing First Light, the UK Film Council's scheme for young filmmakers, and in setting up digital storytelling exchanges between marginalised communities across Europe. He also teaches documentary at the Met Film School. He is currently working on *Town of Runners*, a documentary about young athletes in Ethiopia.

Toby Haggith

Toby is a historian and works in the Film and Video Archive of the Imperial War Museum, where he is in charge of non-commercial access and devises the cinema programme. He has a PhD in Social History from the University of Warwick and has written essays on various aspects of history and film. He is, with Joanna Newman, the co-editor of *Holocaust and the Moving Image: representations in film and television since 1933* (Wallflower Press, 2005). He also conceived and is the organiser for the Museum's annual Film Festival for student and amateur filmmakers (now in its tenth year) and the associated Student Documentary Master Class.

Mary Agnes Krell

Mary is a digital artist and educator based in the UK. She is the Head of Media Practice and a Senior Lecturer at Sussex University, where she conducts practice-based research across film, performance and digital media. Mary's work in theatre and digital media has been widely exhibited and she has been creating interactive projects for the web, CD-ROM and installations in the UK and internationally since the early 1990s.

Jean Martin

Jean is Senior Lecturer in Digital Music and Sound Arts at the University of Brighton. He has studied in Zurich and Berlin and is a freelance composer and writer. He has created music for numerous TV documentaries broadcast on BBC 1 and 2, Channel 4 and Discovery. He moved to London in 1993, and during the 1990s also worked as a radio producer for German public radio, reporting on British contemporary art music; see www.soundbasis.net.

Acknowledgements

Authors' acknowledgements

To Tony and Romany and those I have ever worked with in the last 25 years. You documentary filmmakers are a passionate, intelligent and creative bunch and our world would be different without your relentless ambition to highlight visible and invisible, but always complex social worlds. Keep on banging on those closed doors!

Wilma de Jong

To Janet, Tara, Noah and Rasmus, who have encouraged and inspired me all the way, and to my graduates and students, who have taught me filmmaking.

Erik Knudsen

To my family & to colleagues at Met FIlm, Hi8us and APT Films who, over many years, have shaped my ideas about what documentary is and enabled me to try to put those ideas into practice.

Jerry Rothwell

Publisher's acknowledgements

The publishers would like to thank the panel of academic reviewers, whose constructive comments have helped shape the development of this project throughout. We would also like to thank the authors for the dedication, skill and hard work they put into making this project a reality.

Introduction

Introduction

This book sets out to explore the field of documentary production and documentary theory in ways relevant to contemporary hybrid documentary filmmaking. In doing so, we draw on the body of knowledge and experience that has been built up by academics and documentary filmmakers over the last 100 years. We also strive to be different from other books about documentary production and to capture the ways in which documentary is currently being transformed, in its content, audience, production, financing and distribution.

Creative Documentary: Theory and Practice has been edited by three authors, each with different experiences and perspectives on the documentary form. Wilma de Jong teaches documentary theory and practice in higher education and, prior to this, owned her own independent production company for 14 years. Erik Knudsen is a filmmaker and teacher in higher education, working across fiction and documentary, who also runs his own company. Jerry Rothwell is a documentary director who has worked within television, interactive production and cinema, whose work also draws on his experience of participatory and community arts practices. Together, we try to build a portrait of the ways in which documentary is changing and propose approaches to filmmaking which combine both theory and practice. We hope that, by bringing together these different perspectives in a single book, we manage to capture the diverse, often fragmented and sometimes opposing practices that comprise contemporary documentary production.

The book is intended for students and filmmakers in the early stages of their careers. We intend to equip readers with the ideas, methods and information that will support critical documentary making, an approach that both understands the contemporary institutional, practical and financial contexts for documentary production, and which encourage innovation and originality.

This is not a book about production technology, about particular equipment or software. Digital technologies are developing so quickly that such information quickly loses its relevance. However, one of our core aims is to address the impact of digital technologies on the production process, on the documentary film text and on distribution.

Our era has been described as an 'age of narrative chaos'. The internet and digitisation have not only transformed film consumption patterns and production methods, but have also demanded new, non-linear and interactive storytelling techniques. In the age of YouTube and web streaming, many people's experience of documentary material is in the form of short clips, snapshots of events or opinions, and an audience's journey through a documentary text may no longer have a set chronological path. Documentary makers have also embraced these new platforms, so whilst we address classic realist narratives, we also explore emerging narrative forms.

Digitisation has also had an impact on more traditional documentary forms, for example on archival films, by making many archives more readily available and resulting in a resurgence of historical documentary that uses footage from the past.

The accessibility of digital technologies is also dissolving and reconfiguring the boundary between subject and filmmaker. Today's documentaries draw more frequently on self-shot material by subjects, perhaps also favouring personal and autobiographical films by those who are part of the events they are filming. Documentaries that deploy this more subjective approach can be seen as a challenge to the disembodied knowledge and facts that classic documentary discourse claimed to present. Instead, these films emphasise more uncertain, incomplete and complex, unstable patterns of knowledge in our world.

These developments may also explain the increased emphasis on the 'voice' of a documentary and the prevalence of strongly authored films. Documentary as a mediated representation of the 'real' always indicates a point of view on the world but in classic mainstream documentaries it has tended to be hidden or denied – particularly in observational and expository documentaries.

A common feature of many contemporary documentaries is that they are driven by an authorial 'voice' that illustrates and indicates a specific ideological position.

The total filmmaker

The focus of the book is the figure we describe as the 'total filmmaker': the filmmaker whose work embraces these new developments in production and distribution, who crosses traditional boundaries of role and ownership, who is likely to be centrally involved in conceiving, researching, producing, shooting, editing and distributing their film, who may in that process collaborate with other skilled professionals but whose engagement with all aspects of the production process is perhaps more all-encompassing than that of documentary makers in the broadcast past, working with larger budgets, crews and institutions.

The emergence of the total filmmaker could be ascribed to four broad trends in the current documentary environment:

1. The most significant past source of finance for making documentaries – broadcast television – can no longer support large budgets for one-off creative documentaries. This is, in part, a consequence of the huge investment in digital infrastructure, channel proliferation and decreasing advertising revenue for commercial broadcasters and a stabilised licence fee for the BBC, but changing audience patterns have also contributed, as has the shift in marketing and scheduling approaches to reaching those audiences. As we write, the economic downturn further exacerbates this trend. Documentary makers increasingly need to seek financial support from other sources, from online platforms, from trusts, foundations and campaigns, or from private (often their own) investment, in order to reduce production costs and find their audiences through different channels.

2. Advanced digital technologies support the total filmmaker by making the tools required for high-quality, high-definition production as available as the domestic computer. Digital camcorders, new sound-recording technologies and editing software make it ever more possible to shoot with reduced, or no, crew. This, in turn, opens up the potential for shooting in situations which are less accessible with a crew or with more elaborate equipment, perhaps also supporting more autobiographical filmmaking or shooting by those who are the subjects of documentary, for example, using home video footage.

3. The institutions which hitherto largely controlled documentary production and distribution channels – broadcasting companies and large independent production companies – are increasingly either turning away from documentary production altogether, or working with micro-companies and freelancers to make these films. There is a consequent shift in working practices, away from industrial production methods and towards multi-skilling, small, flexible teams and cheaper technologies.

4. Distribution platforms have proliferated – today's documentary makers are more likely to see their films watched on social media such as Facebook or YouTube, on internet platforms such as Hulu, Jaman or joiningthedocs, in non-theatrical screenings, and through video-on-demand or DVD than on broadcast television. The total filmmaker is far more likely to be actively engaged in promoting their film on these platforms and needs to have the skills and knowledge to do so.

Examples of the films and filmmakers that typify these new approaches are Franny Armstrong's *Age of Stupid*, Deborah Scranton's *The War Tapes, Rice N Peas, Bang! Bang! in da Manor* and the films of Daisy Asquith (*Fifteen, Kimberley*) and Luke Holland (*A Very British Village*).

Documentary: an umbrella category

Although production methods have changed, the total filmmaker inherits the century-old traditions of documentary filmmaking. Contemporary documentaries continue to provoke debate in the public domain and aspire to an informed citizenship, just as the filmmakers of the documentary film movement did in the 1930s. In the words of investigative filmmaker John Pilger, the documentary desire 'to tell people things they don't want to know' persists. Contemporary documentaries unearth hidden lives and reveal dark and hidden corners of our societies, whether abuse in the family (*Capturing the Friedmans*), the human exploitation of natural resources (*The Cove*), or corruption in Africa (*Darwin's Nightmare*). Highly personal films such as *Daughter's Rite* or *Tarnation* are autobiographical versions of this quest to find answers to, or explore, childhood traumas, or to raise ontological questions about mental health and family relationships in our society.

> Autobiographical films and videos bear witness to our lives in all their variation, and these lives are untidy and contradictory: we have passions, both creative ones and destructive ones; we betray each other and do surprisingly heroic things; we experience profound joy and almost crushing emotional pain; we are both cruel and compassionate. All these experiences and feelings fuel the autobiographical act. Because of this, the autobiographical film or video can break a silence and by doing so lessen the isolation and despair that we often experience, both personally and culturally.
>
> (Michelle Citron, director of *Daughter Rite*)

Documentary is increasingly an umbrella term for diverse formats, narrative forms and different distribution platforms, with one generic aim: to record and represent fragmented realities to their audiences. The ambition to reveal 'truth' or 'reality' has been rightfully challenged, but the aim to 'be truthful' and to reveal experiences ('realities') is central to the documentary ambition.

Defining 'creative documentary'

At the boundaries of this umbrella category – of what should or shouldn't be defined (at least for the purposes of this book) as a 'creative documentary' – are television's factual entertainment programmes, portraying everyday experiences of food, animals, houses and gardens, child rearing and personal relationships. Often presenter-led, factual entertainment is sometimes frowned upon by those who consider themselves 'purer' documentary filmmakers, but these programmes are important sources of knowledge and insight into both personal life and the wider historical world.

In some ways, factual entertainment has thrown off the shackles of the documentary past to create formats that are more accessible to mass audiences, using classic narrative structures and drawing on the aesthetics of intimacy pioneered by documentary makers (see Biressi and Nunn, 2004). Factual entertainment programmes might be cheaper to make but they can be appreciated for informing audiences in an entertaining and engaging way. Information-heavy expository documentaries have turned off many audiences and are still part of documentaries' dull reputation. It might be more useful to create a continuum of documentary filmmaking based on narrative structures, and their accessibility to a variety of audiences.

Classic realist narratives—————————complex narrative structures
Popular culture———————————————High (brow) culture

For the most part, however, this book focuses largely on the making of single films rather than formats or television series, and on films that start from an existing situation rather than a situation specifically constructed for the production.

Documentary ethics

As Roscoe and Hight argue, 'documentary holds a privileged position within society' as it promises to present the 'most accurate portrayal of the social-historical world' (2001: 6). As with, for example, anthropology, this relationship to the social-historical world and with its subjects creates a constant array of ethical dilemmas for the filmmaker. Incidents such as Channel 5 UK's film *The Connection*, in which the filmmaker was alleged to have faked sequences in the story of a Columbian 'mule' smuggling heroin into Britain, and the BBC editing of the trailer for their programme *A Year with the Queen* in which the chronological order of shots was reversed, changing their meaning, highlight these dilemmas for audiences and perhaps undermine documentary's privileged relationship to truth telling. Our view is that this relationship is one that documentary filmmakers should honour with passion, critical analysis and care.

But this is not to say that only those techniques which are seen to mimic our perceptions of reality – the handheld cameras, minimal editing, direct sound of cinéma vérité which signify the immediacy of the 'real' – are the only tools the documentary maker should use. Actor reconstruction, the use of music and the computer manipulation of images are widespread documentary techniques and key methods through which the medium of film can communicate meaning. Digitisation has provoked many debates about the indexical warranty of the documentary image and has placed the burden of truthfulness on the shoulders of the filmmaker, and specifically on the way ethics and values play a part in the relationship between the film text and the socio-historical world it describes.

Documentary films are tainted by, on the one hand, a claim to be truthful and, on the other hand, by the process of selecting and representing realities. The tension between these two aims defines the genre and at the same time opens up possibilities for creative and critical approaches. For Ohad Landesman, documentary filmmakers explore the space between 'story' and 'fact' (Landesman, 2008). A 'story' is a narrative device to link 'events' in the historical world. Stories give facts meaning.

Honour thine ancestors

In this book we will focus on documentary filmmaking as a hybrid form, using a variety of digital technologies. But we honour both the tradition of our documentary ancestors and the many forms they have created, as well the filmmakers who want to challenge those forms. Contemporary documentary filmmakers come in many shapes and may express very different intentions through their films.

Although the word *change* seems to dominate the modern world, much has stayed the same. In Britain, for example, many documentary filmmakers are still white and male; only 8 per cent of the nation's documentary filmmakers are female and most of these are white. Documentary filmmakers from minority backgrounds are slowly making inroads into the field but the 'industry' remains white and male-dominated. We hope that, with the availability of more documentary courses in both Higher Education and Further Education, and the availability of cheaper equipment, the dynamics of documentary production may change this demographic.

Learning 'to move in the world'

Teaching documentary filmmaking in the contemporary education system is dancing a tightrope. Acquiring knowledge – in particular, rational knowledge – seems to be still the main focus of our educational system. It includes setting targets, drawing up standards, regular written assessments and an emphasis on the 'rational' and the quantifiable. This discourse goes throughout our education system from primary to higher education. It raises the issue whether too narrow a formulation of educational aims undermines the intellectual, personal and emotional development of students. We are more than a collection of information and skills. Teaching filmmaking, in particular, requires an environment that nurtures experimentation and fosters discovery and inquiry. A documentary filmmaker really should 'learn to move in the world as if it were your lover' (Macy, 1991: 9).

Or, in Donna Haraway's words:

> Rather than privileging too narrow a range of texts through standardizing the curriculum, might it not be more beneficial for students to have multiple and different tools so that they can converse in the world as coding tricksters, and become actors themselves, agents in the mediation of their own knowledges and subjectivities?
>
> (1991: 201)

We have tried to incorporate both theory and practice and to describe the old and the new. We hope to expand the boundaries of thinking of students and aspiring documentary filmmakers and to support their tutors by providing interviews, bibliographies and exercises that might be beneficial to their teaching practice. We have included various teaching and learning methods and ideas, as well as ways of critically and creatively exploring documentary practices. Exercises, interviews with professionals and suggestions for further reading are intended to stimulate the development of self-directed and self-reflective students who can truly engage with the ambitions, historical framework and creative and critical aspects in the field of documentary production.

The book uses different styles of writing and different approaches to certain subjects, depending on the writer, but all authors have worked with the same chapter template so the role and function of the different chapters is coherent and can be used by students, documentary filmmakers and tutors alike.

Undoubtedly, we will disappoint some readers, including ourselves. Documentary is a huge and varied field, and we have had to exclude some of the breadth of areas it encompasses. We may have to agree with Woody Allen when he talks about his films:

> I write them, I produce them and I direct them and it is still only 60 percent of what I had in mind.

Part 1

The creative documentary

Still of dancer Seol-Ae Lee, as seen in KIMJONGILIA directed by
N.C. Heikin. Photo courtesy of Green Garnet Productions

Chapter 1

What is creativity?

Wilma de Jong

" Creativity depends on interactions between feeling and thinking and across different disciplines and fields of ideas. "

(K. Robinson, 2002: 20)

Introduction

This chapter will offer you different ways of thinking about the magical word 'creativity' and of examining the creative process. Like the concepts of 'freedom', 'free choice' or 'democracy', 'creativity' is a word that has an inspiring yet also an obscure quality. It is frequently used loosely, without a precise definition. The most common notion of creativity is in relation to the creation of art. Those who are creative are considered to have innate personal qualities which other people lack. Those few gifted, creative souls are different from the rest of us mortals.

The notion of creativity as an individual gift, possessed by few, is still very common. This 'gift' seems to express itself in the arts and in our dealing with the hurdles of simply living or, for instance, the sciences. At the moment, much of the literature on creativity incorporates activities such as problem-solving, new inventions or innovations relating to existing products and ideas or problems. Inventions or innovations often refer to a commercial, scientific or technical environment. For instance, the much-used description: the 'creative industries' links creativity to a commercial environment. Florida (2000: 5) states: 'Creativity . . . is now the decisive source of competitive advantage'. Where once quality or availability were a decisive source of advantage in competition, this has now been overtaken – according to Florida – by creativity.

Until recently, it was considered that creativity could flourish anywhere but in a commercial environment. Industry's demands would undermine 'real' creativity. But it could be argued that new media entrepreneurs and games developers, new technological inventions such as the iPod and iPhone, and the successes of 'creative' films in an industrial environment, have challenged this idea. Conversely, Hollywood blockbusters, reality TV and game shows may confirm that creativity in this context means 'creative ideas that attract big audiences', a creativity that could be described as a 'commercial' creativity. The term 'creativity' on its own seems almost meaningless when it is divorced from its environment or the cultural field to which it is applied.

Creativity: 'novel' and 'value'

Contemporary psychological research has taken 'creativity' away from the context of the gifted and talented few who create masterpieces. It is increasingly described as an innate human capacity which can be developed through education or creativity-enhancing environments. A continuum approach might be helpful to allow for exceptionally creative people and for people who show very few signs of creative ability. Creativity can be developed or stifled by teaching or social environments where conformism and the regurgitation of existing knowledge or vision are most appreciated.

The two following definitions might help you think about creativity creatively. 'Creativity is the ability to produce work that is both novel (i.e. original, unexpected) and appropriate (i.e. useful, adaptive concerning task constraints)' (Sternberg, 1999: 3). This definition is the result of about 30 years of research in psychology. A society needs creativity to solve its problems in social, economic and political terms. The 'creative leader' or 'creative management' are commonly used words in today's world. The word 'creative' is now used in a much wider context than just referring to the production of art.

Dewulf and Baillie define creativity as 'shared imagination' (1999: 5): 'Imagination' is novel. It is 'shared' with an audience: colleagues and other students or teachers who become part of it.'

The two most important aspects are *novel* and *value* or *purpose*. The latter aspect might not be familiar, or might even meet resistance among artists or filmmakers, but a documentary, or a piece of art are parts of certain fields of cultural production (Jenkins, 2002) in which certain traditions prevail and norms and values exist, against which these creative products are being judged. We all know the stories of artists whose work is acknowledged as original and novel only after they have died. Picasso's *Les Demoiselles d'Avignon* was only identified as original and maybe even revolutionary long after he had painted it. But the essence seems to be that a product tends not to be considered creative because an individual thinks it is creative. Creative products are part of a field of cultural production. They are not islands in themselves, neither are they produced in a vacuum.

Notwithstanding the importance of the social and cultural environment of a creative product, a work of art, a film or a music composition is at the same time also a product of an individual mind. It is an expression of individual creativity and therefore has an intrinsic value which is not influenced or changed by the field of cultural production. In this context, it is also important to realise that creative people tend to be driven by intrinsic motivation. This means that extrinsic motivators, such as money and recognition, are less important than their individual driving forces of wanting to create. This might also explain why creativity for such a long time has been considered a non-commercial activity.

In today's workplace, and certainly in media production, a team is also expected to be creative. Production teams engage in brainstorming, associative discussions or use other structured discussion techniques to generate new ideas, to improve existing ones or to find unusual combinations of ideas. Comedy series or soaps tend to be written by teams of writers who come up with the jokes or dialogues. In these situations there is no one 'source' of an idea; team members bounce ideas off each other and build up ideas brought in by other group members. The same is the case with documentary production in which a production team – even if it is just a director and an editor or a camera person – bounce ideas off each other.

Synergy between people and the courage to think what one *should not* think as well as a resistance to thinking what one *should* think will create possibilities to explore and imagine the novel. But it is important to realise that 'creativity' is neither a magic wand nor a gut feeling; one needs a certain level of knowledge and intelligence to create the novel. To know the old is certainly necessary to create the new.

Bourdieu defines a field of cultural production as:

'a series of institutions, rules, rituals, conventions, categories, designations, appointments and titles which constitute an objective hierarchy and which produce and authorise certain discourses and activities'.

(Jenkins, 2002: 21)

Aspects of creativity

It may not be possible to teach creativity, but it can be stimulated, nurtured and fostered

In order to help you to develop and be aware of your own creative abilities and not merely rely on divine inspiration, we have listed some aspects of creativity. At the end of this chapter you will find also some exercises with which to practise all kinds of aspects of creativity.

Research on creativity (Sternberg, 1999; Dewulf and Baillie, 1999) concludes that a combination of characteristics defines creative potential. The following aspects of creativity potential are described:

- **Good memory** – The ability to retain information, and to access that information when needed, is important because it will give you the possibility to use and evaluate information from varied sources and to recognise new patterns or unusual combinations.

- **Flexibility** – The ability and willingness to approach situations, concepts and problems from a variety of angles, and not to be hindered by your existing point of view, will open up more playful avenues.

- **Visualisation** – This is the ability to visualise a concept, idea or situation. In creating the visual image, knowledge, experience and images are needed. Filmmaking is visual story-telling, so a feeling for what images can mean and how you can change their meaning when you change the order is important.

- **Positive attitude** – We all know that when we are negative about our own abilities, we will not write the best essay, give the best presentation or come up with ideas for films. Negative attitudes will close off new avenues of thinking and imagining.

- **The environment and hierarchy** – Abra (1997) suggests that, in order to nurture creativity, a hothouse environment is needed: stimulation, reinforcement, persistence, recognition, respect. A creative culture appreciates and nurtures new ideas. Charles Leadbeater (see http://www.charlesleadbeater.net) discusses innovation within institutions and identifies a need for non-hierarchical places for people to meet and talk who would not normally do so, e.g. Nokia's single canteen for all employees. Unusual combinations of people might spark off new ideas.

- **Collaborative creativity/synergy** – The shift away from notions of creative individuals is accompanied by a great deal of interest in and funding for cross-disciplinary collaborations. These partnerships are thought to be good at producing creative and innovative results. The idea is that bringing different perspectives together is more likely to generate something new. Charles Saumarez Smith (formerly of the National Portrait Gallery and National Gallery, now Chief Executive of the Royal Academy of Arts) emphasises how much time and effort has to be invested in partnership activities. Partnerships are hard work; groups of practitioners often develop their own language and value systems. A certain level of translation and understanding of each other's creative world needs to take place.

The creative process – give inspiration a chance

After looking at creativity and its characteristics, we want to examine the creative process.

The term 'creativity' can be used to describe not only a product but also a process. The latter is important in education and media production because it allows us to identify different stages and their characteristics. This insight will help you to create the optimum conditions to come up with the best ideas. From the variety of approaches we can distil the following stages:

1. Preparation
2. Generation
3. Incubation
4. Verification

(Dewulf and Baillie, 1999: 17)

1. Preparation

A well-prepared job is a job already half done.

At this stage, the idea for a film is redefined and reformulated. It is the stage from 'I'm going to make a film about homelessness' to 'How do young people become homeless?' It can take the form of a question or it can be bold statements. Techniques include:

- Formulate the question in five different ways.
- Use de Bono's hat method to approach the issue or problem in different ways. You can find this method of analysis at the end of this chapter.

2. Generation

If you want to get a good idea, get lots of ideas.

(Linus Pauling, winner of two Nobel prizes)

The essence of this stage can be formulated as the 'collection of ideas and the postponement of judgment in the first instance'. Techniques include:

- **Brainstorming** – This technique leads to a list of ideas, or possibilities, or aspects of an idea. The next step is to arrange the list either in order of importance or as a structure with key themes and sub-themes.

- **Mind-mapping** – There are two ways to start a mind map.

  In the first method, you draw a tree and put the core idea in the trunk, subsequently creating branches which represent aspects of the core idea. If you come up with another core idea, just start another tree.

  Alternatively, you can draw a circle in the middle of a piece of paper and draw new circles for different aspects of your idea. Link related circles either by coloured pens or different arrows or lines.

  These two ways of analysing and interrogating your ideas are a quick method of obtaining a visual representation of all kinds of aspects of a concept of a film. Mind-mapping is a really efficient and easily executed method of working for documentary filmmakers.

- **Hitch-hiking; building on other people's ideas** – One person comes up with an idea; the next person adds another aspect of the idea or a new idea, and so on.

- **Free wheeling; associative thinking** – This is the stage at which you collect information and use it as a springboard into the imagined world of new ideas and approaches. For instance, start with single women or premature babies and just associate, and then associate with the associations. After 20 minutes, stop and see if you can make groups of ideas and identify one specific angle that would be inspiring and interesting and does not conform to existing stereotypes.

3. Incubation

The idea that people come up with ideas while putting out the rubbish or having a shower is not a fantasy or a myth. Research has demonstrated that time to let ideas sink in and be digested is essential. Our unconscious data-processing abilities outweigh the conscious ones and can be seen as the source of our hidden natural creative abilities (Gelb in Dewulf and Baillie, 1999). Periods of rest and dreaming, including daydreaming or doing totally different and distracting activities, will allow the incubation of your ideas to take place. Trust your own unconscious data-processing abilities.

Techniques: at this stage, let it happen. Don't push it.

4. Verification

At this stage, you analyse the different ideas, the different angles and evaluate. The next step is execution or implementation.

We hope that this chapter has clarified and demystified 'creativity'. There seems to be an element of the unexpected and uncertain to creativity. It surely is both a process and a feature of a cultural product, whether a documentary, a painting or new ideas to deal with society's ills.

Key points

- Creativity is creating the 'novel' in a certain field of cultural production.
- Creativity does not operate in a vacuum.

Exercises

Exercise 1 Le menu (Inspired by C. Johnson, 2005)

Students often find it difficult to find their own creativity, their voice, in the approach to the subject they want to film. The following exercise will help you to find your own values and gives insight into what makes you tick.

What I hate	What I fear	What I love	What I believe	What I value	What I want	What I know about	People who made a difference in my life	Discoveries that made a difference in my life	Decisions that made a difference in my life

Take a piece of A4 paper and write down 'le menu' in landscape format. Answer each column with your top five answers, or ten, if time is available.

Use a pencil, as you will erase a lot in the process, and it might be more difficult than you think. Please keep the answers short and specific; do not make sweeping statements such as 'I hate global warming'. Dig a bit deeper and ask yourself why this issue comes up.

This exercise will give an overview of what is important to you. It will put you as a filmmaker in a position to develop those ideas that you feel engaged with.

Exercise 2 De Bono hats

De Bono developed this 'thinking' method to help people to make decisions while taking a variety of approaches to the subject into account.

There are six hats, all representing a different approach to an idea or concept.

- **White hat** – While wearing this hat, you ask yourself what information you have and what information is lacking. You conclude with what you need to find out.

- **Red hat** – Describe your emotional reaction to the idea: what is your gut reaction? Describe your intuitive reaction: what are your feelings about your project?

- **Black hat** – Be critical and describe the negative aspects of your ideas. Be pessimistic and describe what can go wrong and what might not work. Ask yourself how you could avoid some of the difficulties. Do not be scared to alter or adjust your concept.

- **Yellow hat** – Be positive and describe the unique possibilities of your idea and how you can realise these. Describe your achievements in positive terms and avoid any judgemental approaches.

- **Green hat** – Be creative and unleash your fantasy. Describe all the unique and interesting features of your idea and all the solutions you can imagine to certain difficulties.

- **Blue hat** – This represents the role of the producer or the chair of the meeting. They will control the process if fights break out, or, if the group or you run out of ideas or get stuck, they should lead the group to green or black hat approaches.

You can follow this process on your own or in a group. It is mainly a very structured way to come to a decision whether a project is feasible or not, or conclude that you need more information to help you decide. Once you have familiarised yourself with this method, it becomes a way of thinking and decision-making which works well and can be carried out in a relatively short time.

Exercise 3 When were you 'creative'?

Remember the moment when you thought, 'This is a really interesting idea' and were proud of yourself. Come up with at least three such moments.

Interview Luke Holland

Luke Holland (Photo © Wilma de Jong)

You're planting seeds and occasionally you get feedback that assures you that you are on to something.

My formative years were spent in a religious community in the jungles of Eastern Paraguay. We lived among the Indians, the Ling Huo Indians. I had a little dog called Whim, and a sheep called Bella. Both used to accompany me to school. But the sheep was always allowed to come into the classroom, and the dog had to stay outside. One day I plucked up the courage to ask my teacher: 'Why is the sheep allowed to come into class but the dog has to stay outside?' She said: 'There are rules about dogs but no rules about sheep.' I'm pretty sure it's been the template by which I've tested all my other decisions: the nature of authority and the nature of rules.

I studied theatre and German. . . . I was attracted to theatre for all sorts of reasons. Storytelling. I liked the Western ideas of alienation. It probably expresses itself when I occasionally remind the audience that they are watching a documentary. Not too much suspension of disbelief, to keep the intellectual trigger going, not get too subsumed or consumed.

I suddenly discovered in my teens that I was actually Jewish. It made me think about narrative and how we conduct our lives. It's a sort of truism, that we lead our lives according to stories that we tell ourselves. We inhabit our narrative. And if that narrative undergoes, as it did in my case, a certain jump, you have to think again.

I travelled thousands of miles inside Paraguay, visiting representatives of each of the 13 indigenous societies, looking at aspects of conduct: military, multi-nationals, missionaries. I produced an exhibition and catalogue which went on to show at the ICA in London; it was called 'Indians, Missionaries, and the Promised Land'. I've gone back to indigenous communities. They often say that the only virtues of ownership are the privilege of giving things away. An inversion.

So . . . photography, art, framing images, telling stories, thinking in terms of narrative. But also dealing with social issues, trying to say something about other societies. I felt a sense of privilege, that I had access because of my language, that I could act as a sort of interlocutor and tell stories from other worlds.

There's a film I made several years ago now, called *I Was A Slave Labourer*. It's a project about resistance in Auschwitz. I'm very interested in resistance, to give a voice to people who seem voiceless. Partly because I thought the story of Auschwitz had always been told in terms of acidity and pathology, death and darkness. There are also stories inside about resistance but they weren't being told.

I manage, just about, to keep my head above deep water, by pursuing the passion, by being single-minded. It's very good if you want to tell stories, if you're passionately engaged in the world, and if you feel you've got something to say. I've had tremendous satisfaction from that whole process. You're planting seeds and occasionally you get feedback that assures you that you are on to something.

Documentary Dogmas – Luke Holland, filmmaker, ZEF Productions

1. Make sure you have something to say.
2. Don't make excuses.
3. Know why, and for whom, you are making the film – think distribution.
4. Shoot on the medium you can afford.
5. Work with good people – but not too many.
6. Do not lose your focus – or your sense of humour.
7. Curtail your ambitions – but not your standards.
8. Never regard the documentary as the poor relation of drama or feature film.
9. Care about your subjects – whoever they are.
10. Take risks – but not hostages.
11. Fight for length – but remember that less is often more.
12. In moments of despair, remember that your film is not a matter of life or death – it is more important.
13. There are rules about dogs but no rules about sheep (see Luke Holland's interview).
14. Add your own . . .

Chapter 2

The creative documentary

Wilma de Jong

"Any creativity which is intended to entertain, provide pleasure, stimulate pleasure, stimulate emotion or provoke thought is art. "

(Owen Kelly, 1996: 10)

Introduction

What is a creative documentary?

This chapter addresses how we can translate notions of 'creativity' to the art of documentary filmmaking.

We have defined creativity in Chapter 1 as 'novelty' in a certain field of cultural production, but we can distinguish between a 'novel' subject and a 'novel' approach in documentary production. The adage of Grierson, founding member of the UK documentary film movement in the 1930s, that documentary is the 'creative treatment of actuality' suggests that creativity has been at the heart of the documentary tradition. The relationship between creativity and actuality has sparked off a century-old debate on how much 'actuality' is left after 'the creative treatment' has taken place and how the 'real' can be presented, if at all.

Early filmmakers, like the Lumière Brothers in 1895, described documentary as 'life on the run'. We would now argue that a concept of documentary as an unbiased observation and recording of the 'real' is naïve. Just recording does not really exist: different technologies, like film formats or digitally created images, present very different filmic representations of the 'real'. For instance, a 16 mm picture is distinctly different from a digital image: the grain, the colour, the edges of the objects and the format provide a different representation. Add to this mix the selection of framed shots, the effects of the camera and crew on the profilmic events, and editing, and it becomes clear that recording the real *pur sang* and presenting it as 'real' because it has happened is an unattainable fantasy. The related aim of documentary to present disembodied knowledge and an objective reality has been challenged by many authors, but not before it essentially damaged the reputation of documentary, causing it to be seen as 'boring' and information-heavy.

However, it raises the question: if you cannot film the 'real', what is the point of documentary? Before we entered the digital era, it was argued that the indexical warrant of the shot was essential. The audience knew that what had been shot had 'really' happened. Digitisation – in particular, special effects – has undermined that notion, not to mention the cases of deliberate manipulation which entered the public domain. *The Connection* by Marc de Beaufort (UK, 1996), an undercover documentary on drug trafficking between Britain and Columbia, included a claim to have interviewed an important drug trader, which at the end was revealed to be untrue. More recently, the documentary *The Queen* (UK, 2008) entered the debate about fake and untruthful representation of events. A shot which showed the Queen walking out of a photo shoot was really a shot of the Queen walking to a photo shoot. The creation of a sequence changed the meaning of the shot. It is very easy to manipulate shots or sequences or create computer-generated images. In short, film technologies, the act of filming in a certain situation, and the editing challenge an indexical warrant of a shot, while the editing can undermine the meaning of a shot.

We, as documentary filmmakers, are being left almost empty-handed. Reality does not seem to exist outside the perspective of the filmmaker and images can be manipulated. But what do we tell this hungry child suffering from malaria in the developing world: reality or truth does not exist; you can develop a different perspective on your situation? What if you want to make a documentary about this child?

Of course, this question manipulates you as a reader at this moment, but, with all the debates about relative truths, uncertain knowledges and incomplete knowledges, it is important not to

▶

throw out the baby with the bathwater. Knowledge appears to be unstable, incomplete and uncertain, temporary and local. It is for this reason that we speak about knowledges, which opens up the possibilities of different approaches and positions.

As a working definition, we could use a concept which Linda Williams describes as a 'contingency of truths'. This undermines the notion of one truth and offers a strategy where there are overlaps, clashes and contingent truths. It puts the burden of the aim of truthfulness, and a truthful representation of certain realities firmly in the hands of the filmmaker, who should honour documentary's privileged position in the public domain. Audiences have very different expectations of different genres. The *Full Monty*, a film about unemployed workers becoming strippers, is not considered to be 'truthful' by the audience. However, a documentary about unemployed workers seeking employment will be seen as, and is expected to be, 'truthful', as depicting actual people who can be phoned and spoken to.

Catch a falling star

During documentary's century-long history, many authors have tried to describe the perceived essence of the genre as 'the representation of the real'.

In the second part of the twentieth century, Bill Nichols, the founding father of documentary theory, suggested that documentaries present 'an argument about the historical world'. This definition does not seem adequate either, as many documentaries may not analyse the historical world or make an argument at all, even if his focus on the 'historical world' is understandable and crucial for the purpose of documentary filmmaking.

You will find that many authors have tried to define 'documentary' and struggled. The fragmented nature of reality, and the many forms documentary filmmakers have used and developed, have made it difficult to find a clear-cut definition. Even the term 'non-fiction' does not seem to cover our subject; post-modern theorists will argue that a fixed reality outside our own perspective does not exist and that the viewer is part of what is being viewed. You may want to consider this position while thinking about the hungry child with malaria in the developing world.

For the moment, Grierson's definition might come closest to describing our work as documentary filmmakers. The fragmented nature of reality does not allow it to be represented unmediated. Reality does not present itself in a suitable order or structure ready for the filmmaker to document it. On the contrary we create a narrative to analyse, and represent the realities we encounter and are part of.

Documentary is perhaps best described as a hybrid film genre which attempts to represent the 'real' in a creative and critical art form. The history of documentary film illustrates our struggles with the 'real' and our attempts to represent it. Implicit in the act of documentary filmmaking is the representation of the 'real', and the unavoidable act of creating a narrative produces a tension. As aspiring documentary filmmakers, you need critical awareness and self-reflexivity to explore your practice and engage creatively with the opportunities this tension offers.

A slightly different approach is offered by Ohad Landesman:

The genre cannot reveal an a priori self-evident truth, and should therefore assert a more relative veracity by exercising strategies of fiction and exploiting the grey area between story and fact. Hybrid documentaries seek to achieve a higher, more slippery sense of truth, reaching at, but never quite touching, the longed-for Real.

(Landesman, 2008: 44)

Documentary filmmakers basically try to catch a falling star.

You are encouraged to creatively and critically explore the representational modes of the genre. Theoretical principles are implicit in all our social and creative practices. Historically, new forms of documentary filmmaking have occurred in specific political, social, artistic and technological contexts. You are expected to see a wide range of historical and contemporary films to gain insight into the many forms of representation of the 'real' that have been, and are being, used.

Documentary filmmakers have demonstrated a fascination with what happens within our everyday and personal lives: our planet, our history, our obsessions, our relationships, suffering and struggles for food, freedom and resources. Many of these documentaries have provoked debate in the public domain, brought hidden events and lives into the limelight, or changed our perceptions of our world forever. You should never forget that this is the domain in which you are operating.

Serendipity

Documentary filmmaking has a unique feature not found in other forms of filmmaking. Roger Silverstone (1985) describes it as 'arbitrary' but it can also be expressed in the word 'serendipity'. For instance, notwithstanding extensive research, when a documentary filmmaker arrives on location, unexpected events or issues can ocur or can be raised. People's memories are shifting; historic events and experiences are being reframed almost continuously, and perspectives move on. Reality is fluid in people's experiences and ways of talking about it. Often if you come back to a certain location to talk to people they will comment: 'After I spoke to you about . . . I thought about it and . . .' and then come up with new ideas or perspectives.

Filmmakers can sometimes chance upon a specific approach to their film or their own attitude or relation to it. For example, Nick Broomfield discovered by accident how his presence gave a distinct character to his films. When filming *The Leader, His Driver and the Driver's Wife* (UK, 1991), Broomfield was not able to get enough footage of the 'Leader' and decided to include those scenes when he was 'producing' the film as it revealed a lot about his main character.

Marc Isaacs could be seen as a conceptual filmmaker. Intrigued by the inhabitants of a tower block, he spent months in an elevator making *Lift* (UK, 2004). The film offers a sensitive and illustrative portrait of the people living in a tower block in East London, but is made very differently from a conventional documentary.

Many documentaries have unearthed issues that were not discussed before in civil society or were not on the political agenda. Films like *The Dying Rooms* (Channel 4, UK, 1995), *The War Tapes* (Deborah Scranton, USA, 2006), or *Cathy Come Home* (Ken Loach, UK, 1966; remastered BFI, 2003) revealed events or human experiences in corners of societies which were hidden from the public eye, whether deliberately or not. Such films provoke debate in society or lead to the foundation of charities, questions being asked in Parliament or the formation of action groups.

These so-called 'social issues' documentaries play an important role in the discourse of many documentary filmmakers.

Andy Glynne, documentary filmmaker and founder of the Documentary Filmmakers Group: As a clinical psychologist, I think the reason that I felt frustrated doing my clinical work was that it wasn't really making as much of a difference as I wished it would. So I started thinking about making films. And I got obsessed with idea that documentaries can change the world. There are docs out there that have been making a difference . . . I think documentary filmmakers on the whole tend to be slightly left-wing and slightly more caring about the world and social issues.

(Interview with Andy Glynne, 2008)

Anand Patwardan: 'To empower people is to make the unheard voices heard, by recording things that are actually happening, that are not being represented in the mainstream media'.

(Chapman, 2007:19)

Wanting to change the world, to make a difference is, of course, a laudable aim and a dominant discourse in the documentary filmmaking tradition, but it can also have a paralysing effect on the process. Filmmakers are part of contemporary cultures and the aim of representing reality can also result in 'reinforcing existing stereotypes'. Recently, I saw a documentary about homeless people, which aimed to illustrate the thin line between homelessness and having a home: how people could become homeless because they lost their jobs, got divorced or were simply thrown out of the house by their parents. It was just a shame that all the people featured in the film were men. Don't women become homeless? A critical analysis and reflection on what you are filming and how you are editing your film and showing it to an audience are necessary to be sure that the film conveys what you want it to do.

We all know films in which the subjects are portrayed as victims. These so-called victim films have been very popular since the 1980s (Winston, 1995; Chanan, 2007; Basu, 2008), notwithstanding a discourse of 'empowering people or 'giving people a voice'. Filmmakers can't 'give people a voice'. Documentary filmmaking is not the art of passing on people's experiences or ideas. The filmmaker selects and creates a narrative which may or may not undermine 'the people's voice'. Although these aspects can be shown in all films, films about the developing world are notable for it:

Despite the fact that a lot of these filmmakers were very educated people who I still admire, I think traditionally indigenous societies have been characterised either as the exotic other . . . the natives are savage, leading an idealised jungle life, or, at the other end of the spectrum, the passive victims of progress, sitting with arms folded, waiting to cast off clothes of western society, waiting for bulldozers to consign them to oblivion. And I thought, there is another way of telling this, the voice that I heard, that I knew. Indigenous people as protagonists, as humans leading interesting, difficult, complex lives. Trying to make the best. Adapting from our society those things that suited them, that ensured their survival. Making mistakes in that process but also trying to hold on to what it was that they value.

(Interview with Luke Holland, 2008)

Issues of the representation of people are fundamental to documentary filmmaking and filmmakers should be aware of how they represent their subjects. Filming tribes while they are doing their habitual dancing may be entertaining, but might confirm the stereotype of the 'wild savage', despite the intention of giving them a voice. You may ask yourself as well how defining the dancing is and how defining it is in English culture to wear paper hats during the annual Christmas dinner.

For instance, *Sisters in Law* (Kim Longinotto, UK, 2005) or *Divorce Iranian Style* (Kim Longinotto, UK, 1999) are remarkable because the audience is on a journey to experience parts of lives which are unfamiliar to western audiences. The style might be described as 'observational' but it is very different from the observational style of Frederick Wiseman or the Maysles brothers, the prolific founders of the observational film from the 1960s. The film is very directly shot, close to the skin, but it shares with conventional observational documentaries the lack of context. Some will consider this a strength, as it provides an audience with an active role in interpretation of the events. Conversely, it can be argued that the lack of context might confirm stereotypical interpretation of events as no new narrative is being presented and audiences have to rely on their existing knowledge.

The documentary filmmaker Daisy Asquith works with small cameras to get very close to her subjects; she films almost under the skin of her subjects and interacts with them. Often you have the feeling you are part of a personal conversation – or is it eavesdropping? Clearly, this method of working has been made possible by small digital cameras which make it easier for her to work on her own and create a very intimate relation to subjects. This sense of closeness to her main characters gives audiences insight into their daily lives and the choices they make.

Inspired by the possibilities or impossibilities of technology, circumstances or just an idea, a novel approach can be found. Taking risks, daring to experiment, are important features of making 'creative' documentaries.

Information

Documentary is considered to be a genre that conveys information, perhaps even one that should convey information. Many documentaries can and do do this, but quite a few documentaries collapse as an artistic product as the film becomes too information-heavy or the structuring devices used do not offer enough emotional engagement. You might be passionate about a subject, but somehow that passion needs to be translated into a film. Documentaries are not filmed books, nor are they simply a series of visually attractive shots, edited in quick pace and supported by a musical score. A documentary takes an audience to an existing or past reality and is so compelling that they can empathise with mind, emotions and imagination. In that sense, documentary is an ambitious creative and critical enterprise.

How to make a creative documentary

There is no map with clear directions available for making a creative documentary, but we can describe some of the fruitful conditions that underpin this ambition.

- You need knowledge and awareness of different traditions in the history of documentary filmmaking. Creative cultural products generally modify, challenge or are inspired by what has been produced before.
- You need to develop an ability to locate and understand different approaches to the subject, and play with different ideas.
- Creative work tends to borrow and mix technologies or forms from different or related genres or art forms but also from different cultural fields. This process is often described as hybridisation.
- In order to be a creative filmmaker it helps to be an avid consumer (of film/media/multimedia). (See ways of watching documentaries, page 27.)
- Take time to digest; down time is essential in creative production. (See section on Creative practices.)
- Try to collaborate with other disciplines; different skills can contribute to the creative process.
- Be a member of a professional community. Creative communities provide ideas, contacts, venues and access to broadcasters, funders and festivals. (See the website of the Documentary Filmmakers Group or the European Documentary Network.)
- Understand the purpose of the film, for whom is it made and why.

- Take ideas further, find new angles and don't copy others: push yourself.
- Above all, give up the idea that you can create a masterpiece on your own in splendid isolation.

Documentary is in a period of enormous change in the way it can tell stories, so experiment and dare to make mistakes or spend hours in editing rooms to make the film work.

Contemporary creative practices

After looking at the meaning of creativity, the creative process and creative documentary, we look at contemporary creative practices. Documentary filmmaking is increasingly merging with other creative practices. For instance, documentary filmmakers are expected to produce an authored DVD of their film, an internet site, or an interactive documentary for the web or a gallery or museum. Many authors describe the effects of rapid technological changes, the commercialisation of our culture and global media industries on contemporary creative practices. The context for the creative practices of documentary filmmakers is very different from 10 years ago. In the next chapter we will consider the creative industries in more depth, but here we will analyse the practices themselves.

Brad Haseman (in Hartley, 2005: 167) distinguishes five different characteristics of creative practices in the contemporary creative industries.

1. Creative practices involve interactivity

YouTube, 4Docs, MySpace are typical examples where audiences can interact with media content. As a consequence, the relationship between author/filmmaker and audience changes and a power shift takes place. It is hard to imagine making a documentary without having a website where one can see the whole or selected sequences of the film, or a DVD which shows interviews with the makers and scenes not used in the final edit. Creating a website during the production process, where interested people can follow the 'making of', or after the film is finished, where audiences can find background information on the film, has become a common practice to engage potential audiences and is a de facto part of a marketing strategy.

It has been argued that the arrival of the cinema and television in the twentieth century denied audiences an opportunity to interact with their media. For centuries, the theatre was a place where artists could express their ideas in the form of theatrical productions and audiences had the possibility to cheer, to boo or to shout 'Encore'. However, it has been one of the characteristics of new digital technologies that the audience, as a group or individually, has become more influential. Some documentary filmmakers like to show their films in different locations in order to obtain feedback. Writers discuss their work in literary festivals or reading events. As already described, artists learn about their work through reaction from their audiences and their peers. Audience reactions can sometimes be very surprising and unexpected.

But the focus on the interactivity of contemporary media production drives the creation and integration of content across different platforms.

2. Creative practices are intrinsically hybrid

The history of documentary filmmaking shows an increased usage of elements traditionally belonging to other forms of media or cultural production: for example, fiction, literary tradition, news or other technologies. Technically, the form has evolved by incorporating other technologies, such as photography, animation, and graphic design. Blurring the boundaries between genres has always been a characteristic of documentary production. Early documentaries used re-enactment (*Nanook of the North*, Robert Flaherty, USA, 1922) and dramatisation to depict a wide range of realities. In fact, the documentary filmmaker's toolbox, which allowed audiences to experience other people's lives, social situations, cultures and introduced them to unfamiliar topics, has always used 'tools' from other genres or technologies. Documentary history can be described as a 'melting pot' of a wide range of storytelling devices and a variety of technological tools.

Hybridisation implies that it is not only the product that is a hybrid but that the production process is hybridised as well. (See Chapter 14.)

3. Creative practices embrace new sites and forms of cultural production

The unique capacity of digital media focuses on its ability to receive and transmit content. The computer screen is seen as the third screen, after the cinema and television, which are used to distribute media content to large audiences, while the computer screen distributes content to the individual or the few. Multi-media, which blurs the boundaries between genres, performance pieces that use video projection, documentaries that enter a museum or a gallery environment, that use websites or DVDs, all mean that the formats of contemporary documentaries and their distribution are undergoing a rapid change. New forms and formats of documentary production challenge the old idea of the 'documentary' as just a film. Thinking across different media platforms and considering how these platforms influence both the content and form of documentary projects seems to be one of our contemporary challenges.

Examples of documentaries across different platforms are *Against The Tide* (ATT.org.uk), *From Zero* by Stefano Strocchi and *Out my Window* by Catherine Sicek, which is one of the world's first interactive 360° documentaries. It's a journey round urban areas throughout the world, recounted by people who look out of windows in high-rise towers.

4. Creative practices are oriented towards multiplatform, cross-promotional means of distribution

In the contemporary climate, emerging filmmakers need to take into account complex and innovative distribution systems which may influence the production of the work. Making a documentary for the cinema is different from making a documentary for television, as distribution and its consequences are already being considered in the conception stage.

Interactive documentary projects and non-linear documentaries use different scripting techniques and require different ways of approaching one's subject. (See Chapter 13.)

5. Creative practices are not approached as if they are commercially irrelevant

Haseman argues that the production of cultural artefacts will not operate separate from but within commercial environments and realities. In his view, it's no longer helpful to distinguish between films funded by state agencies and arts organisations and those cultural products produced and distributed by private enterprise. This argument challenges a long-standing division between 'commercial' and 'artistic' work. It does not imply that commercial work is not creative but approaches it as popular cultural product and, therefore, attracting bigger audiences, while 'high' art is appreciated by relatively small audiences. Documentary traditionally could be situated on the fringe of popular culture. Both content and format demanded very different media literacy from its audiences. Contemporary documentaries have become more popular, as filmmakers have developed different and more accessible formats to tell their stories. However, it is not very likely that a documentary on, for instance, child soldiers will ever get the same audiences as *Touching the Void* (Kevin Macdonald, UK, 2003) or *Supersize Me* (Morgan Spurlock, USA, 2004) did. At present, broadcasters and national funders use far more commercial criteria and popular cultural values to judge film proposals. It might be argued that 'high' art is more marginalised in the contemporary funding and distribution climate.

In conclusion, what is considered 'novel' in a certain field of cultural production is time-bound, culturally specific and related to the experiences and social position of the filmmaker. The term 'situated knowledge' may help you appreciate that you know, feel, react as a person in a specific position in society. Historically, documentary filmmaking has been socially one-dimensional; most documentary filmmakers have been male, white, and middle class as these were the people with access to the technologies and the field of production. There have been a limited number of female filmmakers, especially documentary editors, but they have been hidden from history (see Chapter 20). It illustrates the fact that the aim of representing the real has been tainted by fundamental ideological positions of that period in history and those documentary filmmakers' preoccupations and ambitions. Notwithstanding their aim of 'representing the real', they were not free of these ideological notions. It meant that what was represented in the documentary tradition was also the concerns most relevant to men. However, more women and filmmakers from different ethnic backgrounds have started to enter the field of documentary film production.

It is important to reflect on your social position and be aware of your interpretation of certain realities, rather than presenting your ideas as the one and only truth. This might actually help to make films that make a difference – or change the world, if you so wish.

Ways of Watching Documentaries

The following formal criteria for the analysis of a documentary might help you to form your ideas and find a way of watching films in a professional way. You are not just an audience. As a documentary filmmaker, you have a dual position and multiple gazes: you want to be engaged by the film but, at the same time, you look at how the story is being told, the formal structure of the film, how the film is technically created and, above all, at what is new, creative or original in subject and form.

Please try to apply the following criteria to the documentaries you are watching:

- Mode of address: how the audience is being addressed by the film
- Camera style/shot sequences
- Choice and treatment of subject matter
- Narration/voice-over
- Use of sound, special effects and music

In addition, it might be useful to ask the following questions.

- Which interests have been served?
- Which specific voices have been heard?
- Which are being silenced?

Key points

- Narrative shapes the 'realities' you are filming.
- Representation is always mediated.
- Awareness of the potential bias of one's own social position is essential.
- Working, thinking and imagining in an interdisciplinary context and across media platforms feeds the contemporary climate on documentary filmmaking.
- Being creative and critical go hand in hand in a documentary context.

Exercises

Exercise 1

Look at the following documentaries:

Heavy Load (Jerry Rothwell, UK, 2007) How far does this film undermine or confirm existing ideas about people with learning disabilities?

Lift (Marc Isaacs, UK, 2001) How would you describe the narrative form of this film and how has this influenced the representation of the inhabitants of the tower block?

Hold Me Tight, Let Me Go (Kim Longinotto, UK, 2007) How would you describe the representation of the young people in this film?

The Lie of the Land (Molly Dineen, UK, 2007) How would you describe the role of the filmmaker and her impact on the interviewees in this film?

Exercise 2

Dream about the film you would like to make. Picture yourself with an audience and imagine what you would tell them about the film. After this guided fantasy, write down who your audience was and why you wanted to tell them that story.

Exercise 3 Association – what are the issues you are interested in?

Draw a circle and write in it the things that interest you. For each word that comes up, write down another that is connected. Circle it. See if you can create clusters of interests or affiliations and passions.

Dogma 2001: Kill the Documentary As We Know It

Jill Godmilow

Jill Godmilow

Jill Godmilow is an American director-producer who continually pushes the boundaries of both realist and fictional filmmaking. A well-known film is *Far from Poland* (USA, 1984) about the role of the Polish Solidarity movement and its role in the fall of communism. She was denied visas for herself and her crew to shoot in Poland so she created a form which did not require access to Poland. At the centre of the film are three re-enactments of key texts, three imaginary conversations with Fidel Castro, a letter to a hungry Polish friend, a fantasy tale about the end of the Polish struggle and her own considerations and deliberations about both Solidarity and documentary as a realist film text.

The following is a shortened version of her 'dogma' about documentary filmmaking, from an article she wrote called *Kill the Documentary As We Know It*:

1. Don't produce the surface of things: have a real subject and real analysis, or at least an intelligent proposition that is larger than the subject of your film.
2. Don't produce freak shows of the oppressed, the different, the primitive, and the criminal. Please don't use your compassion as an excuse for social 'pornography'.
3. Don't make films that celebrate 'the old ways' and mourn loss.
4. Don't produce awe for the rich, the famous, the powerful, the talented, the highly successful.
5. Keep an eye on your own middle-class bias and your audience's. Don't make films that feed it.
6. Find a way to acknowledge your authorship.
7. Leave your parents out of this.

Source: For full version, see Jill Godmilow, 2007, *Far from Poland: Documentary without Walls*, Facet Cine-notes, Facets Multi-Media Inc.

Question

Godmilow's 'dogmas' challenge conventional realist documentary filmmaking. What do you think she means by social 'pornography'?

Chapter 3

The creative industries and documentary

Wilma de Jong

❝ The idea of the creative industries seeks to describe the conceptual and practical convergence of the creative arts (individual talent) with cultural industries (mass scale), in the context of new media technologies within a new knowledge economy, for the use of newly interactive citizens-consumers. ❞

(Hartley, 2005: 5)

Introduction

This is a theoretical chapter and will introduce you to key developments in the media industries and the many forms and contexts in which documentary production takes place. It intends to make you aware of contexts in which contemporary documentary filmmakers are operating and production conditions you may encounter. The first part describes the developments in the broadcast industry and the chapter finishes by showing how documentary production is moving out of the broadcast environment.

Given that the digital era started only 30 years ago, when the first PCs were introduced to the workplace, and that we are now walking around with mobiles with internet connection, Blue Tooth, MP3 players and full-blown computers the size of the palm of a hand, it seems justified to conclude that technology and related communication cultures change at a fast pace. Media production technologies, distribution possibilities, the position of audiences, the working conditions of those involved, and funding, all seem in flux. This chapter tries to capture, describe and analyse these changes and their relevance for documentary production.

Analysing the creative industries

The concept of the 'creative industries' is ubiquitous at the moment, but it is actually relatively new. It is not an academic concept but one that was introduced by the Blair government at the end of the twentieth century. It is now often used as an umbrella term to describe media production in its many forms and, as the quote at the beginning of this chapter illustrates, it emphasises the commercial application and, some may argue, the exploitation of creativity.

This concept pushes notions of 'creativity' out of its conventional context of art production and takes it into an industrial and commercial environment. The combination of creativity and industry often seems a contradiction. When we think of industries we see big steel factories, car and fridge production, producing goods for a mass market – after all, the word 'industry' entered our dictionaries with the arrival of the industrial revolution. However, it is not the first time that media production has been conceptualised as an industry. In the 1940s, the German sociologists Theodor Adorno and Max Horkheimer, who belonged to the Frankfurt School, formulated their critique of what they described as the industrialisation of 'culture', which they claimed would lead to 'cheap' and 'inauthentic' mass-produced media products. Standardisation of media products is seen as an important concession to an industrial context. It explains why feature films tend to be one and a half hours long and songs last about 3 minutes.

The Frankfurt School coined the concept of the 'culture' industries; this industrialisation of culture was denounced as the commoditisation of 'the human mind'. Art production and creativity in this concept were relegated to what they described as the 'amateur', who would produce the 'real' creative artefact. This approach has been, and is still, very popular, but the idea of art production not tainted by industrial requirements or money is a romantic notion. For an artist to get their work shown in galleries or museums or to have it published, they need to meet certain requirements, related to the values and institutional norms of the field of production in which they operate.

The idea of creativity without boundaries, operating in a vacuum – most of the time envisaged as a draughty loft – seems to be an illusion, as we have seen in Chapter 2. Art has been subsidised either by the state, rich industrialists or patrons. Recent history shows that the defining lines between art and mass-produced art have fluctuated.

The concept of the 'creative industries' conflates the creative arts and the 'culture' industries. It is argued that the new technologies transform the conventional dichotomies between art and mass media: '. . . art needs to be seen as something intrinsic, not opposed to the capacities of contemporary global, mediated, technology-supported economy' (Hartley, 2005: 9).

The new creative worker is seen as a worker in the new 'creative' economy. Although releasing 'creativity' from the narrow shackles of art production to include a much wider range of 'creative' activities can be appreciated, it can also be seen to reinforce concepts of high and low culture through the back door by focusing on 'excellence'. It fails to challenge the existing hierarchy in art production.

Art is appreciated for its humanising and civilising influence on audiences. It is exhibited in publicly funded museums, national institutions of education and shown on public broadcasting.

> Documentary has always been considered as having high 'art' value and less of a 'commercial' value. The arrival of reality TV in the early '90s' commercialised' documentary production to reach bigger audiences. It therefore became more attractive for broadcasters and created a global market in 'documentary' formats. Some may argue that the Frankfurt School argument is more relevant now than ever and whether 'reality TV' might be appreciated as 'documentary' production is a widely debated issue in the documentary theory.
>
> (Austin and de Jong, 2008)

One can identify a two-tiered system of documentary production: easy, accessible documentary, often described by broadcasters as 'factual' entertainment, and documentary. The concept of the creative industries, which was meant to open up existing ideas about creativity and include more creative activities, became a reinforcement of a long-existing dichotomy.

The 'market' discourse in broadcasting

The increased commercialisation and digitisation of the broadcast culture has made 'programming' more technologically and commercially driven while at the same time attempts are being made to realise the public remit. The tension between these different developments has caused one of the most significant cultural conflicts of our time, one which Hartley's definition of the creative industries glosses over.

Broadcasters, distributors and filmmakers don't produce programmes any more; they produce content. Filmmakers have become producers of a product. At the end of the twentieth century, audiences became customers, and the former couch potato is now often described as a producer of viewer-generated content. The change in language is an illustration of the fast-changing commercial culture in which we are at present living.

Some documentary filmmakers have adopted the corporate language of the market while others consciously refuse to take it on as an act of protest.

> I went to a market and one of the American buyers said, 'Have you got any new products for us, Luke?' And I thought I was a creative artist making documentary films, but I'm making a product.
>
> (Luke Holland, interview January 2007)

Whereas documentary filmmaking once expected to make a contribution to a widely informed citizenship and provoke debate in the public sphere, it has now become a 'product'. Some documentary filmmakers experience this change in discourse about documentary's role in society as problematic. Historically speaking, the discourse on documentary always was located in a more democratic, public service and pedagogic space, described by Nichols (2003) as a 'discourse of sobriety'. It therefore seems alien to the contemporary 'market' ideology. Many documentary filmmakers still draw on those ideas to describe their motivation, while others (such as Morgan Spurlock and Michael Moore) try to push the boundaries to use different, more popular, dramatic narrative strategies to make films that raise important social or political issues, or present different realities, while at the same time being more entertaining. Many 'factual' entertainment formats operate within these parameters. For instance, a popular contemporary documentary format is the so-called 'journey film'. Whether it is Joanna Lumley travelling down the Nile, Michael Palin visiting Eastern Europe, or Molly Dineen embarking on a journey into the English countryside, the concept is the same. The audience is taken on a journey of discovery, led by a filmmaker or presenter. The film still engages with a conventional documentary subject, but the form is more engaging and more suitable for bigger audiences. It could be seen as a documentary answer to the popular and more commercial environment of contemporary television.

The changing economic position of the creative industries

A fundamental shift in the structure of our economy appears to be taking place. The 'creative' industries, incorporating the ICT industries, are one of the fastest-growing sectors of the global economy, with growth rates more than double those of advanced economies as a whole (Rifkin, 2000: 167). Rifkin predicts that cultural production will rise to the first tier of economic life, with information and services moving to the second, and manufacturing to the third position. Certainly, the creative industries have seen an astronomical growth in the last 10 years. In 2000, the creative industries generated £112.5 billion in revenues, and between 1997 and 2003 grew at a rate of 6% per year (DCMS, 2001, 2004; DTI, 2005). These figures are impressive and explain government policies and support for the industry and education. It also explains why creativity has become a key signifier for the description of our economy.

If we go back in time only 30 years, to the 1980s, it was Alvin Toffler who claimed that agriculture and industry would be superseded by 'information' as the driving force in society: the so-called 'information society'. Just as industrialised production had displaced agriculture as a main economic driver, the exchange of knowledge and information had now become a key activity. This explained an increased emphasis on research and development in technology and science. 'Knowledge is power' might be a powerful slogan but it also suggests a degree of control over information which may not always be available in media production. Audience research is strongly emphasised at present, but it still cannot explain why certain programmes or films are successful and others not. The 'nobodyknows' factor (quoted in Caves, 2000: 3) is an important feature of media production in general and documentary production in particular. Could it really be predicted that *Touching the Void* (Kevin Macdonald, UK) or *SuperSize Me* (Morgan Spurlock, USA) would become so successful?

By the 1990s, we had moved on very quickly to a services-based economy, which included a growth in creative industries, such as advertising, marketing and digital communication technologies.

> We need information. But we also need to be active, clever and challenging this information. We need to be original, sceptical, argumentative, often bloody minded and occasionally downright negative – in one word, creative.
>
> (Howkins, 2001: 118)

This short overview of the defining characteristics of our society illustrates how fast changes are considered to be taking place. Those developments will offer related discourses which influence the context, but also the content, of media – in this case, documentary production. The increase in factual entertainment and reality TV could well be considered in this context.

The impression exists that documentary production is becoming de-institutionalised. Film festivals are playing a more and more important role in the commissioning, funding and distribution process. Filmmakers pitch now in front of a few commissioning editors and 'deals' are made on the spot (see Chapter 6). Broadcasters fund only part of the production nowadays and additional funds have to be found elsewhere. One could argue that this would weaken the power of the broadcasters but since the request for documentary broadcast guarantees outstrips the available slots, this is actually not the case.

Documentary production outside the broadcast context is further facilitated by the increased distribution possibilities of the filmmakers, who now own the rights of their film and can sell and distribute films on the net or in alternative venues. For instance, the Good Screenings website promotes films which can be hired at reduced prices to be shown in alternative venues. Smaller venues or picture houses will often show documentaries, whether as a one-off or a part of a themed week. Audiences can see the film, have a coffee in the bar, or a bite to eat, and a public sphere akin to the coffee houses of the eighteenth century is being created. It is not very likely that many documentaries will reach mass audiences. Whether these new developments will lead to viable business models for the documentary filmmaker is not very clear at present.

Mainstream, as in factual entertainment, and a variety of niche markets for documentary production and distribution can be identified. The relationship is multi-faceted – they overlap and sometimes even clash but should be considered as part of the documentary tradition.

Working in the broadcast industry

The developments described above also change the nature of our work and the conditions under which it takes place.

Broadcasters are not only cutting programme budgets, they are also making their organisations leaner and less bureaucratic, with multi-skilled media professionals who can work across different media platforms. For example, in 2007, the BBC made 1,800 staff redundant (mainly in 'factual' and 'news' production) and cut its commissioning budget by £100 million (*The Guardian*, 17 October 2007). At the same time, production is increasingly outsourced to the independent production sector, with lower budgets.

These changes have led to a decrease in employment for terrestrial broadcasters but an increase in the independent production sector and cinema exhibition (Skillset Employment Census, 2009). In the broadcast industry, between 30% and 50% of the workers are now freelance, while a total of 79% of workers in the creative industries are freelancers. The much-celebrated growth in employment in the web design sector is now slightly decreasing, while employment in the gaming industry and production of mobile content is still on the rise. The total of people employed by the creative industries, however, remains stable at 500,000 (ibid.).

At the moment, the creative industries employ 2–8% of the working population in most British cities, and perhaps 10% of the workforce in London. This is changing with the move of the BBC to Salford, and an increase in employment in the North West is notable. Research by the Manchester Institute of Popular Culture revealed that 6% of the Manchester workforce is employed in the creative industries – more than in construction and almost as much as in the well-established transport and communications sectors (Leadbeater and Oakley, 2007: 301).

Nevertheless, the South East and London continue to employ more than half of the workforce in the creative industries. These industries are people-intensive rather than capital-intensive and tend to be interconnected. This interconnection is an essential characteristic of the independent media production sector.

Flexible specialisation

Ever since Storper and Christopherson (1986, 1989) wrote their article on flexible specialisation and the emergence of networks of specialised companies in the motion picture industry, this process has continued to grow and spread to other media production. Some argue that it is a characteristic of our present economic structure. A network of small companies exists which trade with each other: filmmakers need editors or graphic designers or web designers. The scale on which it takes place and the number of people involved make it the most dominant structure of the creative industries at the moment. Leadbeater and Oakley (1999) describe how the 'new independents' determine the structure of the independent production sector.

Hartley (2005) discusses three characteristics of the so-called 'new independents':

- Technology – a new generation of media producers has grown up with new digital technologies which they experience as life- and work-enabling.

- Their values are anti-establishment and anti-traditionalist and, in lots of respects, highly individualistic. They appreciate independence, creativity and operating in social networks, tending to work with friends, family or former classmates.

- They epitomise the notion of what, in a neo-liberalist context, can be described as the 'entrepreneurial' self. Here, the individual is seen as independent and in control of his/her own life. While this is an empowering concept at an individual level, it seems to ignore existing social structures in society. If you fail to get commissioned to make a film, you may attribute this to mistakes you may have made, whereas actually different factors beyond your control may have influenced the decision – for instance, the fact that bigger production companies have established contacts with funders and broadcasters so new kids on the block have to shout very loud to be heard.

New visions of 'work'

The new independents represent a new vision of work which is technology-based and creatively driven, with fluid boundaries between work and private life. Self-employment is growing and portfolio careers are more common. The increase of the new independents, or creative entrepreneurs, can be celebrated, but the relocation of production outside the broadcasters can also be described as a form of strategic outsourcing and a way of reducing costs and relocating responsibilities, mainly in development of projects, though not in the decision structure of programme making.

> I think we are in a changing culture. The 'commissioners' want to be involved in appointing the creative team and the editor, even to the extent of nominating the voice-over or insisting on a voice-over as opposed to relying on the dialogue to tell the story.
> (Luke Holland, interview January 2008)

> Where it becomes more dangerous is where some broadcasters are becoming very prescriptive about the exact nature of the programme they want . . . You know if you don't

. . . remind the viewer every five minutes of the story they have just heard or the story they are about to hear and . . . hold their attention that way, you will lose them, and they'll switch over to *Pimp my Ride* or another channel.

(Louise Osmond, interview September 2007)

These quotes from documentary filmmakers illustrate that, from their perspective, the increase of independent production has also led to increased control by broadcasters who are operating in a competitive industry where audience figures rule.

Conversely, a lot of independents have been set up by successful directors and actors in order to have more creative freedom. Hartley (2005), Leadbeater and Oakley (1999) and Leadbeater (2000) celebrate a lot of potential independents and creativity for the workers in this sector.

Other authors (Dex et al., 1999) are more critical of these developments as they increase uncertainty for those involved. Long hours, irregularity and unpredictability of income create financial uncertainty, and negotiating complex networks of industry professionals such as agents, directors, managers and technical crews (Deuze, 2007: 173) can be time-consuming and often take place at family-unfriendly times.

Most of the independents aim to stay small because they want to retain their independence and focus on their creativity. Often they own a couple of computers and a camera and operate from warehouses owned by manufacturing companies. Their main assets are creativity, ingenuity, and being run by multi-skilled professionals.

Small independent companies are now considered to be the driving force of cultural production. They produce drama series, factual games and educational materials which are distributed via internet, TV and international markets. The big multinationals, such as AOL, Warner, News Corporation, Bertelsmann and Vivendi, aim for big global audiences and new emerging markets such as China, India and Eastern Europe. These tend to focus on entertainment and sport for which international audiences can be found.

In the 1980s–90s, small independents benefited from new policies such as increased production quotas at the BBC. Subsequent legislative changes mean that they now own the rights of their films. Distribution became a more elaborate task for the independent companies, which provided possibilities for generating additional income but also increased the workload of already time-pressed individuals.

Leadbeater (1999) suggests that the independents are taking on a growing share of the employment and output of some of the fastest-growing sectors in the British economy. Growing at twice the rate of the economy as a whole, the independents are an important and influential driving force.

I think that in Britain the independent production community is the powerhouse of the industry, I think it's the small, independent companies that come up with the ideas and the bigger companies often buy those.

(Jonny Persey, Met Film, interview May 2005)

These small companies do not produce the lion's share of the films in the UK, but they are important for the number of people they employ (Hesmondhalgh, 2002) and the possibilities they offer for aspiring directors, writers and producers to have access to the industry. Research by Beacham (1992) at Goldsmiths College concluded that most students who had finished their degrees in media studies ended up in small independent production companies for their first jobs.

You know, new talent can only come through because people take a risk on those people but the only people who are doing that are the independent production companies.

(Jonny Persey, Met Film, interview May 2005)

Sharing offices (Photo Wilma de Jong)

Multi-skilled media workers who are producers or designers are retailers and promoters at the same time, aided by cheaper and more sophisticated communication and computing methods, the spread of the internet and growth of digital networks and new distribution channels.

Working in the independent production sector

The growth of the independent production sector is impressive, and PACT celebrates the 'growth, profitability and consolidation' of this sector.

In their Independent Production Census 2007–08 PACT revealed that revenues of the independent production sector increased from £1.6 billion in 2005 to £1.95 billion in 2007 and in 2008 to £2.14 billion. This marks a 9.4% growth since 2007 and a compound annual growth of 15.6% since 2005.

However, this successful bigger picture does not reveal some of the concerns in the working conditions of media professionals.

First of all, entry to the industry tends to be person-driven. Skillset, the Sector Skills Council for the audio-visual industries, which covers TV and film as well as the gaming and the graphic design sector, carried out an industry survey. The census concludes that only 27% of the 7,000 media professionals had heard of their most recent job through advertisements. Access to the industry takes place through personal contacts in 67% of the cases. The workforce in the creative industries is highly educated – 73% of people working in the media have a degree, compared with 16% of the UK workforce as a whole. Of these, 44% are media graduates, while 56% have a degree in other subjects. Many students offer their labour free, just to become known and be part of a community of practitioners. This method of recruitment is, of course, shameful for any industry in the present day.

Secondly, as a result of the casualisation of the workforce, two-thirds of freelancers report a loss of earnings mainly caused by doing project-work only. This loss of income does not seem to be caused by a lower day rate (Ursell, 2000). Many freelancers are being offered buy-out contracts which mean that they get a lump sum for the work, however long it takes to do the job. This practice means that media professionals on average work 44.6 hours a week, earning a mean salary of £32,239. This compares to a national average of 33.8 hours and £24,300 for the UK workforce as a whole. However, the survey also shows that the majority of the media industries are based in London and the South East, where the average salary is £33,867 and the average working week 44.9 hours. It also reveals that nearly a quarter of respondents earned less than £20,000 in the past 12 months. More than a third earn between £30,000 and £49,999 and a further 11% earn in excess of £50,000.

One can identify the same tendency in the music industry, feature film industry and football or tennis 'industries': a top layer earns big money, and the biggest group of professionals earns substantially less. This polarisation in earnings seems to be a characteristic of our contemporary earnings structures, and fuels many debates about 'fat cats'.

This polarisation can also be identified in documentary production, as Louise Osmond argues:

> Yes, there is a downside to the equipment and everything becoming so much more accessible. It's the fact that I think there's now a polarisation between filming it on a cheap camera, editing it on Final Cut Pro, one person does everything, and kind of high-end stuff, which is glossy, big-budget, CGI. There are numerous documentaries being commissioned now which have bigger budgets than smaller feature films.
>
> You get a very polarised industry and I think what's sad is maybe what's gone is the middle ground where you can find people willing to invest in really interesting stories that aren't necessarily going to get huge ratings but are going to be really good films with a great subject.
>
> (Louise Osmond, interview September 2007)

Polarisation in budgets and the emergence of the multi-skilled documentary filmmaker have created a market for filmmakers which did not exist before. The 'total' documentary filmmaker, who owns their own equipment and has the technical and creative skills, can make a film at a fraction of the costs of broadcast or funded documentaries. In this market, the fledgling documentary filmmaker can make a start to show their talent and skills.

Distribution

The new distribution platforms, such as websites, mobile technologies and interactive TV, have led to what has been described as '360-degree commissioning' by the BBC and other broadcasters.

It implies that each platform of distribution should add value both commercially and creatively to the programme.

The increased commercialisation and digitisation of the broadcast culture have made 'programming' more technologically and commercially driven while at the same time desperate attempts are being made to realise the public remit. The tension between these different developments has caused one of the most significant cultural conflicts of our time, one which Hartley's definition of the creative industries skates over.

BIG indies and small independents

The rapid growth of the industry has led to the independent production sector becoming extremely polarised. The big independents are really big and now often part of a bigger consortium. For instance, All3Media consists of several production companies and Endemol, originator of *Big Brother*, is listed on the London Stock Exchange. In the overview of the emerging 20 'super indies' in the industry, published in *The Guardian* (1 April 2005), Darlow Smithson Productions is a good example. This used to be an independent factual production company, producing 150 hours of factual television per year. It has become part of IMG media group who, in their own words, 'create, distribute and represent compelling content across every medium'. They have just announced that they have signed tennis star Jelena Jankovic and football legend Pele. It is a conglomerate of a range of companies which benefit each other. If a documentary were to be made about Jelena Jankovic's career, it is fairly obvious which company would probably make it.

Regulatory changes and changes in demand may explain this reorganisation of the industry as well as a general tendency of a capitalist economy towards oligopoly.

Being small is being creative

One of the reasons why big consortia buy small independent companies without dismantling them is that creativity needs a small-scale structure in order to flourish. Unlike the production of cars or washing machines, media production – and especially creativity and project development – tends to be small-scale (Hesmonhalgh, 2002).

Moreover, since the Communications Act of 2003, independents own the main part of the rights of their programmes. This makes it possible to sell programmes on an international market but, above all, to sell formats of programmes internationally. The global format market, especially for reality TV, has expanded significantly, and formatted programmes and series have become the main staple of prime-time television.

Policy changes of the broadcasters have also influenced these reorganisations. The BBC has opened up opportunities while closing down many departments. Mark Thompson, Director-General of the BBC, once described the present climate as a 'window of creative competition' and announced an increase of independent production of 50%, allowing external independent companies to compete with in-house production departments. Although initially this policy opened up the possibilities for independents, these quickly narrowed as the broadcasters created 'preferred suppliers'.

As the larger consortia produce big factual series or more expansive docudramas, smaller independents may benefit from their access to commissioning and funding sources by trying to sell their ideas to, or co-produce with, bigger independents. So, far from approaching bigger independents as competitors, smaller companies could try to collaborate with them. This is not always straightforward, however.

> It's harder in some ways to do co-productions with France, Germany. They (broadcasters) want it nationally based and a British presenter, and very often celebrity presenters. Many subjects are going across borders but national broadcast demands may undermine the possibilities.
>
> (Silvia Stevens, Faction Films, interview January 2008)

Co-production might not always be an easy option and the complexities of national cultures do not always coincide with European funding policies.

Documentary production market

Documentary production has blossomed over the last five years. More documentaries have entered the cinemas (Austin and de Jong, 2008) and we have seen some very successful 'block-buster' documentaries such as *SuperSize Me, Touching the Void* and *March of the Penguins*. In addition it could be argued that the sophistication of documentaries has increased: storytelling, visualisation and the use of music and archive material have increased the quality of the films. Documentary is no longer drama's poor cousin.

> . . . I think that people are much more open to the documentary medium now. I don't quite know why that its. Maybe it's because it's been done successfully and people as a result are more comfortable with it as a storytelling device. And it's also shed its slightly woolly-jumper preconception. It has a sexier image.
>
> (Orlah Collins, Pathé, interview 2006)

However, Austin and de Jong (2008) conclude that the boom took mainly place in the USA. While an increase in interest in documentary is notable in the UK, it would be an exaggeration to call it a boom.

The main argument why documentary didn't take off to the same extent as in the USA might be our media system. In Europe, historically, media became part of national and cultural policies and was allocated a role in preserving national culture and promoting national identities and democratic traditions. It is within that context that the BBC obtained the remit to 'inform, entertain and educate' its audiences.

This is still the prevalent position of our public broadcaster, which means that documentaries are being broadcast on national television, although usually much later in the evening, as reality TV has taken over the prime-time slots. The American media system is largely commercially driven. As a result, only a small public broadcast sector suffering from underfunding exists. Underlying this different concept of the media is a different concept of culture. In America, 'culture' seems to be defined in market terms, while in the UK a double route has been created of both public and commercial broadcasters. According to Pathé, one of the big distributors in the UK,

> A lot of films in the last couple of years made an awful lot of money for very little output. There have been a lot of well-received, critically praised and lauded documentaries that have come out recently that have done no business. Some that have done very well in the States have come over here and they've just died.
>
> (Orlah Collins, Pathé, interview 2006)

Despite the expansion of channels, and an increase in documentary production, it is still difficult to get films commissioned. One can identify the following developments:

- The introduction of more channels and an increase in internet distribution without a rise in TV licence income for the BBC or an increase in advertising revenue for the commercial channels have led to a decrease in budgets per programme.

- Broadcasters seem to demand series of programmes. Many documentary filmmakers prefer to make one-off films. Series require a strong format which can be repeated easily. Developing formats is a very different skill from making a single documentary. Format creation operates in a more commercial market of which many independent filmmakers are not part. In any case, many subjects are not suitable for formatting into a series.

> Ironically with more and more channels, there are, in a weird way, almost fewer and fewer opportunities. Because people are watching more of the same thing, and they want what they saw last night . . . Broadcasters want series and they want formatted series.
>
> (Silvia Stevens, Faction Films, interview January 2008)

In addition, many documentary filmmakers develop their structure while making the film. Unexpected developments during shooting may alter the structure of a film. In Chapter 2, this has been described as serendipity, which is considered to be an important characteristic of documentary production. Individual documentaries are reliant on specific slots, such as *Storyville* or *True Stories*, which are also concept-driven but do give a certain freedom to show a variety of documentaries.

- The supply of filmmakers and small independent companies seems to outweigh the demand for new output.

Budgets

As already indicated, the increase in channels and investment of broadcasters in new media technologies and new distribution platforms without an increase in the licence fee for the BBC and a decrease in advertising revenue for the commercial channels has meant that budgets for the different programmes have been reduced.

The other issue is that slots for one-off documentaries, particularly those dealing with more in-depth social issues, have been reduced in favour of series. While the market for this kind of documentary has decreased since its heyday in the 1970s and 1980s, factual production on TV has veered much more towards entertainment (Corner and Rosenthal, 2005). Documentary slots have been replaced by so-called 'factual entertainment' slots. Programmes about food, gardening, fashion and design cater for a variety of audiences but often fall into the category of self-help programmes. The interests of the numerous filmmakers clash with the demand of the broadcasters, for whom audience ratings are an important concern. In addition, there are relatively few slots for one-off documentaries and, even then, the entertainment value is considered as important as the subject. The challenge for contemporary documentary filmmakers is either to find their way within this system or find alternative routes. This will be discussed in Chapter 4.

Key points

- The creative industries are reorganising, with more freelancers and more productions being transferred to the independent production sector. The independent production company seems to be the organisational form for contemporary documentary filmmakers.

- Budgets for programmes are lower, due to investments in a digital infrastructure and channel proliferation without an increase in the licence fee and with a decrease in advertising revenue. There are more repeats. Budgets are tight and do not allow for contingency which could be used for development of new programmes.

- The interest of documentary filmmakers and the demand of broadcasters clash in content and form – formatted series as opposed to one-off programmes.

- Film concepts are expected to work across different platforms. Broadcasters argue that each distribution form should have an added value, both commercially and creatively.

- Mass-produced programming has taken over the television industry. This signals a difficult time for the smaller independents, but original ideas, unique access to certain 'realities', flexibility and the quota system will hopefully see the independent industry continue to grow.

- Networks between different companies with specialist skills and knowledge may benefit both small and large independents.

- The risk of development of new programmes has been transferred to the filmmakers as commissioning is very competitive.

Exercises

Exercise 1

Interview two or three documentary filmmakers and write an essay on how and why they became a documentary filmmaker. Distinguish between so-called individual skills and knowledges and industrial requirements.

Exercise 2

Discuss:

- Is the concept of the 'cultural industries' still useful to analyse contemporary media production or is it hopelessly outdated?

- Is the concept of the 'creative industries' useful to analyse contemporary documentary production or are commerce and documentary alien to each other?

Exercise 3

In the text box that follows you find an overview of what are considered to be characteristics of a successful entrepreneur. Discuss whether you have those skills, knowledge and abilities to set up your own independent company. Identify what you need to learn to be able to run your own independent company.

Running a successful independent company

Leadbeater and Oakley (2005) have done extensive research into small, creative enterprises and they have formulated the following 13 points of advice:

1. Be prepared to have several goes. You are unlikely to make it first time around. Learn from failure; don't wallow in it.

2. Timing is critical. Technology is moving so fast it's easy to be either too early or too late.

3. Don't have a plan: it will come unstuck because it's too inflexible.

4. Have an intuition and a feel for where the market is headed which can adapt and change with consumers.

5. Be brave enough to be distinctive. If you are doing what everyone else is doing, you're in the wrong business.

6. Be passionate: if you don't believe in what you are doing, no one else will. At the outset only passion will persuade people to back you.

7. Keep your business lean. Buy top-of-the-range computers but put them on second-hand desks. Necessity, not luxury, is the mother of invention.

8. Make work fun. If it stops being fun, people will stop being creative.

9. Give your employees a stake in the business: you may not be able to pay them much to start with, so give them shares.

10. Pick partners who are as committed as you. To start with, a business will only be sustained by a band of believers.

11. Be ready to split with your partners – often your best friends – when the business faces a crisis or a turning point. Don't be sentimental.

12. Don't aim to become the next Bill Gates; aim to get bought out by him.

13. Take a holiday in Silicon Valley. You will be convinced anyone is capable of anything.

Interview David Notman-Watt, back2back productions

If you want to come into this business, you've got to treat it like a business.

I started my career at Associated Press Television News, the news agency. I was brought up in Brazil, so I speak Portuguese and Spanish fluently. In my mid-20s I got a job with AP covering their Latin American stories, which I did for a number of years and absolutely loved. I then met my wife, and I realised that I had to make a conscious decision – I was either going to be married to a woman, or I was going to be married to news. I chose my wife. So, I moved to an APTN programme that they ran called *Roving Report*, an investigative magazine programme made up of news pieces of 10–15 minutes' duration. This style of filmmaking worked for me, and the rest is history. From there, I graduated to making longer-format documentaries as the years passed.

The company itself, back2back productions, started in 2000 in my bedroom. I didn't have any financial help, or any mentor as such. But I had a phone and computer, and a long list of films to my name. And it worked. Slowly.

David Notman-Watt (Photo © Wilma de Jong)

If you want to come into this business, you've got to treat it like a business. There are so many documentary filmmakers I meet who don't have a business sense, and that always surprises me. So many work on projects without any budget whatsoever, some for years at a time. That, for me, is unsustainable and I would never do it. I don't ever go on a project that doesn't have some financial commitment to it in place, be that a commission, a distributor's advance, or even a pilot budget. As far as I am concerned, if I'm willing to go and film a story I consider worth making in a place which is potentially dangerous or risky, I expect a broadcaster to honour that and to put up a budget that we can work with. This has been my philosophy from the very beginning. I have been lucky in that, up until now, this has worked for us most of the time. Clearly, budgets are getting tighter now and, with every year that passes, we are looking at newer and more unusual financing routes. There is also the flip-side of course. If nobody wants to put money into the project, you have to ask yourself the difficult question – is the project really as good as you think it is?

I have learnt the hard way, and still am, I suppose. I'm not driving a Rolls-Royce (not that I would ever want to, but you get my point . . .), but the money that we have made from our films over the years is re-invested in the company and we constantly buy more editing equipment, HD cameras, people . . .

I decided when I started the business that, if we were to rely solely on commissions from broadcasters, we couldn't survive. And I'm glad we have kept our options open. We work for a broad selection of organisations – governments, NGOs, companies, as well as TV networks – and the subjects and content of our films have also covered a wide area of subjects, people and countries. And because of that we're still here. That is good enough for me.

Chapter 4

Passionate business: entrepreneurship and the documentary filmmaker

Wilma de Jong

❝ Creativity as the decisive source of competitive advantage. ❞

(Florida, 2002: 5)

Introduction

This chapter focuses on the possibilities and constraints of the different business models that filmmakers have formed to make their films. It will also inform you of alternative routes to break into the industry.

Many filmmakers emphasise original ideas as the determining factor in obtaining commissions or gaining access to funding or distribution. New theoretical notions about 'creativity', expressed by Florida (2002) and Hartley (2005), share this perspective. It might, however, be too narrow a formulation of being successful in this industry.

Research by Skillset (2005) confirms that personal contacts are important to obtain a job in the industry. Certainly, the tendency by broadcasters to create 'preferred suppliers' indicates that 'creativity' might not be the only factor, though it is undoubtedly significant. To unravel these issues is an impossible task as coincidence – being at the right place, at the right time – will also play a role. The whole idea that these processes are rational, predictable and therefore controllable in great detail seems to echo a modern, positivist approach which ignores one of the most important aspects of the industry: it is a people industry. Both personal experience and research confirm that personal contacts within the industry can lead to work. Although Skillset's research refers to getting a job, which is different from being commissioned, it highlights that knowing people is a key feature of the industry. Going to festivals, joining specialist groups (Documentary Filmmakers Group, European Documentary Network) seems to be important. We can argue that this is objectionable in times when equal opportunities and transparent application procedures are advocated and implemented by many industries. However, despite this politically problematic situation, your first step is to make contacts, to meet people at festivals, through volunteer work or working as a runner, or as an assistant of an assistant. You will appear on the radar when a production comes up but it requires ideas, initiative, organisational and communication skills and, above all, persistence to obtain a job or a commission.

The people's premiere – *The Age of Stupid*

Franny Armstrong's *The Age Of Stupid* is one of the documentary successes of recent years, but the story behind the making of the film also gives an indication of how long it took her to get this project off the ground:

> Six years ago a young woman with no film training and just one full-length documentary to her name dropped into *The Guardian* office to ask for some advice. Long before anyone had heard of Al Gore's *The Inconvenient Truth*, she planned to make a low-budget documentary about oil and climate change. Where should she go? Try Iraq and the Niger Delta, two of the most volatile, oil-rich places on earth, the grizzled environmental correspondent advised her – hoping that she would come to no harm.
>
> Blow me, but in 15 days' time, a bright green carpet will be unrolled in Leicester Square and Franny Armstrong, now 35, better travelled but just as single-minded, will trip down it in the company of A-list celebs to a specially constructed solar-powered cinema.
>
> (John Vidal, *The Guardian*, 28 February 2009)

Business models among documentary filmmakers

1. The individual self-employed filmmaker

These tend to be the experienced filmmakers who are approached by broadcasters and the big independents to direct films. The structure they operate may have the form of a company, but it operates more as an invoicing house. While they are free to develop their own films for most of the time, financial necessity means they also need to work for other companies. According to Dex (2000) this group increased significantly in the 1980s and 1990s.

The introduction of the 25% quota of independent productions on all terrestrial channels, the implementation of producer choice in the BBC and the creation of a network centre in ITV created new working conditions across the industry. Due to these changes in regulative conditions, a workforce of more than 50% freelancers was created. These freelancers are not only directors but also include technical staff, production staff and editors.

> I started in news, working for a British news company called ITN as a journalist. Now I have a company of my own with a fellow director but we have yet to do a film purely under our own banner, because at the moment we tend to work for other people.
>
> (Louise Osmond, interview September 2007)

Skillset reports, 'Over the years, both the pull of greater freedom and the push from the threat of actual redundancy have remained common reasons for the workforce becoming freelance' (Skillset, 2005: 83). It is obvious that these are not filmmakers who are starting out, but experienced professionals who know their way in the industry. The same report stated that freelancers in independent production and digital special effects worked 50–54 hours in an average week (Ibid: 89).

Long working hours seem to be a defining aspect of working in the industry. However, many freelancers go through periods of intensive working, followed by periods of relative quiet, during which they try to develop their own work or obtain another job.

Risk management

Freelancers, craftspeople or production companies may avoid risks or even strengthen their positions by joining forces. Faulkner and Anderson's research in the field of film production demonstrated that successful producers and directors work together repeatedly in order to reduce uncertainty and increase profits (1987: 879). Blair (2001) notes that the same is true of craftspeople, camera operators, editors and production managers who work in established groups and gain employment through membership of those groups.

This would indicate that it would be a good idea to become a trainee of a group of camerapeople, or a group of editors (a post-production company) in the hope of working together.

2. The small independent production company, 2–5 filmmakers/producers involved

This is a classic set-up: a few filmmakers/producers who work together or develop their projects while sharing facilities, such as office space, computers, cameras and editing facilities.

> There are four of us. We all came out of the arts one way or another. I was a painter and a performance artist. Most of the others were from St Martins, RCA. We used to make

political, cultural and anti-imperialist posters and a series of poetry posters. And then, out of that, some of us started to make films. Most things we do are for BBC, Channel 4 and international broadcasters . . .

(Silvia Stevens, Faction Films, interview January 2008)

Different financial models operate in this kind of small independent company.

Broadcasting

The time when broadcasters fully funded documentaries seems to be over. Budgets have decreased, due to a drop in advertising revenue or non-increased licence fees, while the costs of running a broadcast organisation have increased, due to the digital infrastructure and proliferation of channels. Many additional causes could be mentioned, but the main issue is not to rely on broadcasters only, but to find funds from NGOs, Art Councils, charities or corporate industries relevant to your project.

Produce first – sell afterwards

It has become more feasible to produce a film independently, pay for the production costs yourself and sell the film afterwards to broadcasters and find a distributor.

Ishmahil Blagrove Jr wrote in Austin and de Jong (2008) that, as maker/producer of *Bang Bang! in Da Manor* (Rice N Peas, 2004, UK),

after three years unsuccessfully attempting to convince mainstream broadcasters to commission the documentary, I was left with no other option but to finance and market the film myself. Free from the conformities of a commissioning brief, the production team found itself with much more creative freedom, enabling us to produce a final result that was more gritty than the sterile products saturating the mainstream.

(2008: 173)

Bang Bang! in Da Manor, which addresses violence within the black community, was later acquired by the BBC and has been screened in over 100 cinemas and theatres in the UK. Rice N Peas developed a market presence without any mainstream support and they continue to finance their films themselves and sell them afterwards. Needless to say, the internet and relentless energy to get their film seen created this market presence.

Crowd funding

Franny Armstrong and producer Liz Garrett, who made *The Age of Stupid* (UK, 2009), used a combination of strategies to get the film off the ground. The concept of 'crowd funding' has been brought to a big audience and managed to get a great deal of attention among filmmakers. Many films have of course been funded by friends, families or remortgaging houses but this concept brought funding into a very different arena: the internet. A website was created and individuals or groups of people who would form a syndicate could buy shares in the production of the film. In exchange, they would be mentioned in the credits and receive a share of the profits. You can find more detailed information, legal documents and the strategy on *The Age of Stupid* website. There are now specialist websites that provide 'crowd funding' opportunities: www.kickstarter.com and www.indiegogo.com

Making the film: £450,000

Getting it seen: £130,000

£150k

Figure 4.1 Selling shares to fund *The Age of Stupid*

3. The artist-documentary filmmaker

> It's a way of seeing. It's a way of being, a way of understanding. It's a language. A way of interpreting the world and telling stories about the world. It crosses borders.
>
> (Luke Holland, interview 2007)

Artist-documentary filmmakers are generally self-employed or have a company to produce their own work, but they do not tend to work for other companies or broadcasters. They consider themselves artists and often have other creative skills (photography, writing). Their work is, to a certain extent, autobiographically driven. The films are an expression of personal interests, fascinations and possible obsessions.

> I have had my own company since 1990. It's small. It's independent. It's a vehicle for me to make the documentary films I want to make. It's partly also so that the company can maintain the rights of the products. Films are commissioned through the company and we maintain the rights through the backend.
>
> (Ibid.)

4. The activist documentary filmmaker

Facilitated by cheaper cameras and editing software, documentaries driven by new global movements such as anti-globalisation and environmentalist resistance to mainstream media and their corporate messages have become more visible on the internet. Documentaries such as *The Corporation*, *McLibel* and *The Yes Men* have reached bigger audiences through the internet and exhibition in independent cinemas or alternative venues. The activist filmmaker uses documentary as a tool to expose social and economic injustice or environmental exploitation. The activist filmmaker is part of a social movement and either personally funds his/her programme or manages to obtain sponsorship from sympathetic NGOs or charities. Although much has been written about the monopolisation of the media industry, the erosion of public values or the intrusion of corporate values in culture, never in history have so many pressure groups been so active in civil society. The internet has provided activist filmmakers with a global distribution channel and the low cost of producing copies on DVD has made this group more prominent in both the public sphere and on the internet.

The characteristics of this group of filmmakers are:

- Independence from existing media organisations
- Radical content, challenging mainstream views or revealing hidden realities
- Alternative forms of distribution: internet, small independent cinemas or alternative venues where one-off events take place
- Belonging to social movements – often production takes place in a non-hierarchical, participatory production group, taking the formal structure of a co-op
- They often take up the role of citizen journalists by reporting on events not reported in mainstream media or hidden from journalists as the footage is shot under cover.

A well-known and successful international activist media network is Indiemedia (Coyer, 2005), which describes itself as 'A network of individuals, independent and alternative media activists and organisations, offering grassroots, non-corporate, non-commercial coverage of important social and political issues' (see Indiemedia website, accessed 20 April 2010).

> The news often presents a sanitised version of events or actions and has a clear bias towards powerful NGOs, corporate industry or government organisations. To get on TV you need to set up visual stunts just as Greenpeace does. I have nothing against Greenpeace, they have been very successful but it is now an established pressure group. We organise ourselves according to our interests – whether it is abuse of animal rights, environmental disasters or abuse of human rights. Big themes but translated into local actions, protesting against another bypass, or a lab which misuses animals.
> It is dynamic and constantly moving. I'm basically a full-time media activist. It's my life.
>
> (Anonymous, interview July 2007)

5. The ambitious amateur

When the Documentary Filmmakers Group (DFG) was being set up, and since 4Docs, YouTube and MySpace have appeared on the internet, it has become apparent that there is a large group of documentary filmmakers who make films in their leisure time, either as a hobby or with the ambition to enter the industry. Channel 4's 4Docs catered very well for this ambition as it selected four documentaries every month which would be shown to commissioning editors. This could lead to an offer of a place on one of Channel 4's training programmes or a film being commissioned as part of their scheme to recruit new talent. After a brief period when it was unavailable, 4Docs was relaunched in 2010.

Amateur filmmaking has boomed since cheap cameras and editing software have become affordable and the internet offered a distribution channel. Many of the filmmakers might have more serious ambitions, but others have integrated footage about their lives as a form of communication in a social network environment.

6. The commercial entrepreneur

> If you want to come into this business, you've got to treat it like a business.
>
> (David Notman-Watt, interview January 2008)

These filmmakers tend to approach their work as a business and operate within the demands of the market, and of broadcasters. This does not necessarily imply that they follow market demands uncritically, but due to their filmmaking experience, contacts and know-how, they are able to navigate through the system and to negotiate more favourable conditions.

The BIG power of small independents

Big independents have development teams that plough through the newspapers, the internet and archives to unearth stories. They will have the personnel who can do basic research, write a treatment and fund a trailer to present to commissioning editors, to whom they have easier access due to a known track record. For them, the online e-commissioning system is not the only route. If they use it at all, it is to obtain access to commissioning editors.

There seem to be three ways in which smaller independents can create a niche in the documentary production market.

Creativity

Powerful big indies and a saturated competitive market demand that documentary filmmakers come up with new ideas and new approaches.

> That's where all the innovation takes place. It is at the edges, so at the moment there's a fashion for heavily interventionist programmes, like *Wife Swap*, which are very heavily constructed, formatted documentaries. I think they're still documentaries; they're still dealing with a situation out in the real world, and they're still trying to reflect a situation in the real world. They're just doing it in a much more tightly controlled, restricted way. That's just the fashion at the moment.
>
> (Ralph Leigh, Channel 4, in Austin and de Jong, 2008)

There is also a demand for authored films, films that show a clear signature from the filmmaker. Filmmakers such as Daisy Asquith, Molly Dineen, Nick Broomfield or Kim Longinotto are recognisable because of their approach to the filmmaking process or subjects. To develop one's own style requires experience. Experimenting with different documentary forms or styles gives the opportunity to develop a personal signature.

Either independents comply with current trends or they try to push the boundaries to come up with new formats or concepts. Incorporating websites and the internet, authored DVDs have become part of programme-making, often described as 'thinking across new platforms'. Small independents could find a niche through their ability to develop a format/programme idea that works across different distribution channels.

Access to 'the story'

Finding a story, unearthing hidden stories and gaining unique access to the people involved, to archived material or to a location is a way for the small independents to create a strong negotiating position in the field. In documentary production, access to the story is a non-negotiable prerequisite for the realisation of the films.

> The first thing is access that no one else has got. That's the trick; the advantage of the small company is often that we are slightly less business-oriented, and are more about building relationships with people. Through networks of friends of friends we find those stories. Those are the films the small Indies get commissioned.
>
> (Andy Glynne, DFG interview, January 2008)

Non-broadcast production

Many documentary filmmakers focus on the broadcast industry to realise projects. The competition with experienced documentary filmmakers, the decrease in budgets for programmes and the availability of other distribution channels might make it necessary to look for other funding and distribution.

> If I think about our present projects, half of the money for one is coming from an EU scheme, the other half from the British Council. We have another one which is funded by Teachers TV, the cable station, and one is funded by the Wellcome Trust, which has started a broadcast development fund. So money is coming from loads of different sources.
>
> (Ibid.)

If your film deals with subjects like the developing world, or illness, or is technically experimental, try to find a trust, a fund, a foundation, an NGO or even corporate industry to help fund it. Now that advertising revenues for TV are decreasing and the licence fee is not increasing, broadcasters are no longer likely to pay for the production of a complete film. Expenditure on internet advertising has overtaken TV advertising and distribution of the existing licence fee over several broadcasters is being debated. The category 'public broadcast programmes' is being introduced, which implies that all broadcasters can apply for public funding for programmes falling into this category.

Co-production

Baltruschat (2003) notes how the surge of international co-production throughout the 1990s can be seen as typical of the increasingly export-oriented television and film industries, which produce commercially viable 'global' products. These are based on entertainment values rather than being the expression of, or a critical reflection of, 'local' issues. The growth of international co-productions is facilitated by international networks and affiliations between small and large media organisations.

For small independents which have the experience and the contacts, this is a mixed blessing. To get co-productions off the ground is very labour-intensive and can add 15–25% of the budget to the costs of the films, but it is a way of succeeding in making a film.

Diversification of income sources

The portfolio career is a much-described phenomenon. Filmmakers teach at colleges and universities, and work for other filmmakers as editors or producers. Others work for big indies for six months a year and develop and make their own films in the months without work. This is not a new development: many filmmakers have, in the course of their careers, worked in other professions, either to save money to develop a project or to make a living between films. Activist filmmakers will often not seek to make a living from their films because of their political aims and their refusal to comply with the demands from funders.

In the present climate, it is not a sign of failure or an illustration of your lack of talent if you cannot make a living from documentary filmmaking alone. Portfolio careers among artists in fine art have existed for many years and there is no reason why this could not work for documentary filmmakers.

An alternative route to obtain experience

It is worth getting a job in the industry starting at the bottom to gain experience. Try during your studies to get some short-term jobs. During the holidays it might be a good time to get a traineeship, internship or a job as a technical assistant or runner. Working conditions tend to be poor, but avoid being exploited – do not work without pay or do ridiculous hours for £50 a day.

Join BECTU (www.bectu.org.uk). If you are currently a student, you are eligible to join when you have finished your course. They hold meetings at which you can meet media professionals and, as a member of BECTU, you will be sent *Early Bird*, a quarterly list of forthcoming productions, free of charge. This will provide you with contact details of people to approach. A short email stating your experience and interest followed up by a phone call might draw their attention to you.

You might also want to try to obtain a job with a camera rental company, a post-production company, as a cameraperson or sound technician. For instance http://www.kays.co.uk offers a list of companies.

Check the websites of the different broadcasters for internships, trainee programmes and 'talent scouting' initiatives.

If you want to work for an independent production company, it is worth visiting the Kays website, which provides a list of 1,700 production companies. They will receive a lot of applications, so it might be better to obtain an introduction from someone you have met at BECTU or DFG meetings.

Make a short, show it at film festivals and use it as a way to establish contact with the big independents when you have another idea which you would like to develop.

Look at www.broadcastfreelancer.com. This website is aimed at broadcasting jobs but they ask for runners, and assistants for assistants.

If you find a job, try to make it work for you, so that you do not leave at the end without anyone even knowing your name. Do not become invisible, show them your commitment and interest and of course do your job well. You might be lugging gear around, driving around picking up bits of kit, or making tea. Have chats at appropriate times and make very good tea.

However, you may feel that in this situation you have to bend over backwards, and that the route of making a film and trying to sell it or use it to obtain finance for another film might be a more inspiring and rewarding way to approach your future as a documentary filmmaker.

Key points

- The conventional way of financing documentaries solely via broadcasters is changing. Budgets have decreased and additional funds need to be found.
- There are several funding possibilities: produce first, sell afterwards; crowd funding; broadcast funding and in addition NGOs, arts councils or other funds and foundations.
- Co-production is limited due to the national demands of broadcasters. Subjects may be international, but there is demand for national presenters or celebrity presenters, which complicates the production process because of working with different presenters for each country. It is more expensive and time-consuming but the project can get off the ground.
- Filmmakers sell ideas but also sell ready-made programmes.

- Portfolio careers seem to be prevalent.
- The interest of filmmakers and the demands of broadcasters clash in content and form, with demand for formatted series as opposed to one-off programmes.
- Film concepts are expected to work across different platforms; each distribution platform should have an added value.
- Mass-produced programming has taken over the television industry, therefore the smaller independents are entering a difficult time. Howevers, original ideas, unique access to certain 'realities', flexibility and the quota system will see the independent industry continue to grow.
- Commissioning is very competitive. Budgets are tight and do not allow for contingency funds, which could be used for development of new programmes.

Exercise

Analyse the funding strategies of *The Age of Stupid* (Franny Armstrong UK, 2009), *Black Gold* (Marc and Nick Francis, UK, 2006). Consider the time and risk involved.

How to be a successful freelance documentary filmmaker

According to research (Lorenzen and Frederiksen, 2005) and our own experience, you should do the following to keep in business as a creative freelancer:

- Consider yourself as a professional who is running a business, exploiting your talents, skills and aspirations. You may want to change the world, but you will only be employed if your skills are needed for a project that will change the world.
- Try to obtain a variety of employment in order to avoid dependency on only one source of income. It could be teaching, crewing for other projects or teaching English as a foreign language . . .
- Develop and nurture networks of filmmakers, producers or relevant professionals in your field who might be interested in your skills or ideas. Mingle in circles of professionals in fields you are interested in – mental health, international development, fashion, etc. You have to become part of a community of practitioners.
- Become a member of professional organisations: DFG, EDN, crewing agencies or a union.
- Read professional magazines to see who is doing what and phone them to offer your services.
- Attend film festivals to keep in touch with new developments or get in touch with other filmmakers.
- Manage your reputation. It is essential that you create an image of yourself as reliable, meeting deadlines and delivering a good job.
- Above all be prepared to answer the question: why would someone hire you?
- Be prepared to do some cold calling and don't take a refusal as a personal offence.

Interview Andy Glynne – Documentary Filmmakers Group (DFG)

Andy Glynne (photo © Wilma de Jong)

When I studied psychology and became a clinical psychologist, I guess I became frustrated with working in the NHS – my aspirations of making much of a difference felt continually hampered. I started thinking about making films. There was one specific example that was happening in Australia at the time. I had a patient who was transgender and had undergone gender re-assignment surgery. But because of the legislation they couldn't go to a bar and they had no employee protection. No lobbying and nothing was happening. I thought someone should make a film about this. If that got on TV then maybe that could make a difference. I realised there was a way film could make a big difference in making people aware about issues, and hopefully change the way people feel.

I came to England, still working as a psychologist, and went to a few filmmaking courses and bought myself a tiny camera and started making stuff. But I didn't know anybody at all, so I put some fliers out in Soho, saying: 'Who wants to talk to another documentary filmmaker? I'll be in this pub', thinking five people might come. About 40 people came. What do I do? We decided to do a couple of screenings in Soho for documentaries that weren't getting on television – or for documentary filmmakers who wanted to show their film to a live audience to get feedback.

We hired a pub and 80 people came down – and, in the following two weeks, 100 people. Then we rang up a commissioning editor at Channel 4 and said 'Look, we've got 100 documentary filmmakers who want to hear what you're looking for.' Then 150 people came. We moved from a pub to a theatre space. There was this huge community of people who wanted to make docs. It was great. Our 'office' was above Bar Italia in Soho. They gave us their restaurant for two hours every Thursday afternoon. There were about five or six of us who all had full-time jobs. At the end of the evening, we looked at how much we charged at the door, and divided it up. That's how it started. It continued like that for six to eight months. Through this process, this community of filmmakers said that what they really wanted was some kind of training. We want industry-led, vocational courses. So we designed a set of courses. At that point, it had to become a business venture. All the people who were involved turned around and said, 'I'm not prepared to give up my day job.' So I was the only one left who was prepared to give up my day job and invest money into it. I carried on with our screenings, and started doing training. Within two years, the training had grown, the membership had grown to 4,000 and back then we were the only organisation doing this kind of training. Ten years later, the landscape has changed dramatically.

Part 2

Development strategies

Heavy Load's drummer, Michael White (*Heavy Load*, Rothwell, 2008)

Chapter 5

Developing ideas
Jerry Rothwell

"I would say that I don't care about the subject. The subject . . . is totally secondary. You can make, I think, a great film with a very tiny subject. I'm convinced that you can make films in the next café, because in the next café there are men and women and stories and suffering people and all of life. It's a question of a way of looking at reality, much more than the subject, which is important for me."

(Nicholas Philibert (director, *Etre et Avoir*), BFI NFT interviews)

Introduction

Ideas are everywhere. The key to a great documentary is how you develop an idea into something uniquely filmic. This chapter looks at how to build your idea into a treatment for a film. It explores the ingredients of a strong film idea, how to approach research, the importance of access and permissions and writing a treatment.

Ideas

When we talk about documentaries, we often begin by saying what the film is about, its subject matter: 'a film about the coffee industry' or 'about the US health system' or 'about a man with memory loss'. So, in some ways, it is surprising when a documentary filmmaker like Nicholas Philibert says he doesn't care about the subject. But subject matter and films are not the same thing and, for a subject to become the basis of a strong documentary idea, it needs to be developed into more than simply a topic, more than 'a film *about* x, y or z'.

When filmmakers are asked about their starting point for a particular film, their answers are more likely to describe an image, a meeting, a juxtaposition or an intuition, than an interest in the broader subject matter. The sources of ideas for documentaries are no different from those of any other creative idea: a character, an event, a situation, something you've heard or read about, been told or experienced first-hand. The world is not short of starting points for possible films. But ideas that can turn into strong documentaries tend to require a few common ingredients: a compelling narrative; a strong concept or form; engaging central characters and the depiction of a particular world. There are some basic questions you can ask yourself about your idea, which will indicate its potential as a film; this is thinking you need to do before you begin in-depth research, or negotiate access, or discuss the project with potential funders.

Is there a story?

Stories are human constructs. Experience doesn't neatly arrive with a beginning, a middle and an end until we make it so. But film is a time-based medium and, whatever the subject of your film, it needs to have the potential to unfold in a compelling way. Not all documentaries follow a conventional story structure, but successful films develop their themes, characters or events over time. This might be a progressive series of actions, or a steadily unfolding revelation of character or place, but it will need the potential to take an audience by surprise or to deepen our understanding. An interesting situation, on its own, is not enough to sustain a film.

A later chapter (Chapter 8) deals with narrative techniques in depth – but here are some initial questions which might help you establish whether your idea has the potential for a story and find where the heart of that story might lie:

- Does the idea suggest a person, a world or a set of relationships at a point of change?

- Define this change. What are its causes? (Where might your idea begin?) What are its key turning points?

- What might happen? (Where might your idea end?)

- Can you find within this situation central characters who want something, for themselves, or for others – for example, to take action to change something? What are the obstacles they face?

- Are these changes significant or meaningful enough to compel our attention? What is it that you yourself find compelling about them? Thinking closely about why you yourself are drawn to a particular idea will give you clues about how to develop your own fascination into something revelatory for other people. As the artist Louise Bourgeois said when asked for her advice to younger artists: 'Tell your own story, and you will be interesting.'[1]

Whether a story is unfolding in the present, and you can only guess at the outcome, or whether it covers a set of historical events, these questions point you towards the narrative potential of your idea. You're testing your idea to recognise whether it can take your audience on a journey, one that will engage them, take them to places they've never been to and tell them things they don't know.

Crafting a story is a process of selection and editing – and deciding what to leave out is as important as what you keep in. As Samuel Johnson said, 'Seldom is it that any splendid story is wholly true.' For documentary makers, who are making a claim that their film represents real events, crafting stories also has an ethical dimension. When does omission, for the sake of a good plot, mislead the audience about actual events? To what extent do we have the right to rework reality to tell a compelling story? Documentary ethics imply a commitment to 'truth telling' and to honesty. In finding the story, you don't have the freedom of a fiction screenwriter.

What form might your film take?

The camera – indeed any image or sound – implies a point of view, a vantage point from which the subject is seen or heard. A strong documentary idea will build on this to create an 'angle' which takes us beyond the obvious – a different 'way of looking at reality', as Philibert describes it in the quote that starts this chapter.

Already, in discovering its potential for story, you've begun to give your film idea a form, its distinctive viewpoint. You need to be able to develop that viewpoint with a consistent set of decisions about structure and style. It has been suggested that a director is like the film's immune system: the role is to prevent elements creeping into the film that damage its integrity. As your idea takes shape, you're presented with a dazzling array of possibilities (and often plenty of unsolicited advice) and, as the development process progresses, you need to narrow these down to a set of choices which best express your film's content.

So in this first stage of development, at the same time as learning more about the story potential of the film, it is helpful to think about its ideal form: what kind of film you might be making. This will also help you decide where best to seek funding. For example, you may need to decide, early on:

- the timeframe in which you tell your story;
- key aspects of visual style and sound design;
- the context for interviewees or witnesses;
- any use of reconstruction;
- your approach to filming current events;
- how the film addresses the viewer (through a presenter, a voice-over, a poetic combination of sound and image, etc.).

These choices also dictate the kinds of visual language your film will use and so the way in which you shoot and edit.

Some of these decisions will be forced by pragmatic considerations – for example, whether and how the key elements in your story are filmable. You might have a great idea about a little-known event in the seventeenth century, but, given that you will have no film or photographic archive, you'll need to find ways of representing the story for the camera. What of your story is visible in the present – or could be made so?

What is the world of your film?

The most successful films take the viewer into a specific world – and documentaries are no exception. Ask yourself how the world of your film works – who are its lead characters, what is its mood, what does it sound like, what colours dominate, what laws govern what happens in it? Again, this will point you towards stylistic choices so you can create a distinctive, out-of-the-ordinary experience for your audience.

One way of thinking about form is that you are giving yourself a set of rules about the making of your film, which will govern how you will bring the idea to the screen. From Vertov to Dogma, documentary history is particularly rich in manifestos and rule-bound approaches to production. Often these sets of rules are about finding a way to break with the conventions of the day. Albert Maysles, a pioneer of direct cinema, said he was reacting against the rules he was taught: You have to use a tripod. You have to shoot in 35 millimetre. And you have to have a point of view. He threw all of these out of the window and set his own rules: Shoot on portable 16 mm equipment, with no tripod, no music, no 'treatment' – to distance himself from his own point of view, giving his work an immediacy and leaving, he hoped, the audience to make up its own mind. What would be your manifesto for your own film?

As we'll see later, stylistic rules are always challenged by the realities of the production process, but they do offer the filmmaker a guide to the particular approach they want to adopt.

Who are your central characters?

Most documentaries have central characters and your choice of 'cast' is a critical creative decision. Documentaries are built on the relationship between filmmakers and their contributors, and a strong central character can carry an audience into the world of the film, and keep us there because we care about what is going to happen to him or her.

Your central characters need to be willing to undertake the sometimes exhausting, emotional and difficult journey of making a film – but not so willing that they're constantly second guessing what you want of them. They need to want something that relates to the central premise of the film, and to follow that desire during the filming. They need to be people who 'work on camera', an indefinable quality that sometimes you'll only appreciate when you view back rushes of them. And they need to be people who are complex enough to have aspects of themselves they keep hidden or that surprise us when they are revealed.

In some ways, all documentaries are a joint exploration between filmmaker and subject, especially as digital technologies have broken down many of the more formal traditional divisions between subject and maker, those in front of the camera and those behind it. Contemporary documentary will often use footage shot by the contributor themselves, either diary or archive, and, at times, work with them as joint author of the film.

There has been a strong resistance in broadcast documentary culture to any meaningful control being given to documentary subjects. The legal framework in which productions take place usually requires contributors to hand over all rights by the signing of a release form. Editorially, it is rare to involve subjects in any filmmaking decisions once the edit has started. Current BBC guidelines state cautiously that:

> We do not normally allow contributors a preview of BBC content. However, when a
> preview is offered to a collaborative contributor for editorial, ethical or legal reasons, we
> must be able to demonstrate the terms under which it was granted. It is best to do this in
> writing in advance. We should always make it clear that we are not surrendering editorial
> control and that any changes made as a result will generally only relate to the correction

of agreed factual inaccuracies, concerns about the welfare of children, or for reasons of personal safety, or national security.[2]

But the nature of contemporary filmmaking – especially films which draw on the subject's own footage or use their lives as the substantial content of the film – often mean a broader collaboration and more detailed consents than simply the signing of a release form.

Consent

At some point in your development process you will need to formalise your main contributors' consent to your film. If you're hoping for a sustained contribution from them over a long period, and perhaps also that they undertake not to do other films which might clash with yours, you will need to do a longer contract, which sets out your expectations and their commitments. You may need this contract in order to reassure financiers that you have the access you say you do, and that it is legally binding. Where relevant, you should also include in that contract the releasing of any personal footage, recordings or photographs belonging to the contributor that are an essential part of the film. Your funders will want to know that there is no danger of a withdrawal of consent to these materials during production and that the contributor has the right to give them.

Informed consent

Most broadcasters use a notion of 'informed consent' to establish whether contributors have given their permission to be in a programme. Informed consent requires the contributor to:

a) have the **capacity** to give consent (a legal and medical definition);

b) give their consent **freely** (i.e. without compulsion or inducement);

c) have sufficient **knowledge** about their contribution and its context to accept or decline.

The need for consent is judged to be a balance between the individual's right to privacy and the public interest. So there are circumstances where consent may not be required – for example, people recorded clearly committing a crime or behaving anti-socially in a public place.

The level of information and dialogue needed for informed consent will depend on how significant the contributor's role is in the final programme. The BBC, for example, offers a list of categories of contributor, with different consent requirements for each.[3] Consent can be either written or recorded, but needs to be in a form that can be used as evidence of the decision the contributor has made.

Research

Film research differs from other kinds of research in that it is targeted towards finding the people, situations and archive material needed to realise a film's premise. Whilst discovering information may be a crucial aspect of the research, it will also be about securing the permissions and relationships necessary to shoot.

Researching context and contributors

One of the pleasures of documentary filmmaking is that it requires you to find out about and understand many radically different areas of human knowledge and experience. Each film takes you into a different world, often with its own codes, language, history, celebrities, science and myths. The filmmaker necessarily becomes a generalist, understanding enough to make his or her way through a subject without – with a few exceptions – becoming an expert who dedicates their life to a particular subject matter. Film is a relatively simplistic medium – at least in the information it is able to convey – and it is more important to find people, situations, stories and images that can represent your subject than to embed yourself deeply in its minutiae in the way that you might need to if you were writing an academic book. But it is important to know enough to be able to represent those who know more, and to understand the context for the subject you are filming.

The internet has, of course, revolutionalised film research, not only as a means of discovering information, but as a method of finding potential witnesses and contributors, or of visualising a particular location. The more complex and controversial your subject is, the less reliable the internet and the more you need to verify what you find there against other sources.

Some filmmakers have created websites for research before their film goes into production – and some films have been based around the contributors to websites such as YouTube (a good example of this is Sarah McCarthy's film *Murderers on the Dancefloor*, the story of a provincial jail in the Philippines which was catapulted into the global media by a series of YouTube clips of its inmates dancing to Michael Jackson's *Thriller*).

Contributors are themselves often the filmmaker's principal guide into their world – though it is important to supplement this with other sources such as organisations and associations dedicated to information about particular subject areas.

Where appropriate, your research should take you to the places and people which are part of your film's world – seeing and hearing things for yourself is the richest source of ideas about the form your film should take. You need to start working towards a trailer to promote your film idea (see Chapter 6), so your research should include shooting with key people and places.

Much of this research will be taking place before your film is fully financed, but there are some sources of funding, principally those with a social agenda, which will contribute to the development of films with certain themes – for example, the Sundance Institute (human rights), ITVS (global issues), the WorldView (documentaries about the developing world) and the Wellcome Trust (films relating to bio-medical science).

Archive research

Research for archival footage and photographs falls into two categories:

- Archive material that gives a feel for an era and can stand in as a general illustration of some aspect of a story.
- Archive material of specific events which are the substance or even, in some cases, the subject of your film.

The search for the first category is relatively easy. Working through image libraries and archives, it is straightforward to find generic or iconic footage to evoke, for example, a particular era or place. The search for specific footage can be much more difficult, and, if your film depends on it, needs to start long before the film is financed. Once you've exhausted the various film archive libraries that might be relevant, if you know that film has been shot, you need to start behaving like a detective.

First, identify what material you need that is original and, in your view, essential to your film. Next weigh up the cost of the search, the likely technical quality of the footage, the time spent looking for and clearing it and its importance for the film. Then start gathering clues (names of people connected to the filming, dates, film can references, production companies) – any piece of information that might take you to whoever holds the footage. Most film archive databases only partially document what the archive holds. You need to find those archivists who have a detailed knowledge of their own material, beyond the database, and recognise which of them might be an enthusiast who will help your search. Be persistent and believe that the material you need is out there somewhere.

Exercise

Love on the Streets

A filmmaker who also works in a London hostel for homeless people has become interested in making a film about homeless couples. She's noticed, to her surprise initially, that a number of the residents in the hostel are in long-term relationships with each other, and also that the hostel has no facilities for couples to share a room. She's interested in how the story of a relationship might shift an audience's perception of homelessness.

So she has an initial idea, a subject area, but not yet a film . . .

Make a plan of her development process to the point where she will be in a position to pitch her idea to funders. Creatively, what does she need to find in order to develop her idea, and, practically, what consents will she need in place? What kinds of film might be possible for her? And what might be impossible?

Key points

- Develop your idea by thinking about its potential for story.
- Decide what kind of film you are making and what are its stylistic and narrative rules.
- Look for characters who can become the central focus of the film.
- Understand what defines the world of your film.
- Make sure you have the necessary story rights and consents for your central characters before you approach funders.
- Know your subject well enough to be able to represent it accurately.
- Begin research for archive footage which is fundamental to the film as early as possible.

Notes

[1] Doland, A. (2008) 'Artist Louise Bourgeois: Still at work at 96', Associated Press archive.

[2] BBC Editorial Guidelines: Fairness, Contributors and Consent, see http://www.bbc.co.uk/guidelines/editorialguidelines/edguide/fairness/fairnesstocontr.shtml (accessed 4/6/2010).

[3] BBC Editorial Guidelines, see http://www.bbc.co.uk/guidelines/editorialguidelines/page/guidance-consent-who (accessed 2/11/2010).

Chapter 6

From idea to pitch

Jerry Rothwell

"Never give commissioners
what they ask for – because
they won't thank you for it."

(Robert Thirkell)[1]

Introduction

When you have established the central premise of your idea, and understood how it can work as a film, you can start to think about creating a proposal for potential funders. It's crucial to move to this stage relatively quickly. If you delay too long in the initial ideas stage, you risk losing your contributors, or another film being made on the same subject, or missing that zeitgeist moment when the idea seemed to speak to a wide audience. By developing your film for a pitch, you will in any case learn much more about what the film should become. This chapter looks at how to put together a documentary proposal for funders, make a trailer and prepare for pitching your film.

Audiences

Once you've a clear sense of your film idea, it's time to think in more detail about audiences. The decisions you take in developing your idea will determine the audience your film is likely to reach – and the types and amounts of funding you are likely to attract (because funding is usually attached to audiences). The same content might appeal to a wide range of audiences, but its form will determine how generalised is its appeal.

Audiences are constructed by distribution systems; film distributors and television broadcasters already have strong ideas about who their audience is and what their tastes are. On the whole, they aren't going to change those ideas for the benefit of a single film. Instead, they're looking for ideas that will work for their audience. So you need to find the methods and channels of distribution which are closest to your ideas about your film's intended audience.

Broadcasters and distributors tend to think of their audience in terms of age (for example, children; 16–24-year olds; 25–34-year olds; 35–54-year olds and over-55s), gender and social group. They might subdivide according to other basic characteristics which might influence lifestyle – for example, those who are parents, or who live in cities. Using these categories, they look at how these audience segments use media. This kind of research will shape their scheduling and commissioning decisions.

Think about who your film speaks to, the audience you want to reach. What does the film bring to that audience? What do you want them to do, think or feel? For example, is it a film that inspires people to take action? Does it speak to the experiences of a specific social group? Find out where your audience 'consumes' its media and so how you can best reach them (cinema, web, television, private screenings, DVD distribution). If your film is intended for broadcast, what slots contain documentaries similar to your own?

Once you've established a clearer idea of how you might reach your audience, you're in a better position to approach those who commission media for that audience.

Sources of finance

The only concrete market for [documentary at] the moment is television. They buy, they pay you. From now on, I'm looking for two types of films – TV hours with a short life that you can sell in six months and some arts programming. Only very rarely feature-length. There are almost no more feature slots in prime time. They get bought but no-one sees them because they are shown after midnight.[2]

This bleak view encapsulates the difficulties of seeking sales for single documentaries, from the point of view of a distributor. For the filmmaker, looking for finance before the film is made, there are broader options. Depending on the kind of documentary you are making, there are a number of different paths you can follow.

Broadcast commissions

Perhaps the most straightforward form of documentary funding – and the one that the distributor quoted above sees as the most viable commercial platform – is that of broadcast commissions. A production company or filmmaker will pitch an idea to a broadcaster, which will provide the finance to make it in return for some or all of the rights in the programme. Broadcasters divide their schedules into slots or strands, overseen by different commissioning editors, and before pitching you need to research thoroughly which strands and which commissioners are most likely to be interested in your idea. There are increasingly few slots for single documentaries as most broadcasters prefer to schedule factual programmes in series. The reasons for this are predominantly financial: it is easier to market to and build a consistent audience for a series of programmes than for a one-off film. It is even more cost-effective to market a format, which can be repeated, sometimes over decades, and in different forms internationally. So if you are interested in broadcast commissions, you need to think about how your programme will work in the broadcasters' schedule and whether what you have is a series idea rather than a single documentary.

International co-production

The larger television markets – USA, UK and Japan – are still able to commission and fully fund a documentary for broadcast in a single territory. Increasingly, however, with the proliferation of channels and the tightening of production budgets, production companies need to seek funding from multiple broadcasters across the world. The most effective way to do this is through international co-production, working with partner companies who intimately know the commissioning process in their own territories.

Feature film funding

The success of a few theatrical documentaries such as *Touching The Void* and *SuperSize Me* has interested financiers who more usually fund fiction features than long-format documentaries, which could play successfully in the cinema. Funding for features usually combines deals with regional development and production funds, national tax incentives (for example, in the UK, the Producers' Tax Credit, which allows a tax rebate for spend in the UK on theatrical documentaries), broadcasters, distributors and exhibitors. You need to understand how and why your film could work best in the cinema and on DVD as well as on television. Putting together a feature funding package is complex and takes a long time. It does, however, enable an ambition and depth to projects which is often impossible on television.

Social funding

Increasingly, organisations which have a social agenda (for example, around international development or human rights) are seeing documentary film as a means of raising awareness of an issue and as an effective catalyst to social change. A range of international funds have been established specifically to fund films which support social aims (for example, the Ford Foundation,

ITVS and the Sundance Institute). There are also national funding agencies which will support work that gives a voice to particular social groups (for example, marginalised refugee communities or disabled people or young people). If your film focuses on these issues and works in an empowering way with its subjects, it may well be eligible for these funds.

'Crowd' funding

Crowd funding is an emerging internet-based funding method where subscribers contribute small amounts of money towards the production and distribution of a film in return for privileges or rights. It is most appropriate for films with a campaigning agenda, where supporters of that campaign want to see the film made in order to advance a cause.

Cultural funding

In many countries, funds exist to support national media and cultural industries. In Europe, funds such as MEDIA, and in the UK the funds managed by the UK Film Council are examples of two such funds – and there are many smaller regional funding bodies, including local authorities and regional screen agencies, which support documentary production.

Pre-sales

You may be able to pre-sell your film to different national broadcasters on the basis of the strength of the idea and the team behind it. Invariably, the more evidence you can show of existing commitments to fund, the more likely others are to join in. Pre-sales, because they imply additional risk and more limited rights for the broadcaster, will be worth less than commissions.

Distribution deals

Some distributors will offer production finance to documentaries in return for distribution rights – though this is increasingly rare, as it carries a high risk for the distributor. More usually, distributors will make judgements on the basis of a rough cut or finished film.

Whatever your sources of finance, you need to have a clear understanding of why they are funding the film, and hence their expectations of the finished product. There's little point in promising a film you're not going to make in order to obtain funding – you may well end up being pressured into making a completely different film from the one you set out to make, or even losing control of it altogether.

The documentary proposal

Your written film proposal is the first introduction potential funders will have to your film. Many documentary filmmakers find it difficult to write convincingly about a film they haven't yet made. But writing your idea can be a way of flushing out potential problems and clarifying your thoughts. Keep in mind that those who fund documentaries have many extremely strong proposals to choose from and you need to find ways of making your idea stand out on paper. Documentary filmmaking is a crowded market with an endless supply of good ideas and a limited number of funded slots, channels and audiences for them. Think about how you might use photographs as well as words, perhaps going as far as designing a brochure to convey both the content and the look of your film.

The proposal needs to include:

- Synopsis
- Film idea and your approach
- Filmmakers
- Budget and finance plan (covered in Chapter 7).

Note that the proposal is not the same thing as a treatment, which is a much longer document explaining how you are going to make the film and might be needed to persuade interested funders finally to commit, but which should not be required as part of an initial pitch.

The synopsis

A synopsis is a short summary of the film (describing what the film is about and what is its focus). Imagine it as the billing a film might get in a TV listings magazine. How would you describe your film to its audience in a paragraph?

> **Example**
> Donor Unknown is the story of one man and the fourteen children conceived with his donated sperm, who want to discover who he is in order to know themselves.

The film idea and your approach

This is the main body of the proposal and should ideally be about a page long. It should describe:

Content

The essential points of the film's story, highlighting its unique attractions as a film: an extraordinary character, humour, a big name, its immediate relevance, its unique access. It is important to be aware of other films on the same subject and to know why yours is different.

Approach

A description of how you are going to realise the film. Be specific about the film's tone, its focus and its technical requirements. If the film offers something unusual – for example, a particular approach to CGI or a narration told in song or verse, support this by describing who will be involved and their proven expertise in these areas. You should give a sense of the film's style – for example, is it observational or does it involve drama reconstruction or is it led by a presenter? Describe your visual approach, and how you will work with sound, if these notably set your film apart.

Format

The type of film you're making. Is it a series or a single? What length are you aiming at? Is it a recognisable documentary genre? What kind of audience is it aimed at? Back this up with reasons why you are taking this approach and why the approach is achievable.

Timescale

Does your approach dictate a particular time frame? For example, do you need to shoot for six months in order to cover a given set of actions? Don't give time ultimatums (e.g. 'I need to have funding by July or there's no film'). These may be true but they are your problem, not your funder's!

Access

If your access to the people, archive, places, events or music in your film is unique, explain why and prove that you have secured it. Access to untold stories is a strong selling point for documentaries and you need to think about whether this is true for your film. But if you use access as a selling point for your film, make sure you have it.

Awareness of potential problems

All documentaries have potential pitfalls and it strengthens your proposal to show that you are aware of them and have thought about how you will surmount them. Examples might be:

- Language issues – how will you work in a language you don't speak?
- Financial issues – if you need to raise a large budget, have you ideas about the multiple funders you will approach?
- Ethical issues – how will you work with sensitive stories or with subjects for whom the filmmaking process is potentially damaging or life-threatening? Are you aware of the consequences of exploring a contentious subject?
- Complexity – for instance, if you are working with a difficult scientific subject unfamiliar to most audiences, how will you explain the necessary science?

Give details about your team if it helps prove you can resolve these issues, and avoid highlighting problems that are insoluble.

The filmmakers

Funders fund filmmakers who they know can create something special, as much as they fund great ideas. You need to show that you are uniquely qualified to make the film. Include a one-paragraph summary of the director, producer(s) and any key personnel whose specific experience strengthens your case for making the film. You should also include a paragraph about the production company, its relevant track record and contact information.

Trailers

Creating a short 'taster' for your documentary is becoming increasingly important in the search for funds to make it. In the absence of a script, trailers are an excellent way to communicate why your film should be made. You're aiming to make something that lasts a maximum of 4 minutes and which:

- introduces the characters;
- introduces the subject area and the world of your film;
- communicates the potential of the story and its arc;
- gives a sense of the film's style and visual approach.

Making a pitching trailer will involve you in shooting with your subjects, usually before you have funding on board. However, you need to bear in mind that your audience of funders and commissioning editors are still likely to draw conclusions from your trailer about the style of the film itself, so it is worth investing time and money, if you can, to make the trailer as close to the production values of the final film as possible.

A pitch trailer should not be confused with a short film. It is almost always shown with further explanation of the documentary or an accompanying document, so you need to decide what is best communicated through these other media.

The pitch

Putting together a good pitch for your film is an essential part of finding the money to make documentaries.

The pitch is the moment that you take your idea and offer it to a potential financier. Usually you've already been through some kind of selection process based on a written proposal, so you can feel encouraged that your idea is at least in the right zone for the funder you are meeting.

For broadcast documentaries the pitch is likely either to be in a meeting with a commissioning editor or, increasingly, at one of the public pitch forums organised by international documentary festivals. In either case, you need to shape the presentation of your film idea into something like a 3-minute spoken pitch and a 3-minute trailer – and be able to anticipate and answer the difficult questions that are likely to come up about your film's subjects and your approach to making it.

Preparation: Pitching to broadcasters

In pitching to broadcasters it is important to understand your potential commissioner's perspective. Commissioning editors are responsible for selecting programmes that fit the brand of their channel and are usually limited to a pre-existing set of 'slots' – strands of programmes that recur at particular time slots and play to the interests of a specific audience. Whilst to the filmmaker the commissioner may seem all-powerful, the truth is that commissioners are constrained by the requirements of schedulers and channel strategy. With this in mind, it is essential to research the current output in the strands commissioned by the person you are meeting and to have seen at least some of their recent notable programmes. These programmes are highly likely to come up in the meeting as reference points for your own film. You should also understand how your documentary or series could work with those slots and audiences.

Preparation: The pitch forum

The pitch forum is a public pitch to a group of broadcasters, usually held at a documentary festival or market (for example, IDFA in Amsterdam, Doc/Fest in Sheffield, Hot Docs in Toronto or Sunny Side of the Doc in La Rochelle). They have grown increasingly prevalent – in part due to the increasing need in Europe for international co-production in order to finance documentaries. For the filmmaker they are a fantastic opportunity to pitch to a large number of broadcasters at the same time, to build a 'buzz' about your film idea, and to promote your credentials as a documentary filmmaker. Usually entrance to a pitch forum is competitive. Ideas are solicited and sorted down to a select few to go in front of the commissioners, so the fact that you're pitching your idea at all means you've a good chance of funding.

Prepare for the forum by researching the broadcasters who are on the panel and the slots they control and, if possible, set up immediate follow-up meetings with those you are particularly targeting in advance of the forum. If you leave it until the forum itself to organise this, they are likely to be booked up, and you lose the momentum you've created by a successful pitch.

Anticipating questions

Commissioning editors are experienced at listening to proposals and identifying their weaknesses. Try to put yourself in their shoes and assess the potential weak points of your proposal. How might you give reassurance that you can overcome these?

Is your access secure? (It's better to be honest about this and to be able to show how you will get the access you need.)

Is there a mismatch between your experience and the ambition of the project? Could you bring on board members of your team who will bolster your ability to make the film and who you could name in answer to any doubts raised (for example, a very experienced executive producer, director of photography or editor)?

Research (and ideally watch) any other films that have been made on the same subject – if any – and be able to speak about why yours is different.

Have a back-up plan for anything in your proposal that is uncertain.

The pitch itself

You can think of a pitch as having six essential parts:

- introducing the filmmakers;
- describing the project;
- showing the trailer;
- explaining your unique approach;
- outlining the film's timescale and finances;
- questions from financiers.

Pitching checklist

Introducing the filmmakers

- Who is pitching and your roles on the film.
- Your track record as filmmakers (for example, a couple of examples of other relevant films you have made, any awards you have won and whether you've worked together successfully before).

Describing the project

Content

- Film title.
- By-line (a brief description of the film idea in a sentence).

- The programme format (single or series, anticipated length, different versions, cross-platform potential).
- Why your idea is unique (for example, your access to the subject, unseen archive, an untold story, etc).
- What is the story?
- What is at stake?

Approach

- The approach and style (whether you will use narration, what we will see and hear, the setting, the storytelling).
- Any technical considerations that specifically enhance your approach (e.g. a particular use of sound, or stills or graphics or camera technology).

Characters

- The characters and what makes them captivating.
- How they will be revealed.
- The point of view of the storytelling.

Audience

- What makes your subject universal?
- Why your subject is important to a wide audience.
- What compels them to watch it?

Why you?

- Why are you uniquely qualified to make this film?
- What added value do you bring to the project?
- Does the film carry a sense of your authorship?

Showing the trailer

- Decide when in your pitch to show the trailer. What needs to be set up for the viewers before they watch it?
- Avoid repeating in your pitch what is said in the trailer.

Projected timescale

- Your planned production period.
- Your planned date of completion.
- Your planned date of release.

Finance

- The overall budget.
- The amount of funding still needed.
- What broadcasters and 'soft' funding you have already committed.

Case study: *Men Who Swim*

Men Who Swim is a feature documentary following the fortunes of a Swedish men's synchronised swimming team, through the eyes of documentary director Dylan Williams, who is a member of the team.

Based in Sweden, Dylan began filming the members of the group and wrote a proposal, which caught the interest of a UK production company, Met Film. As co-production partners, Dylan's company AMP Films and Met Film reworked the project proposal for the UK and European market. With a trailer that showcased the film's humour and his own role in it, Dylan pitched the project at the Leipzig Documentary Campus Pitch (winning 'Best Pitch' in the process), and gained interest from broadcasters in Germany, Finland, Israel, the Netherlands and Austria.

Following up this interest over several months, the project secured commissions first from a Dutch broadcaster, and then from a BBC documentary strand and Swedish and German broadcasters. Together, these commissions brought approximately two-thirds of the total funding needed to make the film.

With this finance in place, Dylan and his producers Al Morrow and Erik Pauser were able to apply for an EU MEDIA Production grant for 20% of the budget, and to the Nordisk Film Fund. With some fee deferments, and smaller pre-sales to Finland, Israel and Italy, this meant that the film was fully funded.

The film went into production 14 months after Dylan first started shooting material for his trailer, and just in time for the European Synchronised Swimming Championships in Milan in 2009.

Key points

- Be clear to yourself about the kind of film you are making and the audience you want to reach.
- Understand the range of funders available for this kind of film.
- Research which funders are most likely to be interested in your film. Understand the slots and strands they commission, programme formats and past commissions. Attend festival pitch forums to research their current interests.
- Prepare a 4-minute trailer which is as close to your end film's production values as possible.
- Write a proposal which clearly sets out your ambitions for the film and the reasons you have the right team to make it.
- Develop a verbal pitch of 3–4 minutes and practise it.

Exercise

Taking the case study above (*Men Who Swim*), explore the commissioning websites of broadcasters in the various countries mentioned and research the different potential sources of funding for the film. Draw up a table of which broadcasters would be most likely to fund the film – and what kind of film they're looking for.

Which broadcasters would you go to in order to avoid making multiple versions of the film?

Notes

1 Thirkell, R. (2006) 'The secret of making popular programmes about business', *The Independent*, 19 June.

2 Jan Rofekamp, Films Transit (international documentary sales company).

Chapter 7

Budgets and schedules

Jerry Rothwell

"We had access to too much money, too much equipment, and little by little we went insane."

(Francis Ford Coppola)[1]

Introduction

In the initial stages of pitching a film, you might still only have a very broad idea of the film's budget. Soon, however, both you and any prospective financiers are going to need a more detailed breakdown of the cost of delivering your completed film. This chapter looks at some of the principles behind film budgeting, presents a standard budgeting format, and looks at how to control, manage and report on costs. It looks at issues in fees for filmmakers and subjects, how to structure financial deals and the contractual and rights issues this will involve.

Why budgets?

A budget is an item-by-item list of all the costs involved in making the film, usually prepared on a spreadsheet. A film production budget is intended serve a number of purposes at different stages of production:

- Before you start production, it is a detailed and realistic prediction of the cost of making the film.

- During production it becomes a tool to control expenditure and to make decisions about how to use available resources. It is also used to predict cashflow, and so to ensure you have the cash you need when you need it.

- Both during and at the end of production it is a means of reporting on and accounting for money spent to those who have supported or invested in the film.

There's a great temptation to create several different documents to accomplish these different purposes, as well as different budgets for different funders, but the more you can organise production finance in a single accurate document, the simpler the life of the producing team will be.

Budget categories

Film budgets are typically broken down into categories (also known as 'schedules') (see budget template). The budget overview template shown in Table 7.1 is based on a standard television budget, but is an appropriate format for most other contexts, even though it may include many items that the low- and no-budget filmmaker will either need to do without, do themselves or find for free. However, whatever your budget, the exercise of thinking through the cost (in both time and money) of all anticipated activity is essential. The categories in a standard television documentary budget include:

- **Development costs** – These are necessary costs prior to the film being financed, and might include: any rights costs (for example, to option a book on which the film is based); the production of a fundraising trailer; initial research and a treatment. Most production financiers will not support large amounts of development costs retrospectively, so stick to those that you can argue are absolutely essential prior to finance. You might also need to see these costs as an investment by the production company in the project.

- **Producer and director fees** – Fees for producers and directors are usually calculated either by the amount of time they will be working on the film during production or as a fixed fee, based

Table 7.1 Budget summary

Category Ref.	Direct costs & overheads
500	Story/Script/Development
600	Producer/Director
700	Artists
800	Presenters/Interviewees/etc.
900	Production Unit Salaries
1100	Crew – Documentary Camera
1200	Crew – Sound
1300	Crew – Lighting
1400	Crew – Art Department
1600	Crew – Editing
1700	Crew – Natural History
1800	Staff NI
1900	Materials – Art Department
2000	Materials – Wardrobe/Make-up/Hair
2100	Production Equipment
2200	Facility Package Arrangement
2400	Other Production Facilities
2500	Film/Tape Stock
2600	Picture/Sound Post Production – FILM
2700	Picture/Sound Post Production – TAPE
2800	Archive Material
2900	Rostrum/Graphics
3000	Music (Copyright/Performance)
3100	Travel/Transport
3200	Hotel/Living
3300	Other Production Costs
3400	Insurance/Finance/Legal
3500	Production Overheads
	Total direct costs
	Production fee (10%)
	Insurance: 0.9%
	Total costs

on a percentage of the overall budget. Fees for assistant producers and researchers are also usually included in this category. (See also section below on rates of pay.)

- **Crew wages** – This includes fees for camera and lighting crew, sound recordists and assistants, editor and assistant, any art department staff, production assistants, runners, etc.

- **Production office costs and unit salaries** – You may well be working from your own home, rather than an office, but making your film will still involve administrative costs, even if just for phone and internet, stationery and postage. For larger-budget productions, this schedule includes an assessment of the proportion of office costs and wages paid by the production company to its staff who are working on the production. Office costs could include a proportion of rent, heat and light, stationery and telephone costs (and, if you are working from home, can be a reasonable proportion of home 'office' costs towards your heating, electricity and rent). Office-based staff could include production executives, the production manager, production co-ordinators and a production accountant (responsible for producing the interim and end-of-production reports to financiers).

- **Equipment hire costs** – The hire costs of camera, lighting and sound equipment, any specialist equipment (for example, steadicam or underwater cameras), and consumables (such as batteries, bulbs, etc.). (See also section below on equipment hire rates.)

- **Fees for subjects and presenters** – Any fees for those who appear on screen, whether presenters or subjects. The ethical issues of paying subjects for their participation in a documentary are dealt with in more detail below.

- **Art department/construction costs** – The costs of any constructed environments and props – for example, interview backgrounds in a studio or reconstruction.

- **Studio and location fees** – Any payments you will need to make for studio hire or for the use of particular locations.

- **Post-production facility costs** – The costs of offline edit equipment hire; online, grade and final sound mix facilities; the creation of final master copies for delivery; subtitling.

- **Film and tape stock costs** – Includes the costs of film or tape shooting stock (or cards and drives if shooting direct to digital file) and costs for stock for the various masters required by financiers and broadcasters.

- **Archive costs** – Payments for rights to use archive, and the associated production costs (for example, viewing copies, duplication or telecine transfer).

- **Graphics and visual effects costs** – Costs of graphics and visual effects elements, from scanning stills or name credits to complex visual effects.

- **Music and performance costs** – Typically, your film might include some copyright music and some composed music. Any rights costs for music and fees for composers and performers or original music, including studio hire, should be included here.

- **Travel and transport costs** – All travel during production, including public transport, taxis, car and van hire and fuel costs.

- **Hotel and living costs** – Accommodation and subsistence costs during production. This might include crew daily allowances (per diems) for living away from home.

- **Insurance, financing and legal costs** – Production insurance (this might be a reasonable proportion of a company's annual production insurance), any bank or loan charges associated with financing the production, and legal costs for the film.

- **Production overheads and fees** – The convention has been to charge a 'production fee' (ranging between 5% and 10%) which represents the production company's profit from production. Some broadcasters expect this, others don't.
- **Contingencies** – An allowance for unexpected costs, usually set at 3–5% of the total budget.

Estimating the cost of your documentary

Working out these detailed costs involves estimating the time each element of production is likely to take, and the maximum rate you are likely to pay for it. You should start by creating a schedule for the production – an assessment of the time required to fulfil each stage of pre-production, production and post-production. If you have a detailed outline of a pre-existing story you should be able to make a very accurate assessment. If your film is an observational documentary, with a story unfolding as you shoot, you'll need to make a reasonable estimate of the time you need to give you room to manoeuvre. A schedule for a 60-minute film might look something like this (Table 7.2). Making a detailed budget involves breaking down each of the budget categories shown in Table 7.1 into seperate items needed (see exemple in Table 7.4).

Table 7.2 Schedule example

28/04	Wk 1	Pre-production
05/05	Wk 2	Pre-production
12/05	Wk 3	Pre-production / Shoot
19/05	Wk 4	Pre-production / Shoot
26/05	Wk 5	Pre-production / Shoot
02/06	Wk 6	Pre-production / Shoot
09/06	Wk 7	Edit Wk 1
16/06	Wk 8	Edit Wk 2
23/06	Wk 9	Edit Wk 3
30/06	Wk 10	Edit Wk 4
07/07	Wk 11	Edit Wk 5/Rough cut viewing
14/07	Wk 12	Edit Wk 6/Feedback
21/07	Wk 13	Edit Wk 7
28/07	Wk 14	Edit Wk 8
04/08	Wk 15	Edit Wk 9/Fine cut viewing
11/08	Wk 16	Feedback
18/08	Wk 17	Edit Wk 10/Picture lock
25/08	Wk 18	Online
01/09	Wk 19	Audio mix
08/09	Wk 20	Layback and QC (technical Quality Check)
15/09	Wk 21	Delivery

Typically, you might expect a 60-minute film to involve 4–6 weeks' pre-production, 8–12 weeks in the edit and post-production. The length of the shoot will vary widely, depending on the subject matter and approach.

Staffing and time

Once you've created a schedule, you can decide what personnel will be required at each stage of the production – for example, as follows (note that Table 7.3 is an example and shows some, but not all, personnel likely to be involved):

Table 7.3 Production staff schedule

Wk		Director	DoP	Prod Mgr	Editor	Researcher
1	Pre-production	Wk 1		Wk 1		Wk 1
2	Pre-production	Wk 2		Wk 2		Wk 2
3	Pre-production/Shoot	Wk 3	Wk 1	Wk 3		Wk 3
4	Pre-production/Shoot	Wk 4	Wk 2	Wk 4		Wk 4
5	Pre-production/Shoot	Wk 5	Wk 3	Wk 5		
6	Pre-production/Shoot	Wk 6	Wk 4	Wk 6		
7	Edit 1	Wk 7		Wk 7	Wk 1	
8	Edit 2	Wk 8		Wk 8	Wk 2	
9	Edit 3	Wk 9		Wk 9	Wk 3	
10	Edit 4	Wk 10		Wk 10	Wk 4	
11	Edit 5	Wk 11		Wk 11	Wk 5	
12	Edit 6/Feedback	Wk 12		Wk 12	Wk 6	
13	Edit 7	Wk 13		Wk 13	Wk 7	
14	Edit 8	Wk 14		Wk 14	Wk 8	
15	Edit 9/Fine cut	Wk 15		Wk 15	Wk 9	
16	Feedback	Wk 16		Wk 16		
17	Edit 10/Picture lock	Wk 17		Wk 17	Wk 10	
18	Online/Grade	Wk 18		Wk 18		
19	Audio mix	Wk 19		Wk 19		
20	Layback and QC	Wk 20		Wk 20		
21	Delivery	Wk 21		Wk 21		
Total (weeks)		21	4	21	10	4
Rate of pay/week		V	W	X	Y	Z
Total cost		21 × V	4 × W	21 × X	10 × Y	4 × Z

Table 7.4 Example of budget detailed breakdown

1200 – Sound crew					
	Pre-Prod. Wks/Dys	Prod Wks/Dys	Post Wks/Dys	Rate	Sub-tot ex N.I.
1200 Sound Recordist inc. kit		10		£300	£3,000
1201 Additional Sound Kit					£0
			Category 12 total:		£3,000

2100 – Production equipment					
	Pre-Prod Wks/Dys	Prod. Wks/Dys	Post Wks/Dys	Rate	Sub-total
2101 Camera		10		£175	£1,750
2102 Motorolas/radios					£0
2103 Sound : Sundries				£100	£0
2104 Camera : Sundries		1		£500	£500
2105 Specialist Camera Equipment		10		£100	£1,000
2106 Grip Equipment					£0
2107 Specialist Sound Equipment		5		£150	£750
2108 Lighting Hire		1		£1,000	£1,000
2109 Generator					£0
2110 Lighting Consumables				£20	£0
			Category 21 total:		£5,000

Drawing on the information in your schedule, you can break down each budget category into detailed items of expenditure (see Table 7.4 for an example). If you do this in a spreadsheet, changes in the schedule can be linked immediately to changes in the budget.

Rates of pay

Thirty years ago, film and television was one of the most highly paid industries, with a strong union powerful enough to black out the nation's screens in disputes about pay and conditions. Now, the industry is notorious for its low pay and poor working conditions, particularly at entry level. Each year, thousands of media graduates leave college looking for work and many are prepared to work for nothing to get a chance of starting in jobs in film and television.

Rates of pay are now largely a matter of negotiation between producers and their employees, with the union standard rates as a guideline, rather than a non-negotiable norm. As part of the package, particularly where a film is underfinanced, producers will often suggest deferments of pay (until finance is closed or set against any potential profit for the film) and a 'back end' share in any profits made by the film.

For budgeting purposes, it remains a useful starting point to use rates of pay recommended by the film and television technicians' union (BECTU in the UK), which proposes the going rates for different roles, as agreed between technicians and producers' associations (http://www.bectu.org.uk/advice-resources/rates).

A common strategy is to negotiate 'all-in' or 'buy-out' deals, where a fixed daily or weekly rate is paid, regardless of the number of hours worked. This is something that BECTU – and many individual freelancers – oppose, because they argue that such deals encourage excessive working hours and undermine working conditions generally. Whilst some freelancers will be willing to take pay reductions or deferments because they are particularly attracted to the project, it's important to treat those working on the film well and to value their contribution accordingly. A crew which starts feeling underpaid is less likely to give you the extra commitment you're bound to need from them.

Equipment hire rates

Most production facilities will be able to supply a rate card for equipment hire on a daily or weekly basis. Start by using these as the hire rates in your budget, but it's important to realise that such rates are always negotiable and that, to control costs, you should try to negotiate a package for the whole production. If you're using your own equipment, you should still include it as a cost to the production to take account of the fact that you have bought, maintain and house it (though if you have to reduce the budget later, this is one area you may be able to cut – or treat as your investment in the film – without significantly affecting the film's quality.)

Contributor fees

Until relatively recently, the payment of contributors to documentaries was seen as a breach of documentary ethics (although as long ago as Robert Flaherty's *Man of Aran* in 1934 contributors were paid for their involvement[2]). But the culture of factual media generally has shifted and today people with a story are more likely to expect payment for telling it. At one level it seems fair that those at the centre of a story can earn from it in the same way as those making the film will earn from it. After all, the film is likely to have a significant impact on their lives, making their private world public and possibly taking up large amounts of their time.

However, the payment of contributors brings with it some difficult ethical issues, and may have a detrimental impact on the process of making the film. It raises questions about whether your subject is participating in the programme primarily for the money and to what extent this compromises their telling of their story. Is their witness to events impartial or has it been 'bought'? Are they more likely to inflate those areas of the story that they think might be most valuable to the filmmaker, at the expense of honesty? It is clearer to see payments to contributors in terms of rights (over their writings, personal archive, etc.) than as reward for their participation. As far as possible, it is better to tie any financial rewards to the film's completion or to a stake in any profits it might make.

Case study *Etre et Avoir*

Perhaps the most famous example of a court case about the payment of documentary contributors was that of the French film *Etre et Avoir*. The film, about a year in the life of a rural French primary school, had at its centre the sole teacher at the school, Georges Lopez.

Etre et Avoir was commercially very successful in France, attracting 1.8 million cinema goers and earning the equivalent of $10 million at the box office. After its release, Lopez sued the film's director, producers, distributor, and even composer, for €250,000 for 'counterfeiting' his class and his teaching. Whilst Lopez' teaching is absolutely at the centre of the film, a Paris court rejected his claim.

The film's director, Nicholas Philibert, argues that, 'To have paid someone for their presence on the screen, it would have meant the death of the documentary. From the moment you pay someone to appear in a documentary, the people you are filming become your subordinates. They no longer have the freedom to say, "No, stop filming."' [3]

Case study *Fearon*

In 2005, the BBC made a documentary about the case of Tony Martin, a farmer who was found guilty for shooting a burglar who broke into his house.

Brendan Fearon, whose accomplice was killed when the pair tried to rob Mr Martin, was paid almost £5,000 to appear in the one-off programme.

The BBC said the move was justified under its internal guidelines because of 'exceptional interest' in the case.

But the man who wrote those guidelines said he was 'not convinced'. He said: 'I tried to write a guideline which would mean (payments to criminals) would almost never happen, but would leave open the door for that real, genuine public-interest occasion. I am not convinced that today's is one such.

'It seems to me an extraordinarily large sum of money to pay a man who committed not just one crime but was apparently a lifestyle burglar.'

Budgets and the 'total filmmaker'

One of the intentions of this book is to explore the ways in which the landscape of creative documentary production is changing as a consequence of digital technology. In an earlier chapter, we have highlighted the emergence of what we have called the 'total filmmaker' – multi-skilled individuals who bridge the traditional boundaries of production – perhaps producing, directing, shooting and editing material themselves. Often their work will be created on much lower budgets than traditional television commissions, and is undertaken by individual freelancers or a micro company rather than within a large production company infrastructure. Finance may be more piecemeal and cumulative, perhaps obtained in stages throughout production.

What does this mean for the budgeting process outlined above?

The working methods of the 'total filmmaker' have some advantages over production within more traditional structures. Equipment costs are likely to be lower, and there is more flexibility around the employment of crew (because the same multi-skilled individuals can work across a number of traditional roles). One consequence of this is the ability to blur the boundaries between pre-production, production and post-production – the traditional sequential production model of documentary. Editing may not occur in a single block of time, but might take place concurrently with shooting. Some shooting may take place before there is a full budget in place, in order to raise funders' interest.

There are some potential disadvantages of these working methods – for example, a lack of focus to the production process, overshooting and a reduction in specific technical expertise and therefore quality. Because of the flexibility of digital production, it can be a temptation not to do a thorough prediction of budget and schedule in advance of making the film. But resources are always limited – whether or not some of them are free – and to make the best use of them and so maximise their value on screen it is important to manage how they are used. So it will be worth going through the budgeting and scheduling exercise outlined above, even if many of the rates are set at zero or are in-kind contributions.

Despite the dangers of the fluidity of digital production, the 'total filmmaker' can work flexibly in ways that – if well organised – can bring down costs and allow resources of time and money to be spent more strategically on those elements that add significant value on the screen.

The value of your film

Whatever figure you arrive at through budgeting, you need to bear in mind that the value of a film is not the same as the amount it costs to make it. Its commercial financial value is determined by its appropriateness for the international market. If there's a mismatch between the production costs of your intended film and the scale of its audience or market potential, you are creating for yourself a big barrier in terms of raising finance and so making the film. In other words, you need to assess whether the budget you think you need is appropriate for the film's potential audience, and, if it isn't, scale it back. If you want to make an installation which is shown to 100 people in a single gallery, there's little point in coming up with a $1m budget; unless you have a very rich uncle or sponsor. The economics of the project don't work. Most broadcasters have guide prices for their commissions for television documentaries, which can be found online on their commissioning websites. If your budget is above these guide prices, you need either to bring in additional financiers (e.g. broadcasters in other territories) or reduce your budget, while still delivering the concept the financiers are interested in.

Cutting budgets

It's likely that, having first established your ideal budget, you'll need to go through a process of reducing it. Perhaps you have offers from some financiers, which you can take up immediately if you can prove that the documentary can be made for a lower budget, enabling you to start making your film. In order to do this, explore whether you can:

- negotiate lower card rates or fixed-price deals for equipment;
- shoot on different equipment which could give you a cheaper workflow;
- reduce shoot days;
- reduce edit time;
- negotiate deferments in both equipment and fees based on clear agreements about when the deferred amounts would be paid (e.g. at the point at which funds are raised over and above the reduced budget);
- find different ways of shooting the more expensive elements in your film: sometimes budget pressures stimulate creativity!;

- look for in-kind contributions that might be made for some of the items you have costed in your budget;
- be realistic – still leave yourself room to manoeuvre and don't cut the budget to the extent that your film cannot be made satisfactorily. It's better to make difficult decisions before rather than during production.

Reporting costs in production

Once you have reached a budget for which you have raised finance, fix it at that amount and avoid making constant changes to the overall production budget. As you spend during production, code each cost to a particular category in the budget and keep a running total of spends in each category, and of projected spends to completion of the film. This will enable you to make decisions about any changes to the resources you want to allocate while in production.

Key points

- A budget is a detailed and realistic prediction of the cost of making the film, a tool to control expenditure and to make decisions about how to use available resources.
- Create a schedule which predicts the time required for each stage of making your film.
- Use the schedule to predict the amounts of crew time and equipment required.
- Refer to rate cards and establish crew fee levels to predict the costs of each element in your film.
- Negotiate every item in the budget in order to get the most for your money.
- Make sure your film costs reflect its overall value to potential funders.
- When you've arrived at a viable budget, fix it and use it to report costs during production.

Exercises

Exercise 1

Create a schedule and then a budget for a given short film idea, using the budget template provided in Table 7.1.

Exercise 2

Discuss the two case studies about payment to contributors. At what point do you think that contributor payments breach documentary ethics? Where do you draw the line between the appropriate financial recognition of contributors' involvement and payment that compromises the integrity of the film?

Notes

1. Francis Ford Coppola on the making of *Apocalypse Now* (Cowie, 1990: 130).

2. Flaherty paid his main contributors in *Man of Aran* to take a canoe out into a heavy sea and later said, 'I should have been shot for what I asked these superb people to do for the film, the enormous risks I exposed them to, and all for the sake of a keg of porter and £5 apiece.' (Quoted in Rotha, P. (1983) *Robert J. Flaherty: A Biography* (Philadelphia: University of Pennsylvania Press, p. 113. See also Chapman, J. (2009) *Issues in Contemporary Documentary*, (Cambridge: Polity Press).

3. Austin, T. (2005) 'Seeing, feeling, knowing: a case study of audience perspectives on screen documentary', in Particip@tions, Vol. 2, Issue 1 (August).

Part 3

Narrative strategies

Kwasi Akufo in *Heart of Gold* (Knudsen, 2006)

Chapter 8

The nature of stories and narratives

Erik Knudsen

“ The universe is made of stories, not atoms. ”

(Rukeyser, M., quoted in Feldman, C. and Cornfield, J. (1992))

Introduction

We are surrounded by stories and storytelling. As you are essentially going to be a storyteller, albeit using a moving image documentary form, it is very important to try to understand the nature of stories and storytelling so that you can master your medium. Before we go on to the creative mechanics of story and narrative structures, we shall in this chapter try to understand why we might tell stories. We will also try to understand the relationship between story, storytelling and our feelings and emotions.

Creatures of time and space

'Every picture tells a story', so the saying goes. Whether it be Einstein telling a story in order to explain his theory of relativity (Einstein, 1996), an African elder teaching children about the history of their people, Brazilian miners sitting in a bar reflecting on a day's work, young Chinese men and women expressing their feelings around their love lives, doting British parents teaching their children about the challenges of life ahead or a Middle Eastern mystic trying to make us understand the connection between material life and infinity, we are not only surrounded by stories, but we seem embedded in stories and stories seem embedded in us.

Kwasi Akufo being told a story by an elder in *Heart of Gold* (Knudsen, 2006, UK)

The ubiquitous nature of story means that we are actually storytellers most of the time. We are constantly telling stories by employing various narrative forms, depending on context, narrative tools and objectives. We are, of course, here going to be focusing on the particular narrative form of the documentary. Hopefully, it will become clear that 'documentary' is by no means a fixed form, nor is any story dependent on such a concept as 'documentary'. In fact, the very notion of distinguishing between fact and fiction for the purposes of storytelling may be completely arbitrary. For the truth or the reality of a story lies not in the narrative form, but in the feelings and emotions that bring about the narrative and in the subsequent experience elicited in the viewer as a result of engaging with that narrative. Even if one does choose to work within a particular set of cinematic codes which we broadly define as documentary, liberating oneself from inextricably linking truth and reality to the documentary genre can unleash incredible creative potential.

Let us first try to define the terms 'story', 'discourse' and 'narrative'. Think of a story as having no form – as, in a sense, being abstract. Hence the need to tell it. It can be a series of feelings and emotions. It can be a cluster of memories. It can be the memories of a series of events experienced first-, second- or third-hand. It can be the underlying emotional currents of someone's life. It can be a series of events imagined, historical events communally remembered, or even a history of ideas. A story can be huge in scale, depth and consequence, and can have qualities about it that are impossible to specify. Indeed, taken to the extreme, a story has no beginning or end.

Discourse is the mode of telling the story, the process of making palpable what is impalpable, principally through the selection and arrangement of a series of events (we could also refer to the discourse as the 'plot'). The selection of key events, for example, the capturing of appropriate imagery, the introduction of an actual or implied narrator, the organising of plot elements, defining of characters, contextualising the setting, and so on, all form part of the discourse. They form the key events, actions and happenings through which the author, by way of a direct or implied narrator, alludes to the story or particular aspects of the story (see Figure 8.1).

The narrative form is the development of story and discourse into a text – that is, a film, a poem, a novel, a biography, a painting, a ballet or whatever expressive form we choose. Within film, of course, we then have clusters of codes of the medium that we use to define whether we think of something as documentary or fiction. The narrative form, therefore, is the physical communication or artistic form with which we will present our viewer with the discourse that will take them through to the story[1].

It may be useful now to reflect briefly on why story, discourse and narrative are so fundamental as a means of understanding and communication.

Figure 8.1 From story to narrative expression

Emotions and thoughts

Good teachers know well that the most effective way to get someone to understand something is to engage the student's emotions. To wholly engage with a student through the intellect may not be enough or often only yields partial results. To engage someone's emotions, you need to work with something that relates directly to the experience of the student. Often this involves stories, either in the form of engaging with texts or by engaging in narrative situations. In a similar way, the filmmaker needs to engage the feelings and emotions of his or her viewer in order to convey the themes of the story.

Emotions are very complex and powerful features of our physiology and psychology. They are the main agent for action in us, both conscious and unconscious. We are often moved to act and to react without being in conscious or rational control of our emotions and their consequences. Fear can make you react with uncontrollable anger or rage, just as joyful love can make you react with uncontrollable crying. Of course, we often use reason as a basis for action and reaction, but if there is ever a conflict between the two – which is more often the case than we sometimes like to admit – our emotions will always have the final say in how we act or react.[2] We can fear something that profoundly affects our lives, even though our reason tells us there is nothing to fear. Or we can fall in love and make a series of decisions even though reason has told us that it is going to end in disaster.

It would therefore perhaps not be outrageous to claim that most intellectual and reasoned thoughts we have are inextricably tied in with our emotions. When we reflect intellectually on events or a piece of art, for example, we are in fact trying to make sense of what we feel and why. If emotions are so fundamental to how we engage with life, it therefore becomes imperative for the visual storyteller to engage with the viewers' emotions and 'move them' to intellectual reflection and/or action.

But why is it that such engagement usually involves story? Perhaps the answer lies in verisimilitude. Story is itself a close analogous reflection of our lived experience. As creatures of time and space, we are protagonists in our own ongoing story, which has a beginning, middle and end. This lived story also has its aims, obstacles, antagonists, turning points, climaxes, sub-plots, dramatic ironies, supporting characters, settings, moments of revelation and, importantly, involves change. We live this story in intense detail, our emotions engaged at every turn and our intellect trying to make sense of these emotions. Perhaps it is, therefore, not surprising that the fundamental form of communication with each other should be a reconstruction in the image of lived experience and that our minds, intrinsically and instinctively, seek to place any artistic expression into a framework that it understands. When you show someone a picture, their instinctual engagement will most likely be to understand that picture in terms of story, to seek in it a protagonist of some sort and all the other elements they know from lived experience. Through empathy, recognition of a context, aims, obstacles and so on, you then draw the viewer into a structure through which, as in life, their emotions engage.

In life, we human beings probably share more common experiences, qualities and features than not. It turns out that human beings have strikingly similar facial expressions across all cultures (Ekman, 1973); that children across cultures have similar dreams (Jung, 1997); that marriage between a man and a woman is a feature of every culture. You will find that people in all cultures have similar aspirations, which manifest themselves in prototypical ideals. You will also find that, across cultures, we have remarkably similar emotional life cycles; that we all have virtually identical physiologies, and so on. There are, of course, variations, particularly of life circumstance and context, but overwhelmingly we have more in common than not. Unsurprisingly, therefore, story and narrative have universal qualities across cultures that result in prototypical elements and structures (Hogan, 2003). We often refer to such narrative universals as 'classic narrative' or 'classic story' (see A prototypical story, below.)

A prototypical story

Young people fall in love in just the same way in a shanty town in Lagos as they do in Knightsbridge in London. Consequently, one example of a prototypical story is the romantic tragi-comedy in which the aspirations of young lovers is in conflict with the expectations of society around them, typically represented by parental disapproval. This is a prototypical story premise which typically follows a classic narrative pattern seen in every culture and repeated across every documented era.

Not all stories and narratives follow the classic narrative pattern, but the overwhelming majority of films do – including documentaries. We shall consider the creative engagement with this classic narrative form in the context of the documentary genre, as well as look at some possible variations and alternatives.

Emotional engagement

What are the emotions we wish to engage and how may this influence approaches to narrative? There is no conclusive list of emotions, though some psychologists, such as Ekman, suggest that there are five basic universal emotions: happiness, sadness, fear, anger and disgust. He suggests that all other emotions fit in under one of these headings. For the purposes of storytelling, we shall look at emotions slightly differently.

If you think of yourself as a viewer, there will be some films that have you sitting on the edge of your seat, heart beating away, hands grabbing the armrests, your mind alert, all your senses sharpened, very aware of yourself, worried about what is going to happen next. Then there will be other films that will do almost the opposite. You will be relaxed, perhaps to the point of almost being asleep. You will be enveloped in a landscape or a scene and have little sense of yourself. You do not care what will happen next because you are engaging in the moment for its own sake. In the former case, your self-assertive emotions are engaged. They are the emotions of fight or flight, emotions that are about you as a separate being, emotions in which you assert yourself. They are, essentially, emotions of survival. In the second case, your participatory emotions are engaged – let us call these 'feelings'. These are feelings which make you want to participate, become one with what you are engaging with, to lose yourself, your individuality, in which you do not feel threatened, you are not afraid. They are, essentially, feelings of transcendence. And then, of course, you will have seen films that fall somewhere between these, even if they perhaps lean one way or the other.

For the first type of engagement – the self-assertive emotions – we might be talking about such emotions as fear, anger, anxiety, sexual arousal or jealousy. For the second type of engagement – the participatory – we might be talking about such feelings as awe, longing, sorrow, joy or love. These types of feelings and emotions and how we engage with them have a profound effect on how you approach telling your story. Let us briefly return to the issue of verisimilitude with life. There will be parts of the story of your life in which your engagement is with survival (in its many forms). This may involve getting what you want or desire in a material sense; standing out as an individual by trying to assert your individuality; facing up to various situations in which you are fearful, and so on. Then there will be other parts of your life which have been much more about transcendence. These will be moments where you don't care about gaining material possessions or protecting them; where you are engaging with life around you in a way where you want to lose yourself; where you reflect on your spiritual side and seek to engage with what is going on around you in a non-materialistic way. To tell a story of aspects of these different sides of you, and to engage your viewer in the type of feelings you feel or felt, would require different narrative strategies. You would tell the story in different ways, depending on what it is you want your viewer to feel and what it is in the story that you particularly want them to understand (see Figure 8.2).

Most of the time – perhaps particularly in richer societies – we are consumed by issues of survival. Will we get what we want or desire? How can we become richer and more successful? How can we protect ourselves and our children (socially, culturally and physically)? How can we make a mark as an individual? How can we build structures that protect us from our enemies (often unseen or unknown)? Perhaps it is no coincidence that the classic narrative dominates our storytelling. However, there are certain people – or certain moments in our lives – for whom, or when, the notion of individual survival is not so much of an issue. How can I sacrifice myself for a cause that is greater than myself? I don't care about my own wealth – how can I live with very little? How can I sacrifice my individuality for the sake of someone else? How can I rid myself of wanting or desiring material things or success? How can I lose myself in that landscape and be one with nature? How can I lose myself in the beauty of this poem or painting?

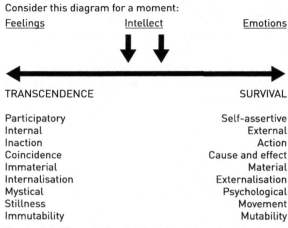

Consider this diagram for a moment:

Feelings	Intellect	Emotions

TRANSCENDENCE ←——————————————→ SURVIVAL

Participatory	Self-assertive
Internal	External
Inaction	Action
Coincidence	Cause and effect
Immaterial	Material
Internalisation	Externalisation
Mystical	Psychological
Stillness	Movement
Immutability	Mutability

Figure 8.2 The relationship between thoughts, feelings, emotions and reactions in story engagement

The ingredients of classic narratives will tend to have certain qualities about them. Often they will involve issues of survival – not just survival in terms of the physical survival of a life, but also the survival of a culture, a people, an ideology, an individual's rights, an organisation or, indeed, an animal species. They will tend to involve the plight of protagonists who in some ways are trying to assert themselves by, for example, setting out to achieve something specific. Protagonists will often be trying to 'protect' or to 'save'. There will be a strong tendency to externalise the themes of the story. Action will be a key feature of the discourse and movement – both within the frame and in terms of the story arc. Events and characterisations will follow an explicable pattern of physical and psychological cause and effect. And, ultimately, there will be some kind of palpable psychological or material change.

Conversely, the ingredients of what we shall here call 'transcendental narratives' will have different qualities about them. They will often involve issues of transcendence. Not just transcendence in the spiritual sense – it could be about how someone comes to terms with a situation that is not going to change. They will tend to involve protagonists who are not trying to achieve anything and have no aims or ambitions in the sense that the protagonist in the classic narrative might have. There will be a strong tendency for the themes of the transcendental story to be internalised. Inaction and stillness – both within the frame and in the arc of the story – tend to be strong features. Events and characterisations could well follow coincidental patterns that do not fit in with psychological cause and effect and which often involve engaging in scenes for their own sake, rather than as part of a plot driven specifically by such causes and effects. And, significantly, there will often not be a palpable psychological or material change in the narrative. The change may be more of a changed state of mind, manifesting itself in a changed perspective or understanding on the part of the viewer of an unchanged story situation. Such a change could involve a renewed appreciation of something timeless and immutable.

At the other extreme, the transcendental filmmaker may be making us look at the same shot for 15 minutes where nothing much, if anything, is happening. Nevertheless, in some strange way, we may be able to engage with the situation on a different level by being awestruck by the beauty of something for its own sake, or by seeing some significance in what at first might seem like random events. Perhaps we are being asked to meditate on a situation or a person's predicament. Here, the filmmaker would not be interested in our being afraid, sexually aroused or anxious, and therefore goes about telling their story in a completely different way.

It is no coincidence that, at the extreme, the classic narrative involves taking its viewer on a journey in which life and death are at stake – whether in documentary or in fiction. The use of the narrative structure and the approach to imagery are designed specifically to engage your self-assertive emotions. This is a process that starts with the choice of story – or component of a story – through the commissioning process and right through to the final cut. At the extreme end, most Hollywood filmmakers take their audience through an experience akin to a roller-coaster ride, with the express intention of engaging their self-assertive emotions, such as fear. There are also plenty of examples of documentary filmmakers who, similarly at the extremes, use the codes of reality to take us into dangerous and pulsating actuality situations with the express purpose of having us sitting on the edge of our seats, gripped by fear. Or, in less extreme cases, the filmmaker will intend us to feel more subtle fears and anxieties for a character or situation.

Having an understanding of the relationship between narrative and emotions is important when it comes to structuring your documentary. For most filmmakers, this understanding is intuitive or has come about from years of experience involving trial and error. This relationship is constantly changing and you will develop your own understanding, with time, of how the two connect. Indeed, creativity itself demands that you constantly engage with the renewal of language, which we shall touch on later. In the next chapter, we shall, as a first approach, start from the notion of feelings and emotions and look at some of the key ingredients of the classic narrative. In the subsequent chapters, we will look at some alternatives.

Key points

- Trust your own experience as the basis for everything you do and create.

- Reflecting on the nature of story and storytelling and relating it to your own experience, feelings and emotions will have a direct bearing on how you make films.

- Being able to place the theme within your own framework of interests, concerns, emotions and feelings will enable you to create a unique work that you will feel committed to.

- To tell a story successfully you must, first and foremost, engage the viewer's feelings and emotions.

- There are different kinds of feelings and emotions in people and you need to think about which ones you wish to engage with in order to communicate your themes effectively.

- Broadly speaking, emotions are responses in you that will tend to move you to self-assertion and action, while feelings are responses in you that will tend to move you to inaction and reflective meditation. Different narrative strategies are required, depending on how you want to move people.

- Understand what your story is about. Is there an underlying issue that you hope this particular set of events will reveal? What key questions do you hope your audience may be asking themselves after they've seen it? What feelings do you hope your audience will be taking away with them?

Exercise

Have a look at a number of media products – TV news, a documentary soap, a Hollywood blockbuster, a novel, a poem or whatever – and try to ask yourself the following questions:

- What kinds of feelings and/or emotions are the creators of the work – the storytellers – trying to engage with in you? In what ways are you moved? How are the storytellers trying to move you?

- If you discover media products that are touching you in very different ways from you would normally expect, is there a difference in narrative approaches?

- Think of a work that has had a profound effect on you. What kinds of feelings and emotions were stirred in you? How do these feelings and emotions relate to how the story was told?

Let's make it a little more difficult. Can you identify a non-arts-based context in which storytelling is going on? For example, if an accountant is presenting the accounts to the Annual General Meeting of a company, presumably they are telling the story of the company's past year. How are they telling the story? Can you think of other non-arts-based situations? Now ask yourself the same questions as above. Do you see similarities?

Further reading

The creative documentary filmmaker is likely to be a curious person who reads and views widely and eclectically. Don't worry about whether you are reading the 'right' texts or watching the 'right' films. The most important thing is that you are reading and viewing – and that you are able to use what you are reading and viewing to contextualise and develop your own work. Some suggested readings emerging out of references from this chapter, by way of a starting point, include the following:

Barthes, R. (1995) *The Semiotic Challenge*, Los Angeles: University of California Press.
Einstein, A. (1996) *Relativity: The Special and The General Theory*, London: Crown Publications.
Ekman, P. (1973) 'Cross cultural studies in facial expressions' in *Darwin and Facial Expression: A Century of Research in Review*, New York: Academic Press.
Hogan, P.C. (2003) *The Mind and its Stories: Narrative Universals and Human Emotions*, Cambridge: Cambridge University Press.
Jung, G. (1997) *Man and His Symbols*, London: Laurel Press.
Rukeyser, M., quoted in Feldman, C. and Cornfield, J. (1992) *Stories of the Spirit, Stories of the Heart*, New York: Thorsons.

Notes

[1] As a creative artist, you will probably be engaged in your work in a much more intuitive and organic way and the separation of story, discourse and narrative merely serves to try to get under the skin of what we instinctively do. It is important to remember that this discussion is not about laying down definitive rules, or about encouraging you to be analytical in your creative processes, but it is about observing and reflecting on patterns in storytelling with a view to harnessing any useful elements for the purposes of creating your own quality creative documentaries.

[2] Meditation is one method some people use to gain control of or to guide their emotions. It takes years of disciplined practice to master any significant amount of control of some of our more powerful emotions.

Chapter 9

Life does not tell stories: structuring devices in documentary filmmaking

Wilma de Jong

" Life does not tell stories. Life is chaotic, fluid, random. It leaves myriads of ends untied, untidily. Writers can extract a story from life only by strict, close selection, and this must mean falsification. Telling stories really is telling lies. **"**

(B.S. Johnson, quoted in Jonathan Coe, 2004: 35)

Introduction

The previous chapter has given you an insight into the nature of stories and our need to make sense of the world we live in. Our realities present themselves as fractured and not obviously coherent, rather than neatly with a beginning, a middle and an end, ready for a filmmaker to record. Reality cannot be found out there but is in our heads, our shared knowledge and experiences. Media play an important role in the distribution of this 'reality knowledge'. Documentary, because of its position in the public domain as presenting 'reality', plays an important role in the shaping of our realities.

This chapter will focus on different structuring devices which will help you create a filmic narrative.

Documentary structures

Documentary filmmaking has a long and complex tradition of structuring footage captured in the historical world into a filmic narrative. There is a wide range of approaches in documentary filmmaking, from strongly interventionist to detached observation, but there is always the question of how to create a structure, how to link events, people and ideas in such a way that an audience can make sense of it and is captivated by it. A narrative structure illuminates the course of events in different ways. It should be appreciated that the form grows best in conjunction with the content during research, the shoot and the editing process. It is very rare that the form you had in mind when you came up with the concept will actually be realised.

You can use the following structuring devices as an initial support to shape the raw data of experiences, ideas and information you have collected.

Please note that it is not only content that will determine your form; the length of the film, the context it will be shown in or the broadcast schedule or slot will also influence the form. A documentary is not made in a vacuum; the organisational and distribution context will influence the final form of your film.

Change and development

Before we look at these structuring devices, you need to realise that development needs to take place in any documentary, whatever narrative structure you choose. Development in this case means change, unravelling or unfolding events and the possible links between them. A film of a still pond on a sunny day is not very likely to engage your audience. Development over time, chronology, is one of the most common dramatic drives, but is not necessarily engaging. The story could move on without any tension, without any key events.

In classic drama theory, 'conflict' is considered to be the central feature that drives the development of all stories, and you will recognise this in many documentaries. This is the case even where you identify a film as being about a social issue, autobiographical or as an investigative documentary. Conflict refers here to a structuring device – for instance, minority group values set against mainstream ideas, East versus West or main characters aiming for goals which alienate them from their social environment.

Table 9.1 Example 'conflict' structure in a documentary

Opening: People used to be happy in this village.	Equilibrium
Then the motorway was built.	Disruption
Noise pollution, more visitors, country community has been affected.	Recognition
A new woodland has been planted between the motorway and the village.	Attempt
It will never be the same but it is a lot better now.	New equilibrium

'Conflict' is the backbone of the classic story structure in the West (see Chapter 10 for a detailed analysis). Often it may be described in the following five stages: equilibrium, disruption, recognition, attempt, new-found or created equilibrium (Todorov, 1977). The disruption in this approach refers to 'conflict'.

But is 'conflict' the only way of structuring a story? Despite its ubiquity, there might be other elements at play. Do you recognise conflict in *Titicut Follies* or in *Etre et Avoir* or in *Lift*? Feminist screenwriter Claudia Johnson was dissatisfied with this conflict-bound approach to telling stories. She felt that it implies, in character-driven documentaries, that the main characters are seen as troubled, aggressive go-getters filled with a desire to do 'their thing'.

In more issue-based documentaries, can we really identify a 'conflict' as being as sharp and distinct as is needed by this storytelling structure? It is a binary opposition where the sharp edges may not always help documentary filmmakers to tell stories with nuance and enough subtlety. Although some changes take place, they are not driven by conflict but can be better described in terms of subtle changes between people and their social environments. (See, for instance, the transcendental narrative.) In short, the conflict model is a way of seeing the world. It is a specific ideological approach.

Johnson argues 'conflict was not incorrect, but it was incomplete'. Read how she came to this conclusion.

Case study Claudia Johnston's story

I had taken a break from researching a documentary film about the most famous murder in Florida, the trial of Ruby McCollum, an African-American woman in my small town of Live Oak convicted of shooting and killing the town's Great White Hope, Senator-Elect Leroy Adams, her doctor and, allegedly, her lover. When she fired the gun – if she, in fact, did it – her life also came to an end. Every major connection was severed; her husband died the next day of heart failure; she was separated from her children, other family, and friends for more than twenty years.

Immersed in Ruby's story, I wondered why it engaged me so deeply. She and I had nothing in common except for our gender and the small North Florida town where we lived. The surface events of her story were the stuff of soap opera – wealth, corruption, infidelity, murder – and this had no connection to my quiet life. There was something deeper at work.

Mulling over what it might be, I saw it was connection itself. Underlying the conflict of Ruby's story, underlying the events of her life and mine – underlying any story, fictitious or true – is a deeper pattern of change, a pattern of connection and disconnection. The conflict and surface events are like waves, but underneath is an emotional tide – the ebb and flow of human connection. It's as essential to story as conflict but it essentially has been overlooked.

(Johnson, 2005: 7)

This approach may help you as a documentary filmmaker to look at aspects other than conflict in the story you want to tell which offer change and development that can drive your film.

Basic structure

The following diagram provides you with a backbone to start to set up your film.

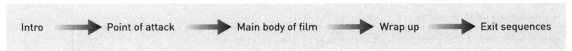

Figure 9.1 Basic structure of a film

- Intro – this provides the hook, main characters, the theme or topic, the framing of the story.
- Point of attack – the moment your story starts.
- Main body – the sequences, interviews that explore your topic.
- Wrap up – the climax.
- Exit sequences – the establishment of a changed reality.

This can be used as a basic timeline on which you can put the different ingredients of your film.

Classic documentary theory

The early documentary filmmakers such as Flaherty, Vertov, Grierson and Ivens (see the filmography at the end of the book) all used very different forms and visualisation strategies, but what they had in common was a strong political drive against Hollywood escapism and entertainment. The main focus was on the historical world, past and present lives in a complicated and unjust world. This often led to an interesting choice of subject but a dull film, and left contemporary documentary filmmakers fighting against the 'dreary' image of the genre.

This and the present cultural landscape in which the spectacular, the special, the unique (*Man on Wire*, *SuperSize Me*) is most appreciated, means that many hidden stories about unknown worlds do not reach the public domain. Funders and broadcasters who are engaged in fierce competition seem to prefer popular and individual stories instead of analysis of societal ills or significant developments in our world. While individual stories of survival, or unique experiences are interesting and revealing, it can be argued that individualising experiences leaves it up to the audience to consider the wider context.

This is not an irrelevant argument because the story structure will, to a certain extent, determine what you can and cannot address in a film. In line with the process described above, the classic realist dramatic structure has become one of the most popular forms in documentary filmmaking. It is remarkable that more experimental forms are currently used in mainstream feature films such as *Traffic* (Steven Soderbergh, USA, 2000) and *Memento* (Christopher Nolan, USA, 2000) than in mainstream documentary filmmaking. Conversely, one might argue that, because documentary filmmakers have used classic forms of storytelling, their films have reached bigger audiences, with the result that broadcasters/funders (de Jong, 2008) demand a classic drama approach in order to reach wider audiences.

The main point here is that each narrative structure will include and exclude certain aspects of the topic or theme you are addressing. Awareness of your choices will help you to develop your structure and play with it.

Reality and creativity

In the UK it was John Grierson (1966) and Paul Rotha (1963) who set up the framework of documentary theory. It was Rotha who argued that documentary should be considered as the 'instruction for the awakening of civic consciousness among the public' (in Aufderheide, 2007: 129). However, both Grierson and Rotha also defined documentary in terms of 'creativity', as they claimed it to be an art form. Grierson's famous reference to 'the creative interpretation of actuality' and the title of Rotha's book *Documentary Film; the use of the film medium to interpret creatively and in social terms the life of the people as it exists in reality* (in Aufderheide, 2007: 129) both illustrate simultaneously artistic and political ambitions and aspirations.

In the USA in 1971 Erik Barnouw published a book called *Documentary* – a truly international study of documentary filmmaking in countries such as Egypt, India and the Soviet Union as well as Western Europe. His influential approach led to a widening perspective of documentary film, creating a continuum in which the poetic, ethnographic, advocacy and propaganda films found a place while also appreciating the role of funders, state-sponsored and commercially sponsored films.

But without doubt it was the American, Bill Nichols, who was one of the most influential theorists of documentary. His *Representing Reality*, published in 1991, was one of the first books to theorise documentary. (See also works by Corner, Bruzzi, Ward, Beattie and Ellis and McLane listed at the end of this book.) It was one of the first attempts to distinguish between different documentaries in what he describes as 'modes of representations'; these 'modes' are different 'constructions of realist representations of the historical world' according to certain formal conventions.

In *Representing Reality* (1991, new edition 2005), Nichols distinguishes between the following modes.

Expository mode

This is often seen as the 'classic' documentary form, which uses a voice-over (often described as the 'voice of God'), to address social issues or explain certain phenomena in our world. Documentaries such as *People's Century* (1995, BBC series), *Windrush* (1998, BBC series), *March of the Penguins* (USA, 2005) and *Wal-Mart: The High Cost of Low Price* (Brave New Films, USA, 2005) are more contemporary forms of the expository documentary.

One of the most distinguishing features of this mode is the narration, which delivers 'the truth of the matter'. It is anonymous, a voice from nowhere, which tends to be male, white, middle-class and identified as part of the establishment. It conveys, according to post-modern theorists, a form of bourgeois representation of our world. Contemporary expository documentaries use a more personal, authored voice-over which situates the film within a certain social field and therefore allows for multiple perspectives on the historical world.

Narration as a device has the obvious advantage that you can give contextual information in an efficient way. Visual coherence can also be manipulated as the narration takes precedence over the image and allows you to use shots/sequences from disparate locations. The narration will pull the narrative into coherence.

Observational mode

In the mid-1950s, lighter cameras with synchronous sound became available and made filming on location more feasible. This mode gained popularity and is often still perceived as 'real' documentary.

Observational, or 'fly on the wall', films are popular at the moment on television, whether the theme is Great Ormond Street Children's Hospital, an accident and emergency department or a police station. These films share the concept of contained social worlds. 'Walled cities' (Rabiger, 2009) are being filmed, especially those where daily routines are continuously disrupted. This provides these films with a strong dramatic drive, as actions and events are continuously unfolding.

In its strictest form, the observational documentary has no commentary and uses no interviews. The camera is directed to record unfolding events, and long takes, synchronous sound, and shaky shots are part of the aesthetics of this mode.

An observational approach eschews intervention in the pro-filmic scene and directly focuses on what happens there and then. This can leave it open to criticisms of lack of context or framing of the film. The assumption that the presence of the camera will not influence the behaviours of the characters in the film has also been contentious. However, this mode of representation conveys a sense of direct access to the historical world which may explain its popularity, though it also raises ethical questions about the representation of individuals in crisis or in stressful situations. Stella Bruzzi sums this up:

> The key issue is that observational cinema has been mis-defined, and has mis-defined itself . . . The core of direct cinema films is the encounter before the camera, the moment when the filmmaking process disrupts and intrudes upon reality of the world it is documenting' (2006: 78).

A contemporary observational filmmaker is Kim Longinotto, who will use interviews in her film, but grounds her films firmly in an observational style – for instance, *Sisters in Law* (UK, 2005; for more films, see filmography).

Interactive/participatory mode

Here filmmakers interview or interact with subjects, either openly, when the filmmaker is on screen, or in masked interviews (we hear or are aware of the filmmaker but he/she is invisible).

This mode allows the usage of archive material and interviews with experts and witnesses, as well as observational footage. It is a versatile form which, when the filmmaker is on screen, can overlap with the performative documentary. The interaction between the filmmaker and the film's subjects is one of its engaging features. In the case of a visually absent filmmaker who is still present, if only vocally, the film's narrative is created in a constant dialogue between filmmaker and subject – for example, *The Lie of the Land* (Molly Dineen, UK, 2008); *Lift* (Marc Isaacs, UK, 2001); *Shoah* (Claude Lanzmann, France, 1992).

In other cases, the film relies on interviews and an almost invisible hand structures the narrative, which can make it an expository documentary without narration. In expository documentary, interviews are often used to create or support the argument of the film; the 'interactive' element almost disappears and the filmmaker hides his/her interventions. In these films it is the comments and questions from the filmmaker that provide coherence to the narrative.

Performative mode

The performative mode has become very successful, both in the cinema and on television, since the 1980s.

Through the performance of the filmmaker on screen, be it Nick Broomfield, Louis Theroux or Michael Moore, the audience learns about their subjects and the social world they inhabit.

They perform different roles to provoke, elicit, persuade, cajole or seduce their subjects into revealing feelings, ideas, fantasies or wishes. Although this form may reveal or posit certain points of view, as in Michael Moore's case, it mostly relies on the abilities of the subjects to deal with the approach (performance) of the filmmaker, who will also contextualise both the content and the performance of the subjects. This mode of representation requires a filmmaker with strong interview and social skills. Experience, control over the narrative (script) and an ability to integrate unexpected events or reactions of interviewees are essential.

Examples of this form include: Michael Moore, *Capitalism: a love story* (USA, 2010); *Sicko* (USA, 2009); *Fahrenheit 9/11* (USA, 2004); *Roger and Me* (USA, 2003); *Bowling for Columbine* (USA, 2002) and Nick Broomfield (*Aileen: Life and Death of a Serial Killer* (UK, 2003); *Battle for Haditha* (UK, 2007); *Fetishes* (UK, 1997); *Heidi Fleiss: Hollywood Madam* (UK, 1995); *Kurt and Courtney* (UK, 1998); *The Leader, the Driver and the Driver's Wife* (UK, 1991, revisited 2006).

Reflexive mode

The film *Man with a Movie camera* (Vertov, Soviet Union, 1929) tends to be mentioned whenever this mode is being discussed. The intention of this mode is to reveal the production process of the film itself, in order to defamiliarise the audience with the film text. This mode echoes a Brechtian approach. This German playwright argued that theatre audiences should be kept aware of the fact they are watching an artistic construction. The emphasis on the artificiality or the constructed nature of plays/films is intended to prevent an audience from losing itself in the story. This mode was originally developed as a protest against Hollywood escapism. An audience's critical awareness was seen to be undermined as, through continuity editing, audiences were being kept in the world of the story.

Although this mode has intriguing elements, the breaking of the engagement of the audience can lead to highly abstract 'idea' films. This mode requires audiences to reflect on the act of representation of reality itself in a variety of artistic forms. For instance, in her well-known film *Reassemblage* (USA, Senegal, 1983), Trinh Minh-ha, a Vietnamese/American filmmaker and academic, not only asks *how* Western filmmakers represent African people but also *what* subjects are being selected for representation. In this film she states that she does not want to speak *about* her subjects in Africa but that she wants to speak *nearby* to question the power of the camera, i.e. the Western gaze.

By bringing to the foreground how documentary conventions represent its subjects, the reflexive mode brings into question the status of the documentary genre as a film form that aims to represents 'realities'.

Trinh Minh-ha, cited in Nichols (1991), expresses the view that:

> Documentary is a colonial approach to the world . . . A conversation of 'us' with 'us' about 'them' is a conversation in which 'them' is silenced . . . Anthropology is better described as 'gossip' (we speak together about others) than as 'conversation'.
>
> (Nichols, 1991: 67–68)

Trinh Minh-ha tries to explore new subjectivities beyond existing stereotypes, since how we frame shots and our selection of subjects are considered to be 'naturalised' ideology.

The reflexive mode may not be a form that will attract you but it might be worth considering its aims as it will make you aware whether you are representing existing stereotypes or are developing new ways of approaching certain topics or subjects.

Other well-known films of this type are: *Far from Poland* (Jill Godmilow, USA, 1984), *Daughter Rite* (Michelle Citron, 1979), *The Thin Blue Line* (Errol Morris, USA, 1987).

Poetic mode

This early form (1920s) of documentary emphasises a personal approach to the historical world. It uses juxtaposition, association and reflection as a transition between a variety of shots and sequences of diverse locations. The narrative is not driven by logic but association, ideas, feelings, fantasies, experiences and reflections.

Joris Ivens, a Dutch filmmaker appreciated for both his aesthetic and political approach in his films, made a film about a rainy day in Amsterdam (*Rain*, NL, 1929). The emphasis is not on getting soaked, or that the rain is good for the gardens but on the aesthetic effects of rain on the image of Amsterdam. See also *Berlin – Symphony of a Great City* (Alberto Cavalcanti and Walther Ruttmann, Germany, 1927), and *On the subject of Nice/A propos de Nice*, (Jean Vigo, France, 1929) and *London* (Patrick Keiller, UK, 1994).

Chris Marker's *Sunless* (*Sans Soleil*, France, 1983), among his other films, not only changes the perspective of audiences on the characteristics of memory but also requires a different way of tuning in to the film compared with other documentaries, a different attitude.

The poetic mode allows the filmmaker to use different ways of linking sequences of shots and can ask a variety of questions about the nature of our lives. This mode offers you a wide range of possibilities for not addressing certain topics but at the same time reflecting on them.

The above 'modes of representation', or ways of constructing realities, are, in their purest form, different styles of documentary filmmaking. One could not describe it as a family tree (Bruzzi, 2000, 2006) but in certain historical periods particular forms of documentary filmmaking tended to be popular.

Observational formats were very popular in the 1960s and 1970s, but at the present time a pure observational film is rare. Most documentaries will be contemporary hybrids which will include, for instance, interviews, or expository films which contain observational footage. Hybridisation defines the contemporary documentary film climate, not only between different 'modes' but also with dramatised scenes, animation, and web-based materials/footage.

It is the awareness of what certain structuring devices will allow you to include in or exclude from your film that will push you to explore and combine different structuring devices. For instance, when you use a presenter/interviewer this becomes a structural device, as he or she will take on a certain role. For instance in *Shoah*, Claude Lanzmann takes his interviewees to the empty concentration camps where they stayed during the Second World War. This approach leads to direct associations and memories of events, around which he structures his film. It is a clear example of how the content and form have grown in the process of filmmaking.

Creating a structure with a drive: change and development

The following list gives you an overview of some general structuring devices used in a documentary context. It is by no means exclusive, but it will help you to focus on how to tell the story and think about how the structure influences, perhaps even determines, the narrative and content of your film:

- chronology – event- and character-driven;
- thematic;
- essay;
- comparative/juxtaposition;
- transcendental (see Chapter 11);

- dramatic (see Chapter 10);
- non-linear/interactive (see Chapter 13).

Chronology

Although common, this is a very difficult structuring device. When you are following events/ people through time, the tendency is to follow them and let it all happen, but this may not be interesting enough or create sufficient tension or drive in the film. You should be careful not to create a film that proceeds like the previously mentioned still pond on a sunny day.

Observational films tend to be chronological but, depending on the attitude of the filmmaker, he/she will choose the most interesting events and may even mix events at different locations without really undermining the impression of chronology of the film. However, it might not be the actual chronology of the events as they have been shot. For instance, in *Titicut Follies* (USA, 1967) by Frederick Wiseman, we follow the daily routines of a secure mental hospital such as bathing, changing clothes and therapy, but it is the special events such as the party at the beginning of the film which create interest and function as a hook for the audience. It may be the hook to engage the audience but it is questionable whether this party took place before the filming of the daily routines in the hospital. The same can be said for the counselling sessions with the psychiatrist, which are intercut within the film's narrative without jeopardising the basic structure of daily life at the hospital. The long take covering the changing of the clothes is broken up by a counselling session between the psychiatrist and a prisoner, after which we return to the changing of the clothes sequences.

In order to avoid a boring chronology of events, you may want to play with certain key events to create development and drive. At the end you may have altered the chronology of the events but does this intervention undermine the aim of the film, any more than the representation of daily life in a secure mental hospital, as in *Titicut Follies*? Frederick Wiseman has always been very clear that he films events in an observational mode but that, when he enters the editing suite, he will create a film, a story, and in that sense reflect his personal experience of events. His position on non-intervention is different from that of the Maysles brothers, Pennebaker or Kopple (see Nichols (1991, 2005), Ward (2005) and *Cinéma Vérité: Defining the Moment*, Peter Wintonick, Canada).

Natural chronology

A film which could be seen as a 'natural' chronological film is *Czech Dream, proceed to check-out* (Filip Remunda and Vit Klusak, Poland, 2003). Two film students create an advertising campaign with the help of an advertising agency for a hypermarket that does not exist. The film follows the production process of the multi-media campaign till the opening, when 4,000 shoppers arrive to get the best deals in town, only to discover that there is only a shop façade. The film opens with the two filmmakers explaining their intentions and how they have built up the narrative of the film.

Following a main character through time

A natural chronology can be found in those films that follow a main character preparing for a great event, whether it is a performance, marriage or moving. This way, you will have a drive and development, but you will still need to delve deep into the personal motives, fears and joys of the main character(s) involved to provide depth and emotional engagement with your story. Quite a few observational films, such as *Primary* (Pennebaker and Leacock, USA, 1960), *Jane*

(Hope Ryden, USA, 1962) are made like this. You may also want to have a look at films made by Kim Longinotto who makes contemporary hybrid observational films such as *Sisters in Law* (2005); *Divorce Iranian Style* (1998) and *Hold Me Tight, Let Me Go* (2007).

These films tend to be described as following an *inductive* model (Hewitt and Vasquez, 2010: 188–92) of storytelling. As a viewer, you enter the story at a certain moment and from then on you see the story unfold. Gradually, more information is revealed and this finally creates a complete narrative.

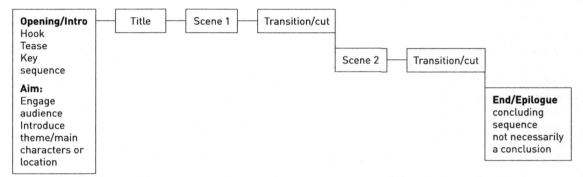

Figure 9.2 The inductive model
Notes to Figure 9.2
Transitions in this structure are important as they indicate time progressing (often a dissolve), or a different location (hard cut), or a fade to black to start a new scene. The number of scenes is not particularly relevant, as long as the chronological development within the film is not disturbed. Alternatively, you can break the predictability of this structure by making short sideways associations or by introducing an event which will get more attention later in the film in order to increase the tension. For instance, if you film someone who is preparing for a great performance, you might introduce the preparations on the day itself, in short sequences in the middle of the film.

Thematic

Many documentaries offer a theme, whether it is unemployment on a housing estate, global warming, domestic violence or changes in agriculture. Your analysis of the theme will determine your structure. Mind mapping (see Chapter 1) is a good way of exploring how to link the different aspects or components of the story. There are many possible links between different elements: logic, association, cause and effect, but also historical factors, political or cultural factors or simply a question which is followed by an answer (see Michael Moore's films). Often personal, individual stories are used to explore different aspects of the theme. This can also be described as a sociological approach as it often deals with the big sociological themes such as individual vs. society or structure and agency.

You may finish with a conclusion, but you can also end with a question or a provocative statement that challenges the perceptions of your audience.

This narrative structure is often described as a *deductive model*, starting with a statement or a thesis, and the rest of the film explores the different aspects of the topic. For instance, the film could start with a thesis such as this: At the beginning of the twenty-first century there are more children living below the poverty line than 40 years ago. You know exactly as an audience what will happen next.

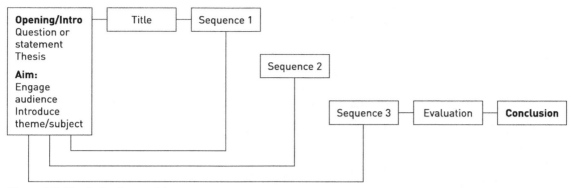

Figure 9.3 The deductive model
Notes to Figure 9.3
In this structure, the filmmaker starts off with a point of view or statement, to which all sequences are related. Each sequence addresses a different aspect of the theme/topic and provides support, through interviews with experts or individual citizens, to confirm the point of view. In the final sequence there is a conclusion: the question will have found an answer. The statement has been proven to be right, partly right or completely wrong. It's a coherent and logical format.

Look at *SuperSize Me*. Morgan Spurlock sets up his film by stating that junk food is bad, especially McDonald's, and the following film sequences all support this basic statement. It's an engaging and important film addressing the quality of fast food but it might be reasonable to ask: who eats McDonald's 24/7?

This structure can operate as a closed system. Once you are drawn into the world of the film, it is hard to think outside its frame of reference.

Examples of the deductive approach include: *The Lie of the Land* (Molly Dineen, UK, 2007) and *Darwin's Nightmare* (Hubert Sauper, France, 2004).

Essay: a journey

The essay film explores one particular question, statement or thesis and finishes with an argument or answer to the question, just like a written essay.

Michael Moore's films follow this structure as he is on a quest to find out about certain events or to talk to certain people, and every step leads to a new question or action. He starts with a question and may or may not find a 'temporary' answer but, either way, this raises a new question. The form of question – (temporary) answer – new question drives the film forward and keeps the audience involved.

The essay film is often used as a journalistic investigation in certain social fields.

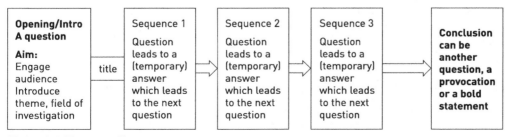

Figure 9.4 The essay film

The above description of an essay film is inspired by the concept of written essay which has been translated into a documentary film form.

> As in written essays, the (essay) films tend to marry the personal voice of a guiding narrator (often the director) with a wide swathe of other voices. They usually address real events, but do so in a fragmentary, non-systematic way, probing and searching rather than channeling the authoritative 'voice of God' that marks so many documentaries.
>
> (David Winks Gray (www.sf360.org/features/the-essay-film-in-action))

Michael Moore's films belong to that group of essay films with a strong political engagement but the essay film can be placed in a much wider context.

Paul Arthur describes the essay film as a 'meeting ground for documentary, avant-garde and artfilm impulses' (2003: 62). This takes the concept of an essay film into a more experimental and creative domain. Nora Alter pushes the essay film even further into what she describes as 'heresy'. The essay film 'strives beyond formal, conceptual and social constraint' (1996: 171). Inspired by Adorno (1991: 23), for whom 'heresy' is the 'essay's innermost formal law', Alter argues that 'the essay film disrespects traditional boundaries, is transgressive both structurally and conceptually, it is self-reflective and self-reflexive' (1996: 171).

This concept takes the essay film close to what we have described as the creative documentary. Films by filmmakers such as Chris Marker, Harun Farocki, Derek Jarman, Patrick Keiller, Werner Herzog, Michelle Citron and Ross McElwee (see Appendix) expand the concept as all of these filmmakers push the boundaries of traditional documentary formats. However, at the same time, the essay film becomes an unmanageably big 'category' as it includes autobiographical, biographical and politically engaged films.

What could be saved here is the notion of 'heresy', whether it concerns form, content or the role of the voice of the author. Another aspect in common is the challenge to the notion of a plot. The essay film is more of a journey, the development of an idea, an exploration in incomplete and uncertain, instable worlds.

Comparison/juxtaposition

Here, the filmmaker follows people or events at different locations and cross-cuts between the different lives or events to make a point. Cross-cutting between time and space is a device also used in feature filmmaking. Every scene is a little study in itself, which leads to a similar or different event or experience of the main characters.

When you make a juxtaposition between two sequences/scenes, you create a clear point of view which may imply conflict, tension and argument. It is up to the filmmaker whether or not the audience is shown the results of the comparison or juxtaposition, or is left to come to its own conclusion. This cross-cutting between different locations/events/people can be used as part of a film, but it can also be used as a structuring device for a complete film. In this case, you create a multi-story structure.

Multi-story structure

To develop a multi-story structure requires significant research and planning of your film as you need enough key scenes of each event/personal story to keep all stories evolving.

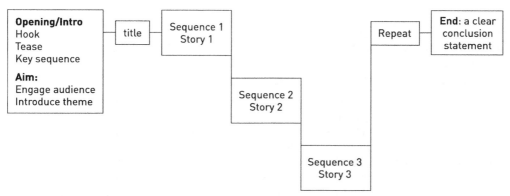

Figure 9.5 The multi-story model
Notes to Figure 9.5
You can use a multi-story structure as an opening in a film, as Wim Wenders did in *Buena Vista Social Club* (Wim Wenders, USA, 1999). Wenders cuts between a recording session, a concert and finding the location of the club. In *Spellbound* (Jeffrey Blitz, USA, 2002), a film about the preparation of a diverse group of children living at different locations in the United States for a national spelling competition, a number of stories are cross-cut through the whole film. The main theme of the film is the preparation for the spelling competition, with each sequence covering a child at different stages of preparation.

This structure often needs a voice-over to avoid the audience losing track of the main theme of the film.

This short overview provides some guidelines about the possible structures for a documentary. Whether you let a story unfold or lead an audience by the hand through an evolving story depends not only on your intentions but also on the access you have to certain locations or people.

Specific documentaries

The following section gives you an overview of different types of documentary – a list of subgenres. The descriptions operate as a tag, a label to describe your film. They do not pretend to be exhaustive and mainly address the strengths and weaknesses of each as an initial framework of your film. Like most 'tags', they fence off a certain area of interrogation and investigation but leave the form open:

- portrait or biography
- diary
- scientific documentary
- historical documentary
- investigative documentary
- archive-compilation film
- travelogue
- going back to . . . (when or where it all happened)
- road movie–adventure–action
- report – journalistic
- one day in the life of . . .

- institution-film
- docudrama (drama inspired by real-life events)
- dramatised documentary (reconstruction)
- oral history.

Making a choice of a specific subgenre will help you during the production process, and provides clarity to your production team and possible financiers/distributors. This overview of subgenres is meant to help you to reflect on your own approach. Most of the structuring devices mentioned can be used in a variety of formats.

When you are making a film you will have in your head a loose idea of form, which will undoubtedly be challenged while shooting or editing your material. It is important to keep this overarching structure in mind and not to become lost in the intricacies of a few scenes.

All documentaries are produced in a certain distribution context, which will influence the format and therefore the content. For instance, a portrait to be seen in a gallery or museum will offer different possibilities from a portrait to be shown in a broadcast environment, where TV schedules and specific slots or a cinema release will provide opportunities but at the same time constraints. Documentaries are not made in a vacuum and the viewing context should be taken into account when you are producing your film.

Portrait/biography

The portrait offers 'human interest' as well as information about a person, and, if made well, will provide insight into a specific historical period or social location. A portrait can offer a 'compassionate' approach but at the same time be 'critical'. The filmmaker does not have to idolise the main character – in fact the film becomes more interesting when the 'gritty' or contradictory aspects of the character are being addressed.

In *The Last Bolshevik* (1993, BBC) by Chris Marker about the Russian filmmaker Alexander Medvedkin (1900–89), who was his friend and mentor, Marker structures the film in the form of six letters sent to him posthumously. He uses his own voice as a voice-over and in interviews, but in a contrapuntal relationship to the visuals. The narrative interweaves feeling, thoughts and analysis of what it meant to be a communist in the twentieth century and a filmmaker in the Soviet Union. The film has many layers: personal, artistic, historical and political.

Biographies are a popular form of historical documentary. Historical information can be presented in an accessible and visually/emotionally appealing way. The danger with this form is a lack of analysis or synthesis if the information presented is purely anecdotal, a celebration of special events. Portraits or biographies often include interviews with people who knew the main character as well as archive material, home movies and photographs.

Examples of this category include:

The Fog of War, Eleven Lessons from the Life of Roberts. McNamara (Errol Morris, USA, 2003)

When We were Kings (Leon Gast, USA, 1996)

The Last Bolshevik (Chris Marker, 1993, BBC)

Grizzly Man (Werner Herzog, USA, 2005)

Thomas Jefferson (Ken Burns, USA, 1997)

Grey Gardens (Albert and David Maysles, 1975)

Diary, autobiographical

This chronological and fragmented approach is very attractive, but keeping the point of view of the 'storyteller' central can sometimes be difficult. This form needs 'intimacy', although a certain balance needs to be realised between the 'inner' experiences and the 'external' events in the life of the storyteller (see *Tarnation*, Jonathan Caoutte, UK, 2005).

It is also a good form to mix with observational or essay formats. Combined with different formats, it allows the filmmaker to integrate different ideas, feelings and experiences in the film without interviewing the different subjects. The audience is being addressed directly and intimately. For instance:

Don't fence me in (Nandini Sikand, USA, 1998)

The Beaches of Agnès (Agnès Varda, 2008)

Who's Going to Pay for these Donuts, anyway? (Janice Tanaka, USA, 1992)

Silverlake Life: The View from Here (Peter Friedman, Tom Joslin, USA, 1993)

NO! The Rape Documentary (Aishah Shahidah Simmons, USA, 2006)

Dialogues with Madwomen (Allie Light, USA, 1993)

I for India (Sandhya Suri, UK, 2005)

51 Birch Street (Doug Block, USA, 2005)

Sherman's March: A Meditation on the Possibility of Romantic Love in the South During an Era of Nuclear Weapons Proliferation (Ross McElwee, USA, 1986)

This form is also used as part of 'The making of . . .' documentary which tells the story of the production of a film and is made in the context of the marketing of a feature film. It is very popular as part of certain reality TV formats (e.g. *Wife Swap*), but can also be part of more conventional documentaries, in which it is presented as a different experience, a different voice which can give another layer to an essay or thematic film. Examples include:

Hearts of Darkness: A Filmmaker's Apocalypse (Eleanor Coppola, 1991, USA) about the production of *Apocalypse Now* (Francis Coppola, 1979, USA); *Dangerous Days*: Making Blade Runner (USA, 2007); *Alien Evolution* (Alien Quadrilogy); *Tribute to Lawrence Tierney/The Good, The Bad and The Bunker* (*Reservoir Dogs*: 10th anniversary special edition); *Other Voices: Creating The Terminator* (*The Terminator*: special edition); *Pursuing the Suspects/Keyser Söze: Lie or Legend/Doing Time with the Suspects* (*The Usual Suspects*: special edition); *Akira Kurosawa: It Is Wonderful To Create* (*Seven Samurai*: special edition).

Scientific documentary

The central focus of this form is a problem or an event and the collection of evidence to explain its occurrence. It is essential to keep the audience involved in your quest for explanations/answers. Very often a presenter, or a voice-over, will keep the narrative of the film together or the programme is set up in a magazine format in which each section addresses a different aspect of the main theme e.g. *Horizon* (BBC series); *An Inconvenient Truth* (Guggenheim, USA, 2007).

Historical documentary

This popular form can sometimes be boring if told as a chronological story. The filmmaker needs to find a drive that moves the story on and a strongly authored approach may help to engage the audience. Re-enactment, dramatisation or an interesting presenter are contemporary TV formats to add an entertaining and contemporary concern to a certain historical event. For instance, *Casualty 1908* (Channel 4, 2009), a film about a hospital at the beginning of the twentieth century, is told from the perspective of a doctor and a nurse. The main characters engage audiences while the living conditions and relationships within a hospital are revealed as in an expository documentary. It provides insight into the healthcare at that time, though some may argue that this 'example' approach will not give the audience the wider context of the health care system.

Watch also the History Channel to have a closer look at how different historical events are represented on film:

Sunrise over Tiananmen Square (Shui-Bo Wang, Canada, 1998) animated *S-21: The Khmer Rouge Killing Machine* (Rithy Panh, Cambodia/France, 2003)

Killing Time (Annika Gustafson, Canada, 2007)

Memories of Berlin: The Twilight of Weimar Culture (Gary Conklin, Germany, 1976)

There are many films made about important historical events such as the First and Second World Wars, revolutions or civil wars. Specialised websites can advise you on specific documentaries (e.g. www.historicaldocumentaries.weebly.com). See Chapter 19 for more information on the role of archive footage in film.

Newsreel series such as *Pathé News* (1910–56), *Paramount News* (1927–57), *Fox Movietone News* (1928–63), *Hearst Metrotone News/News of the Day* (1914–67), *Universal Newsreel* (1929–67) and *The March of Time series*, part of the USA National Film Register, can offer archive footage (see Chapter 19).

Investigative documentary

The audience follows a reporter in his/her quest to reveal 'lies, scandals, and injustice or criminal activities' (John Pilger, Documentaries that Changed the World, UK, 2006, 12 films made between 1970 and 2000).

The reporter will talk to camera but will also use his/her voice as narration to explain events. Narration tends to keep the story together, bridging movements across space and time. Investigative documentary is often seen as a much-admired mythical form, with the conclusion (the truth?) revealed by the journalist. Its credentials are based on the audience's perception of journalism as fair and impartial. As the film constructs an argument, it is often structured around thesis/antithesis/synthesis or cross-cutting between the first two.

This form has been used to explore well-known events like the Bhopal explosion, the Exxon oil spill or Shackleton's expedition to the Antarctic. The film is set up and framed at the start as an investigation; events unfold and additional information is revealed which then provides the backbone and the drive of the documentary.

In the UK, Michael Simkin and Donal MacIntyre (Dare Films, UK) have specialised in undercover investigations and focus on crime, drugs, and other worlds hidden from the public eye. Other notable examples of investigative documentary are:

Bought & Sold: An Investigative Documentary About the International Trade in Women (Gillian Caldwell, UK, 2009)

Outlawed: Extraordinary Rendition, Torture and Disappearances in the 'War on Terror' (Gillian Caldwell, UK, 2009)

A useful source of information is Witness, an organisation that uses video and online technologies to expose human rights violations (https://www.fulfillmentwarehouse.biz/witness/).

Archive documentary-compilation documentary

Although not many have written about archive documentary apart from Jay Leyda (1964), it has become a popular form. Based on archive material and newly shot material, a compilation documentary is created. In the editing, the meaning of the footage is changed, either by an oppositional reading of the material, e.g. *Atomic Café* (Rafferty, Loader, and Rafferty, USA, 1982, reformatted 1995), or by the use of different editing techniques, such as juxtaposition, e.g. *The Fall of the Romanov Dynasty* (Esfir Shub, Russia, 1927, reformatted 2002), continuity (realist narrative) or editing, e.g. *Deep Water* (Louise Osmond/Jerry Rothwell, UK, 2008).

Atomic Café uses training films produced by the military, news broadcasts, and interviews with scientists to conclude that audiences, journalists and politicians were misled in order to support atomic testing in the Pacific.

The Fall of the Romanov Dynasty uses home movies from the tsar's family, newsreels and other 'discovered' footage, and juxtaposes the different sequences in such way that a new story is being told about the beginning of the twentieth century in Russia. A story about exploitation and poverty of the peasant class.

Deep Water tells the story of round-the-world yachtsman Donald Crowhurst, whose public deception during the Sunday Times Golden Globe Race and subsequent alleged suicide may have been due to mental health problems. In this case, the archive material was arranged in such a way that a tragic individual's dramatic story could be told. It is a classic narrative: the hero wants something, but meets many hurdles, and in this case he fails.

This format relies on the ability of the filmmaker to order footage, shots and sequence in a different way in order to create a new meaning. One could also argue that the footage has been taken out of its original context and misinterpreted. It might be worth considering whether documentary filmmaking is not really based on these notions.

As more archive material becomes available and the technical means to transfer the original material to a digital format has become easier, compilation films or the usage of archive footage has become more popular. But archive can be used in very different ways. Very often it is an illustration. You make a film about London and you show 10 seconds of archive footage. However, the historical context of the footage or the reason why it has been shot is frequently not clear. It tends to fit an allocated slot in a completely different film.

Travelogue

The travelogue was one of the first popular documentary forms. Photographers/filmmakers used to travel and collect their material and present their work during lectures at public events, in schools and in town and village halls. Often this work fell into the category of the exotic, portraying images of people in faraway countries who were either admired for their close relationship to nature and having escaped the alienation of an increasingly industrialised western world, or were seen as savage (Basu, 2008). The filmmaker would recount the story of their travels, illustrating the talk with slides and film clips. In the 1960s and 1970s the classic travelogues declined, only to re-emerge in a more popular format at the end of the twentieth century.

At the moment, the travelogue seems to be a popular TV format. A celebrity is sent to a faraway country to show and describe their experiences, for instance *Travels with Michael Palin* (BBC series), where the audience visits various countries and is introduced to different cultural and social traditions via the people Michael Palin meets on his travels. This form is dependent on the engaging qualities of the main character(s).

The travelogue is also explored as a way of following the production of a certain product. For instance, Alain de Botton followed the breeding, catching, transport and arrival of shrimps in the UK. It is an issue documentary but the experiences and comments of the presenter are used to link the events in an engaging way.

In many cases, the travelogue is considered to be a new form of ethnographic film, with the audience learning about different cultural values and traditions through the encounters of the presenter. But the form may celebrate the unique, the bizarre, the odd and reinforce existing stereotypes. For the principles of travel documentaries, watch the *Art of Travel* by Alain de Botton (BBC, 2005 DVD, via Seneca Productions).

Road movie–action–adventure

This form is comparable to the travelogue but is bolder and braver as the main character engages with their surroundings (see Bruce Parry, *Tribe*, 2005–7 complete series, BBC). It is dependent on the engaging qualities of the main character(s) and their courageous nature. A good example of this would be Ewan McGregor and Charley Boorman's motorbike journey from Scotland to Cape Town in South Africa (*Long Way Down*, 2007, BBC series).

Music/concert/live performance documentaries

Since *Don't Look Back* (Pennebaker ,USA, 1967), an observational documentary about Bob Dylan's concert tour in the UK, this approach has become popular to film concerts/behind-the-scenes events.

In 1970, two other observational filmmakers, the Maysles brothers, made *Gimme Shelter* (USA, 1970, remastered 2007), which covered the notorious concert at San Francisco's Altamont Speedway. The Beatles produced their answer in *Let it Be* (UK, 1970), which covered the recording of their last Apple studio album. The multi-talented Martin Scorsese's historical documentary about The Band, called *The Last Waltz* (USA, 1978), really brought this genre to the foreground.

These documentaries tend to be observational and characterised by almost unrestricted access for the filmmaker. The latter seems to be about the biggest issue in the contemporary climate. Further examples of the genre include:

Woodstock (Michael Wadleigh, UK, 1970, remastered 2001)

Stop Making Sense (Jonathan Demme, USA, 1984) about Talking Heads

Buena Vista Social Club (Wim Wenders, Cuba, 1999)

Madonna: Truth or dare (USA, 1991)

Cirque du Soleil: Journey of Man (USA, 2000)

Going back to . . .

In this approach, a filmmaker usually goes back to a place where an important event took place and looks for traces of this event or invites witnesses of the event to describe their experiences – for instance, *Shoah* (Claude Lanzmann France, 1985, remastered 2008).

This device is often used as part of a portrait/biography or autobiography. Saira Shah went to Afghanistan to explore the effects of the Taliban on daily life and in particular the lives of women (*Beneath the Veil*, 2001, Channel 4). The intimacy of this form leads to absorbing and informative films.

One day in the life of . . .

This is a literary/essayistic approach which can be critical but also poetic and dynamic. It can be engaging if someone leads an interesting life or is a compelling character. However, it can lack analysis and become anecdotal. In this form, the filmmaker has to find a moment of 'conflict' within the main character, or with his/her social environment, or find those instances of deep connection or disconnection with the social environment – those moments of tenderness, love, humility or compassion, or the opposite: loneliness, isolation or even despair.

The institution (described by Rabiger as the 'walled city' film)

This is a form which is well developed by Frederick Wiseman (*High School*, 1968, USA), *Central Park* (USA, 1989), *Titicut Follies* (USA, 1967), *Hospital* (USA, 1970). Contemporary versions are the TV series *The Police, Accident and Emergency* or, potentially, any institutional environment where a lot of visually interesting things happen. Most of the time, these are institutions with strict daily routines which are disrupted. An element of unpredictability makes these films interesting. Through editing, the filmmaker makes 'comments' on the events. A good insight and overview of observational filmmaking is offered in the documentary *Cinéma Vérité: Defining the Moment*; by Peter Wintonick (Canada, 2006).

Docudrama

Real-life events form the basis of the storyline here, but the requirements of classical dramatic storytelling mould the real-life events into a certain chronology, or certain characters become more or less prominent. This form can be very controversial, but may have a positive effect on debate in the public domain. Striking examples are: *Bloody Sunday* (Paw Greengrass, UK, 2002), *Cathy Come Home* (Jeremy Sandford, UK, 1976, remastered 2008), *Bradford Riots* (Neil Biswas, UK, 2006). More recently, the BBC's *Five Daughters* (BBC, 2010) retold the murder of five young women in Ipswich in 2006 and Nick Broomfield made the docudrama *Ghosts* (UK, 2007) about illegal immigrants who drowned while fishing for cockles.

Dramatised documentary

This is the reconstruction of certain events in which the film stays as close as possible to real events. Re-enactment has a long history in documentary filmmaking as early documentaries involved re-enactment of real events, whether historical or contemporary. Sometimes if you do not have access to the real 'thing,' you have no choice other than to recreate it.

On television, *Crimewatch* uses re-enactment of crimes to jog the audience's memory and as an illustration of the crime. It is considered highly controversial in this context.

Oral history

Here, the main characters describe the same events or experiences. The personal experience is central to this form. Strict editing can avoid its becoming too repetitive, and an overarching structure or theme is needed to frame the interviews (see Richie, 2003). Memory is an ever-moving landscape and it requires special interview techniques and preparation for interviews. The Oral History Society website provides tips and recommendations for this kind of project (ohs.org.uk).

An example of the genre is *The Life and Times of Rosie the Riveter* (Connie Field, USA, 1980), based on interviews with women who worked in munitions plants in World War II.

Interactive documentary

In recent years, documentary has entered museum and gallery environments, resulting in formats by which the audience decides the order of the different sequences. In this way, the documentary is effectively created by each member of the audience. A good example of this work is *Warte Mal: Prostitution after the Velvet Revolution*, by Ann-Sofi Siden (1999). *Warte Mal* was marketed by the South Bank Centre as a walk-in documentary. Thirteen screens were installed in a museum space. The 'peepshow' cubicles had transparent windows and the audience members could see each other while watching the interviews with the prostitutes, pimps and clients in the booths. The atmosphere of the location was created by wall-sized photographs of the surroundings of the village of Dubi, on the border of Germany and the Czech Republic (Hobbard, 2003; Basu, 2008).

Kuba, by Kutlug Ataman (2004), portrays the inhabitants of the shanty town, Kuba, in Istanbul. Thirty old-fashioned, battered TVs show interviews, talking heads, with the inhabitants (Adrian Searle, *The Guardian*, 29 March 2005). As in *Warte Mal*, the audience select the stories they are interested in and dip in and out of the life stories which are being screened.

The internet has also challenged conventional documentary formats. Interactive documentaries tend to have a non-linear structure. Again, each member of the audience creates their own documentary by the way they navigate through the sequences. Some interactive documentaries on the internet are websites offering a variety of short sequences, photos, animation and text. (See Chapter 12.)

Short documentaries

As mentioned above, the form will also be influenced by the length of the film. Within an educational context, most films that are produced will belong to the so-called 'shorts' genre. We will pay extra attention to these films. Complicated structural devices may not be suitable here, as the audience will lose track of the narrative and the intentions of the film.

Historically, the short documentary (20 minutes or shorter) has always been considered as a site for experimentation, a tool of change (video activism) and, of course, a training ground for a lot of filmmakers, but it has actually received very little attention in the public domain. However, over the last 10 years we can identify an increased attention to the short film by broadcasters, festivals and audiences alike. More public funding has also become available to produce short films. The BBC's Brief Encounters, the Film Councils' Digital Shorts, Channel 4's Short and Curlies and currently 4 thought TV illustrate a higher profile for short films.

Channel 4 and the BBC regularly include short films on their websites and a new website dedicated only to the distribution of short films was launched in 2010: MiShorts. In addition, short documentaries have found more exhibition space in galleries and museums, on the net and, more recently, as podcasts. The short now has its own festivals, and in more established festivals shorts have been allocated their own space.

The short has gained a more prominent place in the documentary film field and has become a 'genre' in its own right.

Making a short

Short documentaries require a different approach to both the structure and content of your film. Whether you have 6, 10, 30, 60 or even 90 minutes to tell a story makes a big difference to your subject and how you can tell the story. It could be argued that the short is particularly challenging as the narrative and visualisation need to be precise and there is not much room for manoeuvre. The whole idea of 'it's only a short' may lead to unexpected problems.

Content: be specific

The subject of a short should be specific. Subjects such as global warming, the credit crunch or love and divorce in the twenty-first century might be too big, but you can translate these themes into specific examples while at the same time still making a point about the wider issue. For instance, global warming can be illustrated by the life of a polar bear or a day in the life of a scientist in Antarctica or a farmer in Africa or the north of the UK. They are brief snippets of a wider issue – the tip of the iceberg, so to speak. Life on a housing estate does not require 10 interviews with social workers, different inhabitants and a great deal of observational footage of life there. Look at *Lift* (Marc Isaacs, UK, 2001) which tells you a lot about this housing estate in East London.

These films work because individual stories are rarely purely 'individual'; they always take place in a wider social, cultural or political context. Our lives unfold at a specific historical moment, which does not mean that there are no individual aspects to our lives but that these might be less significant than we think.

Storytelling: to the point

You will need to get to the point straight away because you do not have time for a long introduction. Your audience needs to understand quite quickly what your theme is and be curious about what the story will be. It requires you to select key issues, experiences and ideas and develop links between these which can be turned into an engaging narrative.

Key points

- The structure of a film develops best in conjunction with the content while being researched, shot and edited.

- A film needs a drive that moves the story forward; this can be a conflict, concept or connection/disconnection, a quest or answers to questions, to name a few.

- Different structuring devices can be used to create a narrative. We have discussed here: chronology, inductive, deductive, multi-story lines.

- Classic realist narrative is often used as the backbone of how we tell stories in the west.

- Different modes of documentary filmmaking can act as structuring devices, as these forms construct presented realities in different ways: narration, participatory, performative, reflective and poetic modes.

- The length of a film influences your structure and choice of topic.

- Broadcast slots or other distribution contexts will influence the structure and content of your film.

Chapter 10

The classic narrative

Erik Knudsen

"Let it be feelings that bring about the events. Not the other way."

(Bresson, 1977: 15)

Introduction

The ubiquitous term 'the classic narrative' describes a broad approach to storytelling that dominates a number of narrative artistic forms. In this chapter, using the context of feelings and emotions as our starting point, we shall explore what the key ingredients of the classic narrative are and then connect this with the documentary genre.

The classic storyteller's key tools

Imagine you are going to tell a friend a story about an experience you had, or one that you witnessed. You want to engage their emotions. You want them to be sitting slightly on the edge of their seat, listening to you. First, you have a reason for wanting to tell this story. You will want it to be somehow relevant to the listener; there will be something you want to draw their attention to or make them realise, perhaps a dilemma you want to present them with. The first thing you will need to get to grips with is: why do *you* want to tell this story *now*? This is not necessarily about being able to put your finger exactly on the answer, but you will need to be able to circle around this question and, to a certain extent, frame it. What is it about *you* that will make the telling of this story unique? Why *you*, and not anyone else who can tell the story? And why *now*? Why do you see a significance in telling that story *now*?

Getting to grips with these issues will help give you the answers to a number of important questions that need to be addressed for the classic narrative. First, it will help you to sort out what it is you're trying to say – the theme – and to identify your unique perspective on this theme. Second, it will help you figure out your premise. Third, it may give you strong indications as to where your key turning point in the film will be – the climax. Finally, it will help give you clues as to who the direct or implied narrator is – the perspective/vision.

You will want to identify a protagonist (or narrative agent, for it need not be a human being), who is trying to achieve something – the aim – and, in doing so, comes up against some conflicts and problems – the obstacles. You will probably try to heighten your listener's attention by pointing out some information in the story that your protagonist is not aware of – the dramatic irony – increasing the tension and sympathy for the protagonist. Then you will take your story to a key moment where the protagonist has to make a critical decision or face a decisive event – the climax – and finally you will wrap up a few loose ends, suggest some implications and new challenges ahead and bring your listener emotionally back down again – the resolution. In a sense, the classic narrative will tend to be linear, starting somewhere and ending somewhere different or somewhere changed. The process of constructing a verbal classic narrative discourse is more or less exactly the same process that will go into the construction of a classic narrative discourse for a documentary film (see Figure 10.1).

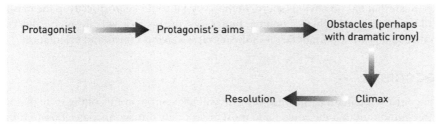

Figure 10.1 The classic narrative

What we have discussed so far applies to a range of narrative texts and applies equally to fiction and documentary film. The differences lie not in the narrative discourse structure or narrative elements but in the use of the codes of the medium, and in the way that the visual and aural material is created and used to bring the discourse structure (plot) and narrative elements to the viewer.

Let us look at some of these classic narrative elements in a little more detail and then we shall go on to briefly identify these elements in an example documentary film.

Climax

The climax is the most critical part of a classic narrative and one that inexperienced documentary filmmakers tend to struggle with the most. One could also use the terms 'key turning point', 'moment of change' or 'decisive moment'. It is usually found two-thirds or three-quarters of the way through a classic narrative. It is the moment in the film where the theme of the film is most powerfully visible. This visibility could be through a key conflict, through an ultimate paradox, through an uneasy truce, through a momentous decision with known or unknown consequences, or something else along those lines. It can be subtle or overt, strong or gentle, dramatic or quiet, but you will find that it is always there in a classic narrative and its presence is critical. This is why you're telling your story: to take your viewer, through their emotional engagement, to this point where they can clearly see what it is you really wanted to tell them. This is often the part of your story that your viewer will remember. It will be their primary way into reflecting on all the other aspects of your film which illuminate your themes and should be a moment in your story which has the profoundest of potential implications. If you're intending to use the classic narrative, never start shooting without a strong sense of where your protagonists might reach this moment in their story and, consequently, how you think you're going to get this key moment across to your viewer.

Premise

Like the climax, the premise is a critical part of a narrative, which should be factored into the preparation of a documentary film before any shooting starts. Reminding ourselves of the fact that a story can be infinite in length, scale and scope, the premise is the key factor in determining the length, scale and scope of the discourse and narrative and can be instrumental in deciding how you start and end your narrative. The premise is the particular event(s) or new or changed circumstance(s) that take us into a story at this particular juncture and moment in time. Why start telling the story here and not there? What has suddenly changed in a particular protagonist's life that has sparked off, or may spark off, a particular series of events? Is something going to happen up ahead which gives us reason to start the narrative at this point? The premise may be diegetic or non-diegetic. (Diegetic elements are sourced and lie within your story – such as music playing from a radio in a scene. Non-diegetic elements lie outside the story – such as music that has no obvious source in the story.) It could figure directly in the narrative or could fall outside it – either before or after. Either way, the premise will always be alluded to in the narrative and is an important factor in the narrative having a focus and orientation.

Protagonist

The protagonist is the main narrative agent who will take part in events of the story discourse. It is therefore important that the correct and most appropriate protagonists are chosen. It is worth noting straight away that a protagonist need not be singular, need not be a human being and, indeed, need not even be a sentient being. Though the documentary film has an entire subgenre devoted to animals, it is not unheard of for a protagonist to be a car, a city, a country, a people or a place. Our powers of empathy are tied up with a range of associations, not least of which relate to being able to identify with a protagonist's aims.

The protagonist may or may not be the direct or implied narrator of the film, but decisions need to be made about who is telling the story and what their relationship is to the protagonist. This also raises the question of perspective, discussed earlier. Are we experiencing events with the protagonist, through the protagonist, or from someone else's perspective, and does this perspective change at certain moments in our story? Where there is a choice of potential protagonists to reveal a particular story, you may want to ask yourself which protagonist's engagement with the story best suits what you're trying to say or reveal. This also involves casting and, as in the fiction film, casting for the documentary is a critical part of constructing a good film.

One important feature of the protagonist in a classic narrative is that they are usually changed by the events of the story, particularly by the climax experience. They have learned something. Their circumstances have changed. They have changed their view of something. Perhaps their behaviour has changed. Perhaps they have learned to come to terms with something. Perhaps they have changed physically or mentally. This change may well relate to the reason for the author wanting to tell the story in the first place and is therefore very important.

Narrator/Narrative perspective

The narrator does not here mean the person, or character, who verbally narrates the film. The narrator here refers to perspective and relationship to the story and its events, an implied or direct person conveying the story. It is often associated with the 'voice'[1] of the film, and has a strong link with what people associate with the 'vision' of the film. The narrator perspective will not only have implications for how the story is told, but also on the aesthetic style of the film; hence its strong connection to the 'vision' of the work.

The narrator could, for example, be a character either directly involved in events, or looking in on the events. It could be an omniscient non-diegetic observer. It could be that the author is also a character. Is the narrator of this story, for example, related to the characters and the events, to the author, or to both? How is this going to be made apparent to the viewer? (See below.)

There are also ethical implications involved in determining the nature of the narrator. The narrator and the viewer enter into an unarticulated and instantaneous agreement, based on current understandings of cultural and cinematic codes. The viewer is more or less guided as to how to relate to the material. That relationship could be a critical factor in determining whether the events are perceived as fact or fiction. Handled conscientiously, and effectively, a creatively deployed narrator perspective could be an interesting tool to marry fact and fiction. A viewer might in one film accept that certain parts have been completely fictionalised, because of the relationship they have with the film through the narrator, while in another film feel thoroughly misled and cheated when fiction was introduced, because the relationship with the narrator did not allow for it.

The narrator perspective is, in many instances, the defining factor in the definition of a number of documentary subgenres. The 'fly on the wall' non-interventionist observational documentary about a particular family would be quite different if it was a 'video diary' documentary by one of the same family members covering the same story events. The same basic events could be different again if made with a 'presenter-driven' interventionist approach. The shooting style may not vary much, but the narrator's relationship to the story is radically different and, therefore, the 'vision' of the film would be radically different.

Another aspect of the narrator perspective relates to whether events are directly witnessed by the narrator or are recollected by one of the characters and conveyed to the narrator. Is it a narrative within another narrative in which the narrator is telling the story about someone who themselves relates a story to the narrator? This has implications, for example, for how to bring to life past events of the protagonist's life and how these past events relate to the narrative present. Or it may have implications for how one can use the narrative present to bring past events alive again for the viewer.

Aims

The aims usually relate to the aims of the protagonist. What are they trying to achieve? The pursuit of these aims provides the main impetus for the narrative and it is the difficulties, oppositions and complications in achieving these aims that is the source of the main emotional engagement you as a storyteller will be evoking in your viewer. Even if your character is bad, has flaws or is confused, if the viewer can understand and identify with the protagonist's aims, that can go a long way in helping establish the necessary empathy for the protagonist. Where there are multiple protagonists, each will have their aims. It could be, for example, that you have two protagonists whose individual aims are in conflict with each other. This conflict then becomes one of the obstacles to either character achieving their aim.

Aims can take many forms. They can be inner aims, such as a person seeking to come to terms with a loss or to overcome a psychological problem. They can be material aims, such as a group of people trying to build something or get somewhere within a certain time frame. They can be social or cultural aims, such as a person trying to preserve a particular cultural heritage or a community trying to overcome a crime problem. And so on. Good aims also work simultaneously on a direct and on a metaphoric level. The aim of an individual, for example, trying to sell their cultural goods on a city street could simultaneously be a metaphoric microcosm of the macrocosmic struggle of that person's entire culture against oblivion.

One of the features of the classic narrative is the tendency for the narrative elements to be externalised and have a material presence. Therefore, if the aims are inner psychological or mental aims, it becomes necessary to think about how to manifest these externally and materially and how they can then allude to the inner world through metaphor. This externalisation will bring the inner struggle into a palpable realm of action, cause and effect and movement – all strong features of the classic narrative.

An aim may or may not be achieved, of course; in that sense, the narrative can be tragic, comic, or tragi-comic.

Obstacles/Antagonists

The obstacles are the problems the protagonist encounters in pursuit of their aims. They could be physical obstacles; legal obstacles; mental obstacles, such as fear or some kind of mental incapacity; social obstacles, such as customs and social expectations. They could be political or historical problems. These obstacles are often represented by people: antagonists, who could be policemen and women, keeping protesters at bay; judges, as the face of the law of the land; parents against their child who are trying to free themselves from social shackles; the political leader blocking change; the practitioners of a cultural custom presenting moral obstacles.

Developing crisis

Because we're on a journey, the build-up to the climax will be gradual. With a clear sense of the aim of the protagonist, as they encounter problems in trying to achieve these aims, there is a developing crisis. This could be in the form of complications introduced through subplots, new knowledge introduced through dramatic irony or the witnessing of a series of decisions being made by the protagonist. The tension between the protagonist's aims and their obstacles is increasingly engaging our self-assertive emotions because of our empathy for the protagonist and their aims.

Subplot

Though there are many classic narratives that do not have subplots, they can be useful for clarifying or highlighting the protagonist's journey, helping introduce a sense of developing crisis, and building dramatic irony into the narrative. It is important that they should not be competing or parallel stories, but stories which complement, augment and strengthen the story of the protagonist.

Dramatic irony

It is not uncommon in certain parts of the world for audiences to scream out at their hero on the cinema screen when they feel he or she is in danger and they have information about this impending peril not known to their hero. This is as a result of dramatic irony: the difference between what the viewer knows and what the protagonist knows. It is a critical tool for suspense, in which the viewer gets anxious because they have information or know something that the protagonist does not know and that may lead to a complication or fatal consequence for the protagonist. While empathy can cross the separation of diegesis and non-diegesis, the viewer has no means of directly intervening in events and this separation is the cause of the tension and emotional engagement.

Resolution

While a story may continue, the narrative needs to be brought to an end. The resolution follows the climax. Whether the aims of the protagonists have been achieved or not, the storyteller needs to tie up a few loose ends. These include what may have happened to other characters whose aims we might have been introduced to in the context of the protagonist's journey. From an emotional point of view, the viewer is likely to be irritated if the storyteller suddenly abandons them in a heightened state of emotional engagement at the climax. It is therefore necessary to help the viewer resolve some of their own emotions and to 'bring them back down' again.

A good resolution will also introduce some new elements. It will suggest new challenges up ahead for the protagonist which are a direct consequence of their decisions or the outcome of the climax. Or the resolution may suggest a paradox – an upside to a defeat or a downside to a win. In such cases, while one component of someone's story has been resolved, the viewer leaves the story with plenty of food for thought, perhaps for years to come, and hopefully these thoughts will revolve around the themes that you intended to bring to their attention in the first place.

Dramatic question

One important aspect of the viewer's ability to identify with the protagonist and their aims is their ability to identify with the dramatic question. What issues become apparent from the tension between the aims and the obstacles? Is the viewer likely to believe in the questions that arise for the protagonist when obstacles get in the way of them achieving their aims? Do these questions, issues and dilemmas ring true for the viewer and do they somehow relate to them? If the viewer doesn't care about the dramatic question that arises from the tensions between the aims and the obstacles, you're going to find it very difficult to engage their empathy in the plight of your protagonist.

Character motivation

Palpable cause and effect is a very important feature of the classic narrative and we see this most prominently in connection with the characters – especially the protagonist – and their motivations. The rational in us insists that all actions have a cause. Consequently, the viewer of the classic narrative will more often than not want to understand characters and the events in which they are involved in the context of identifiable, and often explicable, psychological traits and motivations. The behaviour of characters, the reasons why they take action, and how they respond to events, will need to fit a psychological palette that is, in part, socially and culturally determined.

Case Study *Touching The Void* (K. Macdonald, UK, 2003)

Let us briefly identify all the above narrative elements in Kevin Macdonald's gripping *Touching The Void* (2003). This is the story of two ambitious climbers, Joe Simpson and Simon Yates, who in 1985 set off to climb the, at that point, unclimbed west face of the Siula Grande mountain in Peru. They reach the peak, but on the way down Joe breaks his leg. As Simon helps to winch him down the mountainside, an insurmountable problem occurs which threatens both their lives. This leads to Simon having to cut a rope from which Joe is hanging, knowing full well that Joe would probably fall to his death. Unbeknown to Simon, Joe somehow survives the fall into a crevasse and most of the film is about his extraordinary struggle to come down off the mountain. Not only is this narrative classic in its construction, we can see that, from an emotional perspective, it is concerned with engaging us in the direct issue of survival.

A scene from *Touching the Void* (Macdonald, 2003)

The narrative is a combination of interviews with the real-life characters, Joe Simpson and Simon Yates, whose story this is, and reconstructed sequences involving the use of actors to play the parts of Joe, Simon and their friend Richard.

Protagonists

There are only three characters in this narrative: the mountaineers, Joe and Simon, and Richard, who mans the base camp. As Joe and Simon set off up the mountainside, it may seem that we have two protagonists. However, once the premise has been established, it becomes very clear that Joe is our main protagonist. He is the one who suffers the injury. He is the one abandoned for dead and he is the one whose struggle and journey we follow to a climax. On one level, Simon becomes an antagonist, one of the obstacles to Joe's survival, in that Simon has to cut the rope and abandon him. As they become separated, and Simon makes it back to the base camp, a subplot develops between Simon and Richard, which is used to create dramatic irony. We shall return to both these points.

Premise

Both Joe and Simon were regular climbers and had climbed in the Andes before, even if they hadn't climbed this particular face. Their story of mountaineering was therefore a long one. However, the reason why we're coming into their story at this point is because something specific happened, something that sparked the series of events that constitute the discourse of our narrative. This event was the fact that Joe slipped and badly broke his leg. This premise is shown in the narrative and occurs about 20 minutes into the 100-minute film. Prior to this point, the narrative establishes the characters, the setting and the situation, building in a sense of foreboding of the premise to come. While in a cinema film it is not unusual for the premise to be revealed up to one-third of the way into a narrative, you may find TV commissioning editors less patient. For them the premise is the 'hook' with which they wish to grab a fickle audience within the first five minutes, before they switch to another channel.

Simon Yates in *Touching the Void* (Macdonald, 2003)

Aims

Once the premise has been established, it is quite clear what the protagonist's aims are. Joe is desperate to survive, exemplified by the need to come off the freezing and treacherous mountain and return to base camp before he gets hypothermia, dehydrates or falls to his death.

Obstacles

There are a number of obstacles, many – but not all – provided by nature and circumstance. First, the leg itself. It is badly broken and is at times so painful Joe almost faints from the pain. He cannot put any weight on it. Second, Simon's decision to cut him loose and let him fall. Here the obstacle is someone else's decision, over which he had no influence because, at that moment, circum-stances made it impossible for them to fully understand each other's predicament or to communicate. Third, and perhaps the most significant, nature herself: storms, snow, ice, freezing temperatures, crevasses, darkness and the like prove formidable obstacles. All these obstacles are portrayed in vivid visual and aural detail.

Joe Simpson in *Touching the Void* (Macdonald, 2003)

Developing crisis, dramatic irony and subplot

These three elements are lumped together here because the subplot and dramatic irony are used to heighten the sense of developing crisis. Once Simon has cut the rope and saved himself, his con-tinued role in the narrative provides a subplot which gives us dramatic ironies which help to heighten our engagement with Joe's plight. We know that Simon thinks Joe is dead, though Joe has no way of knowing that, heightening our concern for Joe. And even though Simon insists on staying at base camp a little while longer, we also see how, at crucial stages in Joe's struggle, Richard and Simon prepare to leave base camp – the very place Joe is desperately trying to get to. In fact, at one point, Simon and Richard burn Joe's clothes in a strange ritual of final farewell, but the dramatic irony, which causes us anguish, is that we know he is still alive. The placing of these subplot scenes with Simon and Richard at base camp within the dominant scenes of Joe's struggle is carefully tuned to help augment the developing crisis.

The obstacles that Joe has to overcome seem increasingly difficult. First the fall, then the strug-gle out of the crevasse, the slide down the mountainside, the dangerous negotiation of the glaciers, the painful crawl across the rocky outcrop, the battle with bitterly cold nights and then the final stretch past the lake not too far from base camp. Each stage becomes more difficult and is complic-ated by the dramatic irony of our knowing that Simon and Richard have finally accepted that he is dead and are preparing to leave the base camp. Joe's only hope of survival is to make it to the base camp with Simon and Richard still there.

Dramatic question

The questions raised by the tension between the obstacles and the aim is stark: does Joe have the strength, the faith, the hope, the sheer willpower, not to give up and fight to survive? It is a question most will understand and believe to be legitimate in this narrative. It is a question that engages us in the drama. In this narrative, it is basic, clear and unambiguous.

Climax

We thought all Joe's earlier obstacles were insurmountable, but there is one beautifully profound scene in the film which provides us with a clear climax where all the themes of the story are most visible, where we really do feel he is on the cusp between life and death, where we get a strong sense of what the film is really about. It occurs about three-quarters of the way through the narrative.

We sense, and indeed Joe himself senses, that he is getting close to base camp because he has seen signs of this in the form of human footsteps in the gravel. However, he is not sure. In any case, in the subplot leading up to this moment, we have seen Simon and Richard burn Joe's clothes in preparation for leaving the base camp, so, for all we know, even if he was close, they might have left by now. That night he drifts in and out of consciousness. In the interview he pauses a lot, as this was clearly a profound moment for him. This was his ultimate feeling of abandonment. Earlier in the narrative, he had spoken about being brought up a devout Catholic, but in a sense his situation had made him lose faith. Yet leading up to this last night, he talks about how there was something within that spoke to him, that drove him on, as if a side of himself had taken over that he had not felt before, that was separate from his usual pragmatic self. At this climax moment, even that hopeful force was drained from him as he lay in the rocks waiting to die, completely alone, spiritually and physically abandoned.

It was the smell of urine that made Joe call out into the night with the very last energy he had left in him. For that smell made him think that he might be lying in the latrine area of their base camp. This detail of a smell forced its way into his fading consciousness and prompted his final calls into the night. Remember that the narrative has been constructed in such a way that we don't even know at this point whether Simon and Richard are at the camp or not. These calls into the wilderness are his final efforts to survive, his final struggle against ultimate abandonment. It could go either way at this moment. Will he be heard? Is anyone there to hear him?

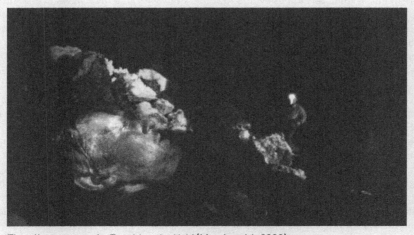

The climax scene in *Touching the Void* (Macdonald, 2003)

It is only at this point that we learn that Simon and Richard are still in the base camp. They have, indeed, not left yet. And they do eventually hear Joe. They find him and he is saved. From there the narrative moves swiftly to the resolution.

It is worth mentioning that during this climax scene the film takes on unusual stylistic elements, as if to heighten and emphasise the importance and significance of what is going on. In some ways it is quite a surrealistic scene, involving flashes of monochrome images of ice, water and rocks, flashes of carcasses in the rocky landscape, surreally drifting clouds, silent stars and various optical effects which contrast significantly with all the other scenes in the film.

Resolution

Joe is made comfortable in the tent and we see him being warmed up and fed. Later there is a shot of the three of them making their journey from the base camp on a donkey. In between, however, there are text titles explaining what has happened to each of the characters since the end of the narrative and the fact that Simon was criticised by fellow mountaineers back in Britain for cutting the rope in the first place, despite the staunch defence of Simon by Joe. In a way, this raises some interesting moral questions for us to mull over after the narrative has finished.

Character motivation and change

In the opening of the film, Joe is presented, partly through comments by the other characters, as particularly ambitious, defiant and confident. There are also suggestions made by Richard that there was something dislikable about Joe. If there is one flaw in the film, it is that the resolution does not give us any hints about how this experience may have changed Joe. At one point, Joe does question why Simon cut the rope and though he later defended this, as indicated in the text titles in the resolution, it seems inconceivable that they, and their relationship, were not changed by these events.

However, it is not an uncommon feature of classic narratives that rely heavily on dramatic action and events that the changes that happen to a character are subsumed by the sheer relief of survival. Nevertheless, the ambition that drove these two men, and Joe in particular, is clearly delineated at the beginning of the film, satisfying this need, in the classic narrative, to understand the psychological causes of character actions.

Narrator/Narrative perspective

The first thing to note about this film is that it is telling a story which happened in the past. Though epic in its themes, it is also very intimate. It is as if the author is saying, 'Let me tell you about something someone else confided to me.' This is largely achieved through the interviews. The three characters tell us in detail their version of events, but it is the way these interviews are shot that give us this sense of confiding. They are very tight shots. We have no sense of location. The lighting is soft and intimate. Importantly, the eye-line of the interviewees is so close to the lens that it seems they are talking directly to us. In fact, Joe, our main protagonist, most of the time talks directly to camera. There is no sense of a presence of an interviewer or any other character except those speaking and us, the viewer. It's as if the author is further saying to us, 'Come closer. See and hear it as I heard and saw it, directly from these people. Look, I'll get them to tell you directly, just as they told it to me.' Even though Joe is our protagonist, each character confides to us, on several occasions telling us things we know the other characters do not know, and this is another effective element in creating the strong sense of shared personal confidences.

Having established that confiding intimacy in which our characters are remembering, it then does not seem unreasonable or unnatural that the author will introduce 'fictional sequences' reflecting those memories. The direct intimacy of the interviews, and the characters' remembering, seems to invite the imagery to come alive before us and it is thus irrelevant that it is technically fiction. For the narrator has established a pact with us that allows our imaginative engagement to accept actors reconstructing the events. The close connection between the imagery and what the protagonists talk about and likeness of the actors to the actual characters give us a verisimilitude with which we can fully engage, without questioning whether it lacks factual authenticity. There is a focused consistency in this perspective, which is in part what gives the film its visionary strength.

Key points

- Understand why *you* are telling this story and why *now*.

- The key ingredients and structures of the classic narrative seem to have the inherent quality of engaging, predominantly, our self-assertive emotions.

- A good place to start constructing a narrative is to identify the premise and the climax. Why is the narrative starting at this moment in the story? Where is the key moment in the film where everything could, or does, change and where your theme is most visible?

- Understand what parts of your narrative perform the functions of these narrative ingredients and be conscious of the fact that – fact or fiction – you are manipulating these elements to engage your audience's emotions.

- Because we speak of 'classic' narrative does not mean that it is necessarily 'conventional' in construct or 'old fashioned'. Far from it. The challenge for you is to work creatively with these elements to engage the viewer successfully.

- Understand who your main protagonist is and how this protagonist's predicament – aims and obstacles, for example – provides you with the right context for your story.

- What changes in your story and how do we see this?

Exercises

The following exercises are based on factual events; however, details have been changed and added, as have names. Imagine that 'Cynthia's story', below, is a summary of your initial research. For the purposes of this exploration, make reasonable imaginative assumptions. Imagine that you are going to construct a narrative and this construction is going to be the basis of further research, the planning and preparation of your production and the skeleton which you will use as a basis for all your shooting decisions. Imagine that you have been given a very tight window to work in and that shooting has to start next week.

Cynthia's story

Cynthia Blake is 67. She is from New York, USA, and is a retired publisher. She has an apartment in New York but has not lived there for two years.

For the past two years she has been living on the luxury cruise liner, the *Mary Rose*, sailing with her across the world on her various cruises. She first came onto the liner when she went on a Mediterranean cruise with her late husband, Ronald, who was an author, essayist and feature writer. During their cruise, Ronald had a heart attack and died. He was buried at sea off the coast of Crete and, ever since, Cynthia has remained on board ship.

In two months' time, the *Mary Rose* is about to dock in Southampton, UK, for the last time, as she is about to be decommissioned. Cynthia's daughter, Catherine, lives in New Hampshire, USA, with her family and is coming to Southampton to pick up her mother and return to New Hampshire. They will stay in London for a few days, see a few sights, do a bit of shopping and then return to New Hampshire together. The plan is that Cynthia will stay with her daughter for a few weeks before finalising what she is going to do next. Cynthia is not sure whether she wants to return to New York to live permanently or

▶

not. Catherine has suggested that Cynthia buy a place near her in New Hampshire. At some point, Cynthia has to go back to her New York apartment and organise a few things and Catherine is always there to help.

The final cruise of the *Mary Rose* is a Mediterranean cruise. In fact, they will be passing the very area where Ronald was buried at sea. Cynthia has a very good relationship with the crew members, including the captain. She is a fairly reserved person, but not withdrawn. During her two years on the *Mary Rose*, Cynthia has had a few of her possessions flown out by Catherine. Consequently, she has been able to create a bit of a home for herself in her cabin quarters. She has her set routines around meals, walking the deck, reading and so on. She has with her copies of all her late husband's work, photographs from the past, photographs from her original cruise, photographs of Catherine and her family, and so on.

In initial interviews, Cynthia is very reluctant to talk about the actual circumstances of her late husband's death. When asked why she has remained on the ship, she has no ready answer. When pushed, she talks about not having anything to return to and says that she has always liked the sea. She mentions that she and her late husband, Ronald, were always fond of the sea and often visited the coast close to where Catherine lives. In fact, she is looking forward to visiting her daughter in New Hampshire and walking along the shoreline again; she is particularly looking forward to walking the shoreline again with her grandchildren. She talks warmly about her Ronald, especially about his writings, for which she has a particular fondness. Ronald was drafted for the Korean War, following which he embarked on a successful career as a writer. She was a young, successful magazine editor and they met through their respective jobs. They moved in literary circles and socialised a lot. She is loosely in touch with one or two friends and since Ronald's death she has deliberately not kept in touch much with her former work circles. She also talks a lot about her grandchildren and how they once came and joined her for a cruise.

Cynthia wishes to be buried at sea, like her late husband, and has already made arrangements.

Exercise 1

Imagine that you have full access to Cynthia, her family and the ship. Construct a classic narrative on the basis of these research notes, making reasonable assumptions about what you think might happen. Write a detailed treatment.

Can you identify all the ingredients of the classic narrative and have you constructed them in such a way that it will engage our emotions?

Exercise 2

Let us make the exercise a little more difficult: imagine that, because of problems with the shipping company, you have not received permission to do any shooting on the *Mary Rose*. Nevertheless, you are contracted to make the film about Cynthia and have to proceed.

Construct a classic narrative, based on the same story, that involves no shooting on the ship. Write a detailed treatment.

Ask yourself the same questions again: can you identify all the ingredients of the classic narrative and have you constructed them in such a way that it will engage our emotions?

Note

[1] For an extensive discussion of the 'voice' of a film, see Nichols, 1992.

Chapter 11

The transcendental narrative

Erik Knudsen

" Nations and peoples are largely the stories they feed themselves. If they tell themselves stories that are lies, they will suffer the consequences of those lies. If they tell themselves stories that face their own truths, they will free their histories for future flowerings. "

(Okri, 1995)

Introduction

Not much has been written about the notion of transcendental narrative. While it has been little written about in the context of fiction (Schrader, 1972) it has been written about even less in the context of documentary (Knudsen, 2008). You will find a lot of literature about the classic narrative, but when it comes to genuine alternatives (as opposed to creative reworkings of the classic narrative) it seems that we lack the appropriate language and tools of interrogation. This term 'transcendental realism' describes a broad approach to storytelling that seeks to engage our participatory feelings, or spiritual feelings. In this chapter, we will explore what the key ingredients of the transcendental narrative are, how they engage different feelings from those evoked by the classic narrative, and then we'll look at how to connect this with the documentary genre.

The transcendental storyteller's key tools

As in the previous chapter, imagine that you want to tell a friend a story. This time, however, you want to tell a story with which you want to reveal things that are perhaps not entirely rational, psychologically explicable or materially palpable. Perhaps you want to get across an indescribable feeling. Maybe you want to engage their more spiritual feelings, their feelings of awe, longing, love, sorrow or hope. To achieve this, the last thing you want your friend to be doing is sitting on the edge of their seat, adrenalin flooding through their system, worried about what is going to happen next or whether your protagonist is going to survive or achieve their aims. In a situation like this, you may want them to relax, forget themselves, lose themselves in the imagery of your story or the setting of your events. Perhaps you want them to link things in a less causal way and reflect on moments in the story with no regard for what might happen next. To achieve this different kind of engagement with your story, you would need to approach your discourse and narrative differently.

As with the classic narrative, there is still a reason for telling the story, an authorial purpose which you should interrogate with the question: why do *I* want to tell this story and why *now*? There will still be a point to your story. There will still be a reason why you should tell it. And there will be a reason why you want to tell it now. At the end of the day, you will still be seeking to reveal something, show someone something or open our eyes to something. You're just going to go about it in a different way, because what you wish to reveal demands that difference.

We are all very familiar with the elements of classic narrative. They are ubiquitous, palpable and make rational sense. Can we use these same elements to describe how one alternative approach – one based on the distinguishing of types of emotions and feelings – might work? Can we talk about defining such elements as protagonist, aims, obstacles, climax, resolution and so on? It should be possible to start with one similarity; namely, for anything to be a narrative it must have events – an 'agent' taking action, or something happening to an 'agent'.

As mentioned earlier, at its extreme the classic narrative is concerned with survival and the alternative narrative approach we have, so far, been alluding to is, at its extreme, concerned with transcendence. If some of the key characteristics of the classic narrative are self-assertiveness, cause and effect, action, externalisation, psychological motivation, movement and change, then some of the key characteristics of the transcendental narrative are self-effacement, coincidence, stillness, internalisation, irrationality, inaction and immutability. What we are therefore talking about is how these events can be structured, organised and presented in such a way as to contain the qualities just described.

Perhaps one place to start to explore this is to recount the story of how a Zen master came to learn about Zen.[1] The Zen master explains that, when he first started learning about Zen, whenever he looked at a mountain, a mountain was just that: a mountain. When he learned a little about Zen, whenever he looked at a mountain it had become more complex: a mountain was not just a mountain because there was more to it than that. When he finally got to grips with Zen and then looked at a mountain, he realised that a mountain was, after all, just that: a mountain. This little story gives us an approach into one prototypical alternative to the classic narrative.[2]

While we have a protagonist, there is no real aim, as we're used to seeing it in a classic narrative, nor a clear premise, nor a climax, nor obstacles or the traditional resolution following a climax. What we have here are a series of events (looking) which are not driven by psychological drivers, but a series of changing states. The master was not looking at the mountain to understand Zen – that would have provided the aim in a classic narrative – but the looking at the mountain (the events of looking) was a reflection of a state. This state started in one place, changed, and then returned to where it started. Nothing has physically or rationally changed, yet there has been a change which cannot be psychologically explained. The relationship to the mountain at the end can only be described as a transcendental one. The process is illustrated in Figure 11.1.

Figure 11.1 Basic tripartite transcendental structure of changing states

What becomes important here is not to fashion a series of events that will take us from one situation to another, in pursuit of a protagonist's aims, but to fashion a series of events that will establish a state of normality, whatever that might be. These events will evolve into ones that then show us a state in which we see some sort of departure from that first state of normality, some sort of schism or crack which establishes a state of disparity or disharmony. It could be that there is a particular event, stage or shift in perspective that signals the beginning of this transition into a state of disparity. However, events continue to be linked by the need to establish this state and not, as in the classic narrative, to further the plot as we follow the protagonist's pursuit of their aims. Likewise, there will be a particular event, decisive moment or turning point that will take us from the state of disparity back to a state of normality, in which nothing has physically changed, yet somehow, because we have been on this journey of shifting states, everything has changed.

With an approach like this, events may seem coincidentally linked, as they do not follow causal patterns. We will be asked to look at these events for their own sake, to link them in non-causal ways, to see elements within these events that do not necessarily serve the purpose of understanding psychological character motivations as we're used to understanding them in a causal context. This kind of linking of events opens up possibilities for reflection and a re-evaluation of our usual engagement with narratives. Our emotions are not tied up with conflicts between aims and obstacles, or with questions of success or failure in achieving those aims or succumbing to the obstacles. Instead, we are invited to participate with our feelings in a series of events that do not direct us in a linear progression, but in a, seemingly, more random series of events that take us into experiencing shifting states of mind. Where events (and scenes) in a classic narrative serve the purpose of leading from one plot point to the next plot point, the events (and scenes) of the transcendental narrative do not lead anywhere in particular in terms of plot.

If the transcendental narrative is about changing states, then let us explore some other possibilities in terms of structure. We could, for example, also be looking at further structures as shown in Figure 11.2.

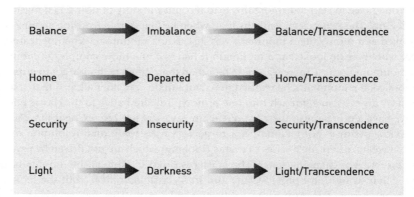

Figure 11.2 Possible variations to the tripartite transcendental structure of changing states

Where the climax of the classic narrative provides us with the clearest moment in the narrative to see the theme of the story, in the transcendental narrative the key turning point brings us back to the state we were first made familiar with and it is experiencing this first state with new eyes that should most powerfully reveal the theme of the narrative. Unlike the moment in the classic narrative where our emotions are at their highest state of engagement, in the transcendental narrative it is in the reflective moments of the final state that the theme should be most clearly visible, engaging our participatory feelings.

Let us summarise some key elements in the transcendental narrative.

Protagonist

As in the classic narrative, the transcendental narrative will also have a protagonist who is the main figure for our empathy. Similarly, the protagonist need not be singular nor, indeed, a human being. However, in the transcendental narrative there need be no aim for the protagonist. What primarily engages us is their state and, perhaps, their predicament. Where palpable change in a protagonist is important to the classical narrative – often manifested in changed attitudes and/or circumstances – immutability in events and circumstances is, paradoxically, a key component of the transcendence element of this type of narrative. While the protagonist may be changed by events, this does not necessarily involve a palpable or psychologically explicable change. Indeed, it is the viewer's changed perspective of seemingly unchanged circumstances, and the often unchanged protagonist, which is at the heart of the transcendental experience of the story.

Premise

It is hard to imagine a narrative without a premise – in other words, a reason for starting the narrative at this moment in time. As we have discussed, in the classic narrative the premise is the event – past or future – which tells us why we are coming into the narrative at this point and, as such, it is this event that triggers an aim and a subsequent series of other causal events. In the transcendental narrative there will also be a reason why we are coming into the narrative at this particular point. This event is likely to be associated directly with the change of state – i.e. we are coming into a particular narrative at this point because the protagonist is going to go through a changing state of some kind. This is, however, a little different because it need not be dealt with separately. It is not a precursor for events to happen, but perhaps a reflective narrative feature to be understood in retrospect.

States and events

The role and treatment of events in the narrative is one of the key variations between the classic narrative and the transcendental narrative. In the latter, the primary purpose of events is to engross us in the state of the protagonist, rather than in the causal pursuit of an aim. These events can therefore be linked more coincidentally and can exist without the need to further the plot development. We are invited to engage in events for their own sake, to engage with links that go beyond the psychological motivations that fuel the classic narrative and to see relationships between scenes that operate in different ways from those of the classic narrative. Non-dramatic details often become important, and a key driver of the actions and happenings of the events need not be conflict-based. While, of course, there may be tensions and conflicts, their role is not necessarily to enhance our emotional engagement in a dramatic question, for there are no conflicts between aims and obstacles. Consequently, there is more room for association and metaphysical connections through stillness, inaction and other reflective elements and qualities in events and scenes.

Key moment of departure

Despite the seemingly more random nature of events, there will be key moments of shift: the shifting from the normal state into one of disparity will be indicated in a key moment of departure. This could also be a series of moments, suggesting a gradual shift.

Decisive moment of return

The shifting state from disparity to normality/transcendence will also be marked by a decisive moment. This moment is important because it is in this return shift of states that we most clearly start to see the themes emerge, as we return to our starting state. Unlike the classic narrative where the climax is marked by a key turning point that could go a number of ways, in the transcendental narrative this key moment is not concerned with the possibility of several outcomes as a consequence of a decision which, for example, will determine success or failure.

Narrator/Narrative perspective

As with the classic narrative, someone is telling this story and they are looking at the story from a particular perspective. The same qualities and purpose apply to the transcendental narrative. As discussed earlier, the narrator perspective – and how this is established – is at the heart of the voice and vision of the film and is a key part of the unspoken contract between the author and the viewer.

Case Study *Anything Can Happen* (Marcel Łoziński, 1995)

The works of the Polish documentary maker, Marcel Łoziński, serve as good examples of the transcendental narrative approach to documentary storytelling – none more so than his extraordinary film *Anything Can Happen* (1995). One of the problems of describing a transcendental narrative is that, where with the classic narrative one can describe a causal series of events in which the logic of the progression is clear, with the transcendental narrative, as we have discussed, events may seem coincidental, even random. Indeed, this is how *Anything Can Happen* may, at first, seem. There is no causal plot, no psychological motivation for the protagonist, no aim, no obstacles, no dramatic question and no climax on which the plot turns. Yet it is a highly structured piece of work.

The narrative takes place in what we must assume is a Warsaw park one summer's day. The sun is shining, the beautiful tree foliage and flowers, and so on, provide an ideal situation. A six-year-old boy (actually, the son of the director) is messing about, playing. He uses a scooter for getting about the park and is often distracted by the many natural attractions that such a park offers: a peacock, butterflies, sticks, floating pollen and so on. In the park there are a number of elderly people sitting on benches enjoying the sunshine.

Anything Can Happen (Łoziński, 1995)

Two or three minutes into the film, the boy strikes up a conversation with an elderly couple sitting on one of the benches. So begins an extraordinary adventure into the lives of elderly people. For the film is about a series of casual conversations this boy has with a number of elderly people sitting in the park (at no point do we see anything but elderly people and this boy). At first, the conversations are quite innocent: names; where people live; he tells them a little bit about his family; innocent questions about what is underneath the ground and so on. The boy has no hesitation in walking up to people, or scootering up to them, and striking up conversations. To begin with they are elderly couples, but as the film progresses it is increasingly elderly individuals. These friendly, casual conversations become more profound, sparked off by two elderly ladies telling him that the war (World War II) was a terrible period for them. Soon, the conversations reverberate with more troublesome memories of the Second World War. Then they are about poverty. Soon after, they're about loneliness and isolation, culminating in one key moment when an elderly woman, overwhelmed by loneliness, starts crying and then says to the boy that she doesn't want to talk with him any more. Moments later, he is talking to one elderly man who tells him about how much he misses his deceased wife and they start talking about how he still feels her presence in the house and about meeting up with her again in the afterlife. The boy's questions are childishly direct, simultaneously, and paradoxically, innocent and wise, and strikingly confident. Eventually, the boy returns to enjoying the park and riding around on his scooter – something he has been doing intermittently throughout. We see some of the elderly people rising from their benches and leaving the park. The final shot is of the boy scootering along a path leading out of the park.

Anything Can Happen (Łoziński, 1995)

Nothing palpable has changed, yet everything has changed. We, the viewers, have been moved in ways the classic narrative could not move us and, consequently, have changed our understanding of a stasis. Yet there is no evidence to suggest that the boy has changed, though, of course, the space is very open for us to make our own associations. We see here the clear shifting of states. First, the normality: any day in any park with a random group of people who probably come there every day. Even the early encounters and questions of the boy seem in character and fit in with a sense of normality. Second, a shifting into disparity: we hear more about the troubled memories of the Second World War (which to this day scars the Polish psyche), the struggle with poverty, the sense of life coming to an end. Ultimately, we hear about the suffering of loneliness. Third, the shift back to normality: the sense of hope that thoughts about an afterlife provide, back to the original routines of the park. Everything is as it was.

Anything Can Happen (Łoziński, 1995)

▶

Let us look briefly at the key elements of this narrative.

Protagonist

The six-year-old boy is clearly the protagonist; it is his encounters that we follow and we experience with him the various conversations. Yet we know very little about him and there is no sense that we understand why he is going about asking these questions. He has no aims, as we would expect of the classical narrative, and there are no obstacles to what he is doing. His encounters seem coincidental and it is not clear whether he has changed as a consequence of this narrative.

Premise

Why are we coming into this story at this particular juncture? Where a classic narrative would have a fairly clear answer to that – because it fuels all subsequent events – this narrative could not be said to have a premise in that sense. However, one could say that, in retrospect, the reason why we are coming into this story now is because we are going to witness a shift of state that will reveal something to us. The relationship between the premise and the story is much more a reflective one than an activating one.

Anything Can Happen (Łoziński, 1995)

States and events

The key events of this narrative revolve around conversations between the boy and the elderly people that are very coincidental in nature, interspersed with, and punctuated by, brief scenes in which the boy plays freely in the natural world of the park. The narrative approach invites us to lose ourselves in the detail of the situation, the detail of the conversation, not because it is important for how the narrative will progress, but because it is of itself. The link between the different people and what they are saying is not psychological and causal; it is much more metaphysical in nature. The events are not organised to lead us anywhere, yet we sense a shift in state. This happens because there is a shift in what people talk about. Also, importantly, we start off with mostly couples, while in the disparity section of the film there is a subtle, yet powerful, shift to the boy only talking to individuals about war memories, health problems, divorce, separation from partners caused by death and, the key theme of the film, abandoned loneliness. The events, therefore, are highly organised to facilitate a progressive shift of state from a distant view of normality, through a more intimate view of disparity, back to a view of normality.

Key moment of departure

There is a moment about one-third of the way through the film when two elderly women mention the Second World War to the boy and talk about how it was an unpleasant time. This is the first time a serious or troubling issue is raised and, as the first real moment when we start to sense a disparity, a crack in the veneer of the beautiful summer's day appears. From this point on, we progress to more serious, more profound conversations that truly start to reveal powerful suggestions of what lies behind the façade of these anonymous elderly people.

Anything Can Happen (Łoziński, 1995)

Decisive moment of return

There is a powerfully moving moment, mentioned briefly earlier, about three-quarters of the way through the film, when one elderly woman is overwhelmed by the emotion of loneliness. On the verge of tears, she tells the boy that she doesn't want to talk with him any more. It is a troubling moment, not just because the woman is very upset, but the boy's innocent probing gets to her and the fact that she has to reject such a sweet young boy is clearly, in itself, a problem for the woman. The transition back to normality is taken with one further step: that of a brief conversation with one of the elderly men about how he feels the presence of his deceased wife and one day hopes to be reunited with her. That shift from the elderly woman who starts crying out of lonely despair to the man who dreams and hopes for a reunion in the next life is, in many ways, the most significant inroad into the underlying theme of the film.

Narrator/Narrative perspective

The connection between the boy and the filmmaker is never made in the diegesis of the film. While the boy mentions his parents in the context of the conversations, at no point does the boy make any connection between himself, his parents and the camera. There is also a strong sense in which the elderly people have no idea that they are being filmed. In fact, one of the striking stylistic features of

▶

the film is the consistent use of long lenses, usually through bushes and foliage. While practical purposes connected with a desire to be completely inconspicuous may have been part of dictating this approach, this sense of visual distance, created by the long lens effect, juxtaposes evocatively with the close intimate quality of the sound. This also strongly heightens our sense of being metaphorically distant from the people we're watching: old people, abandoned and lonely, living with their memories and regrets, waiting to die. Another feature that gives a strong sense of perspective is the fact that we see no other people in the park apart from these elderly people with whom the boy speaks. It is striking; for we would normally expect to see a range of people in a park on a sunny day and many other lesser filmmakers would have been tempted to establish the verisimilitude of the park. Łoziński's visual and aural style means there is a consistent and very clear narrator perspective in this film which, combined with the other elements we have discussed, makes this an example of transcendental narrative documentary at its very best.

Key points

- Understand why *you* are telling this story and why *now*.
- The key ingredients and structures of the transcendental narrative seem to have the inherent quality of engaging, predominantly, our participatory feelings.
- While the transcendental narrative may not have a climax as understood in the classic narrative sense, it will still have a decisive moment or key turning point. Understand where that is in your narrative.
- Understand what parts of your narrative perform the functions of these narrative ingredients and be conscious that – fact or fiction – you are manipulating these elements to engage your audience's feelings.
- Unlike the classic narrative, where some form of change or other is usually an essential ingredient, a lack of palpable change is often a key factor in the transcendental narrative.
- Understand who your protagonist is and how their circumstance provides you with a context to situate your narrative.
- Try to identify the nature of the shifting states and decide how your film is going to reveal these.

Exercises

In order to fully appreciate the differences between story and narrative, and to contrast different approaches to narrative, we shall build this exercise on the one carried out in the previous chapter on classic narrative. By way of a reminder, imagine that Cynthia's story, opposite, is a summary of your initial research. For the purposes of this exploration, make reasonable imaginative assumptions. As in the earlier exercise, imagine that you are going to construct a narrative and this construction is going to be the basis of further research, the planning and preparation of your production and the skeleton which you will use as a basis for all your shooting decisions. Imagine that you have been given a very tight window to work in and that shooting has to start next week.

Cynthia's story

Cynthia Blake is 67. She is from New York and is a retired publisher. She has an apartment in New York, USA, but has not lived there for two years.

For the past two years she has been living on the luxury cruise liner, the *Mary Rose*, sailing with her across the world on her various cruises. She first came onto the liner when she went on a Mediterranean cruise with her late husband, Ronald, who was an author, essayist and feature writer. During their cruise, Ronald had a heart attack and died. He was buried at sea off the coast of Crete and, ever since, Cynthia has remained on board ship.

In two months' time, the *Mary Rose* is about to dock in Southampton, UK, for the last time, as she is about to be decommissioned. Cynthia's daughter, Catherine, lives in New Hampshire, USA, with her family and is coming to Southampton to pick up her mother and return to New Hampshire. They will stay in London for a few days, see a few sites, do a bit of shopping and then return to New Hampshire together. The plan is that Cynthia will stay with her daughter for a few weeks before finalising what she is going to do next. Cynthia is not sure whether she wants to return to New York to live permanently or not. Catherine has suggested that Cynthia buy a place near her in New Hampshire. At some point, Cynthia has to go back to her New York apartment and organise a few things and Catherine is always there to help.

The final cruise of the *Mary Rose* is a Mediterranean cruise. In fact, they will be passing the very area where Ronald was buried at sea. Cynthia has a very good relationship with the crew members, including the captain. She is a fairly reserved person, but not withdrawn. During her two years on the *Mary Rose*, Cynthia has had a few of her possessions flown out by Catherine. Consequently, she has been able to create a bit of a home for herself in her cabin quarters. She has her set routines around meals, walking the deck, reading and so on. She has with her copies of all her late husband's work, photographs from the past, photographs from her original cruise, photographs of Catherine and her family, and so on.

In initial interviews, Cynthia is very reluctant to talk about the actual circumstances of her late husband's death. When asked why she has remained on the ship, she has no ready answer. When pushed, she talks about not having anything to return to and says that she has always liked the sea. She mentions that she and her late husband, Ronald, were always fond of the sea and often visited the coast close to where Catherine lives. In fact, she is looking forward to visiting her daughter in New Hampshire and walking along the shoreline again; she is particularly looking forward to walking the shoreline again with her grandchildren. She talks warmly about her Ronald, especially about his writings, for which she has a particular fondness. Ronald was drafted for the Korean War, following which he embarked on a successful career as a writer. She was a young, successful magazine editor and they met through their respective jobs. They moved in literary circles and socialised a lot. She is loosely in touch with one or two friends and since Ronald's death she has deliberately not kept in touch much with her former work circles. She also talks a lot about her grandchildren and how they once came and joined her for a cruise.

Cynthia wishes to be buried at sea, like her late husband, and has already made arrangements.

Exercise 1

Imagine that Cynthia's daughter, Catherine, has refused to take part in the film and your producer now insists that budget constraints mean that you are only getting access to the *Mary Rose* for a period of time

▶

covering the final Mediterranean leg of her voyage (thereby excluding her docking at Southampton). You have about a week onboard ship with full access to Cynthia, crew and guests. No shooting can happen off the ship.

Write a detailed treatment for a transcendental narrative of Cynthia's story.

Can you identify all the ingredients of the transcendental narrative and have you constructed them in such a way that it will engage our participatory feelings? When you compare this with your classic approach, how does it differ?

Exercise 2

Let us make the exercise a little more difficult: imagine that, because of problems with the shipping company, you have not received permission to do any shooting on the *Mary Rose*. Furthermore, your producer insists that, for various reasons beyond his or her control, you are only able to shoot in the United States. Nevertheless, you are contracted to make the film about Cynthia and have to proceed.

Construct a transcendental narrative, based on the same story, that involves no shooting on the ship, no shooting in the UK and only shooting in the United States. Write a detailed treatment.

Ask yourself the same questions again: can you identify all the ingredients of the transcendental narrative and have you constructed them in such a way that it will engage our participatory feelings? Similarly, when you compare this with your classic approach, how does it differ?

Notes

[1] Zen is appropriate because of its philosophical and aesthetic relationship to oriental art, literature, poetry and cinema, where we see many examples of this kind of alternative to the classic narrative. See, for example, Paul Schrader's *Transcendental Style in Film: Bresson, Ozu, Dreyer* (University of California Press, 1972) where this famous story is also told.

[2] It is worth reminding ourselves that separating out classic and transcendental narrative in this way is for exploratory purposes and that there are likely to be various possible combinations and other variations.

Chapter 12

Cinematic codes

Erik Knudsen

"I am moved by fancies that are curled
Around these images, and cling:
The notion of some infinitely gentle
Infinitely suffering thing."

(T.S. Eliot, *Preludes*)[1]

Introduction

We have in this section so far mainly been discussing the discourse – narrative motivation, events and structure. Though we have been looking at documentary examples, the key points about discourse and structure apply equally to fiction as to documentary. We now need to move from the 'what', 'where' and 'when' of a narrative to the 'how' – in effect, the narrative form itself. What are the elements of the moving image form that are available to the filmmaker to get across such things as the protagonist's aims, obstacles, climax, resolution, and so on, in the case of the classic narrative? Or, in the case of the transcendental narrative, the protagonist, shifting states, decisive moments, and so on? What are the unique qualities of the moving image narrative form, and the documentary genre within this form, which allow you to reveal things about life around you in ways that you couldn't do with other narrative forms? After all, it is these very qualities you are going to use to tell your story: the moving pictures and the sounds. In this chapter, we shall explore these cinematic qualities.

Understanding how imagery works

In order to fully understand, and therefore manipulate, the tools of the cinematic form let us digress briefly to remind ourselves, on a simple practical level, about the nature of signs and codes. For the purposes of our discussion, let us start with the simple basics of signs.[2]

We are essentially working with three types of sign: the iconic, the indexical and the symbolic. These signs refer to the relationship between the signified and the signifier; in other words, the relationship between the object and the sign referring to that object. This could, for example, be a tree (the signified) and the photograph of the tree (the signifier). The three types of sign – iconic, indexical and symbolic – relate to the relationship between the photograph of the tree and the tree itself. (While we may be talking about pictures, these relationships are, importantly for us, also relevant when talking about sound.) This is significant because different narrative forms deal with the relationship between signifier and signified differently and we need to have a sense of what it is that is unique about the moving image.

The three types of signs can be summarised like this:

- **Iconic** – The relationship between the signifier and the signified is one of verisimilitude: the photograph of the tree looks like the tree and you can link the two in a direct way by likeness.
- **Indexical** – The relationship between the signifier and the signified is one of association. Imagine you saw a photograph of the shadow of the tree and not the tree itself. You associate the fact that the tree is present from seeing its shadow, so the relationship between the photograph and the object it refers to is one of association.
- **Symbolic** – The relationship between the signifier and the signified is one of specific assigned meaning. Imagine you had a triangular road sign with a graphic drawing of a tree. The graphic may look nothing like a real tree and, indeed, if we hadn't been taught what it meant, it might be meaningless. The symbolic relationship therefore has been assigned. In many ways, words themselves fall very much into this category. The word 'tree' is written down and you know what it refers to because you have been taught English.

Think of these signs as the way your audience is first going to engage with your story, before they make sense of the meaning of what they are seeing and hearing. It is the primary level of engagement with the form. Different narrative forms will have different hierarchies in terms of prioritising which of these signs is most important to that form. For example, in literature the symbolic is critical: the reader cannot start to associate (indexical) and see in their mind's eye (pseudo iconic) before they understand what the words mean (symbolic). Perhaps it might be relevant to look at other time-based arts, like music and theatre, and compare the hierarchy of sign engagement. Such a comparison might look something like this (see Figure 12.1)[3].

In music (let's for argument's sake concentrate on music without words) the form itself is very abstract. A series of sounds with certain qualities and pitches, broken up by different lengths of silence to create rhythm. It is, in fact, hard to think of any human creation more abstract. The first thing we start doing is associating those sounds and silences. Perhaps we start to think of a river, or a place, or a person, or a situation or any number of combinations of associations. Many associations connected with music are primal. For example, certain low vibrations in particular rhythmic patterns can create powerful primal associations that make the listener fearful. Other associations are cultural. For example, in the Western world there is an almost instinctual association of a major chord with happiness and a minor chord with sadness. And yet other associations are deeply personal. This indexical connection between the music and its object is, in the first instance, purely associative. Out of this association we then start to create images in our minds (pseudo iconic). The least important relationship between signifier and signified in music is the symbolic one; while it is possible to think of sounds that have symbolic qualities (an SOS signal, for example), it is hard to conceive of engaging with music predominantly through symbolic signs.

In theatre, by contrast, the most important thing is that we engage with the symbols of the artificial space. Through the symbolic language of the words and gestures of the performer, associations are created (indexical) from which we start to see in our mind's eye a place, perhaps, and its people (pseudo iconic). The least important thing in theatre is that what we're looking at is realistic and looks like what it's supposed to look like (iconic). In fact, one may go so far as to say that the less realistic theatre is, the better. This has significant implications for how one tells a story, how one casts and what discourse elements one feels would be best suited to the medium. One can have women playing the parts of men and men playing the parts of women, people wearing masks, and an empty stage can be Hamlet's castle. Gestures and behaviour can be

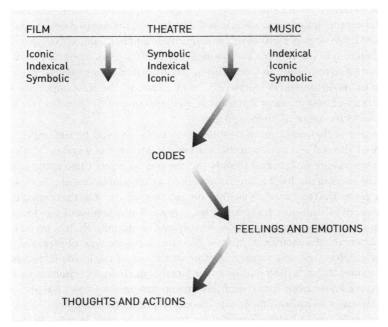

Figure 12.1 The journey of engagement in imagery

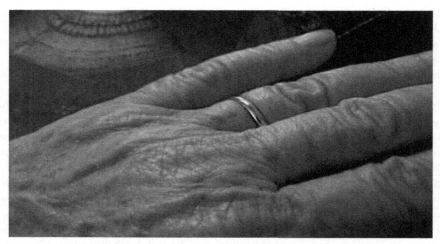

The intimate musicality of *The Gleaners and I* (Varda, 2006)

highly stylised, as can the spoken language. Theatre at its most powerful almost becomes like symbolic ritual, which can have significant historical, cultural and social associations. Through this association emerging out of the symbolic, you then transport your audience to somewhere else.

Imagine filming an empty stage with performers performing *Hamlet*. Your audience's immediate reaction would not be to read that symbolically and transport themselves to Hamlet's castle. Their first reaction would be to see a theatre play being performed and filmed. A papier-mâché tree on a stage will immediately be read symbolically by the theatre audience, whereas in a film it will look like a papier-mâché tree. With film, therefore, the first semiotic engagement is with the iconic. What you see and hear looks like what it is supposed to be. From that initial engagement we start to associate and the indexical is hugely important in film. The camera and the sound recorder capture images and sounds in the likeness of the original objects and it is in how they are captured, the elements within this verisimilitude and in their juxtaposition that we really start to give direction to the viewer's associations. The cultural associations we have built up, for example, around verisimilitude in determining fact from fiction are significant, and therefore important for us, as documentary storytellers, to be aware of. The least important sign element in film is the symbol and in many ways this is, perhaps, one of the reasons you might closely associate the narrative forms of music and film.

What are some of the implications of this? One example would be the implications for the verisimilitude of 'the real' – a notion at the heart of the documentary genre. In other words, the way in which we capture images and sounds and the way we relate these images and sounds to being a direct likeness to our lived reality brings about a cluster of cinematic codes that define the documentary genre. That iconic relationship – the fact that we say, 'Yes, that's what the real world really looks like', or 'This is how real people live' – is a defining feature of the documentary. But it emerges out of the very strength of the moving-image medium itself. It is no coincidence that some of the newer documentary subgenres – the camera phone type of captured moment, for example – are emphasising new ways of reinforcing the use of the iconic relationship between imagery and reality. The style itself reinforces the fact that the imagery is uncensored and close to reality. But, as we know from many viral advertising campaigns from YouTube, this sense of closeness and likeness to reality – the iconic – is entirely manufactured.

Another example would be the implications for words in film. Words are symbols in this context and it becomes apparent that the meaning of words, in themselves, will carry a lot more

Mixing codes of fact and fiction in *Suite Habana* (Perez, 2006)

weight in the context of theatre than in the context of film. Therefore, if you are going to rely heavily on words, there is a danger that you are not going to be playing to the strengths of the medium. To play to the strengths of the medium you need to be thinking more about the iconic and indexical elements: what do we see and hear and what are the associations that emerge out of this? If you are able to place words into a strong iconic and indexical context, then they might be able to play a powerful role. Indeed, in the moving image, it is often the tone of what someone is saying rather than what they are saying that affects the viewer – the indexical relationship to the spoken word as opposed to the symbolic relationship.

Not a single word spoken in *Suite Habana* (Perez, 2006)

Another implication relates to casting. Getting the right characters for your documentary is as important as getting the casting right for a fiction film. The first level of engagement your viewer will have with your characters is establishing that they look like what they're supposed to look like, that they move and behave the way they're supposed to, and this is then followed by associations emerging out of the verisimilitude that you have established.

Associations – the indexical – relate to codes. These are the meanings we invest in actions, gestures and imagery. They operate on several levels: from the animalistic (involving understanding of meanings we might share with some animals) to social and cultural codes of behaviour; and from subcultural codes right through to the finely tuned codes of languages, such as the spoken word or cinema. Codes are not definable, finite or fixed. They are organic and constantly changing and often we're engaging with them completely unconsciously.

When you set off to give your viewer signs via moving images and sounds, you are, in effect, manipulating codes in such a way that the viewer understands what you're on about. One of the first things you're doing is establishing with your viewer a relationship, an aspect of which is letting them know whether they should read this as fact or fiction. As the author behind the camera, you might be satisfied, for example, that you're dealing with factual people or situations, but all your audience have to go by is what you put on that screen, nothing else. Over the years, certain ways of creating cinematic codes have come to be associated with actuality and factuality, while certain other cinematic codes have been associated with fantasy and fiction. In some cases, these sets of codes become entrenched and dogmatic until a filmmaker comes along and breaks 'the rules', thereby helping the subgenre evolve beyond a cliché, refreshing it and preventing its demise.

It is therefore critical that, as a filmmaker, you have some awareness of how your viewer might read your imagery and your juxtapositions. You need to be aware of the clusters of codes associated with certain subgenres and be able to use them and refresh them, evolve with them and, in some cases, rebel against them. There is no dictionary, no thesaurus, but a constantly evolving 'common law' binding us together in shared meanings. (This, in itself, is a good reason to be a student of film history and to try to develop an understanding of your work's place in an ever-evolving language.)

You will be completely manipulating the medium itself, whether as a fiction filmmaker or as a documentary filmmaker. The truth does not lie in the medium, but in your intentions, your integrity and the feelings and emotions you solicit from, and convey to, your viewer. There is always selection, manipulation, emphasis and perspective influencing your work. The fact that you film actual people does not mean that you are going to be more truthful than a filmmaker who is filming actors. However, it is important to be mindful of how your viewer will read your signs. For instance, if you know that they are likely to read certain signs as actuality and you deliberately mislead them, will they, or should they, forgive you for deceiving them? Conversely, if you were to use some actuality footage in a fantasy and lead them to believe, for example, that the suffering within the actuality was fantasy – would they, or should they, forgive you? The blending of fictional and factual codes needs a delicate understanding of not only the codes of cinema, but the cultural codes surrounding you and your viewer. You need to know how to enter into a trusting relationship with your viewer in which they may, on the one hand, be challenged, while on the other not feel deceived.[4]

Key cinematic elements

Let us look at some of the key cinematic elements you will be using to shape your narrative form and briefly suggest some example codes associated with them. In practice, of course, these elements overlap, interact and influence each other.

The shot

The shot holds many of the elements we shall be discussing and, as such, is fundamental to what you're creating. Consideration needs to be given to composition, movement, angle, texture, lighting (which could also be considered under mise-en-scène) and so on. Each of the constituent elements of the shot will have codes attached to them and you need to be aware of what they are and how you will be working with these codes (see examples below).

Your audience will read a close shot following someone from behind as they walk down a corridor differently from if you were following them from in front. This all depends on context, of course, but one can imagine how your viewer might feel that your character is threatened in the former, but less threatened in the latter.

Another example might be different ways of panning. If you pan away from a character to an object they are not looking at, or we know that they are not aware of, this is quite different from your carrying out the same panning when the character is looking at the object. In the former, your viewer would perceive a dramatic irony, while in the latter they would read it as a point of view.

The angles from which you look at characters – high angle or low angle, as well as frontal, side views or rear views – can have a lot of associations connected with power relationships, as well as playing an important role in indicating narrative perspective. For instance, how would you film children – looking down at them or on their level? This would depend on what you want the audience to associate with the situation you're portraying. Is it an adult perspective of a situation or the child's perspective? Is there a power relationship going on and what is it? Combined with the horizontal angle, do you want to suggest discomfort or comfort?

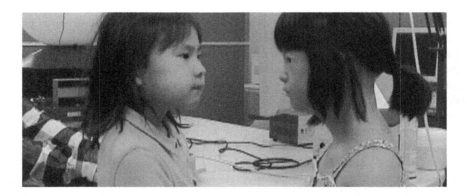

Likewise with composition. The associations linked with composition can reveal a lot. A close, intimate shot of a person carrying out a task, or a wide, distant shot of the same task can yield very different understandings of a situation. The placement of the characters within the shot and where the empty spaces are, again, can have a significant effect on how your viewer will read the situation. Composition alone can suggest tensions and emotions. Additionally, how are the characters placed in relation to each other and what does that tell us about their relationship?

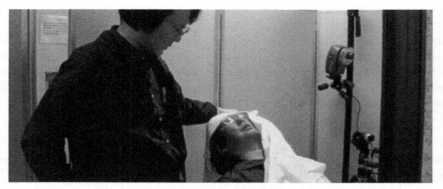

Shots constantly comparing in *Mechanical Love* (Ambo, 2007)

Many of these codes also tell the viewer whether to consider what they are seeing as fact or fiction. If you have wobbly, handheld shots, combined with a raw texture drained of colours, and harsh lighting, they are more likely to associate this with fact and actuality. In contrast, if you light the scene in a particular way, put your camera on a smooth tripod or dolly and carefully compose your shots, and additionally bring in strong, clean colours, the viewer is more likely to define this as fiction. Over the years, of course, filmmakers have used these associative expectations and assumptions to great effect. Unsettling and challenging the viewer's normal way of reading cinematic codes to look with fresh eyes at a situation they have seen many times before is an effective way of engaging them. The adoption by documentary makers of codes predominantly associated with fiction, and the adoption of codes predominantly associated with documentary by fiction filmmakers, has become commonplace and, in many cases, clichéd. However, at one point, each transgression between these clusters of codes constituted a creative departure by a filmmaker well aware of what he or she was doing.

The montage (editing)

The term 'montage' is used here because it suggests building up, or assembling, rather than cutting away. Post-production is essentially about putting the different shots and sounds together to bring a work to life from its disparate elements and, while this does involve some cutting away, it is the bringing together that is the essential aspect. Magical things start to happen when you bring disparate elements together. The whole is more than the sum of its parts and this is at the heart of montage – editing. Montage is also one of the most associative parts of the filmmaking process and therefore complex. The juxtaposition of images and sounds is often far from the way we directly experience life and many codes have been established over time that enable the viewer to understand the progression of time, spatial relationships, shifts in perspective, thought processes of characters and so on. The codes of the montage have come a long way since the early days of cinema in which a single shot captured a slice of life. We now have montages that involve jump cuts, interlocking elliptical narratives and multi-layered transitions. Considerations of montage are numerous and include: coverage, continuity, action, movement, juxtaposition, spatial relationships and rhythm, to name a few. Let us focus here on highlighting some aspects of codes related to coverage, spatial relationships and continuity. (There will be a more detailed discussion of editing later in the book.)

Some purist anthropological documentary makers cry foul when there is a cut in a scene. For them, the cut breaches the covenant of truth and authenticity. The unprivileged eye does not cut, but roves from one thing to the next. Therefore, if one is to maintain documentary authenticity, the filmed sequence should not cut either. However, this is perhaps misguided. Even anthropological documentary makers are involved in telling stories and the telling of every story involves choosing and organising discourse events, deciding on perspective, selecting a narrative form, selecting what to shoot, what not to shoot, where to shoot it from, how to assemble the narrative in its own temporal space, and so on. Even if one were to have a film that was one shot, there are still decisions about the beginning and the end of the narrative, where we are looking, the angles, the textures, the sounds, and so on. These elements all involve the biased decisions of the filmmakers. This is never more apparent than in the montage: the assembling of the images and sounds into a final coherent whole that is going to work as a unit.

Editors are well aware now that contemporary audiences can make the necessary associative interpretations of codes that allow them to be fairly free in terms of which actions and events are actually seen and which are inferred. Do we need to see someone's entire action when carrying out a task? Do we need to see the whole journey that they have made? What coverage can be dealt with through sound and what can be dealt with by the picture? Because we have machines that, to a remarkable degree, can 'capture reality' does not mean that we have to be dogmatic in attempting to reproduce this reality on the screen. We provide the audience with selected bits and have developed a language by which they bring their associations and experiences to fill the gaps. It's similar to the relationship we discussed earlier between story and discourse (see the example below).

> If we see a sequence with a woman shopping for vegetables in a market and the very next sequence is of her clearing food from a dining table and taking the dirty dishes into the kitchen while we hear the sound of children running up the stairs, we will immediately associate that the woman cooked the meal for her family and that they sat down and ate it. It is therefore possible, with two simple shots, to tell the viewer about a much more complex set of actions that are never actually seen. If we were to add to this the fact that the first sequence of the shopping was done with some fast cutting, while the clearing of the dishes was done in one long shot, new associations about the nature and the cooking and the meal will start to emerge; one can therefore look at loading the action not seen with certain qualities and associations.

One of the most effective ways to engage a viewer is to allow them space to use their own imagination, experiences and associations. The question of what one shows, and what one does not show, is therefore important. However, the ambivalence that might emerge should not be a question of not being clear about the story (ambivalence is not about hiding). The ambivalence emerges out of the fact that the clear narrative elements one does include have powerful and far-reaching associations and consequences.

It is not just the shot which gives us a sense of space and context. One of the most common codes associated with spatial relationships relates to what is known as the 'action line' or 'crossing the line'. While this is an issue that needs to be dealt with at the shooting stage, it is at the montage stage that one sees the importance of considering this 'common law rule'. Some filmmakers and cinematic traditions do not adhere to the codes associated with the 'action line' and, indeed, some filmmakers deliberately set out to challenge this code for specific purposes. As with any set of codes, they are there to be challenged and adapted.

Editing at the heart of working with archive footage in *Capturing the Friedmans* (Jarecki, 2004)

If you cut together two people talking to each other, you would expect them to appear as in Figure 12.2.

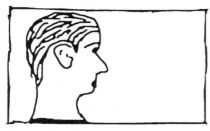

Figure 12.2

Spatially, they seem to be talking to each other, even though they are in separate shots. This has been achieved by shooting them as in Figure 12.3.

Figure 12.3

The dotted line is the action line, an imaginary 180° line between two main points of interacting action. What would it look like if one of the camera positions were to cross to the other side of this invisible action line as in Figure 12.4?

Figure 12.4

The consequence would be assembling two shots in sequence that would look like Figure 12.5.

Figure 12.5

To our sense of understanding space, this would not seem right; it would look as though one character were speaking to the back of the other, as though they were not facing each other. However, in the 'real world' they were facing each other. Here we see the importance of spatial compositional codes, such as those associated with looking into empty space, and montage codes, when linking people in space through assembling of shots in a sequence.

Continuity and coverage are, of course, linked. The moment you break up a scene into shots, you are, in fact, breaking the continuity of real-life actions. Nevertheless, viewers still need to order events into a coherent time-line in order to allow them to fill the gaps and, in the final assembling of your narrative, continuity is an important factor. Continuity is not simply about covering action in an expected order, for there is plenty of scope to play around with this order; it is also about emotional and psychological continuity.

Earlier we looked at the cause and effect of the classic narrative, as well as coincidence in the transcendental narrative. Many of the same issues are relevant for the editor in terms of continuity. The editor not only needs to understand how each cut and each sequence work in terms of continuity of action, but he or she also needs to understand about the continuity of emotion and the continuity of psychological behaviour. In the classic narrative, each cut needs to serve the purposes of the linear cause and effect, while in the transcendental narrative the cut must serve the purpose of establishing a lateral state.

The mise-en-scène

The mise-en-scène refers to all the elements within the scene: the props, décor, the clothing and even the lighting. It would be a mistake not to consider this aspect of the tools at your disposal as seriously as the fiction filmmaker. While the fiction filmmaker will tend to put these elements in their scene, the documentary filmmaker may be more inclined to think of finding them. Having said that, some fiction filmmakers like to work in factual situations, using what they can find, and some documentary filmmakers like to put things in, or construct the mise-en-scène, for their films. Either way, the visual and aural information that contextualises the main action is an important associative factor in the viewer getting information and impressions.

Mise-en-scène in *The Five Obstructions* (Von Trier/Leth, 2003)

Consider a simple interview situation in which you are interviewing a doctor, say, about an important medical breakthrough that he or she has been involved with. Seeing this person talk about the breakthrough wearing jeans and sitting in their garden at home, surrounded by their children playing, would be quite different from seeing them in a laboratory, wearing their lab coat and surrounded by assistants working away.

Not only do we glean much information from the mise-en-scène, but it is an important factor in influencing our mood, our attitude to the characters and, even, our belief in the situation. It can also tell us about the state of someone's mind, about their feelings and provide subtextual information about the theme. Likewise, the mise-en-scène can be used to give reminders of past events and hint at things to come.

The mise-en-scène should, therefore, be considered to be one of the key elements of telling your story.

The characters

As mentioned earlier, casting is as important in a documentary film as it is in a fiction film. The strengths of the medium mean that your viewer is first going to deal with them on an iconic level – their likeness to what they're supposed to be – and then on an indexical level – what the viewer associates with what they are seeing and hearing from your character. This is, of course, particularly important with the protagonists. Think of it this way: it is important that your characters are what they are, rather than seem what they are. You are, in a sense, experiencing your characters through their surfaces and these surfaces need to be genuine in their likeness.

Your characters should also be embodied in the story itself; that is, visually and aurally placed in the story. Do the mise-en-scène in which they are situated, the setting in which they live, the other people with whom they are engaging provide you with an opportunity to visually and aurally capture your characters in a context where you can film them engaging with the discourse events you need to tell your story? Can you, additionally, visually establish a premise for these particular protagonists that can evoke some events through which we will see their predicament? One important aspect of making sure you cast characters who are embodied in the story is to ensure that you engage the viewer through the particular, rather than through the general and generic.

The dramaturgy

Another tool you will be using to construct your narrative is dramaturgy – the dramatic interaction between the protagonist and other characters. This is particularly clear in the classic narrative, where the embodiment of the conflict or struggle that your protagonist is engaged with involves, for example, antagonists – people who represent the obstacles your character is encountering. When casting your main protagonist, one consideration might be whether there is sufficient scope for dramaturgical interaction in that protagonist's particular circumstances to allow you to tell your story to best effect. You may want to think how you can embody the obstacles of your protagonist and what kinds of situations might therefore emerge that provide you with the necessary encounters and interactions that can lead to an effective and engaging narrative (see the following example).

> If you were making a film about a young woman's struggle to free herself from certain social and cultural norms, how could you, dramaturgically, bring this to life? Do you have access to the very people who are the face of these norms? Who could provide encounters, conversations and visual contexts for the necessary dramatic interaction that would engage us in the dilemmas? If such characters are not available, how else could you visually engage us in the dramaturgy of the experiences of the protagonist?

Dramaturgy does not just apply to human interaction. Indeed, we can imagine dramatic interactions between animals, between human beings and animals, between human beings and nature, and between human beings and material things. In any of these circumstances, dramaturgy provides opportunities to engage your viewer in your narrative by bringing inner and outer struggles to life in highly visible ways.

The sound

It could be argued that sounds affect people more deeply and profoundly than pictures do. There is something very primal about sound that makes it capable of creating powerful associations in people, often without their being conscious of it. When sound and picture are combined effectively, we can truly see the documentary brought to powerful life. It is usually the case that, while you can get away with technically imperfect pictures in the cause of good dramatic action, for example, this is far less the case with sound. Sound usually transforms an image and can play an important part in conveying discourse information. It is not just about information, though. The texture of sound can have a significant effect on mood and on associations, and one can therefore use sound to give some direction to the viewer's reading of events that are happening visually.

More often than not, sound is used to legitimise the verisimilitude of the picture by paraphrasing the action of the picture. However, sound can also be used to tell us about things we do not see. It can play a role in creating dramatic irony. It can create a contrapuntal role to what we are seeing. It can help us link to other parts of the narrative. It can remind us of past events and give us a sense of foreboding or hint at things to come. It can help provide a cultural and historical context, and many other things. Used creatively, sound can transform a documentary film.

The role of sound is something the filmmaker should, therefore, consider during the conceptualising of the film. If one is restricted visually, there are good opportunities for using sound creatively to enrich the visual images and bring a work to life.

While we are considering sound we should perhaps mention music. There are instances where it is hard to distinguish between the sound effects of a film and the music, and many sound designers will not do so. There is diegetic music and non-diegetic music. Diegetic music resides within the story, while non-diegetic music resides outside the story. Traditionally, many documentary makers shied away from using non-diegetic music because it detracted from the authenticity of the factual experience and had very strong associations with fiction. However, non-diegetic music is now widely used in documentary.

The power of music to move us is, in a way, evidence of the power of sound. While this can be useful, it can also be a curse. Music is so powerful that you can use it to disguise poor filmmaking. For example, the power of the music can be almost wholly responsible for moving the audience and there are many instances where a film has non-diegetic music driving the emotional engagement of the viewer from beginning to end. In such instances, one could argue that the viewer has little space to engage with the full range of elements in the film as their emotions are being strongly directed.

In addition, for most people, certain pieces of music have personal and cultural associations. The use of well-known music, therefore, has to be handled with care. If you do use well-known music, use it for its specific cultural associations and contextualise it as such. Imagine if your viewers all start to reminisce about quite different things and have very different experiences associated with a particular famous piece of music; you will lose them. In view of the associative power of music, unless you're using a well-known piece of music for specific cultural associative purposes, try to commission original music and use it with care.

Poetry and renewal

As with any language, the documentary form would die if it did not continually evolve. Approaches to narrative, modes of discourse and the use of cinematic codes gradually become clichés and, in order for the documentary artist to prevent their work becoming stale and empty, they must continually refresh the language with elements of originality and innovation. What in part distinguishes the poet's expression from idiomatic expression is the fact that the poet plays with language and metaphor, making new and unusual combinations that will help us see even familiar things in a fresh way. Many of the expressions and metaphors we see in idiomatic spoken and written language originated in poetry, found their way into ordinary everyday language and then became embedded in the core of our culture.

Likewise with the documentary language. Many components of a contemporary documentary which we take for granted were originally introduced by 'poets' of the form: the jump cut; the stylishly lit interview; the presenter-led interventionist style; the video diary; the non-diegetic use of music; even the observational style – these are examples of components of the documentary that were introduced by innovators and original creators. At any given time, the norms of the genre, the routines of the trade and the idioms of expression need to be renewed, refreshed, evolved and developed. There is not, and never was, an agreed documentary genre. The genre exists merely as a cluster of cinematic codes, the combination and use of which are constantly shifting.

It is therefore important that, as a creative documentary filmmaker, you do not fall into the trap of becoming a hack, someone who merely repeats the routines of the trade and form. If you want your audience to see afresh you will need to play with the form, with metaphors and imagery and with the processes you engage to create your work. This is clearly not something that can be taught or prescribed, as only you will know the answer through your own unique exploration. However, perhaps it is possible to identify a few qualities in yourself that you should try to encourage: these may include intuition, gullibility, playfulness and courage.

Intuition

We are both rational and irrational beings, as evidenced by the science of the right and left brain. Part of us wants to explain everything, to understand everything in a linear, causal chain and for all relationships between phenomena to fit a rational pattern. Another side of us does not adhere to this rational engagement, but wants instead to engage with feelings. It does not seek to understand, but perhaps merely to experience. It can accept paradoxes and coincidences without a need for explanation. It allows 'gut feelings' to come to the fore, works with imagery and metaphors and is generally considered to be our 'creative' side. We live most of our lives in a world constructed by our rational world view and it can be very difficult to break out of this to engage with aspects of our experience which lie outside it. The arts, in general, play a vital part in opening us up to our other side and the documentary filmmaker, too, needs to engage with their irrational, intuitive and feeling side. You may be familiar with the expression 'Listen to your intuition': perhaps this is a quality you can work on developing.

Gullibility

This might at first seem like a strange quality to encourage. People often associate gullibility with a character flaw. However, gullibility suggests an open mind. It suggests a mind prepared to accept things initially at face value, a willingness to consider possibilities and notions that, at first glance, the rational or conditioned mind has dismissed as unreal, unfeasible, fantastical or plain ridiculous. Like a child's mind, the gullible mind is willing to listen to people's stories without making judgement, will recognise feelings without dismissing them out of hand and, above all, will be willing to try to make playful connections between phenomena and elements our schooling and rational constructs have long dismissed. A mind that is always sceptical is a closed mind. Try to encourage yourself to play with 'impossible' notions, 'ridiculous' ideas and 'fantastical' postulations. You will be surprised by how close to the truth the imagination can be.

Playfulness

We often think of children as being 'creative' and perhaps even remember ourselves as having been more creative as children than as adults. There is an openness – a gullibility – about a child. Their mind has not yet been schooled and socialised into more fixed patterns of associations and thinking. This allows them to imaginatively combine notions and ideas that we, as adults, have long since learned do not belong together. And it is through play – the playful combination of images, ideas and associations – that the child learns and discovers. Perhaps, as adults, we need to unlearn many of the fixed notions and associations we have adopted, with a view to playfully questioning many of these assumptions. We can do so by breaking patterns of thinking and reconnecting phenomena and elements in new and evocative combinations.

Courage

It requires courage to successfully allow scope to the attributes of intuition, gullibility and playfulness mentioned above. Courage to challenge one's own preconceptions and habits, courage to challenge the dominant norms of the genre and form, courage to stand alone in the face of ridicule and criticism, courage to listen and take criticism when relevant, courage to embrace what your rational mind says is a crazy idea and play with it. In other words, as a creative practitioner, you must have the courage to take risks.

Key points

- How are you linking your narrative form and style to your theme?
- How are you using the combination of sound and picture to tell your story? Your sounds, your pictures, your composition, style, texture, editing rhythm, music, and so on – all are components you are going to manipulate and you should be in control of them all.

- Everything you are putting in place should have a reason for being there, even if you only know that reason intuitively.
- Be aware of how the cinematic codes work; play with them, juxtapose them, explore.
- Remember: the fact that you may be working with factual roots does not mean you do not engage your imagination in creating your work.
- Remember that this medium is particularly successful when working with associations – partly because you are encouraging the audience to participate by using their own imagination.
- Don't hide information from your audience, but think of the most powerful way you can share it with them, through which they can themselves wrestle with associations, ambiguous consequences, paradoxes, and so on.
- Be courageous and take risks.
- Listen to your intuition.
- Play is an important part of the process of creation.

Exercises

Exercise 1

Choose one of the treatments you prepared for an earlier exercise and identify a particular scene in it. Now imagine how that scene may unfold and storyboard that particular sequence twice: first with a view to shooting the whole sequence in one continuous hand-held shot; second with a view to shooting the same scene with one static shot.

- How would you, or could you, use sound differently in the two scenarios?
- How is the pacing and rhythm of your scene affected?
- How would you approach your editing differently?
- What effect do your different approaches have on our emotional and feeling engagement with the scene?

Exercise 2

Choose a simple process or activity – such as the building of a campfire.

Prepare in two different ways how you are going to make a little film about someone making a campfire: first, prepare for a short documentary that is going to be more classical in its structure and approach; second, prepare an alternative documentary that is going to be more transcendental in its approach.

- How will you shoot each version differently in terms of shots, editing, sound, pacing and so on?
- What choices will you make to strengthen the differences?
- What choices will you make that will create a visual unity to each film?
- Do you see your differing approaches touching the viewer in different ways? And if so, how will that affect their relationship to, and knowledge of, building campfires?

Now make the two films and see how they live up to your predictions and expectations.

▶

Exercise 3

Identify a very personal theme, feeling or emotion that you would like to get across to an audience without having to reveal anything autobiographical.

Now construct a short narrative film using entirely found footage – i.e. footage you have not been involved with shooting yourself, such as footage from the internet, family archive, footage from movies, stills from magazines etc. Screen your completed film to your friends and colleagues without telling them anything about the themes, feelings or emotions that inspired the work and let them talk about it.

Do you feel that you have managed to engage them in the themes, feelings and emotions that you hoped for initially? How has your approach to narrative structure and your approach to imagery succeeded, or not, in achieving a connection between your intentions and the reactions of your viewers?

Notes

[1] Eliot, T.S. (2002) Preludes in Selected Poems, Faber and Faber.

[2] For a more comprehensive study of semiotics, see Roland Barthes (1995) *The Semiotic Challenge*, Berkeley: University of California Press.

[3] Remember that we are only separating these elements out for argument and understanding; in the real world things are likely to be blended, mixed and act upon each other.

[4] Some of you may be familiar with the incident around the broadcast of Orson Welles' adaptation of H.G. Wells' *War of the Worlds* (1938). Orson Welles used all the codes of the factual news programme to create a drama, but the consequence was that 300,000 San Franciscans took to the streets in an effort to evacuate the city and Orson Welles had to apologise the following day. What do you think he was apologising for?

Chapter 13

New media, new documentary forms

Mary Agnes Krell

" Though much emphasis currently is placed on collaboration between artists and technologists, the real trend is more toward one [person] who is both artistically and technologically conversant. "

(Youngblood, 1970: 193)

Introduction

Digital technologies, and specifically the internet, have introduced radical changes to the way we make, distribute and archive film. They have consistently expanded the range of tools, competencies and expectations required of all filmmakers. In response to that ongoing state of flux, this chapter will explore the nature of certain changes, considering the effect on issues raised elsewhere in this book (such as narrative) and suggesting a series of taxonomies for (re)considering and engaging with emerging media technologies. We will explore a range of tactics for engaging with the constant evolution of film production, consumption and transmission in the twenty-first century.

Film in a changing media landscape, or evolutionary media and tactics

Technology has historically introduced change to the way we make, view and present films. With the introduction of personal computers and the internet, that state of change continues and, many believe, is accelerating. Computers regularly compress information, reducing it to a series of binary data (ones and zeros) to transmit across communication channels. This fragmentation occurs not only in a literal manner in relation to film and video as it is compressed for viewing online and on a range of portable devices, but also in conceptual ways. Just as, when editing, you constantly (re)arrange narrative and visual sequences within your films, sequencing together distinct film clips, film viewers are increasingly able to reconfigure films. It can be argued that computers and, by extension, websites that allow groups of users to build custom experiences by groups, sound, image and video have led to the development of a kind of empowered user or viewer.

It is dangerous to assume that audiences will continue to retreat to the cathedral of a darkened cinema to view a film. They may first view a film while on a plane or a train. They may see only a fragment of the film or may be distracted by surrounding information onscreen. The very location in which films are viewed has become unstable. In addition to trains, planes and theatres, films may be seen on televisions, laptops, mobile phones, on large screens in public spaces and elsewhere. You might argue that films are increasingly being viewed in these diverse environments *instead of* in a cinema. With the fluidity and instability of multiple environments comes a range of expectations that the film form itself should do more and *be* more than it once was. Just as average computer users have evolved to develop a range of skills that allow them to reorder and alter documents on their computers, audiences increasingly expect to be able to enact a degree of agency when interacting with films. They may want access to pre-production materials or to alternative shots for scenes. They may wish to reconfigure a film or add a different soundtrack. In the interest of film criticism, viewers may wish to use fragments from the film alongside other materials to contextualise, explain or explore themes and ideas within the film.[1] That notion is key – the nature of interacting with a film at a granular level, exploring and even remaking it.

Narrative interventions

Much time has been spent in previous chapters exploring narrative in a range of forms. Digital technologies, specifically the internet, continue to introduce change to the nature and expectation of narrative. Linearity is no longer as rigidly demanded and a range of interruptible, interactive and expanded narrative possibilities emerges.

Interruptibility

Once removed from a traditional cinematic space, film falls prey to the unstable lighting, sound and architecture of the environment in which the film is seen. Consider, for a moment, the radical differences between viewing a film on a mobile phone and watching it on the internet or on a television in your own home. In each of those situations, your viewer may be interrupted by a range of environmental intrusions – from the sound of the telephone ringing to the loss of battery power, among many others. Your user may also simply choose to pause the film and return to it later. While much has been written about the seismic changes that video and DVD formats have introduced to film viewing, I wish to focus only on the idea of the interruption as leading to interaction.

Interactivity

Playing and pausing a film, particularly on the computer or the internet, is literally a form of interaction. Interacting with a film in a space where you also create, edit, publish and alter texts introduces some interesting expectations. Writing about film in the early days of the internet focused on a kind of interactive cinema where users might choose their own endings. Such discussions have evolved to include the practices of making and remaking films and responses to them. In addition to the kinds of video essay mentioned earlier, other patterns of remaking films have emerged. It is not uncommon for viewers to produce altered versions of films or re-cut scenes for comedic or artistic value and then post them online. These methods of audience interaction can be expected to increase as the technology required to produce videos continues to become more affordable and accessible. You can expect your audience to employ interactive methods to view your films, often choosing to participate in them in a range of ways.

Through the increase in use of the internet, new models of narrative construction have been introduced and embraced. The term 'interactive narrative' is one used to describe a range of these and is worth exploring briefly here. If more traditional models of narrative are linear and contain branching structures of a story told/experienced over time, interactive narrative could be seen to be non-linear and to exhibit a range of structures such as nodal, episodic, recursive or others.

An interactive narrative differs from other forms of narrative in that its plot structure can be described not as a single trajectory or arc but as a series or system of connections that users/viewers may choose to follow. When planning a project with an interactive narrative, it is useful to visualise/draw out your intended story. Interactive narrative is most commonly illustrated as nodal and is generally illustrated using a star map or similar diagram that places a central episode or idea in the midst of supporting information and/or possibilities. In interactive settings, you may choose to construct an experience that hinges on events, themes or objects. The maps below show two ways of illustrating/planning a narrative about a female war photographer during World War II. In these examples, users might choose to explore any number of paths from a starting point. First, users can choose to explore largely through individual events or via a more traditional timeline (see Figure 13.1). In Figure 13.2, access to information is grouped by type of objects. None of these routes is exclusive and many projects will employ some combination of structures that uses both events and objects to construct narrative experiences. Figure 13.3 shows another way of mapping a more complex interactive narrative.

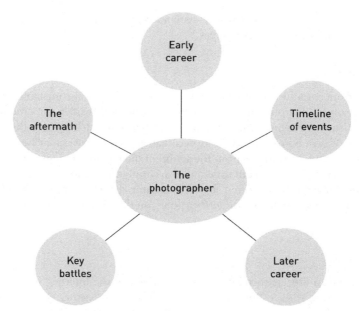

Figure 13.1 Narrative about a WWII photographer using key events as structure or navigation

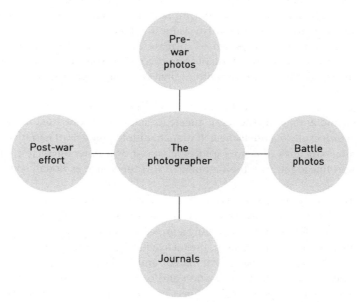

Figure 13.2 Narrative about a WWII photographer using key objects as structure or navigation

Mark Stephen Meadows provides two useful systems worth considering when constructing an interactive narrative. He articulates the steps a user will take to interact with a story (or film or website or other project) as observation, exploration, modification and change.[2]

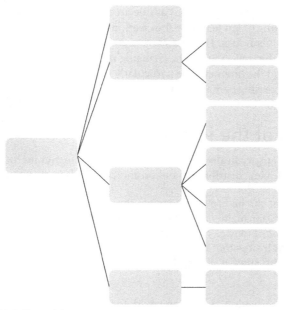

Figure 13.3 Branching structure which may use a cambination of events and objects as navigation

Expansion

As we move from traditional forms of film creation and distribution, we see changes to the kinds of static documents that remain the same each time the film is delivered in canisters or on DVD. Digital technologies and the kinds of possibilities afforded by them lead to films that exist in a range of forms. In addition to the film itself – something a viewer may choose to view in a single sitting or in fragments – there is the range of additional material available online and offline. While video essays and other reconstructions of films have been mentioned, it is also worth mentioning other materials your viewers may seek out. It has become commonplace for viewers to search the internet for trivia and other data related to a film at the same time as watching it. Filmmakers would do well to consider what a viewer might find when doing an internet search using the title of a film because many viewers (and producers) will do that very thing.

Not *if* but *how* – a key question

In order to face the ongoing state of change that the internet and other digital technologies bring to filmmaking, you may wish to begin by asking not *if* new technologies change what you do but *how you might use them* to expand what you do.[3]

Transmedia convergence and participatory culture

In his writings, Henry Jenkins has repeatedly engaged with questions arising from the convergence of technologies in our everyday lives and the ways that audiences and practices of participation come together. He suggests that, in this convergence culture, old and new media collide.

He cites the (inter)action of fans and films as one area where we see interventions and transformations, from the writing of fan fiction to the creation of video responses to films, as mentioned above. In addition to his books, Henry Jenkins maintains a blog where you will find a series of articles and entries that reflect upon the changing media forms and spaces emerging through digital technologies and the internet. One particularly interesting article explores the 'transmedia generation' and its increasing demands for participation in the culture of (film)making.[4]

Film on and of the internet

Donato Totaro, writing specifically about the internet and cinema in 2007, proposed that the web is a space for archiving, distributing and promoting film. He suggested that,

> Film on the internet can be broken down into three broad categories: 1) Web sites that function as archives for mainly non-commercially viable films 2) Web sites that function as distributor/exhibitor of movies made exclusively for the internet (which I will call 'internet cinema'), and 3) Web sites that function as promotional material for theatrical film releases (official film sites, trailers, electronic press kits).
>
> (Totaro, 2007)

While these categories provide a useful framework for considering the place of film on the internet, they neither engage with other digital media (mobile phones, public displays, other portable devices) nor do they emphasise the role of the audience/user in these practices of archiving, distribution and promotion. For that reason, you may wish to consider the effect that the internet *and* other digital technologies and emerging practices have had on film. New technologies persistently introduce questions of transmission (portability), archives (sustainability) and distribution (translatability).

Portability

Whether in canisters or on DVDs, films are physically portable, though new technologies lead to films being moved about in increasingly diverse and smaller (even miniaturised) ways. As the circles in Figure 13.4 begin to overlap with each other, questions arise about how changes to the

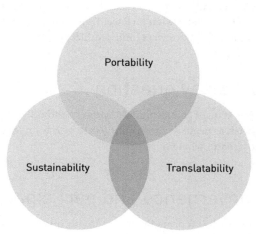

Figure 13.4 Digital technologies and emerging practices raise a number of related questions about film

way a film moves around may be tied to its translation or its sustainability. Through the use of digital media, film can be translated into a range of formats (for viewing on computers, mobile media, televisions and in other spaces). The film can also become something that viewers and others may wish to keep (in whole or in part), archiving it in personal and communal spaces as well as public and archival spaces.

Translatability

At a basic level, a film itself can be viewed in and from a range of languages and cultures. New technologies, however, introduce questions about how your film might be translated to different digital forms. Technical questions of compression and decompression sit alongside questions of linked and/or interrelated content.

Sustainability

Questions of sustainability and the traditional archive remain concerns for filmmakers. However, when one considers questions of translation and (increasingly portable and unstable) transmission, those questions shift and expand. You must consider not just how you might keep your own film and its constituent parts on your own computers and other digital media but also how the film and its form might exist as a record. Who might archive your film and where? Questions of both authoritative documents and archival forms emerge.

Citizen journalism, cell phones and Iran

In 2009, the internet and mobile phones were used in unexpected and novel ways to document events in Iran. Videos and images from mobile phones arrived on websites and in inboxes all over the world, documenting and responding to the death of Neda Agha-Soltan, a young Iranian woman who was killed during an anti-government protest in Tehran. The BBC covered the events and the rising phenomenon of digital citizen journalism in Iran on their *Digital Planet* series. It can be found online at: http://news.bbc.co.uk/1/hi/8176957.stm (accessed on 01 May 2010).

To Shoot an Elephant

Directors Alberto Arce and Mohammad Rujailah have created a film that documents a significant chapter in the history of imperialism in the Middle East. It provides a rare insider's account of Israel's invasion of Gaza in 2008/9. The film is challenging to watch, as repeated violence and acts of barbarism are documented. They include attacks on schools, homes and hospitals.[5]

The filmmakers describe their film as an embedded film (they were embedded with the paramedics) and a collaborative film, citing the contributions of the Palestinian Red Crescent Society and Health Worker Committee as well as others involved locally and internationally. The film's collaborative element is extended by its Creative Commons licence.[6]

The film is truly a new documentary form. It occupies a shared space between what documentary has been for the first century of its existence and what documentary films

▶

are becoming. The film uses traditional and digital channels for distribution (it is pos-sible to obtain the film by purchasing the DVD, emailing the production team, or down-loading the stream). There is also a website that is used not only to promote the film but also to help raise funds, as it affords visitors a chance to make a donation at the *To Shoot An Elephant* website.[7]

The piece has been featured at a number of film festivals and its form and content have provoked a range of strong reactions. It has received numerous accolades, includ-ing the award for 'Most Innovative Filmmaker' at Florence's Festival dei Popoli. The voting committee had this to say,

> After we watched this film we engaged in a long passionate discussion. This film never left us. We want to award the filmmakers for sharing with us an emotional, physical and stressful experience, for being there and witnessing the horrors and destruction of the siege imposed on the Gaza Strip earlier this year.
> (taken from http://creativecommons.org/weblog/entry/19263 Accessed on 15 May 2010)

Tribe and crowd funding

One increasingly common use of the internet for many contemporary filmmakers is as a space to raise funding. No chapter on the internet and documentary film would be complete with mentioning online film finance. In the twenty-first century, filmmakers are increasingly using online spaces and social practices to take part in activities referred to as tribe- and crowd-funding. Networks of filmmakers, funders and other interested individuals use these often cool or innovative spaces to get projects off the ground and through production and post-production.

A few of the sites that received attention at the time of writing were those directed at filmmakers and funders and include: Biracy, IndieGoGo, Kickstarter and Massify.[8]

Practicalities

While it is important to consider how the internet and other technologies change the way your film is made and viewed, you must also engage with the practical side of things. To produce a step-by-step guide to preparing your film and additional related materials for online publication and/or distribution would be to print something that was out-of-date before you even read these words. However, there are questions you can (and should) ask as a filmmaker and certain tactics you can employ when putting your film out into a wider/digital world.

Putting your film on the web

There are many places to put your film on the internet and, at the time of writing, 4Docs was one of the best resources for documentary filmmakers.[9] You may also choose to put your film up on websites such as YouTube (one of the most popular sites for video on the internet), or Vimeo (a site often preferred by filmmakers for the increased control you gain over your layout and video quality). One of the advantages of placing your film (or even just a trailer or other part of it) on sites such as those mentioned above is that they often take into account the range of formats required for the main devices from which people may view the web.[10]

Digital distribution

In addition to posting your film on websites such as 4Docs, YouTube and others, you may wish to distribute it in other ways, whether traditional or novel. Designing, producing and shipping your film all over the world can be fun and can also be very expensive. There are, however, a number of digital download services for films today. You should take time to explore the ones most relevant for you and your intended audience. You will want to take note of the costs, formats and benefits of these services.

Your website

Do you have a personal website? Is it up-to-date? Some filmmakers have personal websites where they feature all or some of their project in development. Will you do so and, if so, have you planned and incorporated times for updating the site into your overall production plan? Will there be a specific site dedicated to your film? If so, have you considered the cost and time of building and maintaining such a site?[11]

Getting attention

Once your film, or some part of it, is online, you will want people to be able to find it. You may even want to try to get the attention of as many people as possible. When trying to attract web traffic to your site, you must remember two key rules. First, nobody likes spam. It is fine to use your website and social networks to promote your film. Unsolicited emails and comments, however, are considered spam and are highly unwelcome. If you plan to pay someone to promote your film or your site, ask about the practices employed and about how they avoid spamming people while promoting films. Secondly, there are some things that truly do help people find your site. One school of thought is that you might employ search engine optimisation (SEO) tactics to make your site and its content as accessible as possible to search engines such as Google. It is worth spending some time exploring ways of optimising your content for the web (you might even try typing the phrases 'optimising web content' and 'SEO' into an internet search engine).

Once you've got the attention of viewers, you may want to know who is visiting your site and where they come from. There are a number of ways to track that kind of information. One of the most common at the time of writing this chapter is the use of Google Analytics to keep track of traffic to your site. Useful information such as what pages are most/least visited can be obtained, as well as details about the areas of the world your visitors come from.

Key points

- The media landscape continually evolves. As a filmmaker, it is important to ask how these changes impact your own production process.
- Increased user interaction with films online, on mobile phones and elsewhere leads to increased expectations of participation by those users. It is important to consider, from the outset, the nature and level of interaction you hope your viewers/audience will have with your film.
- Planning an interactive narrative should include the creation of a nodal or star map to show connections or pathways through your project.

▶

- The internet and new technologies that follow will change the way that films are made and seen. The important question to ask is: How can you use new technologies to expand your own filmmaking and your film audience?
- It is important to distinguish between simply putting your documentary online and making an internet documentary.
- Mobile media and social networks continue to change the way films get made and seen. It is important to look out for new and novel events such as the citizen journalism events in 2009 and the rise of crowd-funding for films.
- When putting your film online, think twice about where you will put it and at what point in your overall production timeline.
- Make time to plan for updating material online and investigate ways to save time and money by using online film distribution channels.

Exercise

The task

Consider the various ways digital technologies might affect your film and ask yourself the following questions.

1. What is the structure of your film? Draw out a map for a non-linear narrative, using a nodal or star map to illustrate key moments or connections within the story.
2. How will you use the internet and other technology to create your film? Will you use a blog or other website to document the making of your film? Will you create or use a structure to facilitate user engagement with your film through comments, mash-ups or other interactions?
3. How will you use the internet to promote and distribute your film? Will it be a place where you promote your film by making a website or publishing it on another site for distribution?
4. Will you use the internet to archive your film in some way? Will you post it to YouTube or Facebook or some other site? Will you create multiple formats so that your film can be seen on a number of internet-enabled devices?
5. How can users interact with your film? Will you make the film available for reuse? Will you publish supporting images or other materials for your audience to use?
6. As always, with changing technologies come new expectations. Can you think of a new or novel way to use the internet or other digital media to grow the audience of your film?

Notes

[1] The twenty-first century has seen an increase in the production of video essays as film criticism. In producing such essays, filmmakers and scholars create videos containing scenes from an original film and a range of elements such as images, sound, text and voice-over that relate to a particular critical question about that film. Catherine Grant's 'Unsentimental Education' is an example of this kind of video essay and it can be found online at: http://filmstudiesforfree.blogspot.com/ (accessed on 10 May 2010).

[2] According to Meadows, during observation, the viewer/user makes an assessment. During exploration, they do something. At the point of modification, the viewer/user changes the system and then reciprocal change occurs as the system tries to change the viewer/user. Taken from his book, *Pause & Effect: The Art of Interactive Narrative* (Peachpit, 2003).

[3] As a filmmaker, you might consider your film as a constellation of ideas and materials. In addition to the film itself, you will often be asked to participate in the creation of images, texts, sounds and other materials for the internet and other contexts. Increasingly, film and television projects are linked to web-based and mobile content such as games, comics and other materials.

[4] Jenkins publishes and comments on an article about the transmedia generation on his website. The article is useful both for the way that it addresses international engagement with digital film and for the references it makes to other filmic and internet developments of relevance to you as a filmmaker: http://henryjenkins.org/2010/03/transmedia_generation.html (accessed on 12 May 2010).

[5] http://toshootanelephant.com/ (accessed on 15 May 2010).

[6] *To Shoot an Elephant* begins with a Creative Commons statement:
'This work has been registered under a Creative Commons license.
You are free to download, redistribute, translate
And build upon this work non-commercially,
As long as you credit it,
And license your new creation under identical terms.
So any derivatives will also be non-commercial in nature.
PROTECTING CREATIVITY THROUGH SHARING.'

[7] The film's title comes from an essay by George Orwell: 'Shooting an elephant', originally published in *New Writing* in 1948:

'. . . afterwards, of course, there were endless discussions about the shooting of the elephant. The owner was furious, but he was only an Indian and could do nothing. Besides, legally I had done the right thing, for a mad elephant has to be killed, like a mad dog, if its owner fails to control it.'

George Orwell defined a way of witnessing Asia that still remains valid. The project's website frames the film with the following information provided by the director: To shoot an elephant is an eyewitness account from the Gaza Strip. December 27th, 2008, Operation Cast Lead. 21 days shooting elephants. Urgent, insomniac, dirty, shuddering images from the only foreigners who decided and managed to stay embedded inside Gaza Strip ambulances, with Palestinian civilians.

[8] URLs for these sites can be found in the Further reading section at the end of this book.

[9] The UK's Channel 4 has produced a website called 4Docs that hosts a wide range of documentary films and related resources. In addition to films, there is a blog containing useful (and regularly updated) information about opportunities, resources and contemporary debates relevant to documentary filmmakers: http://www.4docs.org.uk/.

[10] At the time of writing, there was much debate about and movement from Flash video formats to HTML5 video formats. The latter allows video to be seen on popular devices such as certain mobile phones including the iPhone, and other computers that do not have (or choose not to use) Flash, such as the iPad. Both YouTube and Vimeo have taken steps to ensure that their catalogue of films is rendered in HTML5-friendly h.264 format (leaving you to worry about your film and not its format).

[11] There is ongoing debate about whether or not films should have dedicated websites. Often, sites developed only for a specific film become quickly dated and often forgotten. It is important to consider the time and resources you can contribute to maintaining a website for an individual film. Nothing is worse than an outdated website containing information about a 'New film! Coming soon in 2002'.

Part 4

Production
strategies

Enid Briggs (1898–1973) one of the first female filmmakers
(see Against the Tide, www.tide.org.uk)

Chapter 14

A good waltz or a nasty tango: individual qualities of the 'total' filmmaker and teamwork

Wilma de Jong

Introduction

This chapter will address the basic skills necessary to work as a 'total' filmmaker as well as what it means to work in a group or a team and the nature of group work.

The 'total' filmmaker

The filmmaker who works on their own or with just a few other professionals, such as a producer or an editor, has become one of the most prevalent features of the present media landscape. The key words for the 'total' filmmaker appear to be: *multi-skilled, multi-talented* and, above all, *driven* and *persistent*. The last of these seems essential. Documentary filmmakers tend to believe strongly in their film projects. There is an urge or a strong belief that the film needs to be made. And this will help them to jump all kinds of hurdles to achieve their goal. On the other hand, pure nosiness or simply being intrigued by people's lives or why they make certain decisions is also a motivating factor. Whatever underpins the desire to make a film, it needs to be a strong emotion, a strong drive, a passion that signifies the 'total' filmmaker.

Negotiating skills are also necessary. Imagine negotiating with people to obtain access to a location, with broadcasters to obtain a broadcast guarantee, with accountants, with solicitors or, above all, with your subjects. It is obvious, too, that good people skills, and good communication skills, are essential for a documentary filmmaker. Somehow you must be able to convince people to co-operate, to trust that their ideas, feelings and experiences will reach the screen in a 'truthful' and recognisable way.

An ethically sound approach is of high value in contemporary documentary filmmaking as interviewees or the general audience have become more aware of possible 'manipulations' by the media. More than ever, the burden of being truthful has become the responsibility of the documentary filmmaker.

Being *multi-skilled* implies having creative, social, analytical, negotiating and technical skills. This may sound complex and demanding but many of us have these skills. In this sense documentary filming has become closer to the position of painters, who combine artistic vision and technical skills with the business skills needed to negotiate with galleries and museums.

However, in an educational context, and for bigger films, production teams are a reality and this might well be your experience at the start of your career. The following paragraphs will give you basic tools to analyse group processes and provide awareness of how a group can work efficiently and co-operatively.

Working in a team or group

There is an art to being a successful member of a group. It can be quite a different process from individual study at a university or in any other form of education.

Joe Lister is a web developer and works for internet development companies and for the marketing divisions of large media companies:

'I've always worked in large companies, or medium to large web design or multimedia companies and it is always team-based. As the technology has become more and more complicated, it has become almost impossible for one person to make a website all on their own. You need lots of different and complementary skills.'

(Dewdney and Ride, 2006: 121)

In media production, the ability to work well as part of a team is essential. Most bigger media projects are produced by a team of people with specialised skills and knowledge. You might be responsible for one specific part of the project, but all information will ultimately be referred back to a team that will digest it and take decisions on how to proceed.

Being part of a team involves learning interpersonal skills, such as speaking, listening, negotiating, as well as leadership, the art of managing a project and working with and motivating others. It is also an opportunity to learn more about your personal strengths and weaknesses, such as being too dominant, or being too reserved. Working in a team represents a steep learning curve for most students and starting filmmakers.

Group dynamics

Groups tend to go through different stages during their lifetime. The literature describes the following stages:

First stage: the start

Forming: the group works well, all members are polite and co-operative.

Second stage

Storming: the first cracks in unity appear. Disagreements and even conflicts arise. Depending on the skills of the team members, this stage can be very short. It is important to focus on the task and not be tempted to stop communicating or to let the group get out of control.

Third stage

Norming: the group focuses on its task and follows its ground rules. Members find their place and contribute accordingly. This is an important stage because members need to find a common way of operating but, if the 'norming' becomes too strong, creativity might be stifled. 'Group think' may occur in this stage.

Fourth stage

Performing: the group works dynamically together, and differences are accepted and channelled through working procedures. Members operate independently and co-operatively towards the realisation of the film project.

Fifth stage

Adjourning or mourning: the group completes its task and is proud of its achievements but has not dismantled the team. Sometimes euphoria occurs and members promise to work together on other projects, which may or may not happen. In retrospect, good and bad experiences are evaluated and can lead to life-long partnerships!

It is important for filmmakers to keep these different stages in mind in order to be able to deal with conflicts and serious arguments. The 'conflictual' (Storming) stage is part of normal group development, and research has shown that actually a bit of 'storming' will take place at many stages. Awareness of these processes helps you to put certain events in perspective and not to interpret certain incidents as due to your own or someone else's mistakes. Try to avoid 'blaming' people as it undermines those concerned and the group process.

However, in many cases there might be a producer or director who calls the shots, which will affect the group process in a different way. Most producers/directors will listen to different kinds of contribution but in the end they take the decisions.

Forming production groups in education

Groups are formed in different ways. This is a much-debated issue as some tutors prefer students to choose their own groups, while others insist on randomly chosen groups or those based on the common interests of students.

Randomly chosen groups

The most random way to form groups is for the tutor to give all students a number – 1, 2 or 3 – students with the same number are a production group. It is often argued that in the industry one cannot choose one's colleagues; on the other hand, conflicting interests and commitments might distort the production process.

Students select themselves

In this case one or two students select the rest of the group. Most of the time they will choose the most useful/popular members first, while the rest of the students are waiting to be selected. This can be a confidence-sapping experience for many students.

Based on the topic

This is often a fair way to form a production group. Based on the assignment and the different topics of the film, students decide which production group they will join. This way students join the groups they are interested in – either because of the topic or because of the people in the group.

Different cultural backgrounds

As many international students study at British universities, it is highly likely that a production group will consist of people from different cultural backgrounds and nationalities. This will affect both the group process and communication, as cultural differences and different educational backgrounds may lead to communication problems.

Going out for an informal meal, or meeting at home to get to know each other better is often an effective way to engage with each other. Discussing favourite films/music or books is an opportunity to illustrate the different cultural references you are all using.

Some cultures observe very different notions of politeness in communications. Looking someone in the eye when talking may not be common to all cultures, and there might be different protocols surrounding agreeing and disagreeing. In the UK, discussion-based learning seems to predominate. Some foreign students will need time to familiarise themselves with this style of learning, as many may come from a background of more teacher-led forms of education. It is good practice to note these differences as part of the preliminary meetings. They should become an issue which can be openly discussed and may even be the subject of jokes.

As documentary filmmakers, we should be able to find ways to work within different cultural contexts and with people from different cultural backgrounds. After all, our job and interests are deeply related to issues of 'difference', otherness and different social cultural traditions.

To agree a way of working as a group will help you to find common ground and focus on the task, which should facilitate the group process.

Ground rules

Ground rules are important in any group/team and in the first instance three aspects of your production team should be discussed:

1. How the group should operate.
2. Clarification of the task in hand and time planning.
3. Availability, interests and experiences of individual members.

How should the group operate?

The issue of how to operate as a team needs serious attention. Most teams rarely have conflicts about the task in hand; they generally tend to be about how the group is operating – for instance, members not doing their work or punctuality issues.

Formulating ground rules will help you to find a way of working together. Examples of common ground rules are:

- Members should attend all meetings or send apologies by email, text or phone.
- The work should be shared fairly between team members.
- Members should encourage everyone to contribute.
- Individual tasks should be completed by agreed deadlines. If problems occur with a task between meetings, members should be informed by email, phone or text.
- Members should check their email or phone messages every day.
- Responsibility for chairing meetings and taking notes should be rotated or allocated as a task to specific members.
- Before the end of each meeting, the time and place of the next meeting should be arranged.

Each production team can add rules according to the nature of their team or their project. The most important issue here is that all members agree on the ground rules. It should be considered a signal of good intentions to contribute to the production process of the film project.

Meetings

Regular meetings are essential to check the progress of the project and share information and ideas about the content of the project. Email or texting cannot replace face-to-face communication. Electronic communication should be used as a tool for quick updates or urgent messaging. Brainstorming, taking decisions and planning the project should take place face-to-face.

Avoid forming subgroups and developing ideas for the film project of which the other group members are not aware. This will allow ideas to drift apart and conflicts to emerge.

Agenda

There are two ways to create an agenda for each meeting: an agreed agenda or an ad hoc agenda.

A quick brainstorm will lead to a simple list of agenda items which will provide all members with the opportunity to put their issues on the agenda.

The main issue is to have a structured approach to meetings so that there is a sense of purpose, but also to maintain a degree of flexibility so that any 'matters arising' can be addressed.

Minutes

It is important to record important decisions and actions. This will help to monitor progress and remind individual members of their tasks.

In difficult situations, the notetaker could regularly ask, 'What do you want me to write down? This will not only help the notetaker to write the minutes but it will help the group to formulate their decisions more clearly.

Communication between meetings

Email is a very efficient group communication tool but can cause problems. For example, it can be difficult to assume the right tone of voice when approaching unknown professionals and institutions and sometimes forget basic salutations. It is not advisable to approach the communications officer of a firm with 'Hi' . . . and end with 'Cheers' or 'Best'. Correct salutations are also essential in emails to friends or colleagues.

The golden rule in responding to a controversial email is not to press 'reply' on receipt, but to wait at least a few hours, or preferably until the next day, before you press the reply button. Maybe just a simple phone call to discuss the matter would be a better solution.

Texts are highly efficient for making appointments and short information messages but do not try to come to major decisions by texting.

Taking decisions

In a professional environment it will be the producer or director who will take the final decisions in relation to the film project. However, in an educational context there are two ways of taking decisions:

- consensus decision-making;
- majority decision-making.

Consensus decision-making is a sophisticated form of decision-making. It does not actually imply that you should all agree. That might be an ideal situation but in most situations different ideas and opinions will exist. Members of a group should ask themselves why they have different opinions from the rest of the team. A team member may not agree with the others but decide that the issue at stake is not important to her or him and go with the flow. The art of going with the flow is an important quality of being a group member in this form of decision-making.

If you find yourself on your own, ask yourself: 'Why do you think that other people should adopt your stance? Are you always right? Be aware of when to let go of an idea that is unpopular. Pushing your vision any further may lead to irritation. Consensus decision-making is like a good waltz that can turn into a nasty tango if you do not have the right attitude!

Consensus decision-making seems the most democratic method but it takes up a lot of time. If there is one person in a team who thinks they are always right then they may try to dictate the outcome of discussions.

(See www.seedsforchange.org.uk/free/consens and www.actupny.org/documents/CDocuments/ Consensus.html and the Wikipedia entry on consensus decision-making.)

The alternative, majority decision-making, does not imply that the minority can be ignored. Those who do not agree may sabotage further decision-making by being obstinate and trying to prove that they were right to disagree. Instead, respect the opinion of the minority and explain why the majority choice would work better for this project. The metaphor of dancing is also appropriate here: dancing is about creating a flow together, but still being able to make clear steps and lead.

The task

Start every production team meeting by reading the assignment carefully so that all members agree what kind of project is to be expected at the end. In case of lack of clarity, ask the tutor for clarification or further information. Write down in your own words the required characteristics of the project that is to be produced. It is surprising how often students start their work before fully getting to grips with the assignment.

Planning your project

Take an A4 piece of paper and draw a timeline for your project. In the case of a media project, it is best to start with the deadline when it has to be submitted and work backwards. Use the following categories as a guideline:

- research script
- pre-production
- production
- post-production
- rough cut
- final cut
- date of submission.

When you have planning to do, fill in the different tasks that need to be done and the time they will take.

Allocating tasks

You need to allocate tasks, according to the stage of the production.

In the first stage of research you may want to keep the roles open and divide them up according to interest or experience. Distinguish tasks that need to be done simultaneously or in parallel with others, from those that can only take place when other tasks are completed.

Later in the production process you may want to divide up the tasks according to specific production roles. Some groups may be resistant to the idea of identifying different functional roles and allocating them to specific people. However, your group is likely to be much more effective if you do so.

Having someone who retains an overall vision of the project, and thinks of how to enable everyone to contribute most creatively, can be of great benefit. It will avoid stress and conflict if the planning allows for some flexibility and the possibility that something may go wrong. Thinking ahead and planning are essential but it is a waste of time for all team members to do so on behalf of the entire group.

Individual members

People take different roles in teams not just according to their own personalities but also to the needs of the group. You may find that in one group you are an organiser, while in other groups you have a listening and reflective role and summarise what is going on regularly.

Meredith Belbin is a well-known researcher who describes the different roles people take up in groups in his book *Team roles at work* (2002). These are outlined at the end of this chapter.

Problems in the group

Groups often experience problems. Some are practical or technical. Others involve the maintenance of the team. The problems may not be easy to identify or solve, but they should be tackled rather than ignored. Ask for help from your tutor if you need it, but remember that learning to solve problems, which will inevitably arise, is one of the major aspects of this type of work. The most common group/team problems and how you can address them are covered below.

- **One member does not pull his/her weight** – The so-called 'free rider' or 'freeloader' is one of the most common problems which lead to frustration and even the anger of other members who work hard to get the work done.

  Very often a member takes on a task but does not deliver. When this problem has been identified, it is important not to address the issue at a production meeting as this will make the 'free rider' feel under attack. There might be understandable reasons why this imbalance has occurred. Some members may meet each other regularly during the week, so the project moves on without others realising it. The best solution might be for someone to discuss the issue with the person in a separate meeting and try to find out what is going on. There might be no malicious reasons at all. The group member involved might feel that their task is too difficult or too big compared with what has been allocated to others. Or personal circumstances may have prevented them from performing the task.

  Addressing this kind of issue requires good communication skills. Ask open questions or express your own feelings, but above all do not accuse. Do not start with: 'I think you are not pulling your weight.' You will meet a defensive attitude which will quite likely make the situation worse. It is better to ask an open question, such as: 'How is the . . . task going?' A constructive approach is best in these situations. Ask what can be done to help the person do the task.

  In the case where someone deliberately takes advantage of the work of others, you may wish to inform your tutors. It is very difficult for students to discuss this matter with other students.

- **Two or three members of the group are doing all the work and others feel excluded** – Some members might be more experienced or have become so enthusiastic that they get carried away and forget the others. If you feel excluded, it is important to raise this point at a meeting. Again, do not blame or accuse but say that you do not feel involved and ask whether there is a way this could be resolved. The allocation of tasks may need to be reconsidered. Maybe the more enthusiastic members should report more frequently on their progress so that everyone in the group knows what is going on. Perhaps the person who felt excluded could take on more responsibilities later on in the production process. Remember, a good group has happy members who feel valued and appreciated. Empathy for the position of other members is as important as doing your own job in a group.

- **Dominant members** – We all know them – the persuasive talkers, the confidence-exuding members who present their arguments with enthusiasm but ignore other visions and ideas. In the first instance, try to solve the issue of domineering members at the level of the management of meetings by organising rounds in which all members can express their opinions and ideas. The chair should try to find which ideas are common to all members of the group and which are not.

- **Working with someone you do not like** – You may not like someone or you may feel that someone does not like you. Do realise that you 'work' together, you are 'colleagues'; you do not have to be friends. A professional attitude, such as focusing on your tasks and on the project, may help you work together. Often we change our minds about people when we get to know them better. One last thing: although it may seem easier to be friends with those we work with, in times of problems it might actually make the situation more complicated. Basically, you need to aim for good working relationships.

Although we focus in the book on documentary filmmakers who film on their own or work with only one or two other media professionals, you can find an in-depth overview of professional production roles in Chapter 16.

Exercises

Exercise 1 (Individual exercise)

Read Belbin's description of team roles in Table 14.1.

Do you recognise your own role or the different roles you have taken on in group work?

Table 14.1 Belbin's team-role descriptions

Team role	Contribution	Allowable weakness
Plant	Creative, imaginative, unorthodox. Solves difficult problems.	Ignores incidentals. Too occupied to communicate effectively.
Resource investigator	Extrovert, enthusiastic, communicative. Explores opportunities. Develops contacts.	Over-optimistic. Loses interest once initial enthusiasm has passed.
Co-ordinator	Mature, confident, a good chairperson. Clarifies goals, promotes decision-making, delegates well.	Can be seen as manipulative. Offloads personal work.
Shaper	Challenging, dynamic, thrives on pressure. Has the drive and courage to overcome obstacles.	Prone to provocation.
Monitor evaluator	Sober, strategic and discerning. Sees all options. Judges accurately.	Lacks drive and ability to inspire others.
Team worker	Co-operative, mild, perceptive and diplomatic. Listens, builds, averts friction.	Indecisive in crunch situations.
Implementer	Disciplined, reliable, conservative and efficient. Turns ideas into practical actions.	Somewhat inflexible. Slow to respond to new possibilities.
Completer finisher	Painstaking, conscientious, anxious. Searches out errors and omissions. Delivers on time.	Inclined to worry unduly. Reluctant to delegate.
Specialist	Single-minded, self-starting, dedicated. Provides knowledge and skills in short supply.	Contributes on only a narrow front. Dwells on technicalities.

(www.belbin.com)

▶

Exercise 2 (At the start of a group project)

This exercise works well at the start of a group project as all members have the chance to explain their experiences and the openness will enhance the group process.

Everyone gets 5 minutes to write down answers to the following two questions.

- Describe your negative and positive experiences of working in a group.

- What do you think is important to make a group/team run as smoothly as possible?

The next step is to discuss both questions and at the end draw conclusions that inform your operations as a team/group.

Exercise 3

This explores cultural differences in agreeing and disagreeing in a group discussion.

All members are requested to describe the different ways of saying 'Yes' and 'No' in their culture, country or class. Do realise that these differences exist not only between different countries but also between different parts of the UK or different social classes.

The aim of this discussion is for all members to be aware of differences in styles of communication. Listening and asking questions might prevent people jumping to conclusions or help to avoid misunderstandings.

Chapter 15

Producing
Jerry Rothwell

" The producer's role is to
be an alchemist – to bring
together the elements of a
project and support them into
a magical reaction. "

(Anna Higgs, interview)

Introduction

In this chapter we look at the role of the documentary producer – the skills it involves and the methods that successful producers use to develop and fund film ideas, to ensure that the best film possible is made and that it reaches audiences. The chapter also explores some of the producer's legal and financial obligations and how small independent production companies can survive and thrive.

The role of the producer

The word 'producer' covers a very wide range of film production activities across fiction, documentary, animation and interactive, and different producers engage with their projects in different ways. All are focused on broadly the same aim – to bring a film idea successfully to the screen – but, just as in an organisation, different styles of management can realise that aim.

In the public imagination – based, perhaps, on our image of Hollywood – the producer's primary focus is money. Producers are typically seen as mercurial figures – ducking and diving and exploiting their way to personal riches and power over the creative process as they build a studio empire. It's not a helpful role model for those who want to produce documentaries. In documentary, producers tend to have a detailed involvement at all stages of production – way beyond that of most fiction producers – ranging from very hands-on organisation to relationships with contributors to distribution. The financial rewards won't usually buy you a poolside lifestyle.

Frequently, the documentary producer and director are the same person: the 'producer-director' who perhaps works to a much more hands-off 'executive producer' within a production company, or even completely on their own as an independent filmmaker. Here we treat producing and directing as separate roles, as though done by two different people. Whether done by the same person or not, it is a useful conceptual separation. Producing and directing are fundamentally different kinds of activity. Whereas the director needs to be immersed in the detail of a creative process, in imagining and then realising a vision of the film, the producer is engaged in a strategic and organisational set of goals and tasks, driven by the pragmatic aim of getting that film to the screen. These very different mindsets do not always sit well together. Total focus on the creative needs of the film can lead to neglect of the strategic development of the project; and the logic of management and administration sometimes needs to be set aside to develop the best creative ideas. So splitting these tasks between different members of a team is often the best and most efficient way forward.

The producer's role is to bring to a film idea all the elements it needs to reach an audience. This will include:

- developing the idea with the director;
- anticipating the key audiences for the film;
- seeking funding;
- creating a budget and schedule;
- working with the director to appoint key crew members;
- overseeing all contracts required for the production (with crew, contributors and financiers);
- managing the financial and organisational aspects of the production;
- reviewing the creative progress of the film, including rough edits;
- ongoing negotiations with financiers – the producer often acts as a bridge between the vision of the director/filmmaking and the needs of the commissioner/financier;

- overseeing delivery and legal and compliance issues;
- overseeing distribution and any financial issues after the film's production (for example, sales, tax credits and dealing with the share of any revenues from the film).

These jobs encompass a wide range of skills. Successful producers tend to be strategic thinkers, good negotiators, excellent at distilling ideas and communicating them, adept at networking and quick to see the financial implications of decisions. Most are motivated by the challenge of getting certain kinds of work on the screen, but are less interested in the nuts and bolts of filmmaking craft.

Ideas

Successful producing begins with a strong sense of what makes a good film idea. Like directors, producers will be attracted towards certain kinds of film according to personal taste, aesthetic judgement, political motivation and business potential. A producer is, perhaps, also more likely to be thinking about the film's audience from the beginning. Producer Anna Higgs (whose edited interview is included at the end of this chapter) comments that:

> As a producer, you've got to look at things practically as well as creatively. On the practical side, you need to do the research – has anyone covered this world already? Is there a key event to tie in a pitch to? Can we prove a hunger or impact for this sort of story? Creatively, it's about how the story will be told. Whose point of view will we see it from? What sort of length and format does the story need to best support the aims of the film? Then the balancing act: are we able to do what we want creatively for the budget we'd likely be able to raise?
>
> (Anna Higgs, interview)

In selecting ideas, most producers look for three essential components:

- a strong story or concept (see Chapter 6);
- a creative team that is able to deliver on the full potential of the idea;
- a range of likely funders (broadcasters, social funders, arts funders, investors, etc.) to match the probable cost of the film, given its content, format and intended audience.

For many producers, the challenge of bringing together these different elements is what motivates them. Producer Julie Goldman of Cactus Three explains:

> It's exciting when someone comes to you and tells you, 'Look, this is what I want to do.' It's a blank slate; that's where you get to begin. We love that. The idea of how we're going to help create something out of nothing and support that effort from inception to completion – just that concept alone is what makes it exciting and challenging. It's actually the best part of it for us. It starts with the question: What do we need to do to get this from right here to distribution, to getting it seen? I love clean slates.
>
> (Julie Goldman, interview[1])

Knowing the documentary landscape

The producer will quickly need to have a sense of where, in the current funding climate, the film might find its first backers. As funds for documentary production become increasingly split across different financiers, funding bodies and distribution platforms, it is essential for documentary producers to develop a good understanding of the fast-changing landscape of opportunities available to them. Currently, few single documentaries are made with the backing of just one funder, and more usually the producer needs to put together a budget from a patch-work of different sources. So today's producer needs more than ever to gain a comprehensive and up-to-date knowledge of documentary opportunities.

There are various ways to do this:

- **Watch documentaries** similar to the films you are interested in and look at credits and film websites to find out who the financiers are. Explore what else they have funded, what they think has been successful and what their latest programme of work is. Most broadcasters have sections of their websites aimed at producers, where commissioning editors specify their current slots, needs, interests and how best to approach them. Most trusts and foundations that fund documentary also have detailed 'How to apply' information online, giving current projects and funding programmes.

- **Go to workshops and events** aimed at producers. Many organisations run short courses and events, a lot of them free of charge, which are ideal to learn about new developments in documentary finance and distribution. You'll also have a chance to share ideas and strategies with other producers. There are many longer courses which enable new producers to work with experienced producers and financiers on a particular idea, such as Discovery Campus, ESoDoc and EAVE.

- **Attend festivals and forums.** Documentary festivals combine screenings of the latest docu-mentary releases with networking events, pitching events and market meetings. Many of the pitching events allow observers and are a good opportunity to hear the major broadcasting commissioners giving feedback on new ideas and revealing their current priorities. Festivals are a means of continuing your own professional development as a producer – and you may be able to obtain funding to attend them from local screen agencies or industry training bodies such as Skillset.

- **Join the mailing lists of major documentary community websites**, which give regular updates on funding and training opportunities, projects in development, and festivals. Examples are: www.reelisor.com, www.britdoc.org, www.shootingpeople.org.

- **Use social media.** Sites like Facebook and Ning have hundreds of groups given over to news about documentary production and specific films. As well as being an important tool to publicise your film and build a community around it, they also act as a useful source of information about funding, festivals and distribution.

- **Join industry associations.** Much of this information is also gathered and disseminated by the major documentary member organisations, such as the European Documentary Network, and producer associations, such as PACT. These usually charge for membership but also offer other services such as legal advice.

Given all these different sources of information available on the internet, it is more important than ever to be strategic about the development of an idea. It is better to make a few well-thought-out approaches and applications than a lot of hurried ones. The competition for fund-ing is extremely high – currently there are far more documentary ideas and proposals being developed than there are funds or broadcasting slots to make them. Talk to more experienced producers about what opportunities are best for your film.

Finally, know when you need to get on and start making the film. Most independent docu-mentary filmmakers start shooting their films without knowing whether they have full finance – and work for little or no money until they have enough material to make a strong case for the film.

As Nick Francis, co-producer and co-director of *Black Gold*, advises:

In 2003, when the humanitarian crisis in the coffee farming areas of Ethiopia was reaching a peak, we couldn't hang around and wait for commissioning editors at television stations to turn round and say, 'This is an idea you should run with.' Because we owned our own equipment, we just put our own resources in, and went out there and started telling the story. . . . [My advice would be] to get on and do it, not thinking too much, just believing in your idea and getting on with it.

(Nick Francis, interview[2])

Independent production companies

Once documentary filmmakers start to approach funders, they usually need to be working within a production company. Most documentary financiers are only be able to release money to and enter into a contract with an organisation with a formal legal structure, which gives the financial and legal accountability they need if things go wrong.

Embarking on your first project which requires a substantial budget, you are faced with a choice, as a new filmmaker: whether to set up your own company, or to work with and through an existing 'indie' (independent production company). It's therefore important to understand the world of independent production companies so you can make an informed choice about the alliances you may need to make.

A brief history of the independent production sector in the UK

Prior to the 1980s, most documentary production in the UK was undertaken either by the two main broadcasters – BBC and ITV – or, in the case of industrial, campaigning and non-broadcast documentary, by freelancers or even documentary units for large public or private organisations (for example, the GPO film unit, the Central Office of Information or the industrial film units of multinational companies). Within broadcast, there were few opportunities for independent companies because of the dominance of in-house production at the major channels. The creation of Channel 4 in 1982 transformed this production landscape, because the terms of its charter set out by the Conservative government included that it should source virtually all of its programming from external companies. This led many documentary producers and directors who had hitherto been employed by the BBC or the ITV companies to leave and set up their own independent companies.

The model pioneered by Channel 4 was one where the broadcaster became a publisher rather than a producer – a quite new formation in British television and one that has had a lasting effect on the make-up of the film and television industry in the UK. Its immediate impact was to stimulate the creation of a multitude of micro companies, based around individual filmmaking talent. By 1986–7, Channel 4 was buying programmes from 360 different companies, two-thirds of which only produced a single programme for the channel in that year (Mediatique, 2005). By 1993, ten years after Channel 4's launch, there were more than a thousand independent production companies in the UK.

Many of these media microbusinesses continue to exist. Often they have been created solely to support the work of one or two filmmakers, have no plans for growth other than around these filmmakers' individual career development and would cease to exist if and when those individuals stop making films. These so-called 'talent-based' companies have proved to be a viable model for production in the short term, but have some significant disadvantages from a business perspective. They tend to have little time or capital (or perhaps desire) for company development, often become dependent on a few relationships with key funders, and are very vulnerable to any changes in funding priorities and personnel. Usually these companies reach a point where they must make a decision whether to try to grow a larger and more viable business or continue a somewhat unstable hand-to-mouth existence, but one which has some compensations in the freedom it gives to the individuals involved to make the films they feel most passionate about.

Setting up a production company requires little investment – but surviving and growing is much harder. In the 1980s, most of these companies frequently gave up all rights in their programmes to the broadcaster who first commissioned them. But they were helped by the 1990 Broadcasting Act, which created a 25% quota for programmes to be sourced from 'indies' from the major broadcasters. In 2003, the new Communications Act changed the terms of trade between broadcasters and programme makers, so that production companies could retain rights to exploit their programmes across other platforms and in other territories – providing important new sources of revenue as multi-channel TV, mobile and merchandising proliferated. In 2009, the BBC extended its quota of indie-produced programmes to 50% of its original programming budget.

These legal changes have led to a consolidation of the independent production sector in the UK over the last decade. The number of independent companies has contracted to about 800 and a pattern has emerged consisting of three tiers of company, as identified by media research agency, Mediatique (2008):

- The 'super indies' – perhaps no more than 15 large bulk suppliers, with revenues of tens or even hundreds of millions of pounds a year, who have grown by acquiring successful smaller companies and becoming the 'preferred providers' of the major broadcasters, integrating a number of subsidiaries from different stages in the media production chain – for example, including post-production facility houses and distribution companies. They make few single documentaries because of the low financial returns, and so their factual production will be focused on returning formats and series that can build audiences across different platforms and be sold internationally. Current examples of this scale of company are All3Media, RDF Media, Endemol.

- The medium-sized companies, described by Mediatique as 'the mid bulge', whose main income is from regular programmes for broadcast television. These are often companies that started as 'talent-based' and have grown usually to specialise in particular kinds of production, but have not diversified into, say, large-scale post-production and distribution. They are big enough to have solid relationships with broadcast commissioners, but are almost entirely reliant on broadcast commissions for revenues. They are important possible partners for documentary makers, because of their status with commissioning editors, who trust them to produce quality programming.

- The microbusinesses – a very long tail of small companies, often focused on a niche style of programme and particular talent, often consisting of two or three individual programme makers. They are not strongly positioned to negotiate on rights and may need to co-produce on more ambitious ideas.

For filmmakers with new ideas but little experience, the choice of what company to work with to produce their work comes down to the following options.

- Setting up and working through their own microbusiness. At least initially, this is likely to have less clout with broadcasters or funders and so adds little to its potential, but gives total control over the production.

- Taking the idea to one of the large 'super indies', who are likely to want to develop it into something more formatted so that it can be sold across different platforms and territories. If you have an idea for a large-scale, documentary format, this may be the best chance you have of seeing it realised. If you have an independent single documentary, it's unlikely to be of interest.

- Working under an 'umbrella' or co-production agreement with a mid-sized company. This might involve ceding control over the funding of the project and recognising that the larger partner will have the primary relationship with the financier (and that often that relationship may be more important to them than their relationship with you). But it may also radically increase the chances of your film being made. Broadcasters often need the comfort of larger companies to mitigate the risk of working with new talent.

For the filmmaker, building successful partnerships with larger companies and more experienced producers requires finding relationships which you can trust, where you feel there is a good understanding of the idea and your vision for it.

Choosing the team

A producer needs to start with the confidence that the director can make the idea into a quality film. They will need to become an advocate of the director's approach to the idea, so they need to believe in it themselves! The best way to understand the kind of film that a filmmaker is able to make is to look at their previous films. If there's no evidence of previous work of any quality, the producer is going to find it hard to persuade anyone to fund the film. Having made an excellent short film – of whatever length – will open up a much wider range of funders, and it is better to have a single film of very high quality (for example, one that has won awards at student or short film festivals) than a lot of average material.

Most directors want to choose their own creative and technical team. But the producer has an important role in selecting this team – and, in many cases, will want themselves to bring a team together which will support the film's case for funding. Anna Higgs, who has produced many first-time filmmakers, argues that:

> We look for other elements you can attach to the project to help the financiers feel more confident. As a young production company ourselves, we've sought mentors and 'big name' technical crew for projects, to balance new talent with safe sets of hands. For instance, we're producing a *Wonderland* for the BBC and it's the director's first hour for TV and so we've paired him with a BAFTA-winning editor who's worked on films like this for 20- or 30-odd years. The director's happy to be with someone so experienced and the commissioner knows the editor's work and so feels more confident too.
>
> (Anna Higgs, interview)

Working with the producer to select a team can also help the director be braver about their choices. There's a great temptation for new directors to work only with the people they know – friends, or those they have worked with before. The producer can encourage the director to look at a wider pool of talent – those who are perhaps more experienced or have proved they have exactly the right skills for a particular vision of the film.

Rights

The producer needs to anticipate the major copyright issues associated with an idea from the start of development. Any financier will need to know that the core rights are available to the filmmaker, and some documentary ideas, however great on paper, are unmakeable because it is impossible to secure all the rights needed.

In some cases, it is very clear what those rights are. Documentaries based substantially on books, for example, will need to show an option on the relevant film rights to the book. Recent well-known examples of this are *Touching The Void*; *Man on Wire*; *Enron: The Smartest Guys in the Room*; *The Shock Doctrine* and *The End of The Line*. But just because a book has been written about the subject of a film doesn't mean the filmmaker has to obtain book rights. Copyright protects the particular expression of an idea, not the underlying idea itself. So if your film is substantially based on the research or form of a book, you will need to obtain the rights. If it covers the same events, but is based principally on your own research, you may not need book rights.

Key to this is an understanding of what is or is not in the public domain. The justification for a public domain is summarised by Patterson and Lindberg (1991) as:

> There are certain materials – the air we breathe, sunlight, rain, ideas, words, numbers – not subject to private ownership. The materials that compose our cultural heritage must be free for all to use no less than matter necessary for biological survival.[3]

As well as including works which are no longer covered by copyright (for example because of their age) and the use of 'insubstantial' parts of a copyrighted work, the public domain also includes the right to portray 'real historical events' – so, for documentarians, copyright is not in the subject matter, but in the form of telling: an interview, a book, archive film, music, the form of a particular piece of research. If book rights are not required, the rights needed will be the contributors' consent to use their words, image and 'performance' on screen, the rights to use perhaps their personal archive footage and photographs, or archive from a library, the publishing and recording rights to any music in the film, and the rights to film in any private location.

If a documentary is heavily dependent on any of these rights, the producer must be able to show that they can obtain them when seeking finance.

The rights you need

The specific rights you obtain over the use of this content are going to determine what you can do with your film. Generally, rights have three parts to them:

territory – the countries in which the rights can be used

duration – the length of time they can be used for

media – the media through which the content can be distributed.

Ideally, the producer is looking to secure rights *in perpetuity* (i.e. for all time), *in all media* (i.e. for broadcast, DVD, video on demand, download, streaming, rental theatrical, non-theatrical screenings, etc. – the clause also usually includes 'all media not yet invented') and *throughout the world* (i.e. in all territories). This frees up the film made using those rights to be used in whatever way the producer chooses. Obtaining such comprehensive rights may be expensive, and rights holders will often reduce fees for a reduction in the time period, or the territory, or the use (for example, for non-broadcast, educational use only, or limiting the number of copies of a DVD). The danger of such compromises for a producer is that it is not always possible to predict how a film will be used and not having the full rights may prevent you from distributing it in the way you want.

A further question to consider is whether you need any exclusivity on your use of the rights – in other words, whether you want to prevent the rights holder from selling the same rights to anyone else as well. You need to balance an assessment of whether another film using the same rights released at the same time as your film will detrimentally affect your film, against the costs of exclusive rights (they are likely to be far more expensive). However, you may well want your key contributors to give exclusive consents to you, at least for the period of making and initial distribution of the film.

Such negotiations with the main contributors and rights holders are key to both producing and directing, with the producer taking a lead on financial and contractual issues and the director on creative and editorial issues. Whatever agreement is made, a continuing relationship of trust and communication, sometimes even of joint authorship, is essential. Simon Chinn, producer of *Man on Wire*, describes the process of securing the consent for the film's main protagonist, Philippe Petit, the tightrope walker who walked between the Twin Towers shortly after their construction:

I first came across Philippe on a famous BBC radio show called *Desert Island Discs* in April 2005. It was a combination of his extraordinary passion and utterly idiosyncratic view of the world that first caught my attention. Then I read his memoir, *To Reach the Clouds* . . . I pursued him with some tenacity – a quality he appreciates. He was pretty sceptical at first but I had the bit between my teeth and wouldn't let go. In the end, he relented! The key to getting him to entrust us with his story was to guarantee that we would involve him in the creative process and make it as much of a collaboration as we could. James [Marsh, the film's director] and Philippe hit it off immediately and they spent many hours together, over the course of many months, discussing the film . . . Philippe was a central creative collaborator in the process – he was brimming with ideas throughout the production and we embraced his best ones. In the end, though, we had to make the film we wanted to make and so there were some disagreements in the last stages of editing. But when the film was locked Philippe looked at it again and – even though it's not the film he would have made himself – gave it his blessing.

(Simon Chinn, interview[4])

Relationships and decisions

Working with the key rights holders is fraught with potential for misunderstandings, often caused by differing expectations. It's not infrequent that the end film isn't liked or supported by the main rights holder. The documentary *The Shock Doctrine*, based on Naomi Klein's book of the same title, didn't meet with the author's approval to the extent that she was quoted as having 'disowned' the film, asking to be removed from its credits.[5] This probably didn't help the film's distribution, but note that Winterbottom's right to make and release the film wasn't in question, because there was a clear prior agreement about rights use.

Relationships with contributors are just part of the network of alliances the producer needs to build for the film's success. We could show this as the producer being at the centre of a triangle (Figure 15.1) of rights holders, financiers and the creative team.

Each of these groups has a different perspective and sometimes different interests in the production. It is up to the producer to keep these in balance and focus them on the same objective – a vision for the finished film. The producer needs to create the space for the director to work at their best, know when to involve financiers in editorial decisions and when to allow the director to take the necessary creative risks which are crucial to make the best films.

Underpinning these relationships is a need for clarity of expectations for each of the different parties, and for legally binding contracts, which set out those expectations and can be used to arbitrate if things go wrong. Keeping the communication going between the different parties is essential.

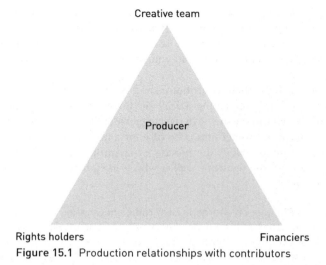

Figure 15.1 Production relationships with contributors

The producer and production management

Usually driven by events taking place in the outside world, the documentary production process is innately more fluid and unpredictable than most media production. Even in a retrospective story, the actual telling of the story unfolds in the present, almost always without a full script, with contributors who cannot always be scheduled and moved around according to the needs of the production, in the way that actors might be in a fiction film.

New technologies have facilitated this fluidity even further: reducing technical costs, allowing a more iterative process for shooting and editing, permitting high shooting ratios and requiring less planning in advance.

The traditional documentary production process aspired to a linear progression from initial concept to final edit (see Figure 15.2). This workflow largely holds for series production and more formatted documentary. For the independent single documentary, however, the workflow is necessarily less of a stepped progression. This is in part because the process of gathering support and funding for the film will need to persuade more than a single financier. This both takes longer and requires more finely produced sample material as 'proof of concept'. So today's documentary maker may well be filming and editing prior to finance and full legal consents. They may shoot, then edit, then shoot again, then rescript, then shoot and so on. They are able to do this because production costs (particularly equipment and facility costs) are lower and crew sizes are smaller.

So the creative documentary workflow in today's production environment may require the different stages of production to overlap and even occur concurrently, as shown in Figure 15.3.

The production is an iterative process of development, content collection, analysis and reflection, at the same time as the producer is fundraising, marketing and planning for distribution. These conditions of production have an impact on the creative process of making the film, in ways that sometimes suit the filmmaker:

> Documentary filmmaking for me is a process of evolution. We will sit and talk about an idea, but after two or three months on the road the idea will still be there but a great deal will have changed. And a lot of our preconceptions will have turned on their heads . . . Things have to grow. That's why the long development period is necessary.
>
> (Grimsby and McClintock, 1995: 6)[6]

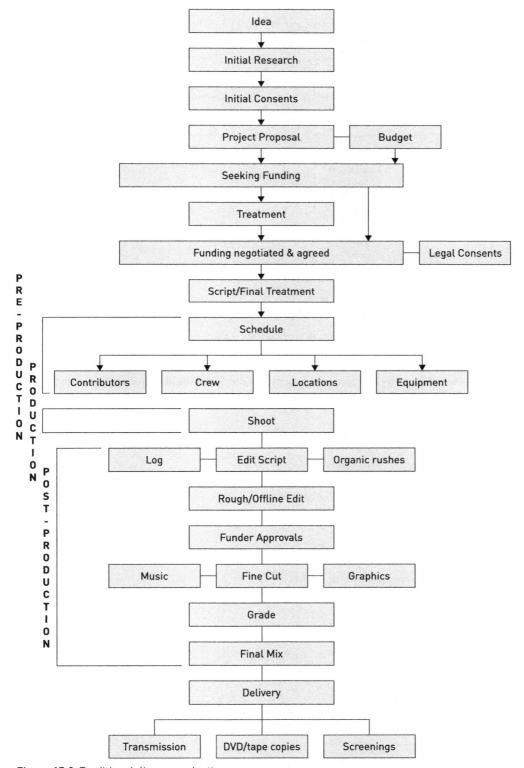

Figure 15.2 Traditional, linear production process

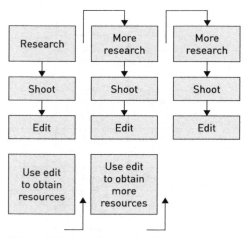

Figure 15.3 Iterative production process

During this process, ideas about the film will change and evolve. The producer needs both to work with and to facilitate these changes and keep the focus and potential of the initial proposal.

Making a schedule for a short film

Earlier in this book (Chapter 7) we've described the creation of a budget and schedule for a film. Once production has started, these become the producer's main tools to make decisions with the director about what the production can afford and how it can be delivered on time.

Once research is under way and a treatment is made, you should estimate a schedule for your film, working backwards from the date it needs to be completed. Decide how much time you are going to allow for:

- final post-production (grade and mix) . . . (in Figure 15.4, 2 days)
- fine cut. . . . (in Figure 15.4, 2 weeks)
- rough cut viewings. . . . (in Figure 15.4, 2 days)
- rough cut . . . (in Figure 15.4, 4 weeks)
- edit preparation . . . (in Figure 15.4, 1 week)
- shoot . . . (in Figure 15.4, 2 weeks)
- pre-production . . . (in Figure 15.4, 2 weeks)

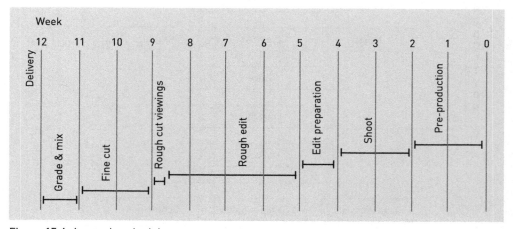

Figure 15.4 A sample schedule

In this example (Figure 15.4), the schedule is 12 weeks long.

This schedule starts from the point at which the film has sufficient funding to complete. As noted above, it is likely that research, shooting and editing will also occur in the process of raising that funding. In a film with no budget at all, you would aim to structure your production as though it were fully funded from the start, because that is the most efficient way to use your resources.

Monitoring the budget

Every creative decision about the film has an impact on the budget and the schedule, and the job of the producer is to get the best value for the resources available. This means negotiating every aspect of the budget while constantly being aware of what the end cost of the film is likely to be.

Keeping an update spreadsheet showing the budget, spends to date and projected future spends is crucial (see Table 15.1). This example takes the travel section for a documentary filmed abroad. As well as the budget column, the producer keeps a 'Spent' column showing spends to date, and a 'Projected' column showing the expected total spend now the production is under way. By doing this for the entire budget and totalling the 'Projected' column, the producer can easily assess whether the production is over or under budget. The 'Difference' column – which is the difference between the projected spend and the budgeted spend – will show this for every item in the budget.

Table 15.1 Budget cost reporting

Travel & transport				Budget	Spent	Projected	Difference
Airfares – Economy	2	Flights	450	900	1179	1179	+279
Excess baggage	1	Allow	100	100	0	0	−100
Vehicle hire (inc. driver)	2	Weeks	300	600	224.72	800	+200
Taxis				100	16.07	50	−50
Fuel		Allow	150	150	108.21	200	+50
Rail fares/UK travel	2		80	160	87.00	125	−35
Visas	1		45	45	30.00	30	−15
TOTALS				2055	1645	2384	329

In this example, airfares turned out to be more costly than expected, but the crew managed to get by without any excess baggage fees on all their equipment. Vehicle hire is more expensive than projected and, although as yet the team has only spent a small portion of that category, the producer knows that they will need a vehicle for more days during the shoot and that there will be an overspend in this category. Fuel is more expensive than expected, but the production team have saved on taxis, rail fares and visas. At this point in the production, the amount spent is £1,645, but it is projected to rise to £2,384 by the end of the production, giving an overspend figure of £329, which will need to be saved elsewhere.

Legal and compliance

As well as managing the production's budget and schedule, another essential role for the producer is to ensure that legal consents are obtained during production. There's a great temptation in the heat of the shoot to think that you can wait to get release forms signed later, but often this is hard to do and involves considerably more work. So the producer needs to ensure that the director obtains contributor release forms and location release forms, and needs to be working on clearances for music, archive and other rights during production.

Interview Anna Higgs – Producer

Anna Higgs, Producer, Quark Films

I started out assisting on interactive 'edutainment' projects for a community arts organisation in my home town of Birmingham, working with audiences to make products that were targeted at them. Over time I became a bit of a specialist and I was hired by Andersen Consulting to work for their Interactive Design Group on audience engagement for big corporate clients like Sony, Telewest and Sainsburys. The media side interested me most, so I quit and got a place on the two-year MA in Producing at the National Film and Television School. The course is for fiction and animation, but it also reignited my passion for documentaries. (I'd grown up in a fairly political family, watching docs all the time.) So I ended up working with directors on the documentary course – and that's how I started producing.

My producing partner Garin Humphries and I are very much creative producers. We don't just raise finance and then take back seats. There's an art to being an all-round producer that I like and believe is essential for the success of films. After all, if all you're only interested in is the story and you're not as thorough on the finance and logistical side, there will likely be problems sooner or later. As the world of documentary development and production gets tougher, I think that producers are becoming more important for filmmakers so they can do what they do best – tell stories.

For me, when I hear an idea, I ask 'Why this story?' and then 'Why is this filmmaker going to be best able to tell it?' It's also got to be something we can be passionate about and I need a strong sense that there's an audience that would like to see this story. Getting docs off the ground is hard enough – without a passion for telling the story and connecting to an audience I couldn't sustain it!

I think the experience of the corporate world made me more conscious of the need to understand audience from the beginning – rather than just make a film and expect it to 'find' an audience later. When you're pitching to a broadcaster, in many ways they're the first audience – do they like the subject matter, have they got the slot for it? But when you're working more independently, there are some really exciting ways that you can both make your idea more robust and build your audience from the start. With *The People vs. George Lucas*, we did this by having an open call for filmmaker, fan and foe submissions to the debate: 'Love or hate Star Wars: what's your view?' We had over 600 hours of footage sent to us from all around the world, giving us a wealth of material and a loyal support base for the film. By truly engaging your audience from the beginning and making the relationship a two-way transaction, you have them interested and excited to see the whole film in ways that trailers or fan sites won't achieve on their own.

For me, producing is driven by a passion to bring stories to an audience, however large or small, that inspire, entertain and engage them. The joys are when you sit at the back of a big theatre and watch your film move people to laugh or cry. It's inspiring to work with creative people – we always have the rule to work with people better than us when we can, so that we're always learning and striving for excellence. It's very tough when a promising meeting goes nowhere and a project stalls, but the days that you get a 'yes' from a big broadcaster tend to wipe the slate clean!

Notes

[1] http://stillinmotion.typepad.com/still_in_motion/2009/07/interview-julie-goldman-executive-producer-cactus-three-films.html

[2] http://susty.com/black-gold-documentary-nick-francis-interview-producer-director-international-coffee-industry-fair-trade-dialogue/

[3] Patterson, L. Ray and Lindberg, Stanley W. (1991) *The Nature of Copyright: A Law of User's Rights*, Athens, Georgia: University of Georgia Press.

[4] Interview with Simon Chinn: http://www.sbs.com.au/films/blog/single/108397/-Man-on-Wire-interview

[5] See http://www.guardian.co.uk/film/2009/aug/28/naomi-klein-winterbottom-shock-doctrine

[6] Cited in Kilborn, R.W. and Izod, J. (1997) *Introduction to Television Documentary: confronting reality*, Manchester: Manchester University Press.

Chapter 16

Directing

Erik Knudsen

"At each touch I risk my life." [1]

Introduction

In this chapter, we're going to look more specifically at the role of the director and what direct-ing actually is. It is one of those 'jobs' in film production that is very difficult to define, partly because it has no natural limits or boundaries. For the director is involved with all elements of a production and virtually all aspects of what you find in this book are of concern to him/her. Here, we shall focus more specifically on the functional aspects of the director's job, rather than the narrative or aesthetic considerations which have already been dealt with in Part 3 and else-where. In this chapter we will explore the role of the director, considerations a director should engage with when dealing with subjects and crews, and identify some of the key challenges that a director is regularly faced with.

The role of the director

The making of a documentary film may involve from one individual right up to fiction-level crewing and casting scales involving dozens. It seems almost absurd to use the term 'director' to talk of the individual making a film that is not character-driven, or perhaps not even driven by live events. The term 'directing' would suggest that there is someone else, or others, to direct. However, even the individual filmmaker will more often than not have to work with a number of other people at various stages of a production. Generally, there is a subject in the film, perhaps a researcher has been employed, maybe the filmmaker is working with an editor, a sound recordist, a colourist or a graphic designer. Each project, no matter how much of a Renaissance man or woman the filmmaker is, will usually involve some other people making a contribution to the film. We must remember that the term 'directing' originates from a time when the tech-nology demanded that responsibilities were divided among a team of people, each dealing with different aspects of the technology, which then became separate crafts. On the crudest level, therefore, directing could be described as giving direction to the creative contributions of a pro-duction team and onscreen participants in order to achieve a coherent and unifying narrative vision. Without such direction, a film is likely to lose its focus and fail to reach a coherent core of a story's purpose, as creative contributors may start pulling in different directions in the vacuum caused by the absence of a unifying vision. (There are, of course, instances where directors collaborate, but they are performing the same function of giving a coherent unifying vision to a film.)

As we discussed in Part 3, at the heart of any story lie some thoughts, feelings and emotions which are impalpable and, perhaps therefore, very fragile. The director's primary responsibility is to recognise and identify these qualities, and underlying story purpose, and to harness their creative energies and the creative contributions of others to bring these thoughts, feelings and emotions to life as a documentary film. To achieve this, the director will be guiding the story through what is effectively a quasi-industrial process involving many complex human relations, political and social contexts, financial complications and technological challenges. At the end of that process, the most important thing for the director is that some in the audience have been moved and that their response somehow has a connection to the original feelings, thoughts and emotions which were part of the film's conception.

In order to achieve the objective of emotionally moving at least some members of an audi-ence, a director needs to develop certain skills and encourage certain qualities within themselves. Some of these include how to work with the onscreen subjects in the film and also with the creative team. We shall look at each of these areas in more detail, but first let us look briefly at the qualities of vision, leadership and management, and understanding the language of documentary film. Qualities in these three areas are imperative for good directing.

Vision

Your team and onscreen subjects will not only demand that you have a vision, but will offer you the respect that will make their contributions so much more valuable if they feel that you have one. Having a vision is not something that can be taught, nor is it necessarily something that can be defined. You may not be able to explain it or clearly articulate it. It does not mean that the film is somehow fixed in your mind or, for that matter, very clear. Having a vision is very much connected with your deepest self, your motivation for wanting to tell a certain story, your aspirations for that story and its themes, and a sense of the shape that the narrative might take. Having a vision is, indeed, about having a dream – a dream of what you aspire for the film to be.

In some cases, you may be able to close your eyes and see the film unfold before you. In other cases, you might have a strong feeling for the film and be able to express that through decisions about what seems right for the film and what seems wrong. Some directors may be verbally articulate about their work in such a away that other team members can see the film in their own mind's eye. Other directors may talk indirectly about their work through discussions about other people's works.

However you convey it, a film production process needs a vision into which a team of contributors invest their creative contributions. The more the team believes in this vision, and the more confident they are about it, the more they will invest of themselves and their creativity into the work and the better the film will be for it.

Leadership and management

Having a vision is essentially what makes the difference between leadership and management. A director will usually have to both lead and manage a team. With a good producer, production manager or assistant director, many of the management responsibilities can be delegated, thereby allowing a director's other strengths to be fully utilised. Not so with leadership.

As a leader, you may well be saying to those around you: 'I have a dream, a vision, of where this film should be . . . This is where I want to take the film and I would like you to help me get it there . . . Are you on board . . . ? How can you help me get us there . . . ?' A leader may well proceed with a project without consensus. As a leader, you will have the courage of your convictions and you will be willing to take risks. You will put your neck on the line and risk humiliation. And when faced with problems, you will not shy away from making difficult decisions. At the extreme, you could end up being a crazed, but inspirational, megalomaniac, leading your production over the edge of a cliff.

Management, on the other hand, centres a lot more around consensus and organisation. Here, you might be saying to your team: 'Right, guys, let's sit down and work this out . . . Are we all agreed that this is how we're going to move forward . . . ? This is the plan. What do you think . . . ?' It would be rare for a manager to proceed with a task without consensus or some kind of instruction. Management is a lot more about a cool-headed assessment of resources – both human and material – organising and deploying those resources in the most efficient way, and making sure that there is a general consensus around procedures and activities. At the extreme, you could end up being a bland, uninspiring bureaucrat managing your production towards soporific mediocrity.

Clearly, having both leadership and management qualities in a director is desirable. Nevertheless, if one had to prioritise, then leadership qualities are the most important. However, let us not confuse leadership strength with loudness, brashness, arrogance or aggression. Quite the contrary. Having strong leadership qualities would also involve having the sensitivity to listen, the courage to respect those who disagree with you, the humility to accept the creative contribution of others, the vision to see the strengths and weaknesses in crew and subjects, the wisdom to understand how to get the most from your collaborators, and the strength to accept that there may be other ways. There is no typical director and no particular style or approach. Strong creative leaders come from many backgrounds, in many shapes and colours, and with many varying personal characteristics. Some are quiet, others loud, some are gregarious and others shy. Trying to be something you are not will not enhance your ability to direct.

Understanding the language of documentary film

We have in Part 3, and elsewhere, dealt with aspects of the language of the documentary form. Here we simply want to emphasise that it is critical that the director has an understanding of the language of the form. While languages always change and there is always more to learn about the language and how to use it, it is, nevertheless, critical for a director to have a good grasp of how the form works and how audiences may respond to it. For it is the director who is going to direct the creative contributions that will give the form a particular expressive shape with a view to moving some members of an audience. Indeed, a great director will add to the vocabulary of the form, thereby keeping the language of the documentary alive and fresh.

A good director is therefore likely to be a student of film – not necessarily in the sense of formally studying documentary with a teacher or in an institution, but in the sense that they take a great interest in studying the work of certain other filmmakers, artists or others that they feel may have a connection with their own. Indeed, a good director will know about what has gone before them in terms of the works of other documentary directors and will have a good sense of where their own work fits into an ongoing narrative about the development of the documentary film. A good director will be studying films to try to understand how they work, just as a child will dismantle household objects to see inside them. That curiosity, and the desire to copy and adapt previous approaches, will be a strong feature of a good director.

Many learn through imitation, but the difference may be that one adds a new element, juxtaposes existing elements in a new way or simply repeats something in a different context. All are opportunities for potentially great invention and the director is therefore always looking, listening and seeking to understand how film works, how it used to work and how it may work in the future.

Additionally, you should have a good understanding of the context in which you are making films; that is, you must appreciate how the codes of the form may affect at least some members of your audience. The cultural associations connected with certain compositional or colour elements in your shots right through to associations connected to your choice of music will all affect how your audience reads your film. You are going to be manipulating cinematic codes and the associations members of your audience bring to these codes. If you lack an understanding of your audience and their relationship to cinematic codes, you could, in extreme cases, cause offence without realising it. More likely, you could end up with a film that fails to take your audience anywhere near the thoughts, feelings and emotions you wanted them to engage with.

This is, perhaps, why the director is often thought of as the author of the film: a critical function of the director is to make creative decisions involving the language of the film, how it is used and, ultimately, how it takes us to the core of a story and its themes.

Your creative team

You may well be setting off to make your creative documentary on your own: producing, directing, shooting, sound recording, editing, sound designing and, perhaps, even composing and recording the music. This approach is increasingly common, given the many changes that have happened to the technology used in production and distribution of documentary films. Indeed, in one shoulder bag you can carry all the equipment you need to shoot your film, edit it, finish off DVDs, project your film and broadcast it to the world. This revolution has changed the way documentaries are made and opened up a range of uses and platforms for documentaries well beyond the offerings of the traditional terrestrial broadcaster. Consequently, there are many changes to working practices.

Traditionally, in British television documentary production, you would see a producer, a director, a camera person, a sound recordist and a researcher. However, in American documentaries, for example, which relied a lot less on television funding, you would often see two-person documentary crews, even in the days dominated by celluloid production. (The Maysles brothers, Wiseman and Pennabaker serve as good examples.) Currently, you may often see a documentary crew consisting of: a producer/director/camera person and sound recordist/assistant. Or you may see a producer/researcher, director/camera and sound recordist. Or a director/sound recordist and camera person. And so on. Generally the trend has been towards smaller, cheaper, more flexible and more intimate crews. In post-production, too, there have been changes. Many directors edit as well. However, most probably find it more useful to work with an editor. The sound designer will often be a different person and, increasingly, colourists, special effects people and graphic designers are involved in the final stages of a production.

Let us assume that you will be working with a separate producer and leading a small creative team who will be carrying out the key functions of camera, sound recording, editing, sound design, graphic design and/or special effects. We will examine some key elements of the director's relationship to these people (see Figure 16.1).

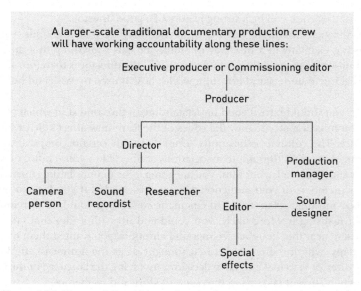

Figure 16.1 The traditional hierarchy of a documentary production team

The producer

The producer is usually responsible to an executive producer or a commissioning editor and has overall responsibility for delivering a completed project, as agreed with these executives. In television, for example, this may be very prescribed and the parameters of what is to be delivered very precise. In line with these objectives, the producer will hire a director and, in consultation with the director, the rest of the team. From an employment perspective, the producer is therefore the boss and the producer can hire and fire anyone, including the director.

The producer will be most careful about the hiring of the director, for there are three qualities they are looking for to match up with the project they have in mind: vision, leadership and management skills, and an understanding of the documentary language and form. Why you, and not any other director? Notwithstanding 'the slings and arrows of outrageous fortune'[2] that bring people together, in a creative documentary the producer will be looking for these qualities to be unique. Every good director has a unique vision, leadership qualities that inspire and a unique creative understanding of the cinematic medium. Usually, a producer will know about the director's potential from other examples of their work they have seen, or maybe they know the director and have had extensive discussions about the possibilities of the project in hand. The producer and the director consequently have a very special relationship, which can be complex and difficult. On the one hand, the producer is clearly in overall charge of the project. On the other, the director has usually been chosen because he or she can provide a unique vision and realise this vision powerfully through the cinematic form by successfully harnessing the creative energies of the production team. Producer and director therefore need each other.

It is important for the director and the producer to have agreed right from the start the parameters of the project and how they plan to proceed. As director, make sure your understanding of what the project is about is acceptable to the producer. Your role is to understand what the producer has to deliver to his or her executives, to make sure that this fits in with your ambitions and dreams for the film, and then to lead the creative effort to realise that dream. A successful producer–director relationship will be built on that mutual respect and understanding.

The producer would not hire you if it were not for their confidence in the fact that you can deliver a product to a certain standard. One of your responsibilities to the producer is, therefore, to be the guardian of quality. To that end, a producer would normally allow the director a final say in who the creative team members should be. It would not make sense for a producer to hire a director because of their confidence in their ability to deliver a quality product and then ignore their advice about what is needed to achieve that quality. As a director, therefore, you should set high creative and craft standards and expect your team to work to those standards. You should be very clear in advance about the constraints, including budgetary ones, under which you will have to operate.

There are as many ways for a producer and director to work together as there are permutations of personal character traits. Some producers and directors work very closely, sharing every thought and throwing ideas back and forth. At the other extreme, a producer may have many projects on the go at the same time and simply let the director get on with it without much contact between them. It is therefore impossible to say where, in the grey area between the two roles, the producer's job ends and the director's job begins, though there may be cultural and national traditions that in part help determine the respective roles and responsibilities.

Because in this book we are focusing on the creative documentary, driven by a notion of the total filmmaker, the director is likely to have been afforded a high degree of autonomy in shaping the film.

The camera person

Good communication with your camera person is essential. A good camera person will try very hard to understand what you, the director, are seeking to achieve and will then bring their expertise, creative solutions and experience to bear to try to realise these aims. However, you must aid them in this process and much of this work will take place during the preparations for the film.

If you are going to shoot actuality, you may not have much time for lengthy discussions with your camera person during shooting. Your communication may be limited to simple signs and you may have to allow your camera person a lot of autonomy in making split-second decisions about what to shoot as a situation develops. In these circumstances, it becomes very apparent whether you and your camera person are on the same wavelength, and almost all the groundwork for this will have been laid during pre-production. Even if you're shooting in a situation where you have a large degree of control over events that you're filming, you do not want to arrive on set and then have to figure out with your camera person what you're going to do. Your onscreen subjects could start to lose faith in what you're doing or could get fed up with unnecessary waiting around. Indeed, you could end up throwing yourself and your camera person into confusion if there are fundamental questions about your approach that you have not prepared yourselves for.

Preparation is, therefore, key. And it starts with choosing the right camera person in the first place. You will be looking to choose a camera person who is not only a skilled craftsperson, but someone who you think will understand what you're trying to do and where you're coming from in terms of your theme and approach. Consequently, this person will not only be able to help you come up with creative solutions to challenges you share with them, they will be able to ask you questions which are challenging to you – ones which test your assumptions and make you more alert and on your toes. Your camera person should feel that they can raise any issue with you, express concerns and have confidence in the fact that you will listen to them and give due consideration to their suggestions. At the same time, your camera person would expect you to have the final say in any decision and will respect that decision and act accordingly. So, while you should expect your camera person to make a positive contribution to creative and technical challenges, you also need to be confident that they will carry out your instructions. You will want to avoid a situation where you have a camera person who has their own ideas that may be contrary to yours and who lacks respect for your decisions.

It is your job to make sure that the camera person has a good understanding of what you are trying to achieve and you should employ a range of strategies to try to ensure good communication. During pre-production you should talk extensively with your camera person about your idea. You may augment this by looking at films or carrying out recces together. You may bring your camera person along to certain research interviews, or perhaps look at paintings and photographs together and discuss them. Depending on the nature of your project, you may even storyboard all or parts of your film. Try to engage with the themes and the practical challenges on many levels by involving your camera person in as many of your pre-production activities as possible; the more varied the ways into the subject, the more likely that you and your camera person will develop an inherent shared understanding of what the film can be. Each partnership will work in different ways and there is no set method or approach, but the more successfully you can create a common understanding, the more the two of you can trust each other. Also, it is much more likely that the technical and creative solutions your camera person offers you will tie in with what you're trying to achieve. It can be very disruptive of a working partnership if every suggestion made by the camera person is wide off the mark. This kind of divergence is a sign that you, as the director, have failed to engage your camera person in the essence of your project and it is likely to lead to an irrevocable breakdown in working relations. As the director, you are ultimately responsible for making sure that the working relationship functions well and brings about quality images.

The sound recordist and the sound designer

The creative deployment of sound is all too often neglected by directors, with sound often taking second place to the images, both in terms of acquisition and of its role in telling a story. Sound can completely change a shot, a sequence, an entire film. As with the images, sound should be a key part of your preparation at the conceptual, the production and the post-production stages of your project. The sound recordist and the sound designer may well be two different people, or your editor may be doubling up as your sound designer. Whatever the permutation of your crewing, bring sound design into your preparation right from the start.

Your sound designer is the person you will work with to develop an overall approach to the sound and its role in telling your story and the aesthetic of your narrative. Sound and picture need to work together and, as with the camera person, you need to ensure that you communicate your aspirations clearly to your sound designer so that they can contribute their creative and craft solutions in the best possible way. While the sound designer may primarily be concerned with post-production, their early involvement may affect the way you shoot something and will also help you give guidance to your sound recordist about what needs recording on location.

Sound recording is, of course, particularly critical if you're going to be using direct sound recorded on location. Quality is paramount; while sometimes if the content is good you can get away with poor-quality images, this is not the case with sound. Distorted or muffled sound, for example, is generally not acceptable, even to the lay viewer, no matter what the content. It is therefore important that you involve your sound recordist from an early stage in the preparation of your project and try to accommodate their needs so that they can record the best sound possible. Like your camera person, unpredictable actuality situations may require the sound recordist to make split-second decisions and, if they have a clear understanding of what you're trying to achieve, they are more likely to make decisions which are in keeping with your aims.

The editor

A strong working relationship with an editor is, arguably, the most important creative relationship for the director. The editing process can destroy or save a film. It is at this point that you finally see whether your dream is going to work or not. Indeed, it is during the editing stage of the process that the film comes alive and you may, as a director, start to see your story in a new light. As the film starts to come together in these final stages, it starts to take on a life independent of you, and the editor will play a critical midwifery role in ensuring that all the disparate elements of the complex production process come together to form a coherent whole. You should therefore never think of an editor as merely a technician pushing buttons; a good editor will have an important creative contribution to make to your film.

It is quite common for an editor not to want to be involved in the shooting of the film. They may want to see the material purely on its own terms, devoid of any emotional component resulting from, for example, the difficulty of getting a certain shot, or the amount of money spent on achieving a particular sequence. That dispassionate engagement can bring fresh eyes to a film which can, in turn, help the director see the real film more clearly.

Nevertheless, the editor does not work in a vacuum. As with other members of your team, you will need to communicate effectively your aspirations and intentions for the film. With a firm grasp of what the film is trying to achieve and how it seeks to do this, the editor is more likely to be able to contribute creative and technical solutions that will help you realise a strong film.

The more you and your editor share a common understanding, the more likely that the solutions that your editor proposes will find favour with you.

Choosing an editor who is likely to be on your wavelength is therefore very important. It is vital that you choose someone with whom you have a good mutual understanding, someone who is not afraid to challenge you in a friendly atmosphere in which risks are encouraged. There are many ways you can work with an editor and your working approach is something you will want to agree in advance. While we have mentioned that many editors like to come to the material fresh, there are also others who like to be involved in pre-production and to look at material while shooting is still going on. This could be useful, for example, in terms of the editor giving advice about coverage, or sequences that will help establish a particular structure, or additional shots needed to establish changes in time. You will do well, then, to discuss and agree with your editor how you wish to work together.

The special effects person and/or graphic designer

Many documentaries may require some graphics, colour grading or special effects. Depending on the complexity of your requirements, your editor may be able to handle these. However, there will be times when you need to bring in specialists in each of these areas. As in the case of other crew members, it is important to think of these issues during the preparation for your film. You may want to consider what special effects, for example, you are going to deploy in your project and then to discuss this with the person who will be responsible for them. It is likely that special effects might require things to be shot in particular ways, and bringing someone in early to talk through these options could make a big difference in avoiding complications later on.

Production designer and/or art director

There may be times where you will work with a production designer and/or an art director. This is particularly the case if you are working with fictional elements, such as reconstructions. They will need to understand your intentions with regard to your mise-en-scène.

Managing your production

Two clear managerial themes emerge from our discussions of the director's relationship with crew members: preparation and communication. Thorough preparation and good communication will significantly enhance your chances of making a good film. The management of your creative team should, consequently, be built around these two themes.

Communication does not just mean a one-way stream of instructions from you to your team. Not only do you need to ensure that you communicate your ideas, your aspirations and intentions to your team, you need to make sure that you invite your team to communicate with you and that you listen to what they have to say. Importantly, you also need to make sure that members of your team are communicating with each other.

Good communication within your production team oxygenates your whole project and fresh ideas and approaches will be more likely to emerge during the process. It will also facilitate good preparation. A well-prepared director and a well-prepared team will enable the project to respond positively to opportunities that arise and meet the challenges that inevitably emerge. When you arrive on location, onscreen participants ready, you want to be in a situation where your team knows what needs to be done, when and why. Ideally, they will need very little instruction from you, with most of any conversation between you and your production team being about minor adjustments. If something genuinely unforeseen crops up, with a well-prepared team you will find it much easier to respond, not least because they will have a good idea of what you're trying to achieve and will therefore be able to make more relevant contributions to the problem solving.

With a well-prepared team, you will also be able to concentrate on the creative challenges and opportunities. For example, you will be able to give your onscreen subjects more attention and spend more of your time with them; or you'll be able to focus on emerging details which you then can bring into your work in an organic way.

What you want to avoid is a situation where you and your team are so unprepared that, when you arrive on location, you are preoccupied with solving basic problems and you don't have time to pay much attention to your onscreen subjects, or can't focus on what is emerging in the scene because you are absorbed in some technical issues. Bad blood between you and a frustrated production team may even come to involve your onscreen subjects. In a situation like that, everyone will begin to lose confidence in you as a director and, once that happens, the whole project may start coming off the rails.

Your producer is, of course, a central part of this preparation. Normally, the producer will take care of logistical aspects of the project: budgeting, salaries, transport, permissions, clearances, and so on. The producer is organising the context in which you will be working, but within that context you are in charge and responsible for preparing the creative process. While the producer has hired you and your team, and is therefore ultimately responsible, your creative team will answer to you, as the director. You will provide the creative leadership and guidance, creative questions should be addressed through you and final creative decisions should always be made by you. The clearer these lines of communication and responsibility are, the more likely it is that your team will work together well to create a stronger work. You want to avoid a situation where your production team, for example, are confused about whether the producer or the director is making the creative decisions.

Examples of some basic pre-production procedures

1. Develop a treatment and discuss this with your producer. Make sure your producer is happy with it.

2. Establish with your producer the exact budgetary situation and make sure that you're happy that you can achieve what you want.

3. Recommend a production team to your producer.

4. Hold regular production meetings with your producer and your production team. Where possible, have an agenda for your meetings and chair these meetings – i.e. take ownership of the process.

5. Have a specific session with your team where you discuss the idea, its inspirational sources and its influences. Invite thoughts, reflections and comments from your team. A clear sense of what this film is trying to be should start to emerge.

6. Establish with your production team how you like to work. How do you want to work on set? When do you want to view rushes? How do you want your team to interact with your participants? What do you expect in terms of attitude and time-keeping? What is the workflow going to be?

▶

7. Depending on the nature of your shooting, establish how you are going to communicate with your team on set. How will a take start and how will it end? How will the camera person and the sound recordist work together? What are the priorities for each scene? What happens if . . . ?

8. Identify any particular psychological, safety or ethical issues that require a particular response and make sure your team understands what these issues are and how to respond to them.

9. Involve your team as much as possible in the research process; where appropriate, delegate research tasks to your team (even technical research).

10. Always involve your team in recces.

11. Where possible and appropriate, introduce your production team to your onscreen subjects in advance of shooting.

12. Take a direct interest in the technical challenges faced by each of your production team members.

13. Together with your producer, prepare a well-thought-out shooting schedule.

Examples of some basic production procedures

1. Make sure your team understands that all creative discussions should be through you.

2. Make sure everyone is clear about the order of shooting and, during shooting, make sure you communicate any changes to this order effectively.

3. Spend most of your time with your onscreen subjects. Immediately before and after takes or sequences, engage first and foremost with your onscreen subjects in order to make them feel confident and comfortable, and to maintain an effective ongoing rapport with them.

4. At the end of every shooting day, review your rushes with your production team and, when possible, with your producer.

5. Try to always thank your onscreen subjects and your production team and leave them with some positive feedback to take away with them.

Examples of some basic post-production procedures

1. Establish with your editor, your special effects person and your sound designer at what stage they will start engaging with the project and in what way.

2. Establish with your editor how you are going to work together – for example, how often you will be in the cutting room.

3. Set out an editing plan, working backwards from your delivery deadline: rough cut, fine cut, colour grading and special effects, picture lock-off, sound post-production, mastering.

4. View and discuss all the rushes with your editor.

5. Supply your editor with a treatment, at the very least, from which to create a first rough assembly. Review this assembly with your editor and producer before you start more detailed editing.

6. Allow your editor creative space – i.e. even if you are spending every hour with the editor, do not think of them as merely a button-pusher.

7. Bring your producer in at key points and, where appropriate, bring in members of your production crew to comment.

At the end of the day, the creative quality of a film is down to you as the director. You will receive most of the praise if the film is successful and, conversely, most of the blame if the film falls short. A director must fully take on that responsibility and never blame the onscreen subjects, the creative team members or the producer. To twist a common proverb:[3] 'The road to hell is paved with excuses.' The director must, therefore, be able to be creative under pressure and sometimes this can be a lonely position to be in.

Your onscreen subjects

One of the most beautiful and profound aspects of making documentary films is that you are working with 'real' people and their 'real' lives. In most cases, these people will be allowing you into their lives, giving you access to often deeply personal feelings and circumstances, from which you will then select elements and mould a narrative. This kind of access places on you a special responsibility to assess the possible implications of your creative decisions for your onscreen subjects and to be able to defend these decisions ethically. This means that you must have confidence in your own motivations for making your film and be satisfied that the narrative purpose of your work justifies the potential consequences for the real lives of your onscreen subjects.

Conversely, you may be teaming up with onscreen subjects who have their own agenda and are trying to manipulate you, the filmmaker, to serve their own purposes outside the context of the film. Such a scenario, too, has ethical implications. Consequently, you need to assess the motivations of your onscreen subjects, whether they impact on your freedom to make independent creative decisions and whether they are in any way going to affect your ability to tell the story you want to tell in the way you want to tell it.

This is quite apart from the fact that every person has a private and a public face; we all show the world one side of us, while there is another side of us that is essentially very private. There is, perhaps, a third face – the face that you, the filmmaker, see, the face that is to be uniquely revealed in your film. To be able to access that special place in a person and their living context requires real skill and life experience. To enter this place requires someone to open up to you, to feel comfortable with you, to trust you. How do you encourage a trusting relationship to develop between you, as a director, and your onscreen subject?

Humility is an important trait you can use to great effect. Not only can it help you see more clearly (as discussed in Part 3); it can show your subjects that you respect them. Even if you are making a film which involves a person with whom you vehemently disagree, if you want that person to open up to you – as opposed to merely showing you their public face – then they will need to feel that you have some respect for them. Add to that an openness on your part, such as telling your subject as much as is possible about why you are making this film and what interests you about them as a person, and you can go a long way to building that trust that can take you into magical places.

Once you have that critical trust, your eyes and ears must be open. The devil is in the detail, as the saying goes. That little remark; that little activity the subject thinks irrelevant; what was not said; the silence at a particular moment – all these little things can be the gateway to a whole new revelatory perspective on a person and their situation. Through sheer instinct, the subject's tendency is going to be to present their public face or the face they think you want to see. What you need to develop is an ability to see what not even your subject can see.

Some considerations when working with onscreen subjects

1. Spend as much time as possible with your onscreen subjects prior to shooting.
2. Be open and honest about your motivations for involving your subjects in your film and in the intentions of the film.
3. Show your subjects respect – this can be achieved in part by showing extended interest in them and their lives.
4. Explain to your subjects what the filming is going to involve.
5. Introduce your crew to the subjects before shooting commences.
6. Give your onscreen subjects most of your attention when on set.
7. Prior to every take or scene, and immediately afterwards, make sure your attention is first and foremost with your onscreen subjects.
8. Do not leave onscreen subjects waiting without knowing why they are waiting and for how long they should expect to wait.
9. Always thank your onscreen subjects for their contributions.

On one level, even though you are working with 'real' people and their 'real' lives, and even though you may be working with some notion of the unprivileged eye, their awareness of your presence essentially makes them performers. You cast them as being most appropriate for your intentions; you have an image of them in a particular narrative in your mind's eye; and you are selectively pointing a camera at them and re-juxtaposing these images in post-production to create a work that is largely rooted in your own motivations and feelings.

Key points

- The director understands the underlying feelings and themes of a film and protects, nurtures and ensures the survival of these feelings and themes through the production process.
- Underpinning a director's work is a vision, leadership and management qualities, and a good understanding of the cinematic form.
- The director is the creative leader of a film production and is answerable to the producer.

- The director gives direction to the creative contributions of others and brings these together into a coherent unifying vision.
- The director facilitates good communication between him- or herself and the rest of the production team, as well as between the team members.
- The director ensures that the film production is well prepared.
- The director develops a strong relationship with the onscreen subjects and is their main point of engagement.
- The director ensures that high creative standards are achieved and is responsible for delivering a quality product.
- The director ensures that the film and its processes are ethically defensible.

Exercises

Get together with a small group of your fellow directors and, for the scenarios listed below, discuss and determine, for each one, the following questions:

1. What are the implications and complications?
2. What could have been done to prevent or modify this sort of situation?
3. What would you, as a director, do about this particular situation now that it has occurred?
4. Can you think of examples, or parallel examples, from your own experience and how does the way you dealt with that situation compare with what you would do with these examples?
   a. It's the first day of the shoot and some of your crew are quite late. However, it is the producer who has brought them and it is hard to work out why they are late. Other members of your crew have been waiting with you and you can sense their irritation.
   b. Your subject, who is 12 years old, is not behaving or performing as you thought and seems to have some inhibitions which you did not experience when you spoke to them initially. The mother has no idea why her child has suddenly 'gone shy'.
   c. You notice that your subject is asking your camera person for advice about how to move across the shot and you overhear your camera person give that advice.
   d. You notice that your producer is giving some advice to subject and crew on set, and this producer has a lot of experience from which to give advice.
   e. Your camera person is setting up a shot that you don't remember asking for and you are told by the camera person that the producer asked to make sure that this particular angle or action 'was covered'.
   f. Your producer starts insisting, on set, that you are not covering yourself and starts having a discussion with you and your camera person about it.
   g. Your subject was going to demonstrate something personal and important for your film but, at the last moment, gets cold feet and decides not to do it. It's an important scene and your schedule is tight.
   h. You want to do a particular shot and your camera person tells you that it won't be smooth and therefore it should not be attempted.
   i. Your subject is very comfortable in front of the camera and talks a lot, but much of what they're saying is not really what you're after.

▶

j.   You discussed the kinds of shots you wanted with your camera person, but halfway through the shoot you realise that you are not getting what you asked for.

k.   Your editor has digitised your material and, when you go for the first session, the editor shows you a sequence they have put together based on their ideas. It is very different from what you had in mind.

l.   Your sound recordist is having trouble sorting out a variety of radio mics for the shoot and is desperately trying to solve the problem on set before shooting. You're just about to shoot and your subjects have arrived and are waiting, watching your sound recordist sorting out their problem.

m.   Your researcher has brought you a lot of background material about your subject and you still don't quite know how you are going to pull it together. The researcher is keen and insists that they can go and interview the subject for further information for you.

n.   You arrive on location and you realise that the room you were shooting in is a lot smaller than you had imagined. You cannot get the shots you had imagined and, as a consequence, you are thrown into confusion.

o.   While on set, your camera person offers you a beer.

Notes

[1] Cézanne talking about his approach to painting, quoted in Bresson, 1977.

[2] Shakespeare, *Hamlet*, Act 3, Scene 1.

[3] The original proverb reads: 'The road to hell is paved with good intentions.'

Chapter 17

Camera and cinematography

Erik Knudsen

" Blind swimmer, I have
made myself see. I have seen.
And I was surprised and
enamoured of what I saw,
wishing to identify myself
with it . . . "

(Ernst, 1948)

Introduction

In this chapter we shall explore the camera – the technology that captures the surface images – and cinematography – the art of helping us see within and beyond the surface images. This is not meant to be a detailed exposition of everything you need to know about the camera and cinematography. It is meant to be an overview of some of the key things you need to bear in mind when capturing images. We will look briefly at the process of looking, how it relates to seeing and then explore how the camera allows us to capture the images that we use to tell a story. In an earlier chapter on cinematic codes, we looked at how imagery works as codes that engage our feelings and emotions. For the cinematographer, it is, of course, crucial to understand these code relationships as they form the basis of seeing. Here, we shall look more specifically at how looking with the camera can help us see. Bear in mind, though, looking is not always related to the visual image. Working exclusively with sound, for example, can also help one to 'see'.

Looking and seeing

There is a difference between looking and seeing. Looking involves directing one's gaze at something, whereas seeing is, effectively, perceiving something. Indeed, you could say that the camera is the machine with which you direct your cinematic gaze to look at something, while cinematography is the art of seeing. We may look at someone's face, but what we see is a personality. The good cinematographer will help us see the personality behind that face by working with the composition, the lighting, the angle, the movement, the colour texture, and so on.

To look, we need to have a technical understanding of how to manipulate and make the most of our technology – the camera. To see, we need to have an intuitive, aesthetic, psychological and cultural understanding of images. You need to bring these two strands together into a seamless process that will enable you to create stories from moving images.

The camera and its legacy

The earliest surviving moving image film is Louis Le Prince's two-second-long *Roundhay Garden Scene* (1888). Compared with other art forms, cinema is therefore very young. The early pioneers of cinema were, in fact, not artists, but scientists interested in developing machines that would somehow capture the movement of life. In just over one hundred years, we have moved from very large mechanical cameras in which very volatile, chemically treated, celluloid-based film was being hand-cranked with the aid of mechanical gears, to digital, pocket-sized mobile phones without any moving parts, capable of recording high-definition moving images.

The introduction of digital technology to the world of cameras, primarily from the 1990s onwards, started a process of convergence that saw the distinction between film technology and video technology become increasingly irrelevant. Digital Betacam, from the professional end, and DV, from the domestic end, emerged as the two most important formats for documentary filmmakers. They provided image quality that could rival that of 16 mm film. As was the case with earlier camera developments, the domestic 'new kids on the block', so to speak, were the formats to lead the developments in camera technology favoured by documentary filmmakers. Mini DV – digital signals recorded on a small tape cassette – spawned the development of a new generation of cameras that came to dominate documentary filmmaking. DV evolved into its high-definition HDV counterpart and we are now in a situation where new tapeless High Definition formats that record straight to flash memory cards or hard drives are becoming the norm.

We now have a comprehensive range of camera technologies and format options available to us. Depending on your objectives, you potentially have at your disposal 35 mm film (colour or B&W), 16 mm film (colour or B&W), Super 8 mm film (colour or B&W), Digital Betacam, DV, HDV, XDCAM, HDCAM, P2, AVCHD, H.264 and a number of other formats. The camera types available range enormously, too. Right from top-end, ultra-high-speed, remotely controlled film cameras used in wildlife filmmaking, to the personal pocket-sized mobile phone, and everything in between, including stills cameras that also record full HD moving images to endoscope cameras capable of filming inside a human body. Whatever the need, there will be a format and a camera designed to deal with it.

Despite this plethora of formats and camera options, the basic principles of filming remain remarkably unchanged since Le Prince shot his first film in 1888. Light is focused through a lens on to a film/sensor, which fixes the image in some way (chemically in film and electronically in digital). It does so, for normal vision, 25 times a second. (In the USA and some other countries it is 23.97 frames a second for film and 29.98 frames a second for TV.) The light intensity is controlled in two ways: first, by the amount of time for which the film/sensor is allowed to be exposed to light – the shutter speed; second, by the amount of light allowed through the lens by an iris – the aperture being the size of the iris opening measured in f stops. The final two elements which you would control are adjusting the sensitivity of your film/sensor to the general light intensity and adjusting the sensitivity of your film/sensor to colour temperature. In film, this would be done by choice of film stock and colour filters. In video and digital, the electronic signal is adjusted in a process called gain (ISO) control, for light sensitivity, and white balancing for colour sensitivity. Whether film, analogue video, or digital, no matter how big or small your camera, how cheap or expensive, you will be working with the same basic elements: shutter speed, aperture, frame rate, light sensitivity, colour balance.

The camera as machine

Formats

The choice of platform or format will not, in any substantive way, affect your abilities as a cinematographer. The creative documentary filmmaker is most likely to spend most of their time shooting digitally. Apart from high-end digital cameras – though this is likely to change with time – almost all digital moving-image cameras involve some compression. This means that the total amount of light information hitting your camera's sensor is compressed using a software algorithm so that the data, on the one hand, takes up less disc space, while, on the other hand, it can be transferred to and from the disc media at speed (see http://en.wikipedia.org/wiki/Digital_cinematography_cameras). (See Notes 17.1, 17.2 and 17.3 for some technical notions you should be familiar with.)

Note 17.1

Frame size

Frame size is the width and height of your image, measured in pixels. Standard definition is usually 720 × 576 pixels. Full high definition is 1920 × 1080 pixels. At the top end, we have digital cinema, where it is increasingly the case that the frame size is described as 4K – that is, a frame size of 4096 × 3072 pixels.

Note 17.2

Bit rate

The bit rate is the rate at which data is transferred to the tape or disc media. This is particularly important, as it is critical in determining how much the data needs to be compressed. This figure can be slightly misleading, since, as compression algorithms become more effective, certain formats such as AVCHD need a smaller bit rate to achieve a similar level of quality as, for example, MPEG2. In standard definition (720 × 576 pixels), for example, the DV format typically works at up to 25 MBits/s, DVCPRO50 works at up to 50 MBits/s and Digital Betacam works at up to 90 MBits/s. In high definition (1920 × 1080 pixels), AVCHD typically works at up to 25 MBits/s and HDCAM at up to 144 MBits/s. Note how, for example, AVCHD, which has to process much more data than DV, does so with a similar bit rate. This is because the relatively newer compression codec, MPEG4, is much more efficient at compressing the information than the DV codec. Likewise, many will say that, in some respects and conditions, AVCHD is not as far behind HDCAM in terms of perceived quality as the figures might suggest. The most effective MPEG4 variant, called H.264, is considered to be such an efficient codec that it is enabling the MPEG4 standard to produce compression quality that can rival other less compressed formats.

Note 17.3

Progressive or interlaced

Tape-based camera recording formats tend to be interlaced, as do most TV sets, currently. This means that, because of the electrical frequencies used for video, each image is based on two scanned fields. To complete an image, both these fields need to be interlaced. The result is that any one frame contains only half the information for the image. This contrasts with progressive scanning, in which each image (of which there are 25 per second) is discrete in exactly the same way as a still image. No interlacing is needed. The current trend seems to be for cameras (and TV screens) to become progressive.

If you are technically adventurous, there are many other factors you could look into. These include: colour depth, the depth at which the colours are recorded (4:4:4:4 being best) and sampling rate, the frequency of digital sampling (measured in Hz). Camera manufacturers usually give all this information in their technical specifications.

Lenses and focal lengths

Probably the most important component of the camera in relation to aesthetic outcomes, including quality of the image, is the lens. The highly complex arrangement of glass inside a lens bends the light to hit the plane where the sensor is situated. This age-old technology needs to be precise and robust. This array of glass affects the field of view, the depth of field, the sharpness, the resolution, the contrast, the colour and the brightness of the image. Many cinematographers talk lovingly about their favourite lenses.

Lenses (see Figure 17.1) are made using a combination of concave and convex glass to bend the incoming light in specific ways.

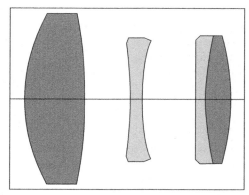

Figure 17.1 Typical collection of concave and convex lenses in a prime lens

There are two types of lens: the zoom lens and the prime lens. The zoom lens can change its focal length – its field of view – while the prime lens has a fixed focal length. The focal length is the distance between the point in the lens where the light is first bent and the focus point on the camera sensor where that light is focused; the scale of the field of view will be determined by the relationship between that distance and the size of the sensor (see http://en.wikipedia.org/wiki/Focal_length). The higher the numerical value of the focal length (such as 200 mm), the narrower the field of view, giving the impression of being closer to the subject. The lower the numerical value for focal length (such as 24 mm), the wider the field of view, giving the impression of being further from the subject. With the zoom lens, the focal length can be changed while filming, typically called zooming.

Note 17.4

Focal length and field

There is a relationship, too, between focal length, focus and depth of field. The longer the focal length (say, 200 mm), the narrower the field of view and the shallower the depth of field. That is, less is in focus in front of and behind the object on which you have focused. The shorter your focal length (say, 24 mm), the wider the field of view and the deeper your depth of field. That is, more will be in focus in front of and behind the object on which you have focused. You will also notice that, the longer the focal length, the flatter the image appears. Conversely, the shorter the focal length, the deeper the image appears to be. These optical illusions are something you should think about carefully when determining the aesthetic style of your film, a particular scene or even a particular cut. The narrative relationship between objects, characters and landscapes can be profoundly affected by your choice of focal length, as can the mood of a film. The way you change your focal length – for instance, as when zooming – also affects how the audience relates to what you are filming.

Most cameras come with a zoom lens as standard, but there are many cameras that allow for interchangeable lenses. The zoom lens is very convenient in that you can change your focal length (field of view) very quickly, thereby needing to physically move less. This can be useful in situations where you need to be mindful of not interfering in events. The flip side of this convenience is that it can lead to visual inconsistency – for example, the jarring that can be caused by cutting between narrow depth of field and deep depth of field, without an aesthetic reason for it. It can also make you lazy by, for instance, making you keep a static distance from the action in a situation where moving to engage with that action would yield better results. The prime lens, with its fixed focal length, will often force you to physically move in order to get a compelling composition. This apparent limitation can, in turn, help give visual consistency and keep you alert and on your toes.

Lenses and aperture

One distinct advantage of a prime lens is its 'speed'. You may from time to time hear the term 'a fast lens'. This refers to the fact that prime lenses need fewer glass elements and can be constructed to have irises that open up wider. With fewer glass components, it is easier to make the lenses bigger to deal with the larger aperture. Additionally, the fact that there are fewer glass components means less light is lost as it travels through the lens. More light means one can have a faster shutter speed, or work in lower lighting conditions.

Quality lenses will have f stop markings, giving you a precise way of reading how large your aperture opening is. A fast prime lens may have an f stop range that looks like the one in Figure 17.2. Every one of these f stops represents a halving of the light passing through the lens for each step going down in value, or a doubling of the light passing the lens for each step going up in value. So, the lens is letting in twice as much light if set to f2 compared with if set at f2.8.

More open								More closed
1.4	2	2.8	4	5.6	8	11	16	22

Figure 17.2 Typical range of f-stop values divided in full stop increments

Each of these f stop stages either halves the amount of light hitting the sensor or doubles it, depending on whether you are opening up the aperture or closing it. The aperture is not only important for controlling the amount of light hitting the sensor. The size of the aperture, the f stop, has an optical effect with far-reaching aesthetic consequences. There is a relationship between focus and aperture. The wider open the aperture (for example, f1.4), the narrower the depth of field – i.e. the less is in focus on either side of the object you have focused on. Conversely, the smaller your aperture (for example, f22), the wider your depth of field – i.e. the more is in focus on either side of the object you have focused on.

If you therefore want to achieve the 'look' that is built on a shallow depth of field in which more is out of focus, a combination of a long focal length and open aperture will achieve that. On the other hand, if you would like a 'look' that is built on a deep depth of field in which more is in focus, a combination of a wide lens and more closed aperture will achieve that.

Sensors

Another factor determines the aesthetic possibilities offered by the lens. That is the relationship between the lens focal length and the sensor size. Typically video cameras have 1/3" or 2/3" sensors. Increasingly, top-end cameras have larger sensor sizes, including full-frame 35 mm sizes. Using the same lens focal lengths, the size of the sensor also plays a role in the field of view and the depth of field. For example, using a 50 mm lens at f2.8 with a 1/3" sensor will give a wider field of view and deeper depth of field than if exactly the same lens settings (50 mm at f2.8) were used with a camera with a full 35 mm sensor. The latter's larger sensor size would give the image a narrower field of view and a shallower depth of field. Again, this can play a major role in a film's 'look'.

Shutter speed

The shutter speed is another tool you have at your disposal to control the amount of light reaching your sensor. You are shooting 25 frames every second (in Europe and many other parts of the world; as mentioned earlier, the USA has a different frame rate). A normal shutter speed is typically 1/50th of a second. Your camera is likely to have other settings, such as 1/25th, 1/30th, 1/100th or 1/200th of a second and so on. Halving the shutter speed (say from 1/200th of a second to 1/100th of a second) doubles the amount of light reaching the sensor. Doubling the shutter speed (say from 1/25th of a second to 1/50th of a second) halves the amount of light reaching the sensor and is equivalent to one f stop change.

The faster the shutter speed, the crisper each image will be in terms of sharpness. This is due to reduced motion blur. It is not advisable to go below 1/50th of a second, unless the action within your frame and the movement of the camera are reduced to a minimum. If you are dealing with fast action, it will help reduce motion blur if you increase the shutter speed.

Note 17.5

Shutter speeds

Another useful thing to bear in mind when it comes to shutter speeds is that in Europe, for example, the frequency of the electricity supply is 50 KHz. This means that when filming with artificial lights or filming TV sets – which both operate at 50 KHz cycles – you can avoid possible flicker in your images by shooting at 1/50th of a second or multiples of that – for example at 1/100th of a second. If you, on the other hand, shoot at 1/50th of a second in the USA, where the frequency is based on a 60 KHz cycle, you may get some flickering in your images or, if shooting a TV screen, a horizontal bar slowly creeping up the screen you are shooting. In this situation, shoot at 1/60th of a second or multiples of that.

ISO (Gain)

Your camera's sensor will have an optimum setting for light sensitivity in which the signal-to-noise ratio produces the best-quality results. However, in some low light situations you may need to increase your ISO setting (add gain), which, in effect, is boosting the signal from the sensor. There is, however, a price to pay for that: increased video 'noise' or grain. The more noise you have in your original footage, the less scope you have for working with it in post-production.

Some cameras, of course, have the ability to let you increase the ISO considerably before visible noise starts setting in. Where this is the case, this is an added way in which you can control your exposure.

Colour temperature

Every light source has a different colour temperature. You may not notice this because your brain works it all out for you and compensates for it so that white really does look white. The sensor

Table 17.1 Colour temperatures for different types of light source

Source	Temperature
Match flame	1700K
Incandescent light bulb	2700K–3300K
Moonlight	4100K
Daylight	5000K–6000K

in your digital camera is like your eyes and records things as they are and, to some extent, if you choose automatic white balancing, the computer in your camera works like your brain to compensate for it. Your camera is also likely to have some pre-sets you can use for different lighting conditions, as well as a manual option. While manipulating colour temperature settings in relation to the actual lighting conditions can be used creatively for aesthetic reasons, it is worth bearing in mind that colour temperature could also be a problematic issue (see Table 17.1). Rather than causing your editor and colourists huge problems in post-production, you may as well get the picture looking right in the camera.

A familiar friend

You should know your camera like the back of your hand. It is important to familiarise yourself with all the settings, in particular those that relate to exposure, focus, light sensitivity and colour balance. Ideally, you will be able to operate your camera without having to think. When in search of particular 'looks', you will know exactly which of the camera's components you need to adjust. It is also important to know what your camera cannot do. Limitations are often the root of many a creative solution. The camera is a tool and, as the saying goes, 'only a poor workman blames his tools' when things go wrong.

Cinematography

In an earlier chapter, we discussed cinematic codes and their relationship to story, narrative, emotions and feelings. Cinematography is very much about dealing with these issues, but using the tool of the camera to capture the necessary images to do so. Being a good cinematographer is therefore not about being good with the camera, per se; it is, principally, about being able to see, and knowing how to use the camera to see. It's perhaps worth noting that most directors of photography on fiction movies hardly ever touch a camera. The camera operator is responsible for this, whereas the DoP is responsible for what is to be captured and how. Once familiar with the camera, your concerns as a cinematographer should be focused on four principal things: composition, movement, lighting and texture. Immersed in the story, narrative and an understanding of the codes of your medium and culture, you embark on using these four components to capture images. What you see is not what you're looking at. You may be looking at actual events unfolding in front of your camera, but what you see is your film.

Composition

Composition is often referred to as 'framing'. While the frame of the image may well be one reference point, others come to mind, such as angle and the relationship of objects to each other, rather than just to the frame. Add to this the influence of optics – such as the relative flatness of image or depth of field – and we have a more three-dimensional understanding of composition.

While one cinematographer may be thinking primarily about flattening the image to give us a sense of being far from the action, another may prefer to deepen our perspective to give us a sense of being right in among the action. You may want to use a narrow depth of field on a face in order to isolate the background and give us a more intimate relationship to the face. You could shoot it with a wide-angle lens with a view to connecting the face with an object in the background which you feel may reveal something about the character. You could shoot it, looking slightly down at it, or slightly up. Indeed, where in the frame would you place the face? What would the difference in our understanding be if the face were looking into space or if the space was behind it? Would we look at it differently if we were a little further away from it or very close?

In other words, you are dealing with a whole range of compositional components which will have a profound effect on how your audience sees. They include:

Field of view

Your focal length determines the field of view. What we see and what we don't see are important decisions that the cinematographer has to make. In deciding what we see and what we don't see, don't forget the complementary role that sound can play. There may be times when an interesting tension can be created between what is seen and what is heard. On other occasions you, as the cinematographer, may find yourself having to make a split-second decision about what to look at. In such a situation, indecision can create more of a problem. Two characters, for example, who are in the same shot suddenly start moving away from each other while the conversation continues. What are you going to do? It is not about simply 'covering the action' but about deciding, in the context of all the other elements that are going to make up the film, what is best to look at.

Field of view may be described as ECU (extreme close-up), CU (close-up), MCU (medium close-up), MS (medium shot), LS (long shot) or ELS (extreme long shot).

Close-up in *The Monastery* (Grønkjær, 2006)

Medium shot in *The Monastery* (Grønkjær, 2006)

Long shot in *The Monastery* (Grønkjær, 2006)

Depth of field

Your aperture and focal length determine your depth of field. Distance of the object from the camera also affects depth of field. What you include in your focus should be a result of decisions you make about how you want your character and action to be perceived. Isolating a character or an action through your use of focus, or connecting characters, actions and objects by including them in your focus can be used very effectively in your compositional scheme. A character in a crowd could be understood very differently depending on whether the rest of the crowd were out of focus or had the immediacy of being in focus. The former could give the impression of isolation and distance, while the latter could suggest connection and closeness.

Use of shallow depth of field with foreground object in *Burden of Dreams* (Herzog, 1982)

Angle

The vertical and horizontal positioning of the camera in relation to characters and action has an important effect on how we understand a situation. Whether we are looking up at someone, down at them or are on their level has many cultural and emotional codes attached. Likewise, following an action from the side can give a very different sense of that activity than if we were looking at it from the front. Choosing your angle is therefore important. Timidity can be a factor that prevents the cinematographer from 'getting in there' – or in the case of shooting with children, 'getting down there' (on your knees) – among action or people, and at times excuses may be made in which the desire not to influence or affect the events is cited. The cinematographer should test these assumptions that lead to timidity.

Deliberate choice of low angle in *Burden of Dreams* (Herzog, 1982)

Framing

It is also useful to think of the two-dimensional space of the frame and to think of the relationship of the key components of the image and the frame. Here we may think in terms of the 'Golden Proportion' or the 'Rule of Thirds' (see http://en.wikipedia.org/wiki/Rule_of_thirds. Accessed 3/11/2010.). These are age-old observations of painting and drawing in which what pleases the eye seems to involve placing key objects of attention in particular parts of the frame. Typically, this involves dividing the frame into thirds and our eye seems to be attracted to certain points within the frame which turn out not to be in the centre of the frame.

Where the lines cross are often parts of the frame our eyes are attracted to in a composition (see Figure 17.3).

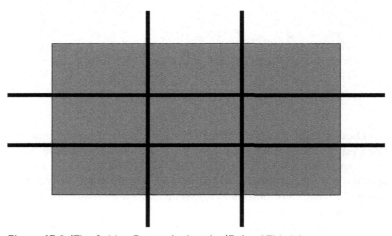

Figure 17.3 'The Golden Proportion' or the 'Rule of Thirds'

Space

How the cinematographer uses space relates to all the other aspects of composition. Whether the two-dimensional space, the perceived three-dimensional space, indeed the space outside the frame, which may be suggested by action within the frame or by sound, this aspect of composition is an important tool for the cinematographer to use. As with all other aspects being considered, codes and conventions play a part in how the cinematographer might use space. The headspace, the space between characters, the single character and their setting and so on can tell us a lot about a situation and a theme.

Relationships

One of the key things a cinematographer can do is tell us about the relationship between elements of an image in the choices relating to angle, depth of field, space, framing and so on, whether this is achieved through intervention or as a result of decisive positioning. The cinematographer always needs to understand the relationship between the various actions, events and characters for this understanding will inform decisions about the most appropriate angle, movement, composition and so on.

Eyes and eye-lines (that is, the direction of looks and gazes of characters and between characers) are critical in the moving image – documentary or fiction – and perhaps therefore need a special mention. It is worth noting here that the importance of eyes and eye-lines in cinema cannot be overstated. Even in real life, and between species of animals, the eyes are the key part of our bodies with which we engage with each other to understand what is going on. The relationship between people and the relationship between people and objects is often revealed and explored through the actions of eyes. Compositional decisions, therefore, often hinge on how you, as a cinematographer, capture these eyes and the invisible links that the eyes establish when they look, or don't look, at people and things. When preparing your shooting, and during shooting itself, you may therefore wish to consider prioritising how you are going to deal with eyes and eye-lines in helping establish characters, themes and situations.

Movement

The moving image is, of course, about movement. Even if the action and frame are still, we are experiencing this stillness through the movement of time. Do not underestimate the simple pleasures of watching movement. Indeed, the juxtaposition of movement and stillness can create evocative metaphors that can stir feelings that rational meanings cannot. You will want to think how you can use movement to evoke the themes and feelings you hope to capture. Different types of movement are at work in a shot:

Pan and tilt

Pan and tilt refer to the movement of the camera when it is at a stationary point. The camera can tilt up or down, or it can pan left or right. Indeed, it can pan and tilt simultaneously. These are by far the most common movements of the camera and we tend to use them to follow action. In some cases you may use them to follow a line of sight or an interesting pattern from one significant object to another. Make sure, however, that panning and tilting are not just random and automatic habits, but that your way of using these movements forms an integral part of your visual approach to the story being told. At times you may find it useful to keep your camera static – this could also be a stylistic decision.

▶

Built almost exclusively on interviews and close-ups of reconstructions, there is hardly a tilt or pan shot in *The Thin Blue Line* (Morris, 1988)

Track

Tracking is when the camera's central positioning itself moves. You could track into something, or away from something. You could track sideways following something, or you could track someone down the street, either from behind or in front.

Part of the same shot, a tracking shot lasting almost 10 minutes in *Bread Day* (Dvortsevoy, 2002)

Handheld vs tripod

Another type of camera movement is that subtle movement which suggests to the audience whether the camera is on a tripod or handheld. In some cases, cinematographers deliberately accentuate this movement, engaging codes of authenticity. The juddery movement of a handheld camera may help give a sense of 'reality' unfolding in an unpredictable manner before the camera. If the same scene were shot with the camera very still and static (on a tripod), this might give a completely different feel and understanding of the same events. In many instances, the question of whether to put the camera on a tripod or not is one of logistics and practicality. However, you should, nevertheless, consider the aesthetic implications and opportunities that these subtle differences in movement can offer.

In-frame *action*

Most of what we film are actions, including those of speaking and looking. Usually we are shooting people doing things. These actions have their own meanings and, as a cinematographer, you set out to capture them in the most appropriate way. All involve movement. The movements themselves can add subtle, yet powerful, layers of meaning to events. Someone's head turning, someone's hands gently stroking another person, feet moving hurriedly through a crowd of other feet, a factory worker carrying out a menial task – there are endless possibilities as to how best to capture the movements within a frame. Always think how you can use the composition to make the most out of these movements.

Add to this the possibilities that movement in and out of the frame can offer. Rather than always trying to follow action, it may be beneficial to allow characters and action to enter and leave the frame – not least because your editor may appreciate the added opportunities such movements allow in the editing. Perhaps the main action moves out of the frame and you hold on a reaction or a consequence. Or, perhaps, the remaining movement within the frame suggests that the main action which departed may be returning.

In-frame *stillness*

Stillness can also be a very effective way of engaging your audience, particularly when working in contrast to, or in synergy with, movement. As a cinematographer, you will also need to have an eye for stillness and how to shoot quiet, reflective or thoughtful moments and situations. Being able to utilise inaction as a way of conveying such moods and feelings can help you a lot in the construction of your imagery. When shooting a film, therefore, think not just of the movements you wish to capture, but also of the still inactions which could play a critical part in the telling of your story. (In the classic narrative structure, for example, how are you going to evoke the 'calm before the storm'?)

Lighting

Image creation is all about light. The intensity, the colour, the texture of light are all necessary in creating the image. Our moods, our understandings, our cultural contexts – and many other things – are determined by the nature of light. It is such an immense subject that it can only be mentioned briefly here (see, among others, Alton, 1995). The way things look, and the many associations that go with these looks, should be at the heart of the cinematographer's concerns. Most documentary filmmakers work with available light, trying to capture it as it really is. In many cases, this is based on an ethics of authenticity in which unspoken rules make filmmakers feel guilty if they interfere too much with actuality. Others feel that the quality of available light provides creative and aesthetic opportunities. Advances in both film and digital technologies mean that our cameras are capable of working in a broad range of lighting conditions, further encouraging the creative documentary cinematographer to work with available light.

Working with actuality and available light does not mean that you cannot make decisions to influence this lighting. Depending on your situation and the nature of your film, you may be able to adjust or adapt the lighting. You may be in a position to determine the time of day the shooting takes place, or the positioning of characters in relation to light sources. You may be able

Using lighting to separate in *The Five Obstructions* (Von Trier/Leth, 2003)

to supplement some artificial lighting with some of your own lighting you bring with you. Perhaps you always carry with you reflectors and black cloths, to help soften or redirect the light in specific circumstances. You may have filters for your lens – such as polarising or neutral density filters – to deal with a variety of harsher lighting conditions.

In short, whether shooting actuality or not, lighting should be at the heart of your concerns and creative decisions.

Lighting and texture in *Five Obstructions* (Von Trier/Leth, 2003)

Texture

The texture of your film is very much connected with lighting. By texture is meant a loose range of elements such as grain, colour scheme, lighting, contrast – all elements that affect the feel of the surface of the image. Prior to the revolution of digital technology in the moving image, it was important for the cinematographer to fix this texture, broadly, at the shooting stage. The film negative would hold all the key ingredients for the final grade of the film. The cinematographer was therefore the critical person when determining the look and feel of a film. Given the extensive developments in digital post-production, this situation has changed. Much of the texturing of the film happens in post-production. The consequences for the cinematographer are profound. Where in the past you would, as a cinematographer, have to make decisions on location about the final look of the film, now the post-production people want you to give them images with as much data as possible for them to manipulate in post-production. This usually means as little grain as possible, median exposures, less contrast and neutral colours. With as much 'raw' neutral data as possible, post-production can completely transform the images to such an extent that the cinematographer may not even recognise them.

The consequences are very clear: as a cinematographer you should discuss with the post-production team, in advance of shooting, what the needs of post-production are going to be. You can then adjust your working methods and approach accordingly.

Preparing for shooting

Being a creative documentary cinematographer, you are most likely to be shooting on location. Most locations have their unique issues that you will need to prepare for, but there are some generic issues specific to the cinematographer that you will need to address when preparing for a shoot and during shooting. These may include:

The director's vision

If you're not the director yourself, it is critical that you develop a good understanding of what the director is trying to achieve. Your job is to serve the film that the director is trying to realise. The more you understand the story, the narrative, its themes and the director's angle on these things, the more likely you are to come up with creative solutions that will be accepted and embraced. If you keep putting forward ideas, solutions and creative opportunities that are continually rejected by the director, this is a sign that either the director is not clear about what they are trying to do, or you have not understood what that is. Either way, positively engage with solving the problem.

There are a number of strategies you could adopt to encourage the understanding you need to have with the director. Talking in its own right, while good, is not necessarily enough. You may want to watch some films together that have some connection to your project and discuss them. Perhaps an exhibition of paintings or photographs might reveal some clues or solutions. Try to attend, as an observer, as many meetings as possible involving the director, even if they are not directly relevant to you. Importantly, visit potential subjects/characters together and listen to what the director is discussing with them. Finally, recce locations together. The observations and conversations about these particular circumstances may go a long way to helping you understand the film you are going to shoot.

A well-prepared film is more likely to be a successful film. In many ways, much of the film is shot in the preparations. Being well prepared, and having a strong understanding of the film's themes and approach will ensure that you are much more likely to be able to deal positively with unforeseen events.

Equipment maintenance and checking

Not only do you need to be familiar with the equipment you are going to use, but you should never take equipment to a location before you have checked that you have everything you need and that it works as you expect it to work. After every shooting day, check your equipment again and prepare it for the following day. You don't, for example, want to start the next day on low batteries or with a dirty lens.

Recces

While it may not always be possible to recce a location prior to shooting, when you can you should always do so. If possible, go with at least the director and the sound recordist. Try to go at the same time of day as you are planning to shoot, so that you have some sense of what the lighting conditions may be like. At the recce, you are trying to determine a number of things. First, it will give you an opportunity to discuss with the director what the actions are going to be, what the spatial context is, how it is going to be filmed and so on. You may have planned some shots already, in which case you will understand them better, or you may find it easier to plan them on the basis of the recce. Second, the recce allows you to work out what equipment you need to use, such as lenses, and what you may need to do about the lighting situation or what the power sources are, should you need to add lighting. Third, the recce visit will allow you to plan logistics such as health and safety issues, where you are going to put equipment that is not being used, and so on. Finally, if you have your sound recordist with you, you may be able to iron out any potential conflicts between your respective needs.

Even if you are unable to recce a location, you should find out as much about it as possible and then imagine and prepare for various issues and circumstances that you may encounter. You need to be in a situation where logistical surprises do not distract you from creative seeing.

Workflow

As mentioned earlier, it is important to engage with the post-production team to understand the needs of post-production. You should also, in conjunction with your producer and editor, determine a workflow for the material being shot. What is the protocol for storing the shot material safely? How is it backed up and who has responsibility for what? How is the material being labelled and logged?

If working with tapeless formats, develop a protocol where the camera's raw material is transferred to a hard drive, checked, then a backup copied to a separate hard drive, prior to deleting material from the camera's storage media. Make sure that, at the very least, the camera raw files and the backups are stored on two separate hard drives and that your procedure for preventing accidental erasure of source material is sound.

Climate and weather conditions

Determine the climate and potential weather conditions of the place where you will be shooting. Not only do you need to figure out how you are going to protect yourself from the elements – such as excessive rain, snow or sunshine – but you need to consider whether your equipment is up to dealing with the particular environment into which you are heading. Obvious examples include very hot or very cold climates. Other less obvious climatic hazards include high levels of dust or humidity. For most situations, you will need to come up with simple common-sense solutions as to how you are going to deal with shooting in these conditions. For extreme conditions, you must seek specialist advice.

Two common problems are heat and humidity. In these circumstances, you will usually have to plan how you are going to protect your equipment – and yourself – from persistent direct sunlight. Also, if you are moving from air-conditioned to hot, non-air-conditioned environments during shooting, you will have to build into your schedule time for your equipment to acclimatise itself.

Travel arrangements

Travel arrangements will, of course, normally be made by the producer. However, you may take a special interest in how these travel plans impact on the shipping of your equipment, for example – particularly where flights and foreign travel are concerned. You will need to liaise with your producer about arrangements concerning what equipment travels as hand luggage and what goes in the hold. Depending on which country you are travelling to, you will need to consider import restrictions and carnet requirements, as well as specialised insurance.

Health and safety and security

While the producer will be making an overall risk assessment for the project, you need to make sure that it adequately reflects the risks associated directly with the camera and yourself as the cinematographer. You need to consider your own safety, the safety of those around you and the safety of the equipment. Where is the equipment being securely stored when you are not shooting, such as at night? What are the external threats relating to the context in which you are going to be shooting and what precautions are you taking to mitigate these? It is important for you in your role as cinematographer to discuss these issues with the producer and to make sure you are satisfied with the arrangements.

Contingency plans

It is particularly pertinent when travelling far from your home base that you have some contingency plans in place. Where possible, take a spare camera, lens and other accessories. Locate where your nearest suppliers of equipment are, should you suddenly develop a serious fault or need additional equipment. Do you have enough battery backup power, in case problems develop with regard to power supply? Have you got the relevant contact details of people who could help you out, including courier and shipping company details?

Watching dailies

It is important that you check your footage on a decent monitor with your director each day, partly to spot technical problems early, and partly to ensure that what you are shooting is in line with what the director is hoping for. Watching dailies can also play an important part in letting the film evolve organically, and the cinematographer can play a major part in this process.

Location shooting

Generally speaking, when shooting, you may find yourself in a 'zone' in which only the film – the composition, the movement, lighting and texture – are alive to you. In a paradoxical way, though you are shooting actuality, you are divorced from that actuality, seeing only the film. All the technical aspects of the camera, the aesthetic components and narrative requirements unconsciously influence your intuitive decision-making. You may think consciously about all these things before shooting. You may think consciously about them after shooting. But never think consciously about them during shooting. The more you practise, the more you will be able to achieve this unconscious seeing with the camera.

Seeing the film also means seeing how it will cut together. Hopefully, you will have had discussions with the director about the types of shot you will be shooting and how they are going to work in the edit. Depending on the nature of the film you are making, the level of detail will vary. Some documentaries are carefully scripted and even storyboarded, while many will leave a degree of autonomy for the cinematographer in the heat of the action.

Either way, there are some key considerations to bear in mind in two key areas: shot size and angle, and coverage.

Shot size and angle

You can make life very hard for your editor if, in any one sequence, you only supply one size of shot and one kind of angle – for example, medium shots always at shoulder height. Covering action and events with just one type of shot can make the whole sequence anaemic and undynamic. Depending on your creative intentions, you may want to ensure that you have a variety of shot sizes to cover a scene: long shots to establish locations and contexts, medium shots to cement an understanding of relationships, and close-ups to take us into the intimacy of the situation. Shot sizes and how they cut together can, in themselves, evoke feelings and emotions that engage the viewer and play an important role in connecting them to the themes of the scene. This means you have to be alert, on your toes, constantly seeing how the film is cutting together as you shoot. You may also need to do some shooting of repeats or other elements after the main events, in order to get the shots you know your editor may find useful. Sound will, of course, play a critical role, as sound itself could, for example, do the work of the long shot. But you will be aware of the intentions and make sure that you are providing shots that in the edit will help the editor create movement in the cuts.

Coverage

There is nothing more frustrating for an editor than not having enough material to properly construct a scene. It is often little things, small actions, that help link scenes or prepare the audience for the arrival of someone, and so forth. Again, you need to be 'in the zone'. As you shoot, the sequence is forming in your mind and you are seeing how it will all fit together. First of all, it is very important that you understand the key elements of the scene and that you ensure that you get good coverage to convey these. If in doubt, these are the key turning points in a scene that you must ensure you cover.

Often this is not enough for an editor, however. Once you are confident that you have covered, or will be able to cover, they key events and turning points of a scene, you should ensure that you cover other useful things for your editor, such as

- your characters arriving at a scene and leaving that scene, if relevant;
- reactions to the main events and actions;
- establishing a location;
- establishing time of day and a season;
- moments – usually quiet – leading up to decisions;
- where journeys and travelling are relevant, coverage of the kind of actions that would suggest and establish this journey or stages in the journey itself.

Remember that real time and screen time are different. What may happen fairly quickly in real life may need stretching out in screen time for it to make sense. You therefore need to ensure you have the coverage to achieve this.

Key points

Looking and seeing:

- *Looking* is a technical process of directing the gaze, *seeing* is in the mind. Your job as a cinematographer is to make us *see*.

The camera and lens have a number of key functions that control the light falling on the sensor and the quality of the image:

- **Lens aperture**, measured in f stops and controlled by an iris determining the amount of light that passes through the lens.
- **Shutter speed**, measured in fractions of seconds, controls the time the light has on the sensor, 25 times a second.
- **ISO (gain)**, usually measured in a range of 100–6400 iso.
- **Colour balance**, the camera sensor's processor compensates for the changing base colour of light, 1500–6500K.
- **Focal length**, the distance the lens takes to bend the light to the focal plane of the camera sensor, measured in mm, high numbers being telephoto, producing flatter perspective and shallower depth of field, lower numbers being wide-angle, producing a deeper perspective and depth of field.

When in action, the cinematographer is primarily concerned with:

- **Composition** – the arranging of elements within the frame, including field of view, depth of field, angle, framing, space and relationships between people and objects. Eyes and eye-lines play a critical role in the composition of images.
- **Movement** – the movement of the camera through tilting, panning, tracking and the judder of the handheld shot, as well as the movement of the action within the frame.
- **Lighting** – at the heart of cinematography; all aspects of the camera are concerned with controlling light.
- **Texture** – in the digital domain it is increasingly important for the cinematographer to understand the post-production workflow in order to supply images that will seamlessly integrate with colouring, grading and special effects.

Good preparation is at the heart of successful shooting. Things to consider in preparing for a shoot include:

- Engaging fully with the director's vision and understanding of the story, its themes and the narrative approach.
- Thorough checking and maintenance of equipment prior to and during shooting.
- Plan and take part in recces of locations prior to shooting and, if this is not possible, evaluate potential issues and situations with unseen locations.
- Establish clear and effective workflows for the logging and safe storage of original tapes and media files.
- Research climate and weather conditions for locations and prepare yourself and your equipment for these conditions.
- Make sure that travel arrangements are conducive to the safe and efficient delivery of the equipment you need to shoot.

- Carry out a risk assessment prior to shooting and during shooting make sure that you implement health and safety precautions.
- Have some contingency plans and arrangements in place, particularly when travelling far. These include plans for spare or replacement equipment.
- Get into the habit of checking your footage on a good monitor with your director on a daily basis.
- Practice will take you to a stage where you can shoot unconsciously and respond instinctively to ever-changing situations.

When shooting, make sure you have an awareness of how your footage is going to cut together and visualise these sequences in your mind's eye. You may therefore want to make sure you consider:

- Variations in types of shots you shoot.
- Covering a scene sufficiently for the editor.

Exercises

Exercise 1

Objective

The objective of this exercise is to familiarise yourself with the basic principles of the camera and, in particular, the lens.

Activity

Have a character sitting in an outdoor setting that gives you an identifiable near foreground object(s), mid-distance background object(s) and a distant background object(s). Place your camera with a zoom lens on a tripod in front of your character. Try to maintain a medium shot for the different sample shots you are going to try. (This will mean you will have to move the camera between some of the shots.) Now shoot about 30 seconds of each of the following settings (for these exercises, we are ignoring white balance, so keep that on automatic or constant throughout):

1. Choose the *widest focal length* and open the *aperture to its most open* state. Adjust your shutter speed to get a correct exposure. If possible, keep the foreground object in the shot.
2. Choose the *widest focal length* and close the *aperture to its most closed* state. Adjust your shutter speed to get the correct exposure. If possible, keep the foreground object in the shot.
3. Choose the *longest focal length* and open the *aperture to its most open* state. Adjust your shutter speed to get the correct exposure. If possible, keep the foreground object in the shot.
4. Choose the *longest focal length* and close the *aperture to its most closed* state. Adjust your shutter speed to get the correct exposure. If possible, keep the foreground object in the shot.
5. Now try an experiment. Take your camera off its tripod and hand hold it. Set your settings to those for number 4 above. Start shooting. Now start walking towards your subject. While tracking into your character, zoom out simultaneously, keeping the same framing. In other words, zoom out at the same speed you are walking in. You can also try this in the opposite direction.

▶

Reflection

Watch your material and ask yourself: how does the focal length affect the image? How does the aperture affect the image? How might the different optical effects affect mood and meaning? Finally, look at your final experiment and try to understand what the effect is and how it is happening.

Exercise 2

Objective

This exercise is designed to get you practising understanding covering action, dealing with shot size variation and making judgements about composition and other components in shooting.

Activity

Arrange for someone to change a car tyre. You are going to shoot the entire sequence of someone changing a car tyre without interfering directly in the action; in other words, it will happen once and you have to capture it.

Using at the very least a range of close-ups, medium shots and long shots, shoot the sequence with a view to putting together a sequence that will make it clear to an audience how a car tyre is changed.

Edit this sequence together and test your results on an unsuspecting audience.

Reflection

Have you captured the key moments and are the details of how a car tyre is changed clear to your audience? Have you used the most appropriate shots? Are your shots engaging and varied? Have you captured enough footage to build your narrative around the key actions?

Having done this first exercise, you may want to carry out another exercise to test what you have learned. Repeat the process, but perhaps this time you shoot a scene in which someone lights a campfire. Do you find that your ability to shoot a scene in an interesting and engaging way has improved?

Chapter 18

Interview strategies

Jerry Rothwell

" Facts and reality
sometimes are not enough.
You need an enhancement
and intensification of it –
some sort of an essential
version of things to make
things transparent. "

(Werner Herzog)[1]

Introduction

Since the advent of sound, interviews have been at the heart of documentary practice. This chapter looks at ways of thinking about documentary interviews, about the choices for the filmmaker, and about strategies for questions and mise-en-scène.

The microphone is yours. No sooner had sound finally reached the documentary (initially in the film *Housing Problems*) than there arose the remarkable idea of including the actual speech of its subjects, and asking them questions in front of the camera. John Grierson's sister Ruby, assistant director of *Housing Problems*, is famously reported to have turned to the slum residents in her film and said: 'The camera is yours, the microphone is yours, now tell the bastards what it's like to live here.'

It took some time for such a direct approach to interviews to filter through to television. The standard television interview for the next 40 years was deferential and strongly boundaried by notions of class, privacy and politeness. But documentary has always privileged first-person witness of events, as revealed through interviews, and as camera and sound technology has progressed, these interviews have ranged as widely as human conversation. Today's filmmaker inherits a tradition of interviewing in which one set of choices – the single camera, medium close-up of a single subject looking just off-camera – has become an all-pervasive norm. But there are myriad examples of other approaches to the interview and numerous possible choices the filmmaker needs to consider.

Your interview strategies depend on the premise of the film and the role of the interviewee in it. You are seeking an approach which complements and supports the other directing choices you are making, so it is important to think through how and why you are using interviews, and to be consistent about the strategies you adopt.

Selecting interviewees

The common question asked in the selection of interviewees is: 'Are they good on camera?' – as though this were a quality people have that is somehow independent of the circumstances of filming. It's perhaps better to see all interviews as a form of improvised performance that depends on setting, on direction, and on representation. The impact of this performance is dependent on the context of the film, not only on personal qualities of the interviewee. A fluent communicator, for example, might be less engaging than someone who doesn't tell you everything and has difficulties speaking about an experience. There are many films in which people who are not especially articulate or fluent on camera hold attention and demand empathy because of their relationship to the story.

As a filmmaker, you make a set of choices about the totality of the interview – who is interviewed, who is asking questions, what is asked, what the tone of the exchange is, where it happens, how it is shot, framed, lit and edited, and so on. It is this totality which conveys the meaning of the interview, not just the elegance of the words spoken or the accuracy of the answers given.

Mode of address

It is useful to start by establishing the role which the contributors are adopting (or which you are asking them to adopt) in relation to the events of the film, the 'mode of address' they use in relation to the events they are describing. Do we see them as an expert or as an unreliable witness, an active participant or a distanced commentator? What status do we give them in the film and how do we relate to them emotionally?

Filmmakers position interviewees in different roles, depending on the circumstances of the interview, where it takes place, the nature of the relationship between interviewer and subject, the questions we ask and the kinds of answers they elicit.

Writing about a different field, Dorothy Heathcote has created a model for the use of role in drama-in-education and for what she terms the 'frame distance' – or sometimes 'role distance' (Heathcote uses the two terms interchangeably) – in a drama context set up by a teacher. Heathcote describes a series of frames through which events are interpreted, which expose different layers of meaning the further removed they are from the event.

Because Heathcote's model explores the relationship between a personal narrative and an event, it is also a useful tool to look at the mode of address in documentary interviews. The diagram in Figure 18.1 is adapted from Heathcote's work,[2] to explore this idea of frame or role distance in relation to interviews with documentary subjects.

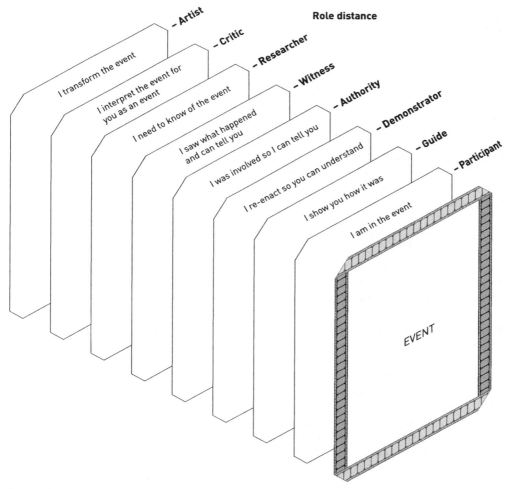

Figure 18.1 Role distance

Source: adapted from Dorothy Heathcote

As you move away from the 'event', the role becomes both less immediate, and more interpretative. If we think about this in terms of documentary interviews, examples of these different roles are as follows:

Participant ('I am in the event')

The interviewee is a key participant in the events being filmed, and is interviewed as those events unfold. Think, for example, of a documentary about the work of an ambulance crew, in which the filmmaker films the ambulance staff as they work, occasionally asking questions of them, perhaps to explain what they are doing, or how they feel about it. This is the standard mode of interview for reality television. Its strength as an interview method is its immediacy; it draws the viewer into the action through the perceptions of its participants. Because of that immediacy, the circumstances of filming, and the fact that the interviewee is primarily focused on another activity, this form of interviewing tends to remain at the level of the action being covered and is less suitable to reach the interviewee's more reflective thoughts or to expand their responses beyond that immediate situation.

Guide ('I show you how it was')

The interviewee guides the filmmaker around a physical space in order to tell their story. The filmmaker has chosen a location significant to the content of the interview and it acts as the starting point for questions and answers – a very common strategy for documentary interviews. An example of this would be Lanzmann's *Shoah* (1985), where Lanzmann interviews holocaust survivors at the sites of death camps, ghettos and executions. They become our guides to those places, but in order to bear witness to a past which is largely invisible in the present-day landscape. The 'guide' role can of course also be used, more prosaically, to explain a physical environment or an organisation – for example, on a journey around a workplace, to which the guide becomes our point of access. Shooting an interview in a location offers the filmmaker both a context and also more choice about the way the interview is edited than, say, a single headshot in a studio.

Demonstrator ('I re-enact so you can understand')

The interviewee re-enacts events while being interviewed (or while telling the story of those events). The re-enactment is usually to demonstrate rather than to dramatise, but blurs the boundary between drama and documentary, using actions, the subject and the location to visualise events. As form of interview, it is not particularly common in documentary – and where it is used, it is often based on a subject who wants or needs to tell their story in this way. Parts of the interview with Philippe Petit in *Man on Wire* would come into this category, where Petit, interviewed in a studio space made reminiscent of a theatre stage, strides around the space, mimes and uses props to describe his tightrope walk between the Twin Towers of the World Trade Centre.

Perhaps the most striking example of this interview mode is in Werner Herzog's *Little Dieter Needs To Fly*, a documentary about German-born Dieter Dengler, a US pilot who is taken prisoner by the Vietcong. Herzog takes Dengler back to the forests where he was captured and held. At one point, Dengler tells the story of his imprisonment while being bound at the wrists and led through the forest by 'extras' dressed as Vietnamese soldiers, prompting him to step out of role to say, 'This is a bit too close to home.' The film's editor, Joe Bini, has remarked on the distinction between these re-enactments, done by Dengler himself, and the drama reconstruction more often used in documentary:

Little Dieter Needs To Fly: Dieter Dengler re-enacts his capture by the Vietcong, while being interviewed (Herzog, 1997)

It puts the audience through the experience, doesn't it? Because in re-creation [i.e. drama reconstruction] you're always distanced from it. But putting that man [Dengler] in that situation made you, as an audience member, somewhere there with him. It's kind of so outrageous that [Herzog] is making him go through this again.[3]

The scene Herzog creates has several layers: the telling of a story from two decades before by one of its protagonists; the physical re-enactment of that story; and a 60-year-old man re-experiencing the trauma in the present as he repeats the actions in the story he is telling. The effect of this is both to understand the past story, and to make us constantly aware of the impact of this story on its narrator even after 20 years.

Authority ('I was involved so I can tell you')

The documentary equivalent of Heathcote's 'Authority' role is the retrospective interview with the participant *after* the event. The 'Authority' interview positions the interviewee as someone who was a key participant in events but who is now recalling it with the benefit of hindsight. Like Wordsworth's definition of poetry as 'emotion recollected in tranquillity', this mode of address combines both intimate knowledge and the potential for much deeper reflection. It is the standard interview mode for retrospective and historical documentaries, more likely to be studio-based, less immediate and more analytical than the 'Participant', 'Guide' or 'Demonstrator' modes, which tend to be location-based. The filmmaker is asking for a first-hand, detailed account, but one that has the distance of time. The subject matter of the documentary is a set of events in the past, and interviews are used to provide first-hand accounts of those events.

Witness[4] ('I saw the event and can tell you about it')

The 'Witness' interview positions the interviewee as someone who has been present at the event but is not a key participant in it. As such, they may be able to describe it, but they may not understand its implications. This is the interview mode of many news stories, of course, where questions are focused on eliciting a brief explanation of what happened (before, typically, cutting to a 'Critic' interview [see below] in a studio where the significance of the event is explained). They are unlikely to be focused on emotional impact unless as an immediate response to the extreme nature of what has been witnessed. In this mode, the interviewee is not important for the purposes of the film as an individual character, only for their ability to bring to life the action of the event for the viewer.

Researcher ('I need to know of the event')

We follow the interviewee on a journey of discovery and the interview questions spring from the experiences and revelations on that journey. The focus of questioning is on the meanings these discoveries hold for the subject, trying to reveal their emotional impact. An example of this interview mode would be the BBC series *Who Do You Think You Are?* in which a well-known public figure explores their own family history. The interviews in the films take place as the subject visits places connected with their family's story, searches through archives, travels and invariably discovers something that makes them re-evaluate their own values and beliefs about their family. The 'Researcher' mode is common in documentaries based around a central character's journey; the interviewee is a kind of cipher for the viewer and, by allowing us in on their investigation, they lead our reactions to the story they are exploring.

Critic ('I interpret the event for you as an event')

When the interviewee's role is that of 'Critic' it's likely that they are commenting on events they have not been centrally involved in, unlike the 'Authority' role. The 'Critic' role asks the interviewee to interpret the event for the viewer, based on his or her own expertise in the subject. Think, for example, of the ways in which interviews with Norman Mailer, Spike Lee, George Plimpton and others are used in *When We Were Kings* (1996), the feature documentary about Muhammad Ali's fight with George Foreman in Zaire in 1974. Although Mailer and Plimpton actually attended the fight, their primary role, alongside Spike Lee, is to provide an additional layer of commentary in the film, beyond the archive footage of the fight and the lead-up to it, and the

Norman Mailer in *When We Were Kings* (Leon Gast, 1996)

film of the concert given in honour of the event. Their contribution is to take us into the cultural and political significance of the events we are watching, so that the Ali–Forman fight becomes much more than a boxing match. As in *When We Were Kings*, 'Critic'-style interviews are usually studio-based, which heightens the sense that they are at a remove from the action, distanced enough to reflect on it with authority.

Artist ('I transform the event)'

It's unusual in documentary to work with interviewees in connection with metaphorical or symbolic interpretations of events, but there are some remarkable examples of this. Of course, it is relatively common in arts documentaries, where an artist's work is combined with an exploration of their life and the filmmaker often tries to find events which have a close relationship to the art and cut between the two. In 'Artist' mode, the filmmaker is encouraging a symbolic reinterpretation of an event by the subject through interview. As Werner Herzog suggests:

> Facts and reality sometimes are not enough. You need an enhancement and intensification of it. Some sort of an essential version of things to make things transparent.[5]

Little Dieter Needs to Fly: Dengler and the freedom of opening a door (Herzog, 1997)

Herzog's own documentaries look for and exploit moments that offer this enhancement. Making *Little Dieter Needs To Fly*, he describes noticing in Dengler's apartment a large number of paintings of open doors. When Herzog asked Dengler about these and about their relationship to his imprisonment in Vietnam, Dengler denied at first that they were significant, saying he had bought them because they were cheap. Herzog suggested to Dengler that they were more than that and Dengler reflected and finally acknowledged that being able to open and close doors was an important freedom to him. In the film, Herzog cuts a sequence of Dengler going back and forth through a door, while he explains that sense of freedom. The scene, Herzog argues, goes deep into the heart of who Dengler is.

A second example of the interviewee in 'Artist' mode is in Nicholas Barker's documentary *Unmade Beds*, about four New Yorkers looking for love in the city's lonely hearts columns. Barker worked with his subjects, using research interviews to construct scripted to-camera accounts of events, which he then filmed in much the same way as a fiction director might work with an actor. The subjects perform a version of themselves, based on their own words. Barker's method gives him enormous control over the shooting and editing of the settings of these performed monologues, and the subjects have the control of rehearsing and enacting an account of their lives through a scripted performance rather than an improvised interview.

Styles of questioning

As in *Little Dieter Needs To Fly*, a film will often use the same interviewee in different interview 'roles', shot in different settings, even within single sequences. For example, a sequence might combine a 'Participant' interview on camera with voice from an 'Authority' interview shot in a studio at a different time. Combining the two enables the filmmaker both to draw the viewer into the immediacy of the action and to step out of that action at times to hear its subjects reflect on it. Usually these interviews will be done at different times because they require a different set of unspoken rules between interviewee and interviewer.

Each interview mode implies a different style and line of questioning. The tone and kinds of question asked by the filmmaker shape the style of answer given by the interviewee, just as in a conversation each party can influence the tone of the encounter through the tone of their own contributions. Aggressive questioning is likely to lead either to more forthright answers (to counter allegations, for example) or to none at all (perhaps even a retreat from the interview); empathetic, open questions will tend to generate more expansive and perhaps less guarded responses. Documentary filmmakers can learn much from other professions where questioning forms a key role – teachers, therapists, market researchers, lawyers, even military interrogators – and it is worth investigating questioning theory and practice in these fields to develop your own skills as an interviewer.

Keep in mind that the interviewer's role is also as a proxy for the viewer, asking the questions that arise from the material in the mind of the viewer during the film. Make a plan of the questions you want to ask, in an order that has a coherent flow from one question to the next. But above all, listen to the answers and leave your plan behind to follow them up in order to deepen and expand the interviewee's story. Listen, too, for the things that aren't being said – and try to probe them through your questions. In a film like *Capturing the Friedmans* (dir. Andrew Jarecki, 2004), about allegations of sexual abuse within a family, it is the silences and gaps in the interviews that sometimes speak loudest.

Preparation

Once you have selected your interviewees, you need to think about preparing for the moment you will ask them questions. In documentary, the filmmaker will usually have already met the interviewee, and in most cases this helps the interview (though there are some films in which the first encounter may need to be on camera – much of the work of Nick Broomfield, for example, depends on seeing this encounter on film). Identify the areas you want to explore with them, and discuss those areas, but be wary of 'talking the interview out' in advance. If the subject has answered all your questions before you start shooting, you may lose some spontaneity on camera. The relationship between interviewee and interviewer is strongest on camera when genuine communication is taking place, not a word-for-word repetition of something they have talked about before. Decide what you need to tell the interviewee about the context of the film and the part their interview plays in it.

The interview mise-en-scène

The role the interviewee is adopting in the film will influence the choice of situation in which the interview is filmed – and so its 'mise-en-scène' for the viewer: how it appears on screen.

In the documentary interview, these choices are primarily over setting (background and location), shot size, lighting and framing, and the attitude of the interviewee to the camera itself.

Setting

Just as in a seventeenth-century Dutch portrait the background gives crucial clues about the sitter, the whole frame of the interview, not just the appearance of the interviewee, shapes its meaning. As discussed above, the closer the interviewer 'role' is to the event/action, the more likely it is that the interview takes place on location. Correspondingly, as the mode of address becomes further from the immediacy of present-tense action, and more reflective, it is more likely that an appropriate choice of setting is a studio. ('Studio' here can mean any room in which you have control over lighting, sound and background.) Think about what else you can see in the frame other than the interviewee, and how this contributes or is detrimental to the meaning of their performance. In a studio you have the option of creating a background – either abstract or perhaps minimally evocative of the settings of the documentary (for example, the studio backgrounds for interviews in *Touching The Void*, which are reminiscent of a mountaineer's tent.)

Shot size

Shot size and framing are also decisions which shape the interview's meaning. Very close shots can create a sense of pressure on the interviewee. A mid shot can feel more analytical and less emotional. You need to decide whether you want to change shot sizes during the interview. This can give you more editing choices and variation (although unless you know in advance what the interviewee is going to say, it is difficult to match shot sizes to meaning with any precision).

Attitude

The feel of the interview will also depend on who the interviewee is talking to, how well they know them and the relationship they have established. In documentary interviews where the director operates the camera and asks questions at the same time, the interviewee can come to see the camera and director as a single entity, which means their relationship to the viewer follows their relationship to the director. In more formal interview set-ups, where the interviewer sits beside the camera, their position will influence the look – the closer the eye-line to the camera, the more an audience will feel the answers are addressed to them. The convention in documentary is that the interviewee should not look directly at the camera as this breaks the 'fourth wall' and undermines our sense of being a privileged witness on an unmediated reality. But many filmmakers break this convention, often through the 'camera-director' set-up above, but also more consciously, for example in the work of Errol Morris.

Morris (*The Thin Blue Line, The Fog of War, Mr Death, Fast, Cheap and Out of Control*) has developed an interview set-up in which the subject could be looking directly at the camera where, using autocue technology, Morris projects a live image of himself asking the questions. For Morris, this system establishes eye contact between the interviewee and the viewer. He explains why this is important in his films:

The Fog of War, eye contact: Robert MacNamara using the Interrotron (Errol Morris 2003)

When someone watches my films, it is as though the characters are talking directly to them . . . There is no third party. On television we're used to seeing people interviewed sixty-minutes-style. There is Mike Wallace or Larry King, and the camera is off to the side. Hence, we, the audience, are also off to the side. We're the fly-on-the-wall, so to speak, watching two people talking. But we've lost something: direct eye contact. We all know when someone makes eye contact with us. It is a moment of drama. Perhaps it's a serial killer telling us that he's about to kill us; or a loved one acknowledging a moment of affection. Regardless, it's a moment with *dramatic* value. We know when people make eye contact with us, look away and then make eye contact again. It's an essential part of communication. And yet, it is lost in standard interviews on film.[6]

Morris calls his autocue-based interview set-up the 'Interrotron'. The direct-to-camera look from the interviewee that results is quite unlike that of a television presenter, creating instead a direct but still intimate and personal address to the viewer.

Working in translation

If you are working with an interviewee in a language that is foreign to you, you need to think about the impact of the process of translation on your interview. First, for all of the nuances of the way questions are asked (tone, phrasing, body language), you are reliant on your translator, who, at least during the period of the interview itself, holds the main relationship with the subject. This means it is crucially important that your translator understands your motives for the interview, its context in the film and the kinds of responses you are looking for; their role extends far beyond language translation. You need to make a decision about whether to translate in full after each answer (which can lead to a stop–start feel to the interview), or to rely on your preparation with your translator and a summary at the end. Often it is better to let the interview flow and then to ask subsidiary questions at the end. You need also to think about the positioning of the translator in relation to the camera, as this may determine where your subject looks. An innovative approach to this conundrum was taken by Jason Kohn in the film *Manda Bala (Send a Bullet)*, in which the translator is in frame alongside the interviewee. The film contains

The translator in frame, *Manda Bala* (Jason Kohn, 2007)

responses from the interviewee in Spanish followed by the translation, which allows us (if we don't speak Spanish) to focus on the subject's physical (body language) response to the question, before understanding the words. Occasionally, there is an interaction between subject and translator, which tells us more about the interviewee and about the context of the interview, as when one of the interviewees refuses to answer a question about money laundering: 'He said he wasn't going to ask me about that!'

The standard interview set-up

The standard set-up for a filmed interview is framed somewhere between a mid shot and a close-up, with the eye-line of the interviewee as close to the camera as possible, but not looking directly into the lens. The framing uses the majority of the negative space (all that space in the picture that is not the subject) on the side of the frame towards which the subject is facing. The image achieves greater depth if the subject is at least five feet from the background – and offers more latitude in grading if the background is darker than the subject.

Standard interview framing

If using lights in the standard 'three-point' lighting set-up, the key light is usually on the far side of the face, so the conventional camera and lighting set-up would be as in Figure 18.2.

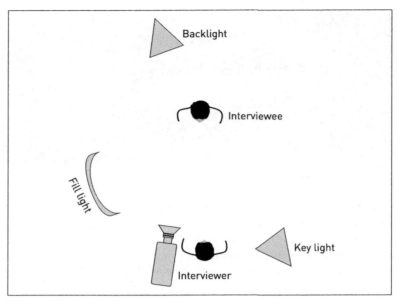

Figure 18.2 Standard interview lighting setup

Using natural light

Many documentary interviews are shot using natural light, but even just using sunlight (and a reflector if you have one) you can use the available light to mimic the rules of this standard set-up, if you think about the positioning of the camera and the interviewee in relation to the strongest light source (usually the sun or, indoors, a main window). For example, see Figure 18.3.

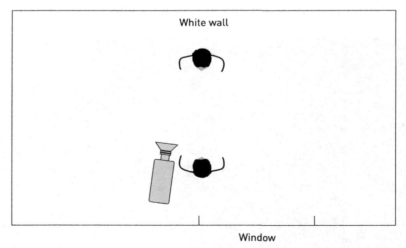

Figure 18.3 Using natural light in the standard interview

Sound

It's obviously desirable to recce the location for your shoot, though this may be something you cannot do in practice. On the recce, as well as looking for possible shots and interview spaces, listen for a time to the ambient sound of the location. Is there an unacceptable level of background noise, which will make the interview hard to edit into a different context? Depending on the mise-en-scène of the interview, you should use either a rifle microphone or a radio/lapel mic, or a combination of both.

Whatever your location, don't forget to record a wild track of the ambient sound to help smooth your audio edits (see Chapter 21).

Key points

- Have preliminary discussions with your interviewee, if appropriate, and use these to inform your decisions about the interview.
- In your research avoid 'talking out' the issues with the interviewee, so that they've told you all they want to off-camera – keep discussions general.
- Think about the role you are asking your interviewees to fulfil in your film and how their relationship to the content will unfold onscreen.
- Make directorial choices about setting and tone, based on your research and how you imagine the interview will work in the film.
- Prepare your interview; think what questions you need to ask in order for your interviewee to fulfil the role you hope for them.
- Plan for how you intend to edit the interview, so that you shoot to give yourself the choices you need.
- Use open-ended questions (unless you are trying to force a particular admission) and avoid questions that can be answered with a simple 'Yes' or 'No'. In the right context, questions can be as broad as 'Tell me about . . .'
- If possible, avoid giving interviewees a list of questions beforehand – if you do, you may well end up with prepared answers – though by all means tell them the broad areas the interview will cover.
- If you intend to cut your questions out of the final film, encourage the interviewee to speak in whole sentences and to include the question in the answer.
- Reassure the interviewee of the elements of control they have over the interview – to redo a particular question, for example, or to ask to pause while they think or reflect on what they want to say.
- Be clear with the interviewee about where you want them to look.
- If the interview is mobile or conducted while the interviewee is engaging in an activity, think about health and safety risks.

Notes

1 From an interview with Alan Yentob, *Imagine: Werner Herzog – Beyond Reason*, BBC1, 1/7/2008.

2 Adapted from Heathcote, D. (1990) Keynote Speech to National Association for Teachers of Drama Conference, October 1989, in *The Fight for Drama – The Fight For Education*, National Association for Teachers of Drama.

3 From an interview with Bini in *Imagine: Werner Herzog – Beyond Reason*, BBC1, 1/7/2008.

4 I have replaced Heathcote's categories of 'Reporter' and 'Recorder' with a single 'Witness' category.

5 From an interview with Alan Yentob, *Imagine: Werner-Herzog – Beyond Reason*, BBC1, 1/7/2008.

6 From an interview with Errol Morris, published in the Winter 2004 issue of *FLM Magazine* and on Morris' website, www.errolmorris.com/ (accessed 13/05/2010).

Chapter 19

The uses and abuses of archive footage

Toby Haggith

" To put it another way,
what's wrong with wallpaper?
It's agreeable to look at, it
helps to move stories along,
and it's useful for covering
cracks in the narrative. "

(Jerry Kuehl, 25 November 2003)

Introduction

The use of archive footage has become ubiquitous and synonymous with films made to explore and conjure up visions of the past. It is so ubiquitous that people in television production frequently just use the term 'archive' and have come to be so reliant on this signifier of 'pastness' that it is now common for television-makers to create a pastiche of archive film where none exists, from vertical lines and scratches to full-blown recreations of newsreel and colour amateur film, as in the 'bio-doc' *George Orwell: A Life in Pictures* (2003).[1]

Archive film is so commonly used in documentaries that we rarely stop to think about its purpose or to question its inclusion in any film. The purpose of this chapter is to outline the uses that may be made of this powerful filmmaking resource; to give a very general overview of the history of archive film in documentary; to examine some of the abuses and to encourage the documentary maker to be more reflective and rigorous when importing archival materials into their films.

Why use archive footage

In most instances, the archive footage used for films about the past is actuality or documentary footage, thus it is the connection of the footage to the real which gives it utility or even credibility. However, feature film and dramatised archive footage has long been incorporated in documentaries when suitable actuality footage did not exist and the dramatisation was effective and powerful. For example, the BBC television series *The Great War* (1964), often regarded as a landmark in television documentary, made free use of feature film material of trench warfare, intercutting this with actuality archive film.

Although we might expect such manipulation from a documentary series produced during the cynical era of television broadcasting, one of the first 'historical' films was made by manipulating actuality footage. This occurred in 1898 when the Lumière cameraman Francis Doublier, travelling in a Jewish area of Russia, re-cut unrelated scenes from 'actualities' to create a film purporting to show the court-martial of Dreyfus in Paris in 1894, a year before the invention of cinema.[2]

Re-purposing archive film

This early example of the genre points to the essential nature of the use of archive footage for films about the past: it is a manipulation of previously shot film – usually of actuality footage – to create a different meaning. Thus we could characterise this kind of filmmaking as an essentially negative or compensatory activity, even a visual deceit, to produce images of an event that went unrecorded or was unrecordable; hence the particularly close association between this style of filmmaking and warfare – because real armed combat is so difficult to film. But it would be wrong to imply that the use of archive footage is a creatively impoverished style of filmmaking; many films have been made about the past in which the archive material has been used accurately and imaginatively. Indeed, as Alwyn Lindsey, one of the sponsors of the 2010 Focal Awards[3] put it, 'Skillfully used archive footage can tell stories and convey ideas in an incredibly compelling way.'[4]

Today, archive film is generally used in short clips, interspersed with other material, such as interviews with witnesses or experts, archival photographs, illustrations or even paintings, explanatory graphics (maps, charts, etc.), contemporary location shots of historical sites and dramatised reconstructions. This might be described as the classical television historical documentary, developed in series such as *The Great War* (BBC, 1964) or *The World at War* (ITV, 1973–4), often with a voice-over commentary.

The value of actuality footage

One of the most attractive and powerful characteristics of film is its verisimilitude, or ability to accurately convey the nature of the world in front of the lens – what is sometime referred to as its indexical nature.[5] As a result, documentary film is often regarded as a vivid and truthful record, with a facility for description which makes words superfluous. As well as being an authentic record, there is an extra attraction because of its actuality – the recording of history took place at the time and in the presence of the event as it unfolded. Some actuality footage of historical events has gained a dramatic power because of the context of its shooting. For example, the difficulties and dangers experienced by Geoffrey Malins and his colleague J.B. McDowell when filming *The Battle of the Somme* (1916) have increased our appreciation of the film and its authenticity. Another important attraction of film as an historical record is that it often has an aesthetic value – it is beguiling as well as informative.

Cameramen and others connected with the production of early actualities and newsreels were quick to grasp the historical value of film. In his article, 'The Wonders of the Biograph', R.H. Mere said that, 'It brings the past to the present, and it enables the present to be handed down to the future',[6] while Lumière cameraman Bolseslas Matuszewski described film as 'seeing the past directly'.[7] It was also observed that, unlike other kinds of historical record, film not only recorded the past but did so in a manner that made the past accessible to the untrained observer.[8]

When *The Battle of the Somme* (1916) was released, its value to future generations was instantly recognised:

> In years to come, when historians want to know the conditions under which the great offensive was launched, they will only have to send for these films and a complete idea of the situation will be revealed before their eyes – for we take it as a matter of course that a number of copies will carefully be preserved in the national archives.
>
> (*The Times*, 11 August 1916)

In addition to these technical characteristics relating to the nature of film and the viewing experience, there are cultural and historical factors that have become associated with film and which make it of interest to filmmakers.

Moving image as legal evidence

Film has inherited from photography a semi-legal status, allowing it to be submitted as evidence in court. In Britain, the first recorded use of moving film as evidence in a criminal trial took place in Chesterfield on 17 May 1935, when the police screened 16 mm film of men involved in illegal betting, which they had shot secretly from an upstairs window overlooking a street in the town.[9] This simplistic use of the moving image to prove an individual's physical connection to a crime or presence at a scene when a crime took place, has proliferated with the development of video cameras, CCTV and digital systems, with even cyclists now routinely recording their journeys from handlebar- and helmet-mounted digital cameras to record hostile driving by motorists.

Film's particular facility to describe or convey scenes which seem beyond words, even human comprehension, made it attractive to those holding trials for war crimes after the Second World War, with the first being that for the guards of Bergen-Belsen at Lüneberg in September and October 1945. Despite the fact that there is much controversy about the real value of the moving image to legal proceedings, this development has given film an authority which lends credence to its use as an historical record in documentaries.

Recording 'everyday life'

Developed by engineers and scientists, and created in the era of mass politics, urbanisation and the rise of the labour movement, film has, from its outset, been a democratic medium for the recording and representation of society. Unlike painting, which did not seriously tackle the lives of ordinary people until the nineteenth century, the first film screened by the Lumière brothers was not of royalty or members of the Parisian elite at play, but of workers leaving the Lumière factory (March, 1895).[10] Other topics of early Lumière programmes were equally universal in appeal: a couple feeding a baby; a train arriving at a station; people swimming; a blacksmith at work; a sack-race at a Lumière workers' outing; men sawing and selling firewood, and so on. Although film had begun as a middle-class attraction, it rapidly became a working-class one, being taken up enthusiastically by fairground showmen and others who developed the medium with a view to attracting working-class audiences. One of the strategies employed by pioneers such as the Lancashire filmmakers Sagar Mitchell and James Kenyon, was to film local events at which crowds could be assured and then show these at well-publicised local screenings a few days later. As a consequence, a rich archive of films recording various aspects of working-class life (people leaving work; civic events; sport; works outings and holidays, etc.) now exists which is a valuable resource for the documentary filmmaker.

While amateur films do cover local and even national events of interest to historians, the vast majority of reels shot by amateurs focus on the domestic world of the camera-operator. Sometimes amateur filmmakers even made a special study of the most prosaic moments in family life, such as dad taking tea up to his wife in bed and the children eating breakfast around the kitchen table.[11] In concentrating on these private rituals and patterns of everyday life, amateur film has bequeathed to us a rich store of images recording the lives of ordinary people to counterbalance the concentration on the 'great and the good' which dominates the newsreel and other professional film collections. Not surprisingly, oral historians take an interest in amateur film, many regarding it as the cinematic equivalent of oral history. This is not just because of its subject matter, but because amateur film is structurally more like memory – it is reflective and subjective, records events spontaneously in a real-time chronology, is whimsical, not premeditated, and is unstaged. As well as its connection to memory and oral history, the unsophisticated way in which amateur film is shot has led many, including amateur filmmakers themselves, to regard the amateur film as a pure form of actuality, more authentic because it is less mediated than the professionally made documentary film.[12]

From record to artefact

The value of archive film has increased as the medium has itself become historical. Now over a century old, many film copies have acquired the patina of age, scratched and flecked from use; the medium is 'old'. Moreover, film ages in a way we associate with 'proper' historical records: old or poorly stored film is brittle, shrunk and smelly. Ironically, even though copies which look 'new' can be duplicated from archive masters of films released many decades, even one hundred years ago, people prefer to use film that looks old and worn with age. There is even software which can be downloaded to give any footage the appearance of age.[13]

Film has acquired its own aura of age, not just in a physical sense, but in terms of the way it is perceived by society. It is no longer the 'new' or 'upstart' recording device, but a mature and respected artefact. As David Francis, former head of the National Film and Television Archive, has put it, 'that film may have started life as a commercial entity, but . . . it has assumed, with time, a new role as a heritage artefact'.[14] Like other artefacts, film has both private and public collectors, who jealously guard their copies in special, purpose-built vaults. The preservation of and access to these films is governed by standards and ethical guidelines, formulated by international affiliations of moving image archivists and curators, notably FIAF (International Federation of Film Archives). Interestingly, the advent of digital preservation and the gradual cessation of the manufacture of film stock, has actually led to the increased value of archive film, with even viewing or distribution copies now coming to be considered artefacts in their own right.[15]

The film archive movement has also long campaigned for film to be given the status accorded to other types of artefact and record:

> There can be no doubt that film archives are equal in cultural importance to the museums and galleries devoted to the plastic arts, and to the great libraries. They have the same task of protecting great works of art and important documents from damage or loss in order to make them accessible for research workers and for the general public.
>
> (Herbert Volkman, FIAF, 1965)[16]

An important milestone in the recognition of film as an historical document was the inscription, in July 2005, of the documentary *The Battle of the Somme* (1916) onto UNESCO's Memory of the World register.[17] Launched in 1992, the programme aims 'to protect and promote the world's documentary heritage through preservation and access'. UNESCO's preamble to the Memory of the World Programme is significant in according film a similar value to the traditional methods by which mankind has documented history:

> If stone, paper, parchment and papyrus are the guardians of an almost legendary past, the language of films and multimedia becomes the testimony of our time and of our future. Documentary heritage reflects the diversity of humanity's languages, peoples and cultures. It is the mirror of the world and its memory.[17]

As with other types of artefact or historical record, film and cinema are now legitimate fields of study for the historian and other social scientists with their own established and dedicated academic journals.[18]

Types of use of archive footage in films about the past

Archive film for illustration and to aid continuity

By giving shape to the unfamiliar, literally showing the viewer what things look like, film can ease the work of the script-writer and support the recollections of a witness. For example, when a military veteran describes some equipment he used or the location he fought in, a relevant sequence can be inserted; in this way the footage operates as a visual glossary for the viewer. Because of the descriptive power of film, illustrative archival inserts enable concision – a really good piece of footage may make words superfluous altogether; experienced script-writers suggest that good archival footage be run without commentary. But archive footage can also add power to the words of an interviewee. For example, when Freddie Tomkins recalls his fear of the jungle during the *World at War* episode devoted to the Burma campaign, the preceding archive sequence of a soldier hacking through the dense foliage stimulates the imaginative powers of the viewer and helps them to empathise with the interviewee.[19]

Archive footage can also be used to assist with continuity, by bridging gaps in a narrative or breaks in editing, or to paper over poor camerawork or jumps in continuity from a witness or speaker. It should be obvious that the archival footage used to patch or bridge the breaks in continuity must be thematically and historically matched with the narrative, otherwise the viewer will be distracted.

A practical storytelling device

Actuality footage can provide a quick and cheap storytelling device to set the scene or provide historical background. This is particularly so in the case of films about warfare, where, as well as helping to set the scene, footage of armies marching to and from a battle, of artillery or of battleships in action can save a filmmaker vast amounts of money in uniform, props and extras. The first three minutes of the historical re-enactment *Ypres* (1925) is entirely composed of archive footage from the First World War, covering the German invasion of Belgium and the arrival of the British Expeditionary Force, up to the start of the Battle of Ypres. At this point, the re-enacted drama and the central focus of the film begin; conveniently, there is no actuality footage of the First Battle of Ypres. Due to the small size of the Soviet Navy in 1925, Sergei Eisenstein was forced to use long shots from 'old newsreels of naval manoeuvres – not even of the Russian fleet but that of a certain foreign power' (ironically, probably the Royal Navy), during the production of *Battleship Potemkin* (1925) – which were intercut with the dramatised scenes on board battleship *Potemkin*, to convey the moments when a squadron of the loyal Russian fleet bore down on the mutinous battleship.[20]

As well as the practical value of archive footage to the feature filmmaker, we must also consider the dramatic power that this historical footage can bring to a film. For studio-bound productions or those where location shoots are limited in scale, actuality footage lends a sense of depth and scale to the recreation of a certain event. Archive film also helps to put the viewer into the mode of thinking about the past, helping the filmmaker to convince the audience of the power of the dramatised reconstruction which drives the main narrative. The archive film is also often beguiling in its own right: the viewer enjoys looking at the historical scenes in the archive film and may experience a frisson of excitement when looking at rare or previously 'forbidden' material – for example, the scenes of 'the field-grey hordes' marching into Belgium in *Ypres*.

More recently, Ken Loach and Neil Jordan made a similar use of archive film in their dramatised historical recreations of the Spanish Civil War and the life of the Irish Republican Michael Collins. Archive footage about the Spanish Civil war was used by Ken Loach at the beginning of *Land and Freedom* (1995), to set the scene for a story about the experiences of a man from Liverpool who travelled to Spain to fight for the Republic.[21] The framing of the archive film in *Land and Freedom* is particularly clever, as it also advances the plot: the archive film is a Republican propaganda film which is screened at a Spain Aid meeting attended by the Liverpudlian, at which point he decides to go to Spain. In *Michael Collins* (1996), Neil Jordan presented newsreel film of the Black and Tans, by way of a cinema screening in Ireland.[22] In addition to the dramatic and narrative utility of the archive film in these two examples, both filmmakers have appropriated the historical authenticity associated with archival documentary footage to lend their films power and credibility. In effect, Loach and Jordan are implying that *Land and Freedom* and *Michael Collins* are more than dramatised feature films; these are serious historical studies, with a status equivalent to an historical documentary. There is even a suggestion that the dramatised sequences are so historically accurate that they have some equivalence to the archival inserts, implying to the viewer that the archival film and the dramatised re-enactment are closely allied.

Witness to the past: actuality footage as historical evidence

In a mode most closely allied to the work of the historian, the filmmaker can use archive film that documents historical events that were not recorded elsewhere or, more likely, for which there is no pictorial record or only an oral account. As was predicted by those who first considered the historical value of film, the best examples of this kind of film have usually been produced by amateur or non-official camera-operators, filming opportunistically or occasionally in a clandestine manner.[23] Due to the secrecy surrounding the German programme to exterminate European Jewry, pictorial records of Einsatzgruppen killings and the concentration camps before liberation are extremely rare. In fact, one of the notable moments in the Soviet film about the Maidanek concentration camp is the sequence of the perimeter fence with a sign in German banning photography. Therefore footage of Jews being shot into a pit in Liepaja, Latvia, in 1941, and of Dutch Jews being loaded into railway wagons at Westerbork camp in 1944 for transportation to Auschwitz, are important visual records of the Holocaust. Because of the rarity and power of such footage they have been used extensively in television documentaries such as *The World at War* (1974) series.[24] When used to illustrate testimony from a person who witnessed such events, this kind of footage becomes more than illustrative material; it is a powerful corroborative document that gives shape and meaning to stories that are beyond most people's comprehension. However, the documentary maker must be very careful before importing such potent material into their film, as the nature of such film evidence is a problematic area. The provenance of footage of 'hidden histories', especially of atrocities, is often unknown; and, partly arising out of the provenance issue, it is not clear what the film is showing other than the obvious – in the case of the Liepaja and Westerbork examples, people being shot into a pit or civilians getting into railway wagons. Clearly, without crucial explanatory documentation, this film is meaningless footage, disturbing for the viewer, but hardly something that could be used as historical evidence.

Montage documentary or compilation film

Esfir Shub is often credited with pioneering the historical compilation film and as the first person to use archive film from disparate sources to create an historical documentary. In fact, examples of this genre were made in Britain in the wake of the First World War (e.g. The World's Greatest Story, 1919 and The Battle of Jutland, 1921) however, Shub was the most creative in her use of archive footage and approached her task from a theoretical standpoint, drawing on her experiences working as an editor in Soviet cinema. She was also partly inspired by Eisenstein's use of archive footage in *Battleship Potemkin*. Her films the *Fall of the Romanov Dynasty* (1927) and *The Great Way* (1927) were commissioned to tell the story of the Soviet Union from the February revolution of 1917 up until the tenth anniversary of the Russian revolution. Due to the fact that so little actuality footage had survived to tell the story, Shub had to rely on a mass of material that did not document the events of the revolution as such but could be used to evoke the feeling of pre-revolutionary Russia and the atmosphere of the revolutionary period. She did this by editing together scenes in a logical structure that made sense pictorially and emotionally, even if each of the actual constituent pieces of newsreel or amateur film had not been shot to convey this new meaning. One of the most powerful demonstrations of her skill is an extended montage of newsreel and other footage, produced around the world, to narrate the story of the growing militarisation of European powers and the build-up to the opening of the First World War.

In addition to creating a descriptive montage, Shub used archive film in a dialectical fashion, which had its basis in Marxist theory of history and political economy. By abutting two different pieces of actuality footage, she created a third meaning which politically subverted the original meaning. For example, scenes of the estate of wealthy landowners, and of the owners of the estate taking tea in their garden, were intercut with views of a squalid rural village and of peasants toiling in the fields, the implication being that the Russian aristocracy were able to decadently enjoy themselves as a result of the exploitation of the poor. The inter-titles also helped the viewer grasp the meaning suggested by the arrangement of images.

In developing this technique, Shub is credited with inventing the idea of 'visual mood', and producing a type of film which, in Sergei Eisenstein's words, resulted in 'the liberation of the whole action from the definition of time and space'.[25] Although Shub herself never used original pieces of footage, always making copies of the archive film chosen for her non-fiction chronicles, philosophically this is a technique which works against the ethos of the archivist and historian, as the original identity and meaning of a film becomes lost when it is absorbed by the process of montage into a compilation. Indeed, the work of today's video artists who make compilation films with the erroneously termed 'found footage', encourages further this process of decontextualising archive film – so it becomes nothing but a cinematic swatch, indexed only by its superficial pictorial content.

The archive compilation or montage documentary has been a popular genre with other film projects that chronicle important episodes in history such as wars (*Victory at Sea*, 1952; *The Great War*, 1964; *The World at War*, 1974), and particularly the reconstruction of a nation's past such as *Mise Eire* (*I am Ireland*) (1959),[26] and even the history of humanity in the twentieth century – *People's Century* (1995). One of the features of projects such as *Mise Eire* is that they are self-consciously nationalist projects, often involving an attempt to recover or reconstruct a national history after an extended period of trauma or suppression of the nation. In the case of *Mise Eire*, the film can be seen as an attempt to reinforce an ideologically approved version of Irish history since independence, which explicitly rejected British colonialism.

Re-purposing of archive footage for ironic purposes

As the use of archive footage matured as a filmmaking technique, it became possible for filmmakers to re-purpose archive film in an ironic fashion. Instead of concealing the misuse or misappropriation of archive footage, the whole point of the ironic use of footage is that the filmmaker draws attention to its inclusion and misuse. This sophisticated technique was particularly prominent during the Second World War, when both German and British film propagandists re-presented captured footage, invariably re-edited with comical music and a new sarcastic commentary, to subvert the film's original meaning. A good German example is *Soldaten von Morgen* (*Soldiers of Tomorrow*) (1941), an anti-British film for the Reich's youth movement, which included British footage of young army officers drilling on a parade ground and of the cabinet ministers Lord Halifax and Anthony Eden, to lampoon the British ruling classes and make them appear decadent and effete.[27] In Britain, Leni Riefenstahl's celebrated propaganda record of the 1934 Nazi congress, *Triumph des Willens* (*Triumph of the Will*), was repurposed in a number of official propaganda films, most notably *Germany Calling* (1941) and *These are the Men* (1943). In the former, also known as *Lambeth Walk* and *The Panzer Ballet*, the newsreel editor Charles Ridley recut scenes to match the popular show-tune 'Lambeth Walk' and, by introducing jump

Newsreel footage of British wartime Foreign Secretary Anthony Eden, re-presented in the German propaganda film *Soldaten von Morgen* (1941)

Source: courtesy of the Bundesarchiv, Filmarchiv/Transit Film GmbH. Still created from the copy held in the IWM collection, IWM FLM 4167

cuts, looping scenes, and reversed sequences of marching troops, the whole spectacle of Nazi power and military precision becomes quite farcical and even camp.

In Britain, film propagandists also used archive film ironically to attack British society and the state. In propaganda shorts such as *Dawn Guard* (1941) and *Wales, Green Mountain, Black Mountain* (1942), footage that documented the ills of the interwar years (poverty, unemployment and slum housing) was presented as a pointed reminder that the heroes of the last war had received little reward when they returned home in 1918, and that the 'people' must not be cheated again. As Dylan Thomas's commentary puts it at the end of *Wales, Green Mountain, Black Mountain*, 'Remember the march of the old young men. It shall not happen again.'[28]

The abuses of archive film

'Generic illustration' or 'wallpaper'

Archive film is mainly regarded by documentary makers as an illustrative material, to be employed for narrative, structural and aesthetic purposes. As a result, terms such as 'generic archive' or 'generic illustration' are now regularly used when researchers request film from the Imperial War Museum.[29] This is a term that bothers film archivists, as it reduces the status of historical footage to meaningless illustrative clips, or 'wallpaper'. The traducing of historical record film to 'wallpaper' is a particular irritant for Jerry Kuehl:

> . . . whenever I hear the term 'generic film' I get extremely annoyed. To be honest, I go ballistic. There is no such thing as generic film. Every centimetre of film was shot at a particular time and in a particular place.[30]

Formerly a film researcher and documentary producer on series such as *The World at War*, Jerry Kuehl is now more aligned with the historian and archivist and, in this role, has become concerned about the use of archive footage in historical filmmaking. As the Office Cat, a nom de plume for his column in *Archive Zones*, he has, since 1997, exposed the misuse of archive film in documentaries.[31]

> The Office Cat is a film researcher. The Cat goes back a long way. Human film researchers are sober and conscientious. If no film of a personality or an event is known to exist, they will say so. The Cat, however, reports directly to producers and directors, and it can find anything they require, whether it exists or not. One of its ancestors discovered film of the Wright brothers' first flight, another discovered the iceberg which sank the Titanic, and a third found film of cheerful passengers on board the Hindenburg seconds before it crashed in flames on May 6 1937. One of its cousins recently discovered film of the marriage of Hitler and Eva Braun in the *Führerbunker* in 1945. If the producer or director wants it, the Cat gets it. It never takes 'no' for an answer.[32]

Kuehl analyses the use of archive footage in documentaries and identifies a range of abuses which undermine what he feels should be the ultimate goal of the maker of films about the past – to produce visual history – films which are the equivalent of the written historical dissertation and to which can be applied the same rules and level of scrutiny by the scholar as would be applied to an essay. Here is Kuehl's useful summary of the principal categories of misuse of archive footage:

1. Film which is claimed to be of one event which is in fact of another event.
2. Film shot in one place which purports to have been shot somewhere else.
3. Feature film masquerading as factual film.
4. Film of an event which was never filmed at all – like the maiden voyage of the *Titanic* or the first flight of the Wright Brothers' aircraft, and finally (though the list is not exhaustive).
5. Film made before the invention of motion picture cameras, like the Battle of Waterloo or Columbus discovering America.[33]

Rather than resort to such measures, Kuehl offes this simple piece of advice for the use of archive footage: 'If there is no such thing as generic film, the only honest way to use material which purports to show historical events is to use it in appropriate contexts.' Only in this way, he argues, will visual history be taken seriously.[34]

In addition to the scrupulous use of archive footage, he suggests that those aspiring to produce visual history should create a website which contains:

1. the script of the programme;
2. a fact check – what print historians call footnotes;
3. a full transcript of any interviews;
4. a detailed shot list of visual material, including photographs.[35]

At the heart of this issue is the fact that, because film is not transparently knowable or self-revealing, it is vulnerable to manipulation or misappropriation. Even footage which seems to show the most obvious scene or piece of action will require some information to give meaning for the viewer.

Many examples of the misuse of archive film can be spotted in historical documentaries and often in some of the most celebrated and respected of broadcast programmes. As I mentioned at the start of this chapter, despite its great reputation and popularity the 1964 BBC television series *The Great War* often used archive footage with little reference to historical accuracy. It also included dramatised material, much to the annoyance of the historians and archivists at the Imperial War Museum, who had collaborated with the BBC on the series, leading them to request that it be made clear to the viewer whenever 'reconstructed or fake scenes' were used.[36]

However, I am illustrating this section with an example of the misuse of archive footage from Alain Resnais' admired film about the concentration camps, *Nuit et Brouillard* (*Night and Fog*) (1955), in which Resnais used British Army, US Signal Corps and Red Army footage shot after the liberation of the concentration camps to illustrate the experience of the prisoners before their liberation. In this instance, it was not just that no cameramen happened to be in the vicinity of the camps when they were operating as labour and extermination camps; filming and photography were expressly forbidden by those in charge.[37]

The sequence in question starts ten minutes into the film and is a rapid assembly of archival images and new colour sequences shot at a depopulated Auschwitz, supported by a powerful musical score and voice-over commentary. It begins with photographs of prisoners at various categories of concentration camps and then cuts to black-and-white sequences of archive footage filmed at Bergen-Belsen and Auschwitz after liberation, at which point the script directly refers to the experiences of the prisoners in the camps.

There are over 100 edits in the 17-minute sequence, making it very difficult for the viewer to identify the location or date of any of the images. Moreover, the voice-over commentary is the viewer's only source of information about the film, and in only a few instances in this sequence is direct reference made to the time-specificity of the archival images: to identify photographs of the stone staircase built by the prisoners of Mauthausen; the photographs of naked people about to be shot by members of the Einsatzgruppen; and lastly, 'When the Allies open doors . . .', to

This still from a sequence in *Nuit et Brouillard* (*Night and Fog*) is accompanied by the commentary: 'Soup . . . each spoonful is precious. One spoonful less, one day less to live', and is used to convey the experiences of prisoners in German concentration camps before they were liberated. The sequence is actually taken from a reel shot on 17 April 1945, after the liberation of Bergen-Belsen concentration camp, by cine-cameraman Sergeant William Lawrie of the British Army's Film and Photographic Unit.

(Film still courtesy of the Trustees of the Imperial War Museum. IWM FLM 4166)

introduce the footage filmed after liberation of the camps, mainly at Bergen-Belsen, of corpses strewn across the ground, of corpses being pushed into mass graves by a bulldozer and of the SS camp guards being marched along by British soldiers. It should be added that the success of such an exercise relies not just on skilful editing and the use of distracting sources like music and commentary, but on the authority possessed by actuality footage to mislead the viewer.

One of the consequences of this particular manipulation of archival images is that, after seeing *Night and Fog,* many people, including even the children of Holocaust survivors, assumed that the bulldozer was being driven by a German soldier at Auschwitz.[38] It is likely also that *Night and Fog* has contributed to the widespread belief that there were gas chambers at Bergen-Belsen.

Conclusion

I hope from the example that I have given of the misappropriation of archive film relating to the Holocaust, that it is clear that the misuse of archive film can have serious consequences. But even without such a cautionary tale, it is deceitful to intentionally mislead the viewer by including archive film which does not illustrate the episode described in the narrative. Moreover, documentary filmmakers have a responsibility to be honest with the viewer and treat them with respect. We are also aware of the power of the moving image: it is so persuasive a medium that, once an erroneous idea has been communicated by a film, it is very difficult to make a retraction or to expunge that falsehood from the minds of the wider community. If, however, a viewer identifies a sequence of archive footage that has been misused or misappropriated, the rest of the film loses credibility – even if the filmmaker has only made one slight and momentary transgression of the 'rules'.

It is also creatively unambitious to be so reliant on archive footage that you will use it as 'generic illustration' or 'wallpaper'. If you cannot find archive film that is directly relevant, think of another method of illustrating the story. If you are absolutely determined to use a piece of archive film to illustrate a point in the narrative, but that film only refers to the point in the story in the most general way, make it clear in the script that this is so.

There is a danger that we have become obsessed with archive film, leading to a 'crowding out' of other forms of historical record which may be just as eloquent about the past, even if they are less easy to interpret. This is beginning to affect the design of museum displays as well as the actual study of history, with some historians complaining that, as television documentaries are now dominated by themes recorded in archive footage, so students show less and less interest in exploring historical subjects that took place before the invention of film. Film archivists may have unwittingly contributed to this trend when they have promoted the value of documentary footage to the historian.

Notes

[1] *George Orwell: A Life in Pictures* (dir. Chris Durlacher, BBC, 2003). Other than photographs, there is no known film or recording of the journalist, author and essayist George Orwell. Later in the year, a researcher found a 1921 clip from Pathé News clip of Orwell as a boy playing the Eton Wall game.

[2] Jay Leyda (1964) *Films Beget Films: A Study of the Compilation Film,* New York: Hill and Wang, p. 13. Another account of the fake Dreyfus newsreel appears in Erik Barnouw (1993), *Documentary: a history of the non-fiction film,* Oxford: Oxford University Press, pp. 25–6.

3 The Seventh FOCAL International Awards ceremony was held in London on 27 April 2010. There were eighteen award categories to which 154 titles had been nominated. 'These awards are intended to reward directors, producers and researchers who use archive material – from film and television programmes alike – in outstanding ways.' (Jerry Kuehl, Supervising Juror for the FOCAL Awards, in the programme of the FOCAL International Awards 2010, p. 4.)

4 Alwyn Linsey, Director of AP International Archives, programme for the FOCAL International Awards 2010, FOCAL, 27 April 2010, p. 2.

5 Elizabeth Cowie: 'The film document as the recording of actuality presents an indexical trace of the reality before the camera at the moment of recording.' (Cowie, E. 'Working Images: the Representation of Documentary Film', in Valerie Mainz and Griselda Pollock (eds) (2000) *Work in Modern Times: Visual Mediation and Social Processes*, Aldershot: Ashgate Publishing, pp. 175–6).

6 Mere, R.H. (1899) 'The Wonders of the Biograph', in *Pearson's Magazine*, February 1899, quoted in Harding C. and Popple S. (eds), London: Cygnus Arts Press, *In the Kingdom of the Shadows: A Companion to Early Cinema* (1996), p. 26.

7 Boleslas Matuszewski (1898) 'A New Source of History: the creation of a depository for historical cinematography', in *Le Figaro*, 25 March 1898; English translation at www.latrobe.edu.au.

8 Edward Foxen-Cooper. 'Historical Film Records: The Life of the Nation: A Heritage for Posterity', in *The Times*, 19 March 1929.

9 The 'films were used to convict street bookmakers. The pictures, screened in court, showed bets actually being received by the bookies' (*World Film News*, May 1936). The filming took place on 15 April 1935.

10 Gustave Courbet's painting *The Stone Breakers* (1849) is widely acknowledged as the first painting in western art to put the working-class figure at the centre of the work and to present the subject, in this case two peasant labourers, in a truthful and unromanticised manner. Proudohn called it a 'socialist manifesto' – a term rejected by Courbet, who saw the subject matter as just a result of his interest in 'realism'.

11 Peter Sykes' film, with the allocated title 'Domestic Scenes at 30 Devonshire Road' (1949), is held in the North West Film Archive. Thanks to Geoff Senior and Marion Hewitt of the NWFA for help with this reference.

12 See Stefan Szczelkun, 'The Value of Home Movies', in *Oral History*, Autumn 2000, pp. 94–8. Also, Laraine Cookson, 'Amateur Film and the Archives', in James Ballantyne (ed.) (1993), *Researchers' Guide to Film and TV*, British Universities Film and Video Council, pp. 5–7.

13 Digieffects sells a product called 'Aged Film', available on disc or as an electronic download, which can 'customize characteristics such as grain, dust, scratches, frame jitter and color and all those little details that tell the viewer that they're looking at historical footage. . . . And with presets such as 8mm, Armageddon, grandpa's attic, old home video, scratched film, shaky projector, speakeasy, 70s and much more.' See Digieffects.com.

14 David Francis, 'The Way Ahead' Open Forum, in the *Journal of Film Preservation*, April 2010, p. 11.

15 See David Francis, 'Art museums display the original artefact, and the public has been educated to believe that a copy, however good, is no substitute. It was hard to make a similar case for films, until now, but with the possibility that film stock will no longer be manufactured and that existing viewing prints will be as much unique artefacts as the negatives from which they were produced, the case has become much stronger.' 'The Way Ahead' Open Forum, in the *Journal of Film Preservation*, April 2010, p. 11.

[16] From Volkman's introduction to *Film Preservation: a report for the Preservation Committee of the International Federation of Film Archives*, FIAF, London, 1965, pp. 3–4.

[17] Although the Battle of the Somme was the first documentary inscribed on the list, the first film submitted and accepted for inscription was metropolis (1927), which was inscribed in 2001.

[18] UNESCO's Memory of the World Programme, in the programme to '*The Battle of the Somme*: 90th Anniversary Gala Screening of the 1916 silent film documentary from the archives of the Imperial War Museum', 22 October 2006, p. 12.

[19] The first issue of the *Historical Journal of Film, Radio and Television*, published by the International Association for Audio-Visual Research and Education, was published in March 1981. The journal describes itself as 'an interdisciplinary journal concerned with the evidence provided by the mass media for historians and social scientists and with the impact of mass communication on the political and social history of the 20th century'. *Film History* was first published in 1988. It is published by John Libbey and Indiana University: 'The subject of *Film History* is the historical development of the motion picture, and the social economic context in which this has occurred.'

[20] 'It's a Lovely Day Tomorrow': Burma 1942–1944, Episode 14, *The World at War* (John Peer, ITV, 1971–1974).

[21] Sergei Eisenstein and Jay Leyda (1951) 'The Birth of a Film', in *The Hudson Review, Inc.*, Vol. 4, No. 2 (Summer 1951), p. 221.

[22] *Land and Freedom*, (Ken Loach, UK, 1995).

[23] *Michael Collins* (Neil Jordan, UK, 1996).

[24] Edward Foxen Cooper, the first curator of the Imperial War Museum's film collection: 'A peculiar feature of the few film records that do exist to-day, and are considered worthy of preservation, is that each one of them appears to have been photographed without any intention of its becoming a record of an historical event.' 'Historical Film Records: The Life of the Nation: A Heritage for Posterity', in *The Times*, 19 March 1929.

[25] See the 'Genocide' episode of *The World at War* (1974).

[26] Eisenstein, S. (1949) 'A dialectical approach to film form' in *Film Form*, quoted in Leyda, J. (1964), p. 27, *Films Beget Films: Compilation Films from Propaganda to Drama*, London: George Allen & Unwin.

[27] *Mise Eire* (George Morrison, Ireland, 1959), sponsored by Gael Linn.

[28] *Soldaten von Morgen* (Alfred Weidenmann, Germany, 1941).

[29] *Dawn Guard* (Roy Boulting, UK, 1941), sponsor: Ministry of Information; *Wales, Green Mountain, Black Mountain* (1942), sponsor: Ministry of Information; producer: Donald Taylor; director: John Eldridge.

[30] A good example of this tendency comes in an article in *Broadcast* designed to advise those seeking to use 'archive content' in a television programme: 'Material gathered for a programme in which archive content is used for generic illustration, for example, can be gathered faster and more cheaply than if archive footage is more central to the programme.' *Broadcast*, 30 November 2007, pp. 28–9.

[31] Jerome Kuehl, unpublished, 'The Historical Value of Archive Film', 4 March 2002, p. 4.

[32] *Archive Zones* was formerly the quarterly journal of FOCAL International, the Federation of Commercial Audio-visual Libraries.

[33] From Jerome Kuehl's unpublished 'IWM Presentation, 25 November 2003' (for the Imperial War Museum student documentary master class), p. 1.

[34] Jerome Kuehl, unpublished, 'The Historical Value of Archive Film', p. 9.

[35] Jerome Kuehl, 'The Historical Value of Archive Film', 4 March 2002, p. 10.

[36] From Jerome Kuehl's unpublished 'IWM Presentation, 25 November 2003' (for the Imperial War Museum student documentary master class), p. 4.

[37] Meeting of the Trustees of the Imperial War Museum, 21 September 1964.

[38] *Nuit et Brouillard* (*Night and Fog*) (Alain Renais, France, 1955), sponsored by: Cocinor, Comité d'Histoire de la Deuxième Guerre Mondiale.

[39] Film scholar Joshua Hirsch, who was himself the son of Holocaust survivors, assumed that the bulldozer driver was a German soldier and that the British Army footage was documenting scenes in the death camps before liberation. See J. Hirsch (2004) *After Image: Film Trauma and the Holocaust*, Philadelphia: Temple University Press, p. ix.

Chapter 20

Zen and the art of documentary editing

Wilma de Jong

" The documentary film editor is an artist who helps endow the film with a richness and resonance that did not exist in the raw materials. By using rhythm and pacing, holding back information, allowing pauses, utilizing music, dialogue and other sounds, emphasizing the emotional character of an actor or subject, using a variety of shots, cross-cutting between scenes and actions, the editor prods the documentary toward the psychological and intellectual domain that we have come to expect from great art and effective communication. "

(Aitken, 2005 Encyclopaedia of Documentary Film)

Introduction

This chapter will introduce you to different editing traditions and to different approaches to your footage and possible editing strategies. However, its main focus is to develop a structure and a 'voice', or point of view, in your documentary during the editing process.

The editor as artist

To describe the editor as an artist, as in the above quotation, seems to be wholly appropriate in today's world. The time when an editor was seen as a crafts/technical person is definitely over. In the early days of film in the twentieth century, editors could be found in the technical department rather than the creative department and were mentioned at the end of the credits of a film. Today, editors have a key position in the credits and have gained an important role in the creative process of filmmaking.

> Historically, the editor was the extension of the laboratory and seen as the person who simply took the pieces and joined them together.
>
> There is a rising status, these days; the editor's creative input is appreciated and specified. The credits on any feature film will now include the DP, the production designer and the editor as the top three status credits. Sometimes . . . the editor will be ahead of the production designer, and very occasionally the editor will be ahead of the DP. On documentaries, the editor is often the main credit.
>
> (Editor Justin Krish, interview 2005)

There is one other aspect that is important in the quotation that begins this chapter: the 'psychological and intellectual domain'. It seems that documentary is operating in this domain. Well, editing certainly is. To structure a documentary, to find its soul, its innate truth, one needs both strong analytical skills and a level of abstraction to understand what is implicitly shown or told in the film. Psychological insight is also necessary to tell the story to an audience, to empathise with main characters and their journey. One could add creativity and a will to find new angles to tell an old story or to create an unexpected narrative. It is not without reason that 'total' filmmakers still often work with an editor to create their final film.

The editor's *lack* of familiarity with the footage and open mind to the story can help the filmmaker to create a film that is appreciated and understood by its audience. Your passion for the subject of your film needs to be translated into a film that is accessible to viewers. Documentary has often had a bad reputation among audiences; it has been perceived as boring and likened to radio with pictures. Too much information and an underdeveloped narrative seem to be the reason. Let's remember the words of Alfred Hitchcock:

> In many of the films now being made, there is very little cinema: they are mostly what I call 'photographs of people talking'. When we tell a story in cinema, we should resort to dialogue only when it's impossible to do otherwise. I always try first to tell a story the cinematic way [. . .].
>
> (Truffaut, 1985: 61)

I am not sure whether Hitchcock was referring to documentaries but it could certainly apply to them. So the first aim of this chapter is try to think about how to tell the story the cinematic way.

- Use images instead of words.
- Edit for a reason. There should be an emotional and narrative drive behind your cuts.
- Create scenes that contribute to the development of the story.
- Edit efficiently. Don't use more shots than you need to.

A documentary needs an impetus, something that drives the development of the story you are telling. Filmmakers often say that they are 'storytellers', but what is a story? *It is the way we make sense of unrelated events, how we create a logic or a link between different events.*

How we tell a story in the West is not how stories are told in other parts of the world. The way we tell stories is driven by our linear and rational way of thinking. The Age of Enlightenment taught us a scientific rationality, which has shaped our storytelling and the creation of linear links between events. But look at the following events and how they are linked together.

Five men are walking on a path in the jungle and the fourth man gets bitten by a snake. What are the possible explanations?

The fourth man committed adultery and is being punished by the gods.

The snake was asleep, was disturbed and unfortunately bit the fourth man.

The snake was slithering through the undergrowth looking for food and waited for his chance.

The snake was scared by the movement of the feet in front of him and bit the man.

Normally those snakes don't bite. It was just a coincidence. The snake might have been protecting its eggs or it may have been mating season.

The man was scared and the snake sensed his fear and bit him.

You may want to argue that there should be a scientific answer which explains the behaviour of the snake. Science is often used as an arbiter of the truth. Documentary filmmaking has been influenced by the idea that rational knowledge about society is possible and that such knowledge can be 'objective', irrespective of who articulates it or to whom the knowledge applies.

Bill Nichols (1991), one of the founding fathers of documentary theory, 'translated' the above-mentioned assumptions into documentary theory. He argues that documentary is located within what he describes as a 'discourse of sobriety':

- seriousness
- accuracy
- knowledge
- social purpose
- comparable to discourses in science, politics, economics or education.

Many contemporary documentaries do not fit this description any more and even expository documentaries are now seen as having a more personal point of view and not providing the one and only truth about a certain subject. The 'voice of God' as described by Nichols (2004) has definitely lost its authority.

In short, there are many ways one can make a link, a connection between events or behaviours and analyse certain realities.

Creativity and the voice of the film

The voice of a documentary will reveal its uniqueness, its distinct position among others in the public domain. It is, therefore, important to watch other films about the same subject to find the angle that makes your documentary different.

At the moment there are quite a few documentaries on climate change on release. But compare, for instance, *The Age of Stupid* (F. Armstrong, UK, 2009) with Al Gore's *An Inconvenient Truth* (D. Guggenheim, USA, 2004). Both films call for action, but *An Inconvenient Truth* uses scientific evidence to persuade us to change our behaviour. The critical viewer will immediately notice that Al Gore himself lives in a mansion and flies around the world non-stop to spread the message.

The documentary *The Age of Stupid* uses both fictional elements and reportage footage and tries to provoke the audience. It shows through short reportages linked by a fictional narrative how our way of life destroys the planet. The film is part of *The Age of Stupid* campaign which addresses wider issues of consumerism and how the Western world exploits people and the environment in the developing world. The premiere took place in a solar-powered tent in Leicester Square and was simultaneously shown in around 50 cinemas around the UK (see *The Age of Stupid* website). It was an attempt to practise what one preaches.

These examples show that a 'voice' can be linked to the way the documentary is structured: how certain events, behaviours or associations have been connected or related together.

The authorial voice can also be identified in the visual style of a film. For instance, poetic shots with a great many dissolves do not seem to be part of the visual tools of a protest film.

> Voice is akin to style, the way in which a film, fiction or non-fiction inflects its subject matter and the flow of its plot or argument in distinct ways, but style operates differently in documentary than fiction. The idea of the voice in documentary stands for something like 'style plus'.
>
> Style in documentary derives partly from the director's attempt to translate her perspective on to the historical world into visual terms, but it also stems from her direct involvement with the film's actual subject.
>
> (Nichols, 2001: 44)

In other words, it illustrates a specific engagement with the historical world. In editing terms it will influence where to cut, how to sequence your shots, whether to use long or short takes, sync sound or narration. It will inform whether you follow a strict chronology to structure your film or rearrange events to illustrate a point or illuminate a specific way of approaching your topic or subject.

Structure and visual style will indicate a 'voice' but the *tone* of voice is as important. Your story needs an emotional drive that takes the story further, that moves the film on, for instance:

- a quest
- provocation
- persuasion
- empathy
- sadness
- alliance
- call for action
- protest
- love
- passion
- desire.

Please note these are all 'emotive' terms; a drive is an emotion. Mere explanation of information will not lead to an engaging film.

You are also working with an audience's expectations of a genre. That a documentary contains information, new perspectives and shows 'real' people is part of the conventions of the genre for audiences.

In addition, Barnouw (1993) mentions the following 'voices':

- advocate
- reporter
- prosecutor
- guerrilla.

You may want to try out these 'voices'. Try to write the story of your film as a BBC reporter, an advocate or using compassion. While writing just half a page you could find a 'voice'.

Intuition and structure

Many filmmakers enter the editing suite with many hours of footage, believing that the film will reveal itself during the editing process.

> I feel like an Inuit or Eskimo carver, who will pick up a horn or a stone and ask, 'What is in there?' And then they carve to reveal the form that they believe is already inherently there in the horn or the stone. Likewise, my editing process is a process of revealing the best movie that is in the material. And like an Inuit carver, I must work to reveal, cut things away and rearrange the order, the sounds, the images, the juxtapositions, the sequences, and thereby find the structure. Often it's not until I have been working on the movie for a while that I start to find the deeper questions and issue. This takes time. It also takes an ability to be open to it.
>
> (Lemle, 1998: 366)

This approach emphasises those aspects of the creative process which have been mentioned in Chapter 1: take time, sit down and let it happen. But Lemle adds:

> One great thing I learned in the process of editing documentaries . . . is that movies are really about the structure of the movie.
>
> (Lemle, 1998: 362)

To find a way of editing that suits you will take time. Some filmmakers prefer highly structured approaches while others edit small sequences and try to find 'the heart' of the film.

Different editing traditions

Editing documentaries has not evolved in a vacuum. There are many links to other cultural products such as novels, poetry, reporting, essays or diaries. The following sections will inform you about important influences in documentary editing.

The American tradition

The American film tradition is based on fictional storytelling informed by a literary tradition. It uses continuity editing and realist narrative techniques, generally described as 'Classical Hollywood Cinema' (Bordwell, Staiger and Thompson, 1988). In Chapter 10 you can read about the realist narrative in detail.

The classic realist narrative has become the most dominant narrative structure in the West. As the boundaries between the different genres have blurred and documentary and other factual formats have become more entertaining and have used more popular ways of telling a story, the classic narrative has also become very popular in non-fiction storytelling.

The most dominant form of editing in feature film is continuity editing, with its main aim being to create the illusion of the continuity of time and space. The audience should be drawn into the story without being disturbed by the editing or the production techniques of the film. In continuity editing, the shots are arranged according to narrative time, chronologically following the story's development and allowing the audience to experience a continuous flow. Good editing is in this case invisible editing.

Continuity editing applies the following techniques.

180° rule – crossing the line

The imaginary line between two actors is followed in continuity editing. For example, if a car drives to the right in one shot and to the left in the next, it will distort the illusion of screen space and time and disrupt the emotional experience of the audience. It will draw attention to the technique of film editing. However, if you want to disrupt, surprise the audience and draw attention to the car or the sequence as part of a conceptual idea, then you can play with this rule. For instance, if you want to give the impression that your main character is lost, you could repeat this sequence several times and replace one of the shots with a shot of a town name or the driver talking to a pedestrian. In this case, your audience shares the experience of being lost with the main character.

30° rule

In order to avoid jump cuts, the angle between two camera positions should not be less than 20°. Jump cuts seem to have become more acceptable recently, and are often seen as a stylistic tool to disrupt the continuity and draw attention to an event or situation. In documentary this rule is less consistently applied. Often when the shots offer a slightly different angle and the transition 'feels' OK, this rule is ignored.

Matching eye-lines

The first shot shows an actor looking in a certain direction and following the 180° line. The second shot shows what the actor is seeing.

Match the action

Different shots are put together in such a way that it gives the impression that an action is uninterrupted and the cuts are invisible.

Shot, reverse, shot

To intensify the effect of a dialogue, shots are edited back and forth between the two actors.

Parallel editing

Although not specific to feature film, parallel editing allows the action to take place in different locations which are cross-cut to indicate that they take place simultaneously. This intensifies tension and increases audience involvement.

In relation to documentary you could have a look at the film *Deep Water* (Louise Osmond, Jerry Rothwell, 2006), which consists predominantly of archive material and interviews but is nevertheless edited as a classic realist narrative. The dramatised documentary *Touching the Void* (K. Macdonald, UK, 2003) is another good example. This film consists of dramatised scenes and interviews, but follows a classic realist drama structure. Have a closer look at most reality formats and television documentaries and you will notice that most of them will follow the basic structure of this narrative style.

But, it could be argued that documentary has lost its critical edge as the 'invisible' editing techniques smooth the narrative and don't allow for different points of view, conflicting ideas, offbeat comments, and juxtaposition when compared with more conventional documentary techniques.

In addition to smoothing the narrative, the classic narrative also ideologically organises the world around us. The protagonist tends to be the hero and the antagonist the villain. We learn to analyse the world by binary oppositions such as black–white, good–bad or hero–villain. These oppositions create conflict, a tension on which much of the classic narrative is based.

> Any narrative that predetermines all responses or prohibits any counter narratives puts an end to narrative itself by suppressing all possible alternative actions and responses, by making itself its own end and the end of all narratives.
>
> (Carroll, 1982)

You might want to think about this issue and perhaps look for a solution which might open up the ideological power and narrative narrowness of this approach.

If you translate this narrative to a documentary format it would follow the following structure. In this set-up, I have omitted the climax, as this is the most complicated element in documentary. When you start developing a documentary you often do not know whether you will meet

Table 20.1 Basic structure

Opening	Where?
The tease	Who?
The hook	What situation?
	When?
	Why?
Main body of the film	Problems/contradictions
	Investigation
	Events
	Conflicts
	Different experiences, points of view, flashbacks, re-enactments
Resolution	Conclusion, amalgamation of ideas
End	Open end
	Back to the beginning – nothing has really changed
	End with a question to your audience or a provocative statement

an event that would neatly fit into this structure, but you know that you will need to create an end. As mentioned before, reality does not present itself as a beginning, middle and end. Some endings are artificially created, either driven by the length of the film or the lack of a real conclusion.

The above structure is the basic storyline structure used in fiction film and documentary film. There are a few variations on the structure with which you may want to experiment.

> Surely a film needs a beginning, middle and an end?
>
> > (Freju)
>
> Yes, but not necessarily in that order.
>
> > (Buñuel)

The classic narrative is chronological. A is followed by B and then C and we end with D:

A. Exposition – establishing situation
B. Complication – the problem, the question, the conflict
C. Series of events
D. Resolution – solutions, answers to questions or open end.

We can change this basic set-up and add more interest and even suspense by using flashbacks or a circular structure.

Using flashback

If you make a documentary which has main characters, you could explain the back story of these characters with a flashback – using photos, archive material or even re-enactment – before you continue to investigate certain events. This would lead to the following structure: D followed by A, B and finally C.

This structure could also be used if you tell the story of a certain location or want to investigate certain events. It would help to make your story more interesting and would subvert the classic structure of chronology.

Circular structure

The circular structure starts at the resolution of the story and goes back to reveal the circumstances, the events that happened before and after the big event – this would give a structure of C followed by A, B and then D. For instance, a programme on riots in a city could start with the big event/riots, followed by an historical analysis before returning to the riots, and the actions/events which followed.

Journalistic practices

Journalists' practices have significantly influenced current documentary editing practices. Some shooting and editing techniques are used in documentary, news and current affairs. We all recognise the following set-up: establishing shot, reporter/presenter on location, talking head interviews and some cutaways – either close-ups of the hands, the back of the interviewee or the well-known nodding shot of the interviewer known as 'noddies'. These are the common ingredients of a television documentary, news reporting and longer investigative documentaries.

Some documentary filmmakers eschew these techniques and distinguish themselves from more reportage-based documentaries by using long takes, interviews where the camera follows the interviewee in their actions (observational shooting techniques), and sync sound instead of narration. This approach relies heavily on the contributions of your interviewees. Through your editing you will support your own analysis or ideas, whether you aim to edit with BBC-style impartiality or in a highly opinionated style.

> I believe that every one of us, every member of the audience has within an 'honest witness' which knows when someone on the screen is telling the truth of their experience. Creating that resonance in the hearts and minds of the audience is what our work is truly about.
>
> (Lemle, 1998: 367)

It is still the case that you, as a filmmaker, ought to be sure that your witness accounts are truthful and that you do not edit in such a way as to change the opinion, feelings or ideas of your witnesses, subjects or experts. When you doubt their truthfulness, you can deliberately edit in such way that it becomes clear that witnesses are not telling the truth (*Capturing the Friedmans*, Andrew Jarecki, 2004).

Researcher James Fallows (1998) describes a tendency in journalistic documentaries for the journalist/filmmaker to become more central. The use of the celebrity journalist, it is argued, seems to be more about appealing to higher audience numbers than informing them. Many TV documentaries use this format: an individual quest, as a drive to visit different locations, have certain experiences or meet particular people.

Think about Meera Syal visiting her family in India, or Saira Shah visiting her family's country of origin, Afghanistan; the individual's social position and experiences are being linked to the wider social and political situation of a country. It is a social issues film but packed in a modern format. It is not a discourse of sobriety but the autobiographical experience linked to wider social issues. This personal angle avoids an absolute truth and a voice of 'nowhere' commentary which leaves an openness, incompleteness and conveys an unstable knowledge instead of the truth or absolute knowledge.

The Russian tradition – montage

The Russian documentary filmmakers at the beginning of the twentieth century have not been given the prominent place in documentary history that Robert Flaherty and John Grierson, the pioneers of documentary filmmaking in the Anglo Saxon world, have enjoyed. However, it is increasingly appreciated that the early Russian filmmakers have been very influential in the editing of factual programmes (Fairservice, 2001; Nichols, 2001).

The Russians experimented with editing techniques such as juxtaposition, voice-over archive material and newly shot footage often used in the expository mode, although now used in many hybrids formats. When sound recording techniques improved, this form was extended, using interviews and ambient sound and live action. These are now all very common techniques in the documentary filmmaking tradition.

Kuleshov experiment

The principle of combining two shots was inspired by Kuleshov, one of the first filmmakers to experiment with sequencing of shots. His experiment was to create a short film consisting of one medium close-up shot of an actor with a bland expression followed by a shot of a plate of soup, a young girl in a coffin and a beautiful young woman. He showed the film to an audience which believed that the facial expression of the actor changed whenever he saw the young woman, the little girl or the plate of soup. The audience attributed this to the acting qualities of the actor (Fairservice, 2001). This famous editing experiment illustrated the basis of montage editing theory and meaning production. It showed that, *when any two shots are joined together, an audience will attempt to establish a meaningful relationship between these shots*. Numerous versions of the experiment, using recent footage, are available on the internet.

Kuleshov's experiment inspired the Russian film movement in the 1920s and 1930s and his editing principles and techniques were often used in documentary filmmaking.

Vertov

Vertov's greatest works combine unstaged footage ingeniously as far as to unleash a tremendous rhetorical force. They distil the sensibilities of newspaper columns, and futurist poems in non-fiction feature films of incredible power and sophistication.

(Hicks, 2007: 1)

Like many early documentary filmmakers, both in Russia and the Anglo-Saxon world, Vertov rejected fiction films and actors, Hollywood narrative structures and direction. This should not be considered a mere technical rejection; it was a political stance against the artificial and illusionary world created in Hollywood films.

Vertov's aim was to record 'life unaware', but he used time-lapse footage, slow motion and reverse action to depict realities that were hidden from normal perception. He believed that the camera could reveal realities which the human eye could not see. But at the same time he drew attention to the fact that the camera eye was an artificial eye.

Vertov certainly never aspired to objectivity. His films and those of many Russian filmmakers at the time were partisan and experimental. The critical and political voice could be identified both in the structure and editing techniques of the film.

Eisenstein

Sergei Eisenstein, like many of the Russian filmmakers, developed an editing style which was more theoretically informed. His principles of editing were inspired by Hegel and Marx. Editing was seen as a dialectical process. The combination of shots with very different, perhaps even contradictory, messages was designed to produce new meaning through the editing. 'Realist images' were edited in such a way that a *new* 'reality' or ideology could be envisaged. For example, in Esfir Shub's film *The Fall of the Romanov Dynasty* (USSR, 1927) juxtaposed images of the dancing Romanovs and the peasants working on the land offered a critique of exploitation which does not exist in the image itself. How can the aristocracy party while the peasants toil on the land? This may not be new information in our time but it certainly was in a period when many peasants accepted the existing social order.

Recurrent juxtapositions of certain events would link disparate events in a coherent vision. This is still an important tool used by many critical documentary filmmakers. To disrupt continuity editing, to distort the naturalness of such editing, can lead to new ideas and critical thought, and challenge preconceived ideas, as in the case of Esfir Shub's film in which the existing social hierarchy was challenged.

In a sequence in *October* (USSR, 1927) where Eisenstein wishes to satirise the mumbo-jumbo of religious ceremonies, he cuts from his title *October* to sets of icons, churches and leaning spires and from these to Egyptian, Chinese and African effigies (Reisz and Millar, 1953: 65). The visual contrast ignores the location and context of the shots and cuts images that have no physical connection but are connected by an abstract concept. He presents his vision through this editing strategy.

The unexpected combination of shots can provoke both intellectual and emotional reactions from the audience, transform ideas and promote new perspectives as well as critique and resistance.

The compilation of shots, regardless of their origin, led to a specific tradition described as the 'compilation film' (Leyda, 1969). The Russian film industry in the early 1920s was not organised on a commercial basis but was state-sponsored. The lack of film stock led to filmmakers often experimenting with existing footage and new footage.

As you can imagine, this form of documentary film will become more popular in the near future as different sources of footage, which are easier to access and edit – although not necessarily cheaper – are transferred to a digital format. You can now edit shot footage, with mobile phone footage or surveillance camera footage or mapping devices from the internet. This will lead to new forms of documentary filmmaking in which new narrative structures will be developed.

Avant garde or experimental film

Avant garde film or experimental films use editing techniques which are informed by fine art traditions from Western European origins. They tend to use different rhythms by editing in shot transitions as well as in shot lengths and explore different narrative styles.

It is not only the Russians who criticised the classic realist narrative; this has been challenged within experimental filmmaking as well. Experimental filmmaking plays with different narrative structures to create different storylines which are less predictable or more critical, and are often described as anti-narrative.

> However ubiquitous, narrative remains a particular method of representation and like perspective (in paintings) it is not a neutral or natural system; its effect is to 'place' its spectator/listener both psychologically and ideologically.
>
> (Le Grice, 2001: 291)

In experimental film, two directions can be identified:

- Visually, there is considerable use of abstraction, with non-representational shots, imaginary visuals and shots which in themselves might be difficult to place. They might be extreme close-ups, urban or rural landscapes, which, through the editing, convey certain associations, emotions, or messages which are not usually connected to those images.

- Experimental filmmakers may break with a conventional realist narrative form but do not provide a clear definition of a new narrative. The creation of a new narrative in each film disrupts the viewer's attention and provokes them to interpret and engage differently with the film. Sometimes the aim is not an actual emotional or intellectual engagement but a physical experience. The audience might feel cold, restless or very calm.

This approach draws on the Brechtian principle of alienation which aims to make the audience aware of the artificiality of the film. The film is portrayed as an artificial construct recognisable in the reflexive mode described by Nichols (2004) and also often used by Russian filmmakers.

Music videos tend to use a great many cuts that are associative but do not follow a direct logic. They use associations, juxtapositions or a range of different angles of a person or an object, which follows a specific rhythm.

Experimental films have explored a variety of 'links' between shots. These may be mathematically and randomly chosen, or use a musical analogy. They may achieve highly personal or dreamlike subjectivity by creating a montage which undermines realist or logical narratives. This means that the position of the audience is very different in this situation. It is not positioned in a familiar or comfortable place as with the classic narrative. The audience is, as it were, on the move.

Non-narrative or anti-narrative forms challenge or undermine the dominant conventions of representation and narrative. It is argued that these conventions are inherently connected to existing power structures, both economically, politically and culturally, and are, in essence, conformist.

Examples you may want to have a look at include the work by Chris Marker (*Immemory*, France, 2008), Maya Deren (Nichols, 2001), Joris Ivens (www.ivens.nl) or Luis Buñuel.

Editing: where to start

Digitisation of your material

Different editors will use the digitising process and the creation of bins to store their material either as a purely technical process or as a way to familiarise themselves with the footage.

Watching while digitising your footage might not be the best way to view your rushes for the first time – because you cannot stop it. You might want to save that all-important first viewing until after the material is digitised. You might also consider it as a process by which you become familiar with your material by making notes and creating bins for specific footage.

The first selection

- Discard footage if it is out of focus, if it is too wobbly, if you cannot understand what people are saying. Do not use shots that do not meet basic quality standards; it will undermine your film.
- Describe the good takes.
- Create bins that make sense to you.

Editors will have different approaches, so it does not really matter what kind of system you develop as long as you can find the footage you are looking for easily. You can make thematic bins, chronological bins, bins for locations, bins for all interviews – whatever you feel will work for you.

The next step is to create sequences on the timeline and put these in separate bins. A scene may contain material from multiple locations or interviews, but it is footage that might have a bearing on the purpose of that scene or segment. Never throw away a sequence, always keep a copy in a bin.

Preparing your edit

The following questions should help you to find the heart, the crux of your film.

- What are the most important elements, events, characters, interviews in the film? Either write them down on a Post-it note or edit them: create scenes and put them in a bin or on the timeline.

- Create the key scenes of the film and play with the order you can put them in.

- Using Post-it notes on which you recorded your key issues, key interviews or scenes, try to group them together on a timeline into certain events, characters and locations. Play with the groupings and try different ways of telling the story. It will happen. Many ideas will come up. You can also do this digitally by creating different bins.

- The start of a film is crucial for your audience. It is the hook, the tease to draw them in. Don't think about quickly edited shots with loud music. Your audience should be intrigued. It is like the first five sentences of a book. They are essential, so pay attention to your first scene and how you address your audience and introduce your subject. The introduction should set up your narrative in a clear and intriguing way.

- Describe the setting, place and time of your film. How will this be conveyed at the beginning of the film?

- Write down what is unique about this film. In what way does it differ from other films on this theme?

- Note down what you want the audience to feel or think after they have seen the film.

You can do much of this work straight onto the timeline. Now that a lot of filmmakers have editing software on their laptops, the difference between preparing for the edit and the edit itself is almost disappearing.

If you are working with an editor, you might want to prepare the edit differently. It will save the editor's time – and your money – if they do not have to look through all your material, so you may want to select the material he/she can work with by creating bins with the footage for the key scenes; the key answers of the interviews; footage to create an opening and an end.

Selecting shots and creating sequences and scenes

Try not to select individual shots but think in terms of sequences of shots. You will need to create sequences of a location, of an event or follow the action of a character and find a way to link the shots together. Try to identify the natural lifespan of the shot, from the moment it becomes interesting up to the moment you lose interest.

- When editing sequences ask yourself the question: What does this scene mean? Introduction of theme or subjects? Conflict? Change or development? Different perspective?

- Where does it fit in the narrative?

- There are different opinions as to where to cut a shot – before, at or after the action. There are no golden rules any more; you have to find out yourself what feels best for your film.

- Every film is an attempt to tell a story using the correct number of shots. Be efficient and do not use five shots if the same message can be shown in three.

- Identify problems with the footage and possible solutions.

- Create a beginning sequence of your film which will intrigue, hook, provoke or tease your audience. Your audience may not be particularly passionate about the subject of your film so grab their attention in the first minute of the film.

- Create bins with different sequences or different beginnings.

- Become used to track-laying and use of different tracks for different forms of sound (NDME – narration – dialogue – music – effects). Each shot should typically have 2–4 tracks, in that order. This will save you a lot of time in the sound edit (see next chapter).

Shot transitions

The way you cut the shots together is not randomly chosen. Transitions tend to have a meaning, whether it is to manipulate time or to make connections between different locations via cross-cutting or parallel editing. Parallel editing involves editing between two sequences of shots of different locations/events to suggest that they take place simultaneously.

Cut

The most used transition is the hard cut: no effects, no suggestion of change of time or place. The audience experiences this as an unremarkable or non-disruptive transition, unless you juxtapose two shots.

Fade in or fade out

This is often used at the beginning or the end of a film. In the middle of the film it would mean the end of a sequence at a specific location or that a new historical period/event is being introduced.

Dissolve

A transition from one shot to another. While the speed of the transition between the two can vary, most of the time it indicates a transition of time or location or an associative or ideological connection between the shots.

Wipe

One shot moves across another shot. Most editing equipment will allow you to use different wipes: a fast straight move, swirly or zig-zag wipes. It is up to you and the editing software you are using.

Ask yourself the following questions when you view your rough cut:

- Does it tell the story you want to tell?

- Is every shot the right length?

- Is the sound right?

- Are the interviews too long or too short?

- Have you thrown away good shots/scenes that do not help the story further?

- Does the rhythm of the film feel right?

- What kind of emotion drives the film forward? What is the emotional effect of the film on you?

- Are there any scenes that appear to be superfluous or too long or too short?

- If there are main characters, how are they introduced?

- Does it become clear that they are main characters?

- Are all shots really of an acceptable quality?

Narration

Narration has had a bad reputation since Bill Nichols (1991) described it as the (male) 'voice of God' in an expository documentary. It does remind many of us of seemingly endless documentaries which waffle on about a distant subject in some quasi-scientific way.

Narration in contemporary documentaries is often personalised and does not try to sell an audience the one and only truth but addresses the audience as human beings who can think, feel and have opinions themselves.

First, consider the gender of your narrator, the age, the timbre of the voice or the dialect. Needless to say, a male with a cockney accent and a female with a northern accent will have different connotations for the audience. Break with traditions and use a female narrator on a technical or economic subject or a male voice for more intimate subjects and you will make your audience aware of your choice.

Rough cut check

'I treat editing as a meditation practice. Each time the movie is going forward on the editing machine, I try to empty myself and see it for the first time – just like your audience will. What do you see in the film? What do you feel? What do you want to see or hear next to keep the story going? Does it hold your interest and attention?

(Lemle, 1998: 366)

Points to consider when you write the narration

- Do realise that commentary can completely change the meaning of the film and is often seen as the 'voice' of the film.

- Do not describe pictures. Commentary has to add something to the visual information. Most of the time, commentary organises the storyline and puts events in perspective. Be careful not to write radio with pictures.

- Do not use written language, but plain, everyday spoken English.

- Avoid writing long sentences, but do not offend the viewer either by making the commentary too simplistic.

- Do not use jargon or other highly specialised words (unless the film is for specialists).

- Keep sentences to the essential information you want to give. Cut out any unnecessary words.

- Tone: Normally one is taught not to use irony, sarcasm or be too theatrical. However, I think that at the right moment and the right place you can use these styles. Just try.

- Read it aloud. Does it sound right?

- Do not use 'I' unless it is a personal piece.

- Call people by their full name – for example: Peter Jones.

- Do not write 20 minutes of commentary for a film of 20 minutes. Allow space for natural sound, music and breathing space for your audiences.

- Less is more. Do not forget that if you try to include too much information it will not come across.

Screening a rough cut to an audience

Screening your rough cut is one of the most important stages in the production process of a documentary. It is the first time that you will show your film to an audience who are not aware of your intentions and who may not share your passion for your subject or main characters. One of the main aims of the rough cut screening is to obtain feedback which will help you enter the last stages of the editing process.

The critical audience

Ask your audience to take on the role of 'critical audience'. Invite them to be critical in a constructive way. Ask them to say if they do not understand the theme of the film, if they lose interest or if they are annoyed by specific shots or scenes, but, on the other hand, also ask them to point out the strengths of the film, scenes they found particularly interesting or engaging. Their role is to help you, the filmmaker, to make the best film possible within the constraints of production and the footage shot. Tell them to ask questions when in doubt about certain aspects of the film.

The filmmaker

This is a difficult stage for a filmmaker. It might be the first time that your film will be seen by an audience. You may feel vulnerable and might become defensive. Don't. Let it happen. Just write down the comments. Have a closer look at them later and decide what you will take on and what you will dismiss. You are ultimately the one who makes the decisions about the form and content of your film. Trust your own creative and problem-solving abilities to move on to the final stages of the editing process.

Key points

- The position of the editor has changed over time from a technical craftsperson to a creative specialist at the heart of a film's creation.
- Try to develop a 'voice' unique to you as filmmaker in your film.
- There are different editing traditions which will influence the ideological content and the editing strategy you use.
- Editing creates sequences of shots which fit a narrative relating to the feelings, associations, information and point of view you want to convey.

Editing exercises

Exercise 1

Take your favourite documentary, copy a sequence on your desktop and edit it in three different ways. Look at the three different edits and ask yourself:

- Which shots feel the right length?
- Are the cuts at the right moment in the shots?
- Where would you need to use a special effect, dissolve, or fade to improve the narrative?

Exercise 2

The film historian Sue Harper argues, 'In general, female editors tend to cut on mood rather than action.' (2000: 232)

Take two films, one edited by a man and one edited by a woman, and describe the difference in editing style. Could this different editing style be related to the gender of the editor?

Exercise 3

Have a look at *Darwin's Nightmare* (H. Sauper, France, 2004) or *Sisters in Law* (K. Longinotto, UK, 2005) and analyse how the filmmakers/editors have edited the opening sequence of the film.

Exercise 4

Watch the famous Odessa steps scene in the film *Battleship Potemkin* (Eisenstein, 1925) and describe the edit techniques and the effects used. The films *The Pillow Book* by Peter Greenaway (1996) and Chris Marker's *Sunless* (1983) are also good examples for analysing editing styles.

Exercise 5

In order to learn to sequence a range of shots, storyboard the following scenes:

- Postman delivers post and is bitten by a dog – 8 shots.
- Driver stops to buy a paper to find on his return that he has received a fine – 5 shots.
- Driver runs after traffic warden, who sees him and runs away – 10 shots.
- A group of people cycling over a mountain – 12 shots.

Exercise 6

The essence of Exercise 5 was to learn to create a sequence of shots conveying a certain action. The following exercise focuses on creating a sequence of shots to convey a concept.

- A cyclist cycles through town. Storyboard a sequence showing that it is very healthy to cycle – 8 shots.
- The same cyclist cycles through town but the sequence should convey the message that cycling in town is unhealthy – 6 shots.
- Using juxtaposition, repeating shots and jump cuts, storyboard the story of a girl going to school for the first time – 12 shots.

Have fun!

Interview Anna Ksiezopolska – Film Editor

Anna Ksiezopolska

When I view rushes at the start of an edit, the thought always crosses my mind that somewhere in all those hours of footage lurks the best film possible. I am excited by the prospect that I will play a role in finding it.

I particularly enjoy the collaborative relationship with the director, and during our discussions will try to understand his or her intention for the film. Unlike the director, I have not been totally immersed in the production for months, so I hope to bring a fresh eye to the material, be the film's first audience.

Especially in the case of documentaries, we'll usually start by working on the narrative, constructing the film's premise with commentary, interviews, sequences, archive. Although the process of writing and rewriting the script continues throughout the edit, we want to be confident the structure of the film works prior to any extensive cutting.

I edit the rushes in a way which I feel will serve the narrative best, constantly thinking about the material and my emotional response to it. Faced with endless possibilities, I need to be decisive but at the same time keep an open mind and continually experiment: it's a voyage of discovery where accidents can be quite fortuitous! I'll frequently start cutting a scene with a clear idea of where I want it to go, only for it to tug me in another direction.

Whenever possible, I fine cut as I go along, so that the scenes can be read as they are intended. My editing style will be influenced by various considerations, including how the film was shot, the director's preferences, then my own. How an audience will respond is always at the back of my mind and, however cerebral a film might be, I believe its main response is an emotional one.

Even when I'm working on my own, the discourse with the director is ongoing: we constantly re-evaluate what we've done, address any notes from screenings and look at ways of improving the film. Discussions can become quite animated, each defending their preference for what works and, in the process, we'll frequently come up with a third, more effective approach. It can be exhilarating to see a film spring to life and begin to exceed expectations – the director's as well as the producer's.

Shrinking budgets and schedules make it increasingly difficult to work in this ideal way. Crafting and fine cutting the film must often be done in my own time after hours. My advice to any aspiring film editor is to be prepared to lock up the building long after everyone else has left.

Interview Alan Mackay – Film editor

Alan Mackay (photo Wilma de Jong)

Editing with a systematic approach; a sense of composition and rhythm.

During my education, I had a strong interest in maths and science, and editing for me does include this way of thinking. A sense of how long a shot or sequence should be, the proportions of the overall film (especially for a fixed-length TV programme); it can be a systematic approach. Also I've always drawn, and a sense of graphic content and composition does come into play when I'm choosing shots.

The grammar of TV has evolved to include jump cuts and shots that are continually on the move. A different editing style comes from finding sections within longer shots, rather than a controlled take, and using the unsteady image from a hand-held camera. This style works best with an emphasis on what's said now, making sense of the sequence. This can also result in shots in the sequence lasting on average less than 4 seconds. But it wouldn't be good if the whole programme was cut like that. Some sequences can be fast, but others should be slower. I'm always looking for the moment where the programme can breathe.

Music in a lot of factual programmes is there to keep your audience engaged, fast-paced cutting, fast-paced music, not giving the audience a chance to think, really. I prefer to make films where the music plays an integral part, where the story wouldn't work without the music.

What I really enjoy looking for in the material is things to do with human beings. I look for human moments, things that might give you the length of a pause . . . a look between people . . . dramatic moments . . . an intensity in the shots. I believe it's an enrichment for the audience.

Editors are often expected to handle more material now and, because of the technology, in less time. If you're working on a half-hour show, you'd be lucky to get four weeks to edit it. On that sort of schedule, you can't get to know all the material. But that's not just a pressure on editors; it is on the directors too. Which leads to more formulaic TV, as it's easier to achieve within these constraints.

What has also changed is the control that's exercised by the broadcaster. To the point where a lot of editors now, if they want to keep working, have to satisfy the commissioning editor rather than their own director or producer.

▶

I recognise this as a model from American TV: market-led ideas to do with branding the channel and its strands in order to aim at particular demographics. So you have to tell people things in a particular way. If a director has an interest in making a programme about the situation in, say, South Africa, it's no longer enough that they have a record of making good films; it won't get commissioned unless it can 'fit in'. I don't believe that the audience in this country has lost interest in seeing such stories on TV.

Chapter 21

Being there: the creative use of location and post-production sound in documentaries

Jean Martin

❝Images without sound – they end up with a feeling of being remote, because you don't feel that you are there. The sense of being somewhere – that is in the sound.❞

(Wayne Derrick, documentary film director, 2009)

Introduction

This chapter focuses on location sound recording and post-production approaches in documentary filmmaking. Location sound recording is analytical in the sense that it isolates sounds important for a film from the general ambience. Post-production sound is synthetic, because it resynthesises the particular location sound recordings into a full sonic environment, which creates the audiovisual reality of the film for the viewer.

There appears to be a wide gulf between theories of film sound and its practice by professionals. This chapter starts by providing some theoretical context. However, most of it explores and explains the practice of documentary film sound. Detailed technical and operational questions are not discussed here, because they are comprehensively explored in specialised books (Sonnenschein 2001; Holman 2002; Holman 2005; Rose 2008) and on websites. (I can recommend the informative texts on the websites of the Danish firm DPA or the German firm Schoeps. Weblinks are given in the bibliography.)

Documentary film strives to be closer to reality than feature film, closer to the object of its observation. Feature films also portray realities through storytelling. As in any film form, sound is crucial for creating a sense of reality for the viewer, the sense of 'being there'. Sophisticated sound technology and approaches are used in contemporary documentaries, matching those in feature films. Well-recorded original location sound is crucial in documentary films, more so than in feature films, where ADR[1] techniques are regularly used. But contrary to the ideology of authentic, untampered with and original location sound, the acoustic reality of a documentary film is carefully synthesised through conscious choices by the location sound recordist and post-production mixer.

Modern multi-track post-production techniques used in documentary films have narrowed the gap to mainstream feature films (e.g. in docudramas). These techniques have also exposed the concepts of cinéma vérité or 'fly on the wall' documentary as ideologies. Digital techniques of sound post-synchronisation make it possible to completely reconstruct a soundtrack from scratch in a realistic and convincing way. Chion termed it 'foleyed cinema' (Chion, 2009: 141). This opens ethical questions of authenticity and originality comparable to the moral issues posed by digital image manipulation through Photoshop. For example, in David Attenborough's film about the Australian lyre bird[2] the question remains, whether technology is imitating nature or vice versa. In many of his films, Attenborough's camera people achieved astonishing close-up shots of animals through cleverly positioned micro-cameras. But when it comes to sound, many sound events would have to be recreated by a Foley artist in the studio. In the film *The Great Salmon Run – Salmon vs bear* (Episode 2)[3] about grizzly bears hunting salmon, the roar of the mountain river would mask any detail sound in a wall of white noise. Yet in Attenborough's film we can hear water pleasantly gurgling, salmon splashing into water or hitting boulders and even a bear. These sounds have been created by a Foley artist.

There are aesthetic differences between documentary and feature films. At first glance, the difference lies in the documentary portrayal of social and environmental realities, whereas feature films tell subjective stories. However, in normal film practice this distinction is constantly blurred: documentary films use storytelling techniques and feature films often implicitly document realities of lifestyle, taste, architecture or community. Both leave the studio in favour of real-life settings.

Texts about documentary film sound

The scope of texts about film sound ranges from basic introductions on technical and practical issues (Prince, 2009) to aesthetic reflections exploring the meaning of mediated sound perception in film (Williams, 1980). The middle ground – and the most useful texts in the context of this book – is represented by writers who put (documentary) film examples at the centre of their exploration (Ruoff, 1993; Chion, 2009). Only very few articles are written explicitly about documentary sound.

The academic debate of (documentary) film sound circles around a cluster of themes: realism, authenticity, aesthetic impact of technological change, narrative. What makes the discussion complex is the seemingly trivial fact that the soundtrack cannot be analysed in isolation. As Michel Chion (Chion, 2009: 226) provocatively put it: there is no soundtrack. What he means is that sound and moving images are perceived in a dynamic relationship, mutually influencing each other.

Sound itself is an ephemeral phenomenon. Even as a recording on film it disappears when the film stops: there is silence, whereas visually we can continue to study the still image. Walter J. Ong (1982, 2002: 32) poetically describes the nature of sound:

> All sensation takes place in time, but sound has a special relationship to time unlike that of the other fields that register in human sensation. Sound exists only when it is going out of existence. It is not simply perishable but essentially evanescent. When I pronounce the word 'permanence', by the time I get to the '-ence', the 'perm-' is gone, and has to be gone.

With digital audio technology sound can actually be frozen, graphically displayed and analysed. But these analytical methods can only approximate to the perceptual complexities of hearing sound and seeing moving images simultaneously. We have to rely on our aesthetic judgement to understand a film.

The question of realism and truth in documentary films is central to the use of sound in documentaries. A simple exercise demonstrates the constructed and selective nature of our perception. When we walk down a street we will be aware of the acoustic ambience, but which specific sounds we perceive can vary greatly even from day to day, e.g. when we are lost in thought. However, if we take a microphone and put on headphones and listen in this way while walking down the same street, we will be surprised at the great variety of sounds we haven't noticed before. So is the natural way of perceiving 'reality' less real than perceiving it through a sound recording device? Or to put it differently: how can we assess whether what we hear is meaningless noise or a significant sound event?

From time to time, feature film directors try to reduce the artificiality of films by reducing them to straight storytelling. The Dogme 95 movement in the 1990s around Lars von Trier should be mentioned here, but also the French Nouvelle Vague (new wave) directors in the 1960s. Godard, for example, plays with the notion of wrong usage of sound in an artistic way and thus creates awareness of the filmic apparatus in sometimes irritating ways. In one instance, he placed an omnidirectional microphone in a Parisian café to record all sounds 'democratically' – i.e. speech is not privileged over traffic noise, pinball machines, radio, etc. This was confusing and provoking for the average feature film viewer.

Alan Williams (1980) tries to resolve the problem of realism in film by comparing sound recording to language in the sense that both construct realities instead of literally reproducing them. Williams rejects the idea that a sound recording is an objective, exact copy of a real sonic event. Instead, he describes sound recording as a signifying practice (Williams, 1980: 55) by stressing the importance of the listening subject for the construction of the audio reality in a film, i.e. the sound recordist.

> My contention is that in sound recording, as in image recording, the apparatus performs a significant perceptual work for us – isolating, intensifying, *analysing* sonic and visual material.
>
> (Williams, 1980: 58)

If one accepts the intrinsic analytical nature of sound recording then the distinction between feature and documentary film becomes purely semantic. In an interview with James Marsh, the director of the docudrama *Man on Wire*, the journalist Guy Lodge observes that Marsh does not recognise much difference between the processes of making a narrative feature and a documentary, claiming that both forms ultimately come down to storytelling. Marsh says:

> There are different skill sets involved, of course, but at the end of the day, it's just filmmaking . . . My job is to put on a good show, whether it's a documentary or a feature.[4]

The idea of sound (and image) recording as an analytical tool used by the director and sound recordist to focus the listener's attention becomes clear when small, insignificant sounds with a low volume are emphasised by being amplified: for example, the lighting of a cigarette or taking a breath. As soon as the sound recordist captures a sound, he makes a selective choice. He has to analyse the general ambience and decide which sound is best suited to support and enhance the moving images.

A good example is the film *Touch the Sound*[5] about the percussionist Evelyn Glennie. The director tried to recreate Glennie's acute sense of perceiving sounds through her body (she is almost deaf). She is shown walking through New York. The sound designer recreated her way of perceiving by highlighting detailed sounds of the city: the rhythm of footsteps, machines and events. The sounds, isolated and recorded in surround, develop a musical quality with their complex rhythms. Instead of taking the eternal city ambience as homogenous noise, the sound designer and director analytically broke down this noise wall into discrete, captivating audio events. The quality of the recordings, the editing, arrangement and mixing are outstanding.

The visual close-up has its exact equivalent in the aural close-up, achieved by varying the microphone distance to the object. But in contrast to the two-dimensional image, sound, whether natural or as a recorded reproduction, is by nature three-dimensional. Instead of remaining at the level of a simple audio-visual parallelism, the soundtrack has the potential to construct highly differentiated three-dimensional sonic spaces independently.

Synchronising sound and moving images

Synchronising analogue reel-to-reel tapes of sound and moving images has been a core problem in filmmaking. When it was first technically achieved, audiences were amazed. In particular, directors of animation films exploited the new possiblities to the extreme. In *Silly Symphonies* (1929–39) Walt Disney celebrates audiovisual synchronicity by having animated animals playing musical instruments.

But making documentaries with sound was still a problem. The sound equipment was cumbersome and intrusive. Huge microphones and heavy, noisy recorders made outdoor location recording very difficult and expensive. Documentary films focus on real live events, which often cannot be repeated. Synchronising sound and images reliably is crucial.

1960: a revolution for documentary filmmaking

The invention of the Nagra, a light, portable sound recording machine, by the Polish engineer Stefan Kudelski in the late 1950s fundamentally changed documentary filmmaking. The Nagra quickly became the industry standard for professional filmmakers. The reduction to a minimum crew of a director/camera person and a sound recordist encouraged new approaches to documentary filming. Small, portable technical equipment was the precondition for getting as close as possible to the evolving, often unexpected live events. In France this new technology inspired the cinéma vérité (cinema of truth) movement, a term coined by Jean Rouch in connection with his film *Chronique d'un été* (1960). It was meant as a tribute to the Russian Dziga Vertov's 'cinema pravda'. Today, though, digital sound design calls the notion of authentic, orginal location sound into question.

The demand for flexible, unobtrusive recording equipment had already been expressed in the late 1950s by the American documentary filmmakers Pennebaker and Leacock. Only after the invention of the Nagra did their aesthetic of 'direct cinema' or 'fly on the wall' documentary become feasible.

Even after the invention of the portable Nagra recorder in the late 1950s camera and tape recorder were initially connected by a cable to synchronise images and sound. This had obvious drawbacks, since the camera person and sound recordist were literally tied together. One of the biggest complaints about the coming of sound to film in the late 1920s was that the cameraman had lost his ability to move around freely to capture the best images. Many critics and directors considered the sound revolution to be the death of silent film art – the only film art they thought there was.

Synchronisation of an independently running tape recorder was reliably achieved by recording onto the tape a pilot tone generated by a quartz pulse. During the transfer from $^1/_4$ inch tape to 16 mm magnetic film tape, the playback speed of the Nagra was controlled by the recorded pilot tone. The start point was indicated by the clapperboard. This guaranteed perfect synchronisation in the alignment of the audio tape with the film clip in each take. Documentary filmmakers like Alan Raymond, who made the widely acclaimed *An American Family* (1973), enthusiastically embraced this invention:

> There was no physical, umbilical connnection between the two of us [the cameraman and sound recordist]. This is absolutely crucial to *Cinéma vérité* shooting. . . . it totally frees the camera/sound team to move as they wish, independently of one another. Camera placement need not be sacrificed to sound position and vice versa . . . the camera/sound team must develop a kind of choreography where both parties are aware of each other all the time. The cameraman must listen to the dialogue and the sound recordist must watch what the cameraman is shooting.[6]
>
> (Raymond, 1973: 604–5)

In post-production the use of multiple, synchronised sound tracks was soon introduced, first on optical, then on 16 mm sprocket magnetic film. Synchronisation was first achieved mechanically and later electronically.

Time code synchronisation

In 1967 the Society of Motion Picture and Television Engineers[7] introduced SMPTE time code, a time reference standard for synchronising sound and images. It was rapidly accepted in the film industry. Time code made the synchronisation of independently running tape recorders and film recording/playback machines reliable and convenient. Instead of having to start a synchronisation with the clapperboard signal, time code-synchronised machines can be locked together at any point in time. The machines will 'know' where they are on the timeline.

The music industry also found time code useful to extend the number of audio tracks by linking, for example, two 24-track tape machines. Multi-track tape recorders were also increasingly used in film sound post-production and dubbing, because it was much cheaper than magnetic sprocket film.

The separation of synchronised sound and moving images during the production process was a great achievement. This approach allowed and encouraged a much more flexible and analytical use of sound. Not only could the camera person and the sound recordist move independently of each other during a shoot, but after a scene was shot, a good sound recordist would always continue to capture useful and interesting sounds and atmospheres on and around a specific location. The rich world of off-screen sound could be analytically explored and recorded. This increased the choice and the creative options during post-production and allowed the enrichment and completion of the reducing effect of the camera framing through sound.

The invention of the digital video camera jeopardised this achievement. The combined recording of sound and moving images on one tape makes the independent capture of sound and images impossible. Although convenient, the DV camcorder is aesthetically a step backward, because it encourages a simple, one-to-one audio-visual duplication: what you see is what you hear. On the other hand, digital audio workstations made the post-synchronisation of sound and image flexible and fast. Digital sound post-production can therefore compensate for some of these shortcomings.

The practice of location sound recording

A sound recordist working on location has to deal mostly with practical problems such as weather conditions of extreme heat or arctic cold and making sure the equipment works reliably (microphones, cables, connectors, batteries, mixer, storage media). His/her core task is to analyse the acoustic environment and make clear judgements about which sounds to select so they match and support the captured moving images.

A location sound recordist normally uses three types of microphone. The miniature lavalier can be hidden on a hat or on the chest of a person. The signal is usually transmitted wirelessly. A shotgun or hyper cardioid microphone has a very narrow focus (see Figure 21.1). It is operated on a boom and has the advantage of excluding unwanted noise from the signal. It needs careful

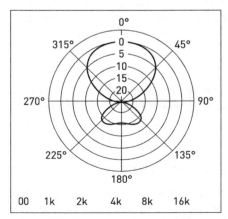

Figure 21.1 The diagram of the frequency characteristic of a Neuman KMR 82i shotgun microphone at 2000 Hertz. If the sound source is at an angle of 90° it will have lost 20 dB compared with the frontal position at 0°.

handling, because a minimal movement to the side from the signal, e.g a voice, will rapidly diminish the signal strength.

Stereo microphones with an MS (mid-side) characteristic or surround microphones are used to record voices and general ambiences either in a stereo field or in five discrete channels.

Sound recording knowledge and how to acquire it

There are two ways to learn to become a film sound engineer. The first is apprenticeship with an experienced practitioner – in other words, learning by doing under professional supervision. The second way is through formal training in an institution, although many of these institutions tend to focus mainly on the operational aspects of complex postproduction studios.

On location, some specific skills, like limiting the volume of acoustic events to prevent a recording from being distorted, have been automated by sophisticated software tools. In computer-based post-production studios, even more tasks can be automated: volume control, equalisation and panning of sound events in the surround field – in effect, the whole mixing process – can be recorded, recalled and changed at any time. These tools become ever more sophisticated. The advantage, and sometimes burden, of digital post-production is the ability to make last-minute changes from the micro level of a single sound, to the level of sub-mixes (e.g. music) to the overall balance between dialogue, sound ambiences/effects and music.

Location sound recordists rarely write about their practice. A good exception is an online text by Dan Brockett, a film and video director, who seems to care about film sound and has worked as a location sound recordist. Apart from discussing devices, microphones and practical tips about how to use them, Brockett tries to articulate aesthetic insights into sound practice in a colloquial style directly addressing the reader. One of his central statements is that 'audio conveys almost all of the emotional impact in the visual medium'. This is confirmed by director Wayne Derrick in an interview with the author (see below). To achieve impact, Brockett demands that sound be 'transparent': 'Your sound is largely what will determine if your project is entertaining to your audience.'

One of the paradoxes of good film sound is its – metaphorically speaking – invisibility. Brockett comments:

> If your location sound is recorded correctly, the easier it will be to work with the basic audio during the post-production process. The better job you do with the sound during video and audio editing, the less the audience will notice it. The only sound that is noticed in a visual medium is usually poorly executed. Great sound works on a subconscious level with the viewer by drawing them into what they are viewing. Great sound supports and enhances the stories you are trying to tell.[8]

Brockett warns against the illusion that a single operator of a digital videocamera (DV) can produce good sound. Despite the democratising effect of affordable digital production tools, division of labour as well as skill and experience is still required to produce good film sound.

A sound recordist always listens to the sound on closed headphones while recording. If the quality deteriorates, for example through the intrusion of environmental noise, he can come closer to the speaker with the directional microphone on a boom to separate the signal from the unwanted noise. This alertness on the part of the sound recordist will guarantee well-recorded speech and location sound, which is crucial for the enjoyment of a documentary film.

An interview[9] with the location sound recordist Paul Oberle, a Berlin-based location sound recordist with many years of professional experience,[10] provided more insight into contemporary documentary sound practice. In documentaries planned for cinema and DVD release, surround sound is standard practice today. Oberle uses a combination of different microphones: lavalier, shotgun, MS stereo, including a surround sound microphone. Only dialogue films, where the main focus is on the conversation between two protagonists, are usually made in stereo, e.g. Derrick's *Horse People* (2009). Equally, TV productions mostly use stereo sound today.

In terms of sound, documentary film is often more complex than feature film, Oberle claims, mainly because of the unpredictibility of the evolving live events. Oberle stresses the importance of the preparatory communication between director and sound recordist ahead of a recording session. In a music documentary about the Venezuelan conductor Gustavo Dudamel[11] the director had failed to mention to the sound recordist that there would be a chamber orchestra playing in one of the rooms. During the shoot, Dudamel moved from room to room. Oberle, who was following the action with a boom, lost the sound of the chamber orchestra after they passed to the next room. After Oberle protested, the scene had to be filmed again with four wireless stationary microphones for the orchestra and a stereo microphone on a boom to follow Dudamel. Oberle recorded the six discrete channels of audio simultaneously on a portable digital multitrack recorder.

For a defined protagonist Oberle uses a wireless lavalier microphone. He always uses lavalier microphones in combination with an additional boom-operated stereo or surround microphone to produce sound perspectives indicating the distance of the point of audition from the sound source, which can be added in the mix. The stereo or surround microphone always has to follow the perspective of the camera frame, in order not to confuse the viewer about the spatial references.

Oberle uses an advanced system which, unlike regular documentary productions, records moving images and sound independently on different machines. In the late 1960s, the French engineer Jean-Pierre Beauviala[12] had the idea of improving synchronisation by simultaneously time marking the audio tape *and* the film stock with time code. This made the alignment of the audio and visual material in the editing process much quicker, more accurate and reliable.

The recording of sound and images separately on location has two advantages: first, the sound recordist and camera person can move freely and independently of each other; second, the sound recordist can continue recording even when the camera has stopped. In this way additional, rich off-screen sound can be captured and used in post-production.

These so-called wild tracks, i.e. audio recordings which are not synchronised to images, are very important to provide the viewer with a sense of being there. Wild tracks can be recorded whenever the camera is not capturing dialogue or other verbal statements from protagonists. For example, the camera person manages to capture a panoramic sweep over a landscape, which is visually stunning, but acoustically spoiled by a passing aeroplane. The sound can be replaced during post-production and enriched by more interesting soundscapes recorded by the sound engineer at a different time. Good location sound recordists will spend time listening and searching for useful or unusual sounds and atmospheres independently. Analysing and isolating certain sound events can musicalise them. Through sampling techniques of looping and layering, they can be organised into soundscapes that can heighten the aesthetic experience of a film scene, as Darren Aronofsky, for instance, has successfully demonstrated in his film soundtracks.

Synchronisation is achieved by a time code generator which is started in the morning on the day of shooting (see Figure 21.2). The continuous time code (TC) signal is transmitted wirelessly and recorded on a separate track of the audio and image recorder whenever a machine is recording. Clapperboards are no longer necessary. Oberle always makes sure that he records a pre-roll of 30 seconds before the action starts to provide more flexibility for editing.

In some recording systems automatic production reports are generated during the shoots, which can be completed with additional information by the sound recordist in the evening during the backup process, e.g. files can be marked as synchronous or as wild track with a few additional notes. This makes the handling of the files during post-production very transparent (see Figure 21.3).

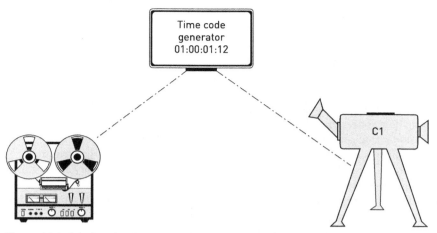

Figure 21.2 Synchronisation by time code generator

Director: Detlef Buck   Title: Same same but different   Location: PP
Prod: Boje/Buck   TC fps: 25.00   Page: 1/7
Sound mixer: Paul Oberle   Media: DVD   Format: S 16/35
Cantar # 537   Type: Mono   Date: 2008-11-24

Filetag	Scene	Take	TC start	TC end	TC state A	T1	T2	T3	T4	T5	T6	T7	T8	Duration	Size
RU3323	36/1		08:01:24	08:02:18:22	08:01:31:03	M front m-6	S	rear	boom			# mix l	# mix r	00:00:54	7 MB
Notes: Sourround, Richtmikro auf track 4 fuer Vordergrund															
RU3324		t2	08:06:02	08:07:02:20	08:06:12:14	M front m-6	S	rear	boom			# mix l	# mix r	00:01:00	8 MB
Notes: Sourround															
RU3325		t3	08:09:56	08:11:02:16	08:10:07:08	M front m-6	S	rear	boom			# mix l	# mix r	00:01:06	9 MB
Notes: Sourround															
RU3325	36/2	t1	08:17:23	08:18:13:19	08:16:05:07	M front m-6	S	rear	boom			# mix l	# mix r	00:00:45	6 MB
Notes: Sourround															
RU3327		t2	08:20:19	08:21:11:13	08:21:03:16	M front m-6	S	rear	boom			# mix l	# mix r	00:00:52	7 MB
Notes: Sourround															
RU3323		t2	08:23:23	08:24:12:16	08:24:02:18	M front m-6	S	rear	boom			# mix l	# mix r	00:00:49	6 MB
Notes: Sourround															
RU3329		w3	08:28:10	08:53:41:16	08:26:40:20	M front m-6	S	rear				# mix l	# mix r	00:05:31	45 MB
Notes: Sourround, Atmo Strasse															
RU3330	37/1	t1	09:04:45	09:05:56:19	09:05:01:22	M front						# mix l	# mix r	00:01:10	9 MB

Figure 21.3 Cantar sound report

In contrast to the myriads of studio production courses, training in location sound recording is difficult to find. Oberle mentions the Konrad Wolf Film & Television Academy (HFF) in Potsdam[13] as an institution which provides excellent location recording courses.

Practical Tips

The list provides some recommendations for location sound recording:

- Use the best possible microphones.
- Use various microphone types: stereo and surround, mono shotgun, lavalier (wireless).
- Separate sound sources.
- Record with great care to produce quality sound: clean, clear, natural. (Even shaky films like *The Blair Witch Project* have good sound!)
- Record additional general ambiences as unsynchronised wild tracks in stereo or surround.
- Use the limiter subtly and be aware of limiter pumping or automatic gain control.
- Listen through headphones while you record so you can judge the quality and usability of the recording. One-man crews rarely produce good sound!
- Use multi-track location sound, if possible, to keep all recorded sounds separate. This makes the synthesising of the film soundtrack more flexible.
- Use pre-rolls and post-rolls, before the visual action starts and after it stops. This makes editing easier.
- Record room tones, i.e. ambient sound when nobody is speaking.
- Avoid reverberant spaces, which create a stressful listening environment.
- Pay attention to background noises: creaking floorboards, people talking, air conditioning, fridge, aeroplanes. This will reduce problems during editing.
- Switch off mobile phones. They radiate signals which interfere with microphones.
- Be aware of microphone noises: (usually lavaliers) rubbing on skin or clothing; stomach rumbles; heavy breathing; mouth sounds (clicking or sticky mouth); certain fabrics, e.g. silk, are noisy; wind noises. This can be remedied by using a microphone with a boom and a windshield.
- The camera person frames whatever they are about to film. The sound engineer has to know how far the frame of the captured images goes. They want to get as close with the boom to the sound source as possible without showing the microphone in the image. (See Figure 21.4.)

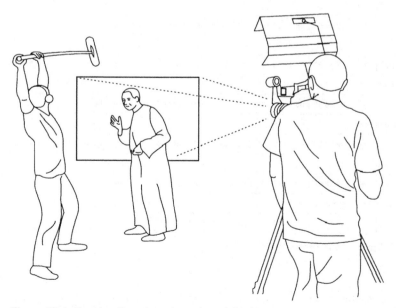

Figure 21.4 Keeping the microphone out of the frame (image by Anne-Claire Martin)

- Be aware that speech has priority in most documentary films. During post-production it is important to be mindful of the core frequency range of the human voice (male: 100–150 Hz, female: 160–250 Hz; for both, the harmonic spectrum around 2–3 KHz is important for clarity) and not mask it with sounds of similar frequency range, e.g. music.

Ear training – creating awareness of environmental sound

Since the early twentieth century, sound recording and reproduction has continually improved. Audio technology has perfected the ability to imitate natural human audio perception in recording and reproduction. What still remains a challenge is to train our ears.

Various artistic and aesthetic movements in the second half of the twentieth century tried to raise awareness of the complexities of sound and its impact on humans. For example, Murray R. Schafer initiated the World Soundscape Project[14] (WSP), together with Barry Truax and others in the late 1960s at Simon Fraser University in Vancouver. Their aim was to create awareness of the quality of the sonic environment by documenting contemporary and vanishing environmental soundscapes all over the world. A major concern was the increasing noise pollution, but the celebration of the beauty of complex soundscapes was equally strong.

Similarly the World Forum for Acoustic Ecology (WFAE),[15] founded in 1993, is an international association of organisations and individuals who share a common concern with the state of the world's soundscapes. Researchers focus on the multi-disciplinary study of the social, cultural and ecological aspects of the sonic environment.

Since the 1960s, visual artists have increasingly become interested in sound. Sound artists – a new category of art practitioners – try to explore sound phenomena in an artistic way, combining sculpture, architectural space and electroacoustic technology. Practitioners and theoreticians of this new art form became very active in the 1990s, particularly in Germany.

The ideas of acoustic ecology and soundart have disseminated into more general sound practice. A documentary film sound specialist who has absorbed some of these ideas is the UK wildlife sound recordist Chris Watson.[16] On his CD *Weather Report* (Touch, 2003) Watson mixed pristine nature recordings from different continents into dramatic soundtracks.

Consuming documentary films: how Is sound affected?

The way documentaries are viewed has changed over time. The composer and writer Norbert Jürgen Schneider (1989) stressed the importance of public television for commissioning and distributing documentary films. Wilhelm Roth, a documentary film theorist and editor of the German film magazine *epd Film*, went even further when he defined television as 'the documentary medium par excellence, even before or below the level of the designed documentary film' (Schneider, 1989: 53). One only has to think of the live broadcast of the destruction of the Twin Towers in New York, or, more prosaically, of the *Big Brother* series. Now TV channels like the Discovery Channel or the History Channel, wholly dedicated to documentaries, have become commercially viable.

Few documentary films are screened in commercial cinemas. Some, e.g. *Etre et Avoir* (France, 2002) and *Touching the Void* (UK, 2003), or two recent films, James Marsh's *Man on Wire* (2008) and Gideon Koppel's personal view of life in Wales, *Sleep Furiously* (2008), have had considerable success with a wider cinema audience. However, most documentary films are still shown on television. And they seem to remain predominantly on the small screen. There are predictions that the internet will soon be the preferred platform for documentary film distribution (Vicente 2008: 271–7).

The TV or small screen setting has compromised the sound quality of documentary films. Soundtrack mixes of films for DVD or television release have a reduced dynamic range compared with the cinema version. This flattens the definition of dynamic depth between loud foreground (speech and special sound events), middle- and background. In a home setting, films cannot be played at high sound levels without disturbing neighbours. Also, in most cases, the loud-speakers do not have the capacity to reproduce large dynamic levels. This puts great constraints on any subtle use of sounds and atmospheres. All sound events – speech, environmental sounds and music – compete for a place 'in the front row'. It is not surprising that most documentary soundtracks are therefore dominated by speech and music. Koppel's film would lose most of its quality – visually and acoustically – in a TV screening. Despite these limitations, television has paradoxically a strong focus on sound – in particular on the spoken word. Images often only illustrate what is said. TV films do not usually narrate in visual terms. The small screen makes this impossible, although flat-screen technology with much larger screens has partly remedied this problem. The emotional and experiential power of sound becomes obvious if one uses a good external sound system instead of the poor-quality TV loudspeakers. The increased depth and definition of sound quality seems to expand the small screen images. In this way one can recreate some of the sensuousness of the medium of film in a domestic environment.

Post-production

In post-production, the audio-visual raw material is edited and assembled. Special care is taken over editing dialogue, which has priority in most films. There are striking similarities between the audio and visual film techniques: the close-up has its equivalent in the acoustic close-up, amplifying normally inaudible, small sounds; the point of view finds its equivalent in the point of audition; the cut is applied both visually and sonically, although sounds have to be treated more carefully so they maintain their identity; synchronicity confirms the mutual influence of the audio and visual signals. But there are major structural differences as well: moving images are two-dimensional and linear, sequential. Sound is three-dimensional, multilayered and simultaneous. Independent sound events can be discretely distributed through a multi-channel sound system.

Post-production of film sound has changed fundamentally since the digitisation of the audio studio. A complete vertical integration of sound control from the micro-level of the sample to the overall mix of the various sound layers has been achieved. The workflow is still divided into distinct tasks – voice and dialogue editing, Foley sound and special effects and music. The difference from the analogue world is that processes of volume control, panning and equalisation can be automatically recorded and changed right up to the last stage of the final mix. Even the arrangement of the sound events in the timeline can easily be adjusted.

The creative selection of special sound effects and synthetic sounds, the integration of archive sounds, the condensing of time through editing – all these techiques have become easier to handle through digital sound technology in the post-production process. As a result, many documentary films have aesthetically moved much closer to feature film. A carefully designed film will always be more powerful than filmed 'reality', an assembly of unedited, original images and sound material.

Structuring time is one of the important tasks during post-production. Sound is crucial for achieving this. Sound always indicates the progress of time. Pictures can be easily reversed without the audience noticing it – for example, a panoramic sweep of a landscape. Sound – wind, birds, rustling of tree leaves – will indicate the normal forward-moving flow of time. As Stephen Prince summarises: 'Sound temporalizes images' (Prince, 2009: 212). Sound can be reversed as well, but this changes its nature fundamentally.

Sound also creates continuity of place and time. Even when the images are cut in unusual ways, continuous sound will indicate to the viewer that a scene is still in the same place and time.

The frequency of edits in contemporary film has increased substantially. On TV, a sequence of images is cut every 2–3 seconds on average. The implications for sound are serious. If the sound-track followed at a similar pace, the viewer would be bombarded with a barrage of incoherent sounds and get highly confused. It is telling that a mock-documentary film like *The Blair Witch Project*, while indulging in shaky camerawork and rough, 'unprofessional' images, used perfectly recorded and mixed sound.

Sounds need time to evolve and decay. Environmental sounds cannot be cut as easily and arbitrarily as images. Sounds and music have their own durations and rhythms: the cry of a bird, a car driving by, footsteps, church bells, etc. Film, like music, is a time-based art. The way time is organised in a film is crucial for the construction of the filmic reality.

A sound designer has to be acutely aware of the rhythm of the cuts. The way a film is edited and the sequences are put together in a montage is directly related to the content of the section: fast, short edits suggest movement, action, speed, whereas long shots with few cuts evoke a more contemplative, quiet, reflective atmosphere or way of being.

The montage can be driven in turn by sound or by the images. Sergio Leone has exploited this in his spaghetti westerns. For example, in *Once upon a Time in the West*, visually there is not much to explore in the desert during the opening title scene. This scene is driven wholly by the *sonic* exploration of the lonely railway station. When the name of the editor is mentioned, a jump cut forces the sound into abrupt loudness. Towards the end of the film, the final shoot-out is staged like an opera scene: the music by Morricone was composed first and the images edited to the music. In many B-movies the music takes over when the structure of the narrative becomes weak.

How can a filmmaker recreate the experience for the audience within one hour, when the presenter, the cameraman and sound recordist have spent six weeks with some people in a remote location? For the BAFTA award-winning director Wayne Derrick,[17] sound has the potential and power to achieve this by providing the viewer with a sense of 'being there'. Images are more abstract than sound. Derrick comments:

> In my series about horse people, what struck me was the amazing power and strength of some of the horses. Particularly in Spain, the horses just had incredible physical ability. What I felt was, you look at them and they look beautiful. But what gave you a sense of their power and strength was the sound of their running and the hooves against the ground as they turn. The same is also true in Montana with the cowboys and the quarter horses – how they were twisting and turning and accelerating and stopping and turning. The image looked good, but you didn't get the same intensity of the strength and power without the sound.[18]

Whereas location sound recording is analytical, focusing on distinct, separate sound events, sound design and sound mixing in post-production have a synthesising function. The aim is to create for the viewer the possibility of a subjective, emotional experience of the story. Given the pressure of ratings of TV stations, documentary films have had to become more entertaining to attract larger audiences, who are not necessarily interested in a particular subject. The focus in these documentaries is often on the presenter and the interaction with people in unusual circumstances. As in feature films, an important goal of the post-production process is to hide the filmic apparatus and suspend disbelief through strong storytelling.

Music

The reluctance to use music has been quite common among 'fly on the wall' filmmakers and cinéma vérité purists. Some feature film directors have adopted a similar approach, as Ingmar Bergman put it in an interview with Ulrich Gregor:

> Music plays an important role in my life: it is perhaps the highest artistic form of expression. I love Bartok, Schoenberg, Stravinsky, Schumann . . . and, above all, Johann Sebastian Bach. But in my films I hardly use music at all, apart from in a functional manner, when my actors themselves listen to music. I find that a film is music itself when it is accomplished.[19]

Most average documentary films shown on TV nevertheless use music to increase emotional impact and make the film more 'entertaining'. Wayne Derrick describes his change from a cinéma vérité approach with no film music at all to a more flexible attitude towards music. While filming for the series *The Real LAPD*, Derrick travelled around with a police officer in LA. One day he filmed the arrest of a gang who had just killed a rival gang member – a terrifying experience, where he feared for his life. When he showed the footage in the post-production studio, the producers and secretaries just laughed when, at one point, the officer shouted at the gang members, who were hiding in their car, 'I wanna see some hands!' and all these hands came up. The editing sound designer then put a dark drone under the scene, which recreated the sense of danger for the viewer. It became clear to Derrick that a camera and sound device cannot record the emotions somebody had during the event. In a film these emotions may have to be artificially recreated.

Sound and music are the primary tools for recreating an experiential reality. In Wayne Derrick's docudrama *Blizzard: Race to the Pole* (2006), a restaging of the race to the South Pole by Scott and Amundsen, the composers Barry Adamson and Howard Davidson created distinct timbral flavours for the contemporary crew and the original footage of Scott and Amundsen. For the latter they used much darker timbres.

Unfortunately, most TV documentary producers don't seem to trust the power of well-recorded location sound. Like many other TV documentaries, Derrick's series *Horse People* (2009) focuses mainly on presenter Alexandra Tolstoy, both on screen and as the off-screen narrator, as well as on music, which tends to be overused. The motivation to do this comes from the perceived pressure to have to entertain the broadest possible audiences.

As a compromise, many film composers have adopted the 'convergent' film music model, a term coined by Stephen Deutsch.[20] Music and sound design blend seamlessly together, partly because they use the same sound material. The Hollywood composer Mark Isham uses a similar approach in feature films. The sound designers of *Touch the Sound* musicalised environmental sounds, e.g. rhythmic sounds of our mechanised world – an escalator, tyres on different surfaces, a cable car and footsteps – to connect them to the percussive sound world of Glennie.

The referentiality of most environmental sounds to their sources (a bell ringing, a door slamming, wind howling, etc.) has the potential to expand the visual frame. This can be exploited to liberate the image track from having to show everything. Spaces and other information can be implied purely by sound. However, this materiality requires careful placement of the sounds – i.e. synchronisation – in order not to disturb the audio-visual balance and unity. Separating or obscuring sounds from what caused them is a core method in electroacoustic music and musique concrète. The resulting ambiguity is also widely used in film sound design, where images can define sounds, and sounds can influence the perception of images in complex, fluid ways.

Voice

It has always been in the interest of documentarists to capture and document the immense richness of human speech and its expressive power, often as pure sound recordings.[21] Frederick Wiseman, for example, recorded the many accents of American English. This makes it problematic and sometimes impossible for non-natives to understand. Subtitling is one solution, but this kind of observational filmmaking is often limited to national or even regional boundaries.

The voice-over is one of the most common tools used in documentary films – if not the key feature in telling a story. Whereas location sound recording has little control over the quality of sound events, voice-over recordings of a commenting narrator allow for maximum control in terms of logical structure, tone of voice and sound quality. In *Blizzard*, the narrator Simon MacCorkindale tells the story of the unfolding drama in an elegant, smooth tone, which is in stark contrast to the hardship and dangers the explorers had to endure.

Sara Kozloff, on the other hand, claims that, in Hollywood cinema, voice-over is still considered 'the last resort of the incompetent' – a stark viewpoint according to Ruoff, but one shared by many observational documentary filmmakers (Ruoff, 1993: 31). Some documentaries, e.g. *Touch the Sound* (2004), avoid a narrating voice altogether and instead use the silent film technique of the intertitle or title card to explain a new setting or chapter.

Interestingly, Ruoff mentions that feature film directors adopted and used documentary film techniques, e.g. Orson Welles in the 'News on the March' episode in *Citizen Kane* (1941). The tone of the commenting voice conveys many implicit meanings. A skilful voice artist or actor can create a sense of authority, calm detachment, irony, emotional agitation or sadness, as can be obeserved in more recent films – for example, *Goodfellas (1990)*, *The Usual Suspects (1995)*, or *American Beauty (1999)*, or the voice of computer Hal in *2001: A Space Odyssey* (1968).

Mixing

The purpose of mixing the soundtrack is to balance all sonic events in a meaningful way and to hide the filmic apparatus (synchronisation mistakes, for instance, are blindingly obvious to even the most unaware film viewer). The dubbing mixer is a highly skilled engineer, who needs technical knowledge to use a complex studio and also a fine ear to make appropriate aesthetic judgements about the balance between all sound events and their relation to the moving images.

Point of audition

Image and sound have to match each other. Usually, the point of view of the camera provides clues about the distance of the object from the camera and the microphone, which both mechanically simulate the position of the cinema spectator. The correct volume is crucial for for creating the filmic illusion for the spectator – the greater the distance, the weaker the intensity of the lower frequencies, in particular. This simple technique can also be used for off-screen sounds to create a rich, layered three-dimensional sound field. There is an ongoing debate whether localisation or spaciousness is more important for recreating a sense of space in the filmic reality. It is more important to be able to localise a sound event on a large cinema screen, whereas a general sense of sonic spaciousness is sufficient for the small screen.

The hierarchy of the sounds varies throughout the film: sometimes the commenting voice is dominant, then detailed environmental sounds or music. At emotional or dramatic moments, directors often add music and remove ambient sounds completely to increase the intensity of the filmic experience – as, for example, in Joe Wright's film *The Soloist* (2009).

Summary of post-production

The first step is tracklaying, i.e. putting all the film images and the location sound on a timeline in a digital workstation and giving it a rough structure. At this point, the director will have developed a draft text for the narrative. After editing and defining the total length, a commenting voice is recorded. Further effects and Foley sound are added and, at a late stage, specially composed music. Through mixing automation, detailed submixes for the effects, music, or voice-over can be built up. In the final mix, all audio elements: speech, sound effects and music are balanced in a meaningful relation to the moving images.

Key points

Most people don't consciously notice environmental sound. In contrast, a location sound recordist has to *analyse* the ambience and select specific sounds to create a differentiated, rich catalogue of discrete sounds, which add value to the images. Dialogue has priority.

Post-production sound is the synthesis of all the elements and materials recorded during the location shoot, edited and completed through additional recordings in the studio. Sound design, i.e. the careful placement of music, ambiences and specially mixed and created sounds, temporalises the image track and gives it pace and rhythm. It can also take over many tasks from the image track, i.e. creating continuity, defining a space, etc. The aim is to create a convincing audiovisual filmic reality, a three-dimensional acoustic space which gives the viewer the feeling of 'being there'.

Exercises

This section aims to inspire greater awareness of sound through a series of practical activities. Most examples can be adapted to the current circumstances of the sound researcher. Doing these exercises will increase your practical skills as a sound recordist and sound designer.

Exercise 1 – Soundwalk

Select a path through an environment (city, nature, factory . . .) and register all the sounds which are there. Listen very acutely and take notes about them to remind yourself later. The separation of sounds can be increased by listening through headphones with a directional microphone. You do not need to record the sounds.

Exercise 2 – Environmental sound without vision

Cover your eyes with a blindfold and listen to your surroundings for 10 minutes. Write down or discuss what you have noticed, as the director Wayne Derrick did:

Years ago, the first time I was in London, I went out with a stills camera to take some photographs of what I thought would make someone feel London. I went by Westminster, I went by all the classic places in London. It didn't really feel like London. It looked like London, but it didn't feel like London. I closed my eyes for a moment and I heard a taxi screeching to a halt and I thought: that is London. It is the sounds of London that really make you feel that you are there. It is not the images, it is the sound! The images are images, but it is the sound that you actually feel you are there and really make you feel the presence of things.[22]

Exercise 3 – Sense of space and/or place

Explore the spatial audio signatures of a space: the reverberation times, direct sound reflections, the emotional quality of reverberant timbres, e.g. in a bathroom or in a cathedral.

Explore the acoustic identities of places: a pub, a shopping mall, a market, a high street, a forest, a small town, a village, etc.

Exercise 4 – Synchronisation

Explore the effect and the power of synchronising audio and visual elements. By combining any sound with a film clip, we synthesise these elements into a new unit. Chion calls it 'synchresis' (synchronisation plus synthesis).

Redesign an existing soundtrack with your own sounds, e.g. for the Honda Cog (2003) car advertising film.

Notes

[1] Automated dialogue replacement: location dialogue is recreated in the studio and replaces the original sound.

[2] http://www.youtube.com/watch?v=VjE0Kdfos4Y [viewed 19.9.09].

[3] http://www.bbc.co.uk/naturesgreatevents/salmon_grizzlycatch.shtml [viewed 19.9.09].

[4] Interview by Guy Lodge (May 2009) about *Man on Wire*: http://incontention.com/?p=3439 [viewed 7.6.09].

[5] *Touch the Sound. A Sound Journey with Evelyn Glennie* (2004), film by Thomas Riedelsheimer.

[6] Ruoff (1993) discusses Raymond's approach.

[7] http://www.smpte.org [viewed December 2009].

[8] http://www.kenstone.net/fcp_homepage/location_sound.html [viewed 24.8.09].

[9] Interview by the author with Oberle by telephone on 3 September 2009.

[10] Paul Oberle films: http://www.imdb.com/name/nm0643276/ [viewed 9.9.09].

[11] *The Promise of Music* (2008) documentary by Enrique Sánchez Lansch about the conductor Dudamel.

[12] http://www.aaton.com/about/history.php#_top [viewed December 2009]. Beauviala had links to the Nouvelle Vague directors.

[13] HFF Potsdam: http://www.hff-potsdam.de/_english/startpage.html [viewed 9.9.09].

[14] http://www.sfu.ca/~truax/wsp.html [viewed 28.8.09].

[15] http://wfae.proscenia.net/ [viewed 27.2.11].

[16] http://www.chriswatson.net/ [viewed 28.8.09].

[17] http://www.bafta.org/awards-database.html?sq=Wayne+Derrick+ [viewed January 2010]. Commercially available documentary films by Wayne Derrick are e.g. *Blizzard: Race to the Pole* (2006), *Tribe*: Complete BBC Series (2007) presented by Bruce Parry; *Horse People* with Alexandra Tolstoy (2009); *Being Neil Armstrong* (2009).

[18] Interview by the author with Wayne Derrick by telephone on 16 July 2009.

[19] Gregor (1966: 106) – quoted from Schneider (1989: 38) in my translation.

[20] Deutsch, S. (2009) 'A Concise History of Western Music for Film-makers', *The Soundtrack 2.1*, p. 35.

[21] The National Sound Archive in the UK and the Library of Congress in the USA have stored thousands of recordings, creating an oral history of the changing usage of human speech.

[22] Interview by the author with Wayne Derrick by telephone on 16 July 2009.

Part 5

Distribution strategies

Home page of the internet documentary *From Zero*,
produced by Stefano Strocchi, Move Productions

Chapter 22

Online, portable and convergence environments

Erik Knudsen

" Film is dead. Long live the cinema! " [1]

Introduction

Much has changed for independent documentary making, distribution and exhibition, even just since the arrival of the seminal camera format, DV, in the early to mid-1990s. In this chapter we shall particularly look at the effect of the development of the internet on distribution and, to some extent, exhibition of creative documentaries. Because we are still in the midst of significant developments in internet technologies and infrastructures as this book is being written, it is difficult to provide an authoritative view of internet technology. We will therefore concentrate on identifying and highlighting a number of trends and developments and exploring some of the consequences for the creative documentary filmmaker in terms of how they think of reaching and engaging with audiences.

Abundance and the digital environment

Like many filmmakers, you may own several cameras. Indeed, cameras are becoming ubiquitous and exist in many different devices, including almost every mobile phone. You may also own several computers. Additionally, you may have access to as many cameras and computers as you could ever want – for example, through a university or other educational source. You are likely to have access to an extensive range of software options with which you can create almost any audio-visual effect imaginable. Increasingly, you are likely to have dozens of films in your personal digital or DVD library and have access to 10,000s of others at the click of a few buttons on your home computer.

Abundance is the ether in which we increasingly live. We are sold the idea that opportunities and career options are abundant and that there are abundant ways of expressing ourselves. Digital technology and the internet are exponentially reinforcing this message.

In 2005, some 206,000 book titles were published in the UK.[2] Between 2003 and 2008, six billion songs were downloaded from the iTunes store alone,[3] representing tens of thousands of artists. In 2006, some 13,000 feature films were shown at US film festivals (Anderson, 2006). What started in book publishing with the Gutenberg press in the 1450s has culminated in the notion of unlimited supply that the digital era offers in terms of arts content. As more people learned to read and write, the Gutenberg press allowed for more diverse voices to emerge. We are now in a situation where, from a mobile phone, anyone can shoot and edit a film and distribute it to the world for thousands, if not millions, to see. In a shoulder bag, you could have the necessary equipment to produce, post-produce, project, make distributable disc media and distribute across the world a cinema-quality film. Abundance of cheap, accessible, digitally based technology is creating unlimited demand (Anderson, 2006), and a lot of that demand is being met by a new breed of consumer-producer, whose ultimate goal is not to build traditional business models, but is, perhaps, simply to be heard.

One consequence of this is that the nature of gatekeepers and gatekeeping to arts content is rapidly changing, as are models of income generation and consequent business models. How many of the 206,000 books published in the UK in 2005 generated enough income for the authors to make a living? Clearly, not everyone writing and publishing a book is doing so to make a living out of it, yet these books will contribute to individuals, to the culture, to the economy of an industry and of a nation. The internet is ensuring that the boundaries between the 'professional' and the 'amateur' practitioner are more blurred than ever. Indeed, these definitions are becoming problematic. In the past, if not clearly an 'amateur', you would be an aspirant seeking to be part of the film and television 'industry' or already involved in the film and television business. Access to these sectors was severely restricted, or built largely on nepotism. If you were not one of the select few receiving public arts funding, you would be deriving a living directly from the profitability of your practice work. This meant working directly to the demands of the few gate-keepers who, because of limitations of technologies, would control the direct access to the audience.

Digital technologies and the internet, accelerated by broadband capacity expansion, are challenging the established institutions and order of the moving image sector. In its day, the Gutenberg press played a direct role in the proliferation of new ideas across Europe, just as the phonogram later helped diversify and engage broader musical tastes. Then video technology, now superseded by digital technology, started doing similar things to the moving image. Digital technology, as the music industry has recently experienced, is seriously challenging the old order of institutions as they lose their monopoly on access to audiences. The key consequence is that independent producers, driven by more complex motivators than profit, can find a context in which they can sustain production and distribution. Notions about sustainability in filmmaking, which had become ingrained in our thinking – such as the belief that one had to reach mass audiences – are being questioned. These were built around models of limited supply and narrow distribution bottlenecks. Long tail business models (Anderson, 2006) are able to satisfy sophist-icated consumer aspirations by responding to more complex tastes. The technology is now able to supply a more diverse palette of products in more fragmented patterns. Consumers who once only had the opportunity to consume what was a mass-distributed product, now have the chance to satisfy their specialist interests, their moral concerns or their plain eccentricities.

> Here's the data for music. Offline, in bricks and mortar retailers, the top 1000 albums make up nearly 80 percent of the total market. (Indeed, in a typical big box retailer, which carries just a fraction of CDs, the top 100 albums can account for more than 90 percent of sales.) By contrast, online that same top 1000 accounts for less than a third of the market. Seen another way, a full half of the online market is made up of albums *beyond* the top 5000.
>
> (Anderson, 2006: 137)

For the creative documentary filmmaker, the abundance of digital technologies, and the con-sequent fragmentation of distribution patterns, allow for more independence: to break with the 'material routines of the trade' (Bresson, 1977); to question the values and tastes of institutional gatekeepers; to question creative assumptions; to challenge working practices; and to speak of things less spoken about.

Online distribution

The combined development of media file compression technology – such as Flash or H.264 – and the roll-out of broadband technology across the developed world, and increasingly in the developing world, mean that it is very viable to distribute a film through the internet. Indeed, illegal movie file sharing using peer-to-peer software has been very active for a number of years and has, in many respects, like music before it, shaped the possibilities of internet-based distri-bution models. With the advent of the compressed mp3 file in music, illegal file sharing in music took hold as the traditional music industry resisted developing online distribution models. Clearly, the young in particular were embracing online distribution of music, partly because they had the devices – the mp3 player – to play the music on and the mp3 player proved flexible, portable and of acceptable quality. It took an innovative company like Apple to take the initia-tive in addressing this demand directly by developing the iPod and iTunes combination in 2001, with the result that they are currently the dominant player in the legal online music market place and the largest music retailer in the United States, if not the world.[4]

iTunes is rapidly also becoming one of the leading players in commercial film distribution in the United States and United Kingdom, with the launch of its movie, TV and podcast download services (including a limited range of documentaries) all delivered to an increasingly flexible range of devices such as the iPod Touch, the iPhone, the iPad, laptop computers, desktop computers and TV sets. This flexibility and diversity of viewing contexts is clearly something the consumer likes, judging by the popularity of these products and others like them. Where once the viewer could only see documentaries in a cinema, they can now carry a device in their pocket that will give them instant access to thousands of movies and other moving image content that they can view on demand.

The phenomenal success of the BBC's online replay service, iPlayer, has led to online on-demand distribution of broadcast material becoming part of every TV broadcaster's strategy. In the UK, ITV, Sky, Channel 4 and Channel 5 also have online services that allow viewers to view what they want, when they want and on whatever device they want. All these services are available, for example, on many mobile phone devices.

These developments in technology have opened up to new independent players what was formerly restricted access to audiences. Until late 1983, the access to audiences for documentary film in the UK was largely restricted to two broadcasters on three channels: BBC One, BBC Two and ITV. Theatrical exposure was, and remains, very restricted for the documentary (though it has to be said that the recent explosion in film festivals across the world offers new ways for documentary filmmakers to show their work theatrically). The corporate and educational outlets were restricted to particular small-scale niche distributors with very local reach. Now, of course, the picture is very different. Using services such as YouTube and Vimeo, a filmmaker can instantly release a documentary to reach a global audience. A range of new types of distribution/exhibition companies have grown up around online platforms, ranging from subscription-based services like Netflix in the United States, to curated exhibition outfits primarily funded by advertising such as Jaman. A range of specialist documentary distributors such as the German-based OnlineFilm, who receive some support from state funding sources and the US-based MediaStorm, sponsored by a major national newspaper, are able to target more niche audiences worldwide. Individual filmmakers also act as independent distributors, such as one of the authors of this book (Erik Knudsen at http://www.onedayfilms.com); Sean McAllister (http://www.seanmcallister.com) and Errol Morris (http://www.errolmorris.com). Groups of filmmakers get together, too, to distribute their work, such as the Danish group of female documentary filmmakers: Pernille Rose Grønkjær, Eva Mulvad, Phie Ambo, Mikala Krogh and Sigrid Dyekjær (http://www.danishdocumentary.com).

Aggregators

The number of online outlets for moving image work is proliferating so much that a new kind of 'aggregator' distributor is emerging. Companies like Brightcove, MeDeploy, TubeMogul, Diva and Content Republic select work to distribute to the burgeoning number of online outlets, manage income from these numerous sources and distribute the income to the content producers. Unlike companies such as Bablegum, AtomFilms and Ameibo, who exhibit work from their own websites, aggregator distributors work strictly behind the scenes to place work in the exhibitor sites. They work, in this sense, a little like a traditional distributor, but in an online environment rather than a bricks and mortar environment.

Distribution models

We have already alluded to the fact that generating income might not be the sole interest of the contemporary total filmmaker. Reaching an audience – perhaps reaching the right audience – may be of primary importance. Nevertheless, income generation is a factor that we will need to consider. It is certainly on the minds of the traditional industry institutions, as they scramble to figure out how to generate the kinds of income they were used to when access to markets was more restricted. Once something is in a digital form, it is extremely cheap and easy to store copy and distribute around networks. The internet was quickly populated by idealists, altruists, enthusiasts and entrepreneurs who embraced notions of open and free access to content. The young in particular, who grew up in a digital era, seem to expect digital content to be free or very close to free. This, coupled with the direct two-way connection film creators and audience can make, means that traditional distribution models based almost exclusively on the exchange of scarce content commodity do not work online.

The issue of defining sustainability becomes more complex. In the traditional film and television industry, sustainability was defined within the context of a direct relationship between the film and income generated from a TV sale (in turn based on public subscription or advertising) or cinema box office. However, sustainability in an age of abundance and easy access to audiences becomes something much more sophisticated. For example, income for musicians from the traditional CD sales has decreased as more readily available, and often free, content is available online. Musicians are having to diversify their sources of income by touring more with live performances, carrying out more varied live activities and developing sophisticated promotion and merchandising strategies. Similar contexts are likely to emerge for the filmmaker, as moving image content becomes as readily available as music content. As online viewing gains a foothold, DVD sales across the film sector are starting to fall rapidly. A range of new distribution models and strategies is emerging, yet, from a monetary income perspective, a lot of exploration is still going on.

Since the development of Web 2.0, the second generation of web technology that allows for more multi-directional interaction, film distribution has become more than simply a one-way flow of content. Audiences and filmmakers are now able to communicate directly and there are even examples of open source filmmaking where audiences and filmmakers are collaborating on the production of documentaries.

The internet is a bit like the Wild West at the moment: many new ideas are being tried and tested and no one is quite sure which of these are going to emerge as dominant models. For the independent documentary filmmaker, it is important to keep up with the debates and play a part in shaping which models and approaches might suit your work and the kinds of audiences you would like to reach. Here are some brief examples of online distribution (though a better word for 'distribution' when talking about online content may be 'engagement') models currently in operation for the independent documentary filmmaker:

Straight sales

Example 1: Amazon.com and Createspace.com

Amazon, through its subsidiary Createspace.com, pioneered publishing on demand. This is integrated into its other subsidiaries, the film information website IMDB.com and automated film festivals submissions site Withoutabox.com. Together, these integrated sites and services feed into the long tail business model of Amazon.com (see the example overleaf).

Long tail business model

In a bricks and mortar situation, where there is limited shelf space for DVDs or limited screens for theatrical exhibition or limited slots for TV broadcasts, as a rule of thumb business models are based on 80% of income being generated from 20% of available products. Bottlenecks in access to audiences and other inequalities mean only selected products can be effectively made available to this audience to generate the income.

Online, however, with ever-increasing storage and bandwidth capacity, certain companies are able to exploit niche interests of audiences to the point where the majority of income comes from products outside the top 20% of those available. By making large quantities of products available, each of which generates small amounts of income, this long tail of products starts to generate the vast majority of the company's income.

For some online distribution companies, such as Amazon.com or Netflix, the vast majority of their DVD sales income derives from DVD titles outside the most popular titles to be found in cinemas and on supermarket shelves. Their business models are based on the principle of the long tail (Anderson, 2006: 130–35).

Amazon encourages any filmmaker to add to the long tail they have created by submitting their film to Createspace. No judgements about content are made, except on issues of decency and copyright. Createspace masters the DVDs and creates a self-service system by which the filmmaker can manage their accounts, including setting the price of the DVDs. These DVDs are then made available through Amazon.com. Only when someone purchases a DVD online is an actual DVD produced. The digital technology allows Amazon to reduce storage costs to virtually zero and production costs are only incurred once income has actually been received. The filmmaker sets the price of the DVD above the costs of production and Amazon's profits. There is also the option to make a film available for download to buy or rent via Amazon.com. As with the DVDs, the filmmaker retrieves a percentage of the income.

Using a combination of cheap cutting-edge printing and duplicating technology and the virtually zero costs of storage and distribution, Amazon can build a business model on thousands of filmmakers making their products available. The small number of sales of each individual product is duplicated thousands of times over, generating large overall income figures. For the individual filmmaker, huge returns may not come from a single source like this – though there is always the chance of a runaway hit! – but it provides a steady flow of income over long periods of time. However, special-interest projects are able to reach significant markets using this distribution strategy, particularly if linked to special-interest portals, social networking groups and blogs.

Amazon also offers the chance for filmmakers, rather like booksellers, to sell copies of their DVDs directly through their Advantage scheme. This follows the more traditional route of supplying agreed DVD stock and resupplying stock as sales happen.

Example 2: IndieFlix

IndieFlix is a US online sales portal run by independent film enthusiasts and entrepreneurs and primarily engaged with the selling of independent fiction and documentary films. They, too, work the long tail model and works are available for DVD distribution, streaming and downloads (see the example opposite).

Streaming and downloading

There is a difference between streaming and downloading and this can have a profound effect on your approach to distribution models.

Streaming means that the moving image content is being delivered to your computer or other device in packets for instant viewing. Whatever material is stored on your computer is merely temporary and is used exclusively as a buffer to help deliver a smooth viewing experience. You will not be able to access this temporary material outside the context of the instant viewing experience and, once you have finished viewing the film, the content will not remain on your device. Examples of services based on streaming include YouTube and Vimeo.

Downloading, on the other hand, involves the actual media file for the film being transferred to your computer or other device. Though you can often watch the film as this process is happening, you will end up with a file you can play again, often even if offline. In most cases, as with movies bought on iTunes, once you have bought the film you keep that file in perpetuity and can play it as many times as you want. Other download options, such as that operated by the BBC's iPlayer for people in the UK, allows the file to be stored on your computer for a specified period of time before it automatically locks or deletes itself. These options allow for a variety of distribution models, though it is often the case that both streaming and downloading will be offered.

As with Amazon's Createspace, IndieFlix works on the principle of print on demand, with no DVD duplication taking place until there is an actual sale. The filmmaker gets a favourable percentage of income from sales and is able to manage their own account through a dashboard supplied by IndieFlix. Unlike Amazon and Createspace, there is an underlying community ethos driving the operation and its marketing strategy. This ethos is built around notions of the independent filmmaker and the worldwide community of independent filmmakers and their friends and lovers of independent filmmaking.

A common feature of all of these online initiatives is the ability to give feedback on the product in the form of ratings and comments. This forms part of consumer guidance and is also a very useful indicator to the filmmakers of what viewers think of their work.

Rentals

Example 1: Netflix.

The US company, Netflix, like its sister equivalent in the UK, Love Film, started life as predominantly a DVD rental company. Based on the subscriber model, the Netflix customer will pay a monthly subscription in order to receive a certain number of DVDs sent out to them each month. Downloads and streaming have now become an important part of Netflix operations and the subscriber model has found its uses in relation to this type of direct delivery to viewers' devices (see the example overleaf).

Subscriber models

We are, of course, very familiar with the subscriber model in television. The indirect taxation involved in funding the BBC, for example, or subscription-based cable TV offer examples of the subscriber model. They work on the simple principle that, with a yearly or monthly subscription, the viewer can have unlimited access to the content available. It is a relatively new model within the online movie and music sectors. Driven by the increasingly widespread availability of fast broadband for a variety of devices, even mobile ones, the subscriber model may become more popular with time. If broadband access does truly become available everywhere, audiences may start to question the need to physically own a copy of the media file on their local hard drives. Media libraries have the potential to become virtually unlimited in size, as the local hard drive will not be a limiting factor to the size of one's movie collection, for instance. Instead of access to half a dozen films on your mobile phone, suddenly you may have instant access to tens of thousands of films. In music, Spotify is just such an example and many industry watchers are closely monitoring the performance of Spotify in comparison with the download-and-own model of iTunes. In this sense, music is more advanced than film, but it won't be long before these two business models will also be competing in online film distribution.

Netflix, and other companies like it, build their portfolio very much on the commercial sector. Though they carry many documentary films, their tail is not as long as that of Amazon, for example. They tend to work with traditional theatrical and TV distributors to make their content available for download and streaming, with the result that, while they can make a large catalogue of work available in perpetuity, there is still a bottleneck in terms of independent filmmakers reaching audiences through these companies.

Example 2: Jaman

Jaman is a curated site dedicated to feature-length art cinema and independent films – both fiction and documentary. Staff view and select films for the portal and films are made available for rental only. Rentals take two forms: on the one hand the viewer can watch many of the films free, streamed with attached advertising at the beginning and end of the film; on the other hand, they can pay to view a film without advertising. The latter option allows the viewer to download the film to their computer and watch it within a limited time frame at their convenience. In this case, the film file is disabled once this period is over and the viewer would have to pay again to watch the film. It is possible in Jaman's case to keep the film file on the viewer's hard drive for as long as they want, but viewing outside the initial given time frame – typically one week – would incur an additional cost for reactivating the file.

Tied in with the viewing possibilities are extensive social networking tools. Viewers are able to leave feedback, engage in debates and participate in a range of other social networking activities. As the filmmaker you would, of course, also be able to participate in discussions with your viewers.

Multiple engagement

Example 1: *The Age of Stupid*

Franny Armstrong's film *The Age of Stupid* (2008) provides a striking example of how a documentary film project can be constructed as a multi-engagement project. While the feature film was at the core of the project, the internet was used, and continues to be used well after the initial the-atrical run of the film, as a vehicle to engage audiences in the wider issues that the film addresses.

Built around one of the core political and environmental themes of the day, global warming, this project engaged its audience from conception to completion and beyond. Investors were harnessed from the internet, by inviting anyone to invest in the film and effectively become one of the team. The internet audience could participate in the debate around the issues that lie at the heart of the film. The internet was used to continually update the participant/audience about pro-gress on the project. Trailers and special limited online screenings were shown. The film's the-atrical release was promoted through the website and linked social networking sites. Subsequent to the film's release, the site engaged with the Copenhagen Climate Conference held in December 2009 and a number of spin-off current affairs documentary pieces were made from this. Many other activities and means of engagement were organised and actualised through the web.

This particular kind of approach to multiple engagement with your audience is particularly well suited to projects that revolve around clearly identifiable political and social themes for which there is already a community of people who are engaging – or who would potentially like to engage – with a particular issue. These are often issues that require, or could benefit from, col-lective action. The ubiquitous nature of the internet and its ability to facilitate multiple direc-tions of communication makes the online environment an interesting and exciting place for the independent documentary filmmaker to interact with their audiences in new and original ways.

Example 2: MediaStorm

One of the barriers that is being broken down by the development of digital technology and the internet is the traditional divide between stills photography and moving image photography. In particular, we are seeing examples of stills photographers taking advantage of recent develop-ments that have seen top-of-the-range stills cameras converge with top-of-the-range movie cameras.[5] At the MovieStorm website, we see numerous examples of news and current affairs photo-graphers venturing into documentary production. Sponsored by a prominent US newspaper, stills photographers are starting to make very personal and intimate documentary films about themes and issues in the news – often stories they may have covered as photojournalists. The photographer/filmmakers then use the site to link their work as photographers with these films, and audiences are able to buy books or DVDs with these works. The site even offers access to training for photographers in non-linear digital editing in a clear recognition that this foray into filmmaking is new for them. The making of these films is not necessarily primarily a commercial venture; far from it. Here we have examples of practitioners in one field, who are probably making their major income as photographers, venturing into another field, that of documentary, as an exploration. The internet provides a mechanism by which they can access an audience in this venture, something that a traditional newspaper or TV news station would never be able to do.

Community action

Example 1: David Lynch Interview Project

We have already seen an example of documentary filmmaking's interaction with the internet being used for political advocacy in *The Age of Stupid* (Armstrong, 2008). David Lynch's Interview Project provides an example of how documentary production and the internet can engage, in an ongoing way, with a more intimate community exploration. David Lynch commissioned a small group of documentary filmmakers to travel a particular route across the United States. The brief was simple: when they saw someone interesting, they were to interview them. A mini documentary would be made out of such an interview and posted on an ongoing basis on the project website for the world to see. What has emerged is a tapestry of small-interview documentaries, each a portrait of a particular person and their story. Taken collectively, they form a fascinating narrative mural of stories of American life.

This is an example of how a fiction filmmaker (of considerable prominence) has used the internet to engage with the documentary form, and parts of the American community, to tell moving stories in an original and engaging way.

Example 2: From Zero

Not too dissimilarly, the Italian production companies Move Productions and Pulse Media have embarked on a large ongoing community documentary production project, From Zero TV, aimed at engaging its audiences in the plight of citizens of L'Aquila, who, in April 2009, suffered a major earthquake. They have chosen a number of characters and build episodes around the characters. These episodes are small-story vignettes of life in the camp and town following the earthquake.

The filmmakers are fully utilising the possibilities of the internet to pursue the production of the social documentary in different ways and can instantly reach a global audience in doing so (see below).

Social documentary

This is an approach to documentary filmmaking in which the documentary filmmakers are engaging directly in a cause and where the narratives being created are designed to effect change and intervention. Such productions can often be sponsored, as in this case, by commercial sponsors wishing to contribute to the regeneration effort, or by non-governmental organisations such as the UN or UNICEF.

Open source filmmaking

Example 1: Open Source Cinema

The internet offers fascinating opportunities in terms of collaborative filmmaking. Using open source concepts developed from online software movements such as Linux and Firefox, some documentary filmmakers are creating collaborative productions using Creative Commons Licensing agreements (see http://creativecommons.org/about/licenses/meet-the-licenses).

Creative Commons licensing

Creative Commons is controlled by a nonprofit corporation, The Centre for the Public Domain, and started in 2002. Given the nature of the internet, its evolving ethos and the emerging possibilities and complications of copyright, the project was created to make it easier for people to share and build upon the work of others, consistent with the rules of copyright.

The Creative Commons project provides free licences and other legal tools. These are designed to enable easier methods for content creators to allow others to share, remix, use commercially, or any combination thereof, material that they have created and made available via the internet.

The Open Source Cinema project is a venture through which anyone can create or participate in a film project using similar tools to social networking sites. Participating creators contribute material under the Creative Commons License and can collaborate in editing a project. Remixing, the reshaping of existing footage, is also possible and can be done in conjunction with a growing number of open source archives.

Example 2: Open archive

Numerous commercial archives exist, such as the BBC's Motion Gallery. Some, such as iStock Photo, allow individual filmmakers to contribute material to the site for commercial exploitation. Others, such as Nature Footage, are sites where groups of filmmakers supply stock footage. If they have the right kind of footage, this is a secondary source of income that some filmmakers may want to consider.

However, changing attitudes to ownership of material, the altruistic and collaborative nature of parts of the internet community and developments in technology are leading to growing amounts of visual and aural material being made available for use under the Common Licensing agreements. One such example is the open source archive at archive.org, where an increasing quantity of footage is available for use within the Creative Commons framework. In some cases, entire collections of material are donated by copyright benefactors and this provides an engaging way for some filmmakers to access, and contribute to, documentary material.

Convergence and portability

Where once the documentary filmmaker had only one screening context to think about – the cinema – this context has now become multi-faceted. The viewer may view your film in many different formats, screen sizes and settings and it is worth considering these when conceptualising your project. Even the traditional TV broadcaster will now always think of any documentary proposal with many different outlets, formats and contexts in mind. In terms of distribution platforms, some of these may include:

- terrestrial TV broadcast (over-air, satellite, cable), may now be watched on a TV, on a computer screen, on portable TVs and some mobile phones;
- online streaming repeat service, viewable on TV set, computer, mobile phone;
- online portal, downloadable to computer and/or mobile device such as a phone;
- single DVD or packaged DVD compilation, viewable on a computer or TV;
- database-driven online archive access to materials generated by the film project.

The viewer may, depending on the platform, view your film in many different types of contexts, including:

- theatrical screening in cinemas;
- at home in front of the TV;
- on their computer on the train;
- on their mobile phone while travelling by bus;
- on a long-haul flight in a plane;
- screening at festivals and other special events;
- at a conference or training event.

It is highly likely that you will need to create a website associated with your film. This could perform a number of functions, including:

- providing a personal, historical and/or social context for the film;
- making accessible additional visual, aural and textual materials not in the film;
- providing teaching materials for schools and colleges;
- providing portal links to supporting services and/or further information;
- facilitating an interactive engagement between viewers and yourself about the film and its themes;
- generally promoting you and your work;
- providing a means for you to sell and/or distribute your work directly to your audience.

The convergence of technologies means that the traditional gatekeepers to audiences are having to incorporate the internet into all their thinking. Traditional distributors, exhibitors and broadcasters will have to become big players on the internet and their operations will see a seamless convergence between theatrical, TV broadcast and online dissemination. Your films will increasingly become available on demand onto any platform, allowing them to be experienced in numerous contexts.

The amateur and the professional

The internet does perhaps throw into question the traditional view of the distinction between the professional and the amateur filmmaker. In the past, we could clearly talk of an 'industry' with definable job descriptions, roles and responsibilities and this made it easier to distinguish between the professional and the amateur. The ubiquitous nature of digital technology, however, has decimated several of these boundaries and left many traditional practitioners concerned about the preservation of certain crafts skills. In other 'industrial' sectors, we have seen developments in technology wipe out entire classes of job, with new job types emerging to accommodate these changes.

As more people over the centuries have learned to read and write, so the written word has become a part of daily life used by all of us for different purposes. Not everyone is a good storyteller, but almost everyone is using the written language on a daily basis for a wide variety of things, including telling stories, documenting and disseminating knowledge and insights. We are not concerned with whether someone is a professional writer or an amateur. We are concerned with what they are writing, what its purpose is and the quality of that writing. Similarly, the moving image is rapidly being used by more and more people; almost anyone in Britain has access to a moving image camera and can place moving images on the internet to be available to millions across the world. Sites such as YouTube become contemporary libraries that many people use as a first port of call in search of knowledge, understanding or entertainment, whether in the form of a documentary, a training film, propaganda or comedy. Organisations, museums, corporations, galleries, interest groups and charities are all producing documentary content of one kind or another for distribution and exhibition online. One person may be employed to do so, another may not. While one may see documentary filmmaking as a political necessity, another is seeking ways of making money. Yet another expresses very personal stories to share as therapy, while others seek to propagate an environmental stance.

In this plethora of opportunities, you have to find your way. While there are a few traditional jobs in what we traditionally call 'the industry', the vast majority of quality content is increasingly being created by people who do not have a permanent job in that 'industry', often moving from project to project. Just as the vast majority of those who write quality books do not make a living directly from book sales, so the modern filmmaker will be looking at diverse income streams.

In many different sectors, there is no longer a rigid distinction between the amateur and the professional. Some innovative mining companies open up their mineral prospecting to people across the internet; software developers increasingly make parts – if not all – of their key software code open source to allow development across the internet; some design companies actively seek contributions from clients and customers across the internet. The question in the digital internet age is more: can someone create good work and can they make a positive contribution? Do you have a good story to tell and can you tell it well?

Key points

- Conceive your projects with convergence and multi-platform distribution in mind.
- Think about how you can use the internet to engage with your audience before, during and after production.
- Consider what kind of business model you can utilise for your project and how you would want your film to have an online presence.
- Be mindful of the kinds of additional materials you are going to generate for your project website and build them into your budgeting and scheduling.
- Be open-minded and creative about how you think you are going to make a living and think of how the internet can play its part in this process.

Exercises

Exercise 1

Objective

The objective of this exercise is to explore how the internet may make you think differently about how you engage with audiences and viewers.

Activity

Identify a documentary project that you are currently working on, or plan to work on.

- Think of three reasons why you would want to engage your audience more broadly in this project.
- With these reasons in mind, identify a strategy that you can employ for a website for your film that will engage your audience prior to, during and following production of your film.
- Consider what additional materials, apart from the footage for the film itself, you may need to generate for your website.

Reflection

Review and discuss the outcomes of your activity with your colleagues and friends. Reflecting on your strategy, do you feel that you are engaging in a way you could not have done without the internet? Why do you think your strategy may or may not succeed in achieving your intentions? And how do your plans impact on how you may make your film in terms of form, process and content?

▶

Exercise 2

Objective

In this second exercise, you will explore a little more about the business potential of the internet for the independent filmmaker.

Activity

Choose three contemporary filmmakers whose work you like or admire. Search the internet and find out how their latest films have an online presence. From this information:

- Outline what you think their online distribution strategy is. Where are their films available? How are they available? What platforms and technologies are in use?
- Do some further research and discover how this ties in with their strategy for the more traditional routes to audiences, such as TV and theatrical. Where do you see convergence?
- Identify which of the approaches being used are also open to you as an independent filmmaker.

Reflection

Reflect on and discuss the outcomes of your activities with your colleagues and friends. In your assessment, do you see sustainable models of distribution for your documentary films? What added value to traditional production activity could help you establish sustainable filmmaking? What kind of business models do you feel might work for you and why? What are the implications for how you may think of shaping your career?

Notes

[1] Francis Ford Coppola quoting George Lucas in interview at http://www.youtube.com/watch?v=-wK9tHKVN80&feature=player_embedded#!

[2] See http://en.wikipedia.org/wiki/Books_published_per_country_per_year.

[3] See http://en.wikipedia.org/wiki/ITunes.

[4] http://www.billboard.biz/bbbiz/content_display/magazine/upfront/e3i12fe2557a9382597671a522cc1cc901d.

[5] A good example of this was the release of Canon's Digital SLR camera, the 5D Mark ii, in 2009. See http://www.usa.canon.com/dlc/controller?act=GetArticleAct&articleID=2667.

Chapter 23

Delivery and compliance

Jerry Rothwell

Introduction

In accepting funding for your film you will have agreed to a contract which specifies the materials that you are now obliged to deliver. This chapter looks at the legal, technical and financial issues in completing the delivery of your film and the paperwork you will need to provide in order for the project to be accepted as complete – and so that you receive full payment.

Delivery

'Delivery' is a technical term meaning the financier's receipt of all the physical elements of your film (such as master tapes, soundtracks and stills), paper elements (such as rights agreements, insurance and crew contracts) and any other requirements of your contract with them. The financier needs these deliverables in order to protect its own legal liabilities, to ensure the technical quality required by their licence, and for scheduling and press purposes.

Each financier may have slightly different delivery requirements, and you may be making different versions of the film for each (for example, shorter versions for some territories). When you are negotiating funding, you should bear in mind that each version of the film will require a different set of deliverables. It will help to minimise your paperwork if you can make the fewest versions that will meet your funders' needs. For instance, it would be better to try to negotiate that all funders who want a one-hour version take a 58-minute cut, rather than make the 58-minute, 52-minute and 50-minute versions they each say they require at the outset.

Delivery is the point at which the decisions you've made as a producer and the records you have kept of them come home to roost. If your management of the production has been thorough, if you've understood what the funder requires from the beginning of production, and you've been efficient about your production paperwork, the process of final delivery can be relatively painless. If your production management has been chaotic, you'll find yourself spending large amounts of time – and probably money – trying to get things right for delivery.

Delivery dates

The delivery date you've agreed with your funder means the date by which *all* delivery requirements (not just the completed film) are due. If your financier is a broadcaster, this will usually be set with a transmission date in mind, and they will be unable to screen your film without the accompanying paperwork and other deliverables. So you need to build into your schedule the time it takes to gather all the delivery materials – and don't underestimate the work involved. Below are some of the typical requirements for delivery.

Technical requirements

In additional to the master copy of your film (usually now required to be on HDCam tape 1920×1080), you typically need to provide:

- one or more Standard Definition (Digibeta) submasters;
- a textless submaster (i.e. a copy of the master tape but without subtitles or graphics, so that these can be added by the broadcaster, if necessary, to comply with their own branding or language needs);

- a submaster with separate M & E track (i.e. a copy of the master tape with all dialogue and voice-over on a separate track from music and effects, so that it can be dubbed if necessary);
- DVD screeners of the film;
- a digital audio file (usually on digital tape) of the film's audio with separated stereo NDME tracks (NDME stands for narration, dialogue, music and effects);
- CDs of all original music.

Technical compliance (or QC)

On delivery, your film will need to pass a technical review by the funder's engineers. If your final post-production was done at a facilities house and completed with reference to the funder's technical compliance guidelines, you should have a master which complies with the necessary standards. Broadcaster technical compliance guidelines are usually available on their websites, and are very specific. (Channel 4 (UK) guidelines currently run to 58 pages!) If you've mastered it yourself (as you might, perhaps, for online or cable channels) you need to be sure it is compliant, using the tools most online editing packages provide. Technical reviews usually cover the following:

- picture formats (for example, whether widescreen or 4:3, and limitations on origination formats as well as mastering formats);
- 'safe areas' for any essential action or for titles;
- standards for audio and video levels;
- frame rates;
- effects such as 'film-look';
- standards conversion (for example, if delivering a documentary shot on PAL to the US market which will need an NTSC conversion);
- subtitling;
- flashing images and repetitive patterns (due to their potential to cause convulsive fits);
- the programme slate and clock;
- subtitling and audio description;
- credit requirements (for example, on the maximum duration of credits and on use of logos).

All of the above need to conform to the specification in the broadcasters' technical guidelines. It is, of course, important to complete any technical quality checks (and get the funders' authorisation) prior to making any of the submasters and copies required as part of delivery, to avoid having to change each of these copies as well as produce a new master.

Publicity materials

Production stills

Most broadcasters will specify publicity stills as part of the deliverables. You need to ensure you take high-resolution stills during the shoot (freeze frames from the film are not usually sufficient), both stills of your subjects and 'behind the scenes' production stills. Some funders require up to one hundred such stills! The stills should be accompanied by a captions list.

Your production stills will be the images by which audiences first get to know about your film. They will be used in the press, in listings magazines and on websites to represent your work. A good production still will increase your audience – and taking them is an art. Documentary filmmaking can be so frenetic – with crews focused entirely on shooting the film footage they need – that it is best, if you can afford it, to plan to use a professional photographer to take additional stills at key moments in the production. Most photographers enjoy the creative possibilities of shooting film stills and, in the case of some of the greatest (for example, Eve Arnold and Henri Cartier Bresson[1]), it has stimulated some of their best work.

EPK

Funders may also require you to provide an EPK (electronic press kit). This typically includes:

- interviews with key subjects and crew;
- footage of the production being made (known as B-roll);
- approximately 3 scenes from the film;
- a trailer.

These need legal clearance for all media used in the EPK, in the same way as you would for your film (usually for all media, worldwide, in perpetuity). This may restrict you from using any music or archive which is not part of a clip from the film itself. Often the material from your EPK may double up as DVD extras, if you decide to produce a DVD of the film, so make sure you retain these rights.

Delivery paperwork

Final programme script

The final programme script is a script of the final edit of the film, including all narration, dialogue and description of action, with time code references. It is used for legal checks on the film and to prepare for signed and subtitled versions.

Chain of title

When applied to a film, 'chain of title' means the documentation establishing your rights to make the film. This will, first and foremost, include any rights required to tell the story – for example, the consents of your subjects, book rights (if the film is based on an existing publication) or archive rights. But the term also covers all contracts relating to crew and participants, location releases, trademark clearances, music rights – or anything used in the film of which others might have legal ownership. The chain of title consists of copies of signed agreements giving you the right to use this material in your film.

Contracts

You will need to provide copies of all the contracts you have made as part of the film, including:

- release forms for all those who appear in the film;
- location releases from the owners of any property where you have filmed;
- contracts with all crew and writers (including details of any residual payments due);
- any option agreements on source material;

- archive film and stills contracts;
- music publisher and recording contracts.

The contracts should assign all copyright to the producer and waive any right to take legal action against the producer.

Insurances

You will also need to show copies of the various insurances required for the film by the funder. This will include:

- Public liability insurance and Employer's liability insurance. These are legal requirements for companies employing staff or whose work may endanger the public – i.e. film companies!
- Errors and omissions – Increasingly, broadcasters (especially in the USA) are requiring documentary producers to provide E & O (errors and omissions) insurance for any omissions or errors in the chain of title. E & O is expensive, depending on the nature and budget of the film. But if you want your film to be shown on US television you may need it.

Music cue sheet

The music cue sheet details all music used in the film, whether composed, recorded or background. The cue sheet is usually in a format provided by the financier, but will include the music title, composer/arrangers, publishers, rights owners, performers, usage category, duration and cues).

You will need to provide copies of your music licences – covering both copyright in the composition of the music (usually held by a music publisher); and copyright in the master sound recording used (usually held by a record company). The licences must show you have the right to use the music, lyrics or recordings in your film for whatever territories, timescale and media you intend to show it in.

Credits

You will be required to provide a full credits list. Many broadcasters have their own unique requirements on credits (for example, requiring them to run for a specific duration, or at a specific speed or size, or in a particular section of the screen). Some will not allow certain kinds of credits (for example, product sponsors, or 'thanks to . . .' credits). Check the funders' requirements before you make any agreements with those involved in the film about the credit you can give them.

Rushes

Some funders will require you to deliver copies of rushes as part of delivery (but, as detailed below in 'What to keep', it is worth holding on to the rights in your rushes and to the originals if you can).

The 'Programme as completed' form

Many broadcasters have a standard pack of forms, known as the PasC (programme as completed) forms, in which to set out and list all the above information. It is extremely useful to know the format of these before you start production, so you can gather information in the right format and save time later.

Financial report

You will usually be asked to provide a final cost statement, detailing the production's expenditure. Depending on the size of your budget, there may also be a requirement to have this audited by an accountant. You will usually have a month or two after the final delivery date to submit this cost report.

What to keep

In an age of digital production, perhaps because keeping copies of films and paperwork is easier, it is correspondingly easier to delete vital materials and even whole master copies. So it is crucially important to decide what the filmmaker and production company need to keep at the end of a production and to archive it clearly for the future.

At the end of an edit you will want to free up media space on an edit machine and so delete the rushes you have been using from the drives associated with the machine. But before you do (i.e. perhaps in the few days after picture lock) you should make and act on decisions about what to archive.

This will include:

Rushes

If you've shot the film on tape, you may not want to keep all of your digitised rushes. After all, if you still have the rushes tapes, you can always redigitise if you need them later. But it is worth creating a media-managed version of the final film (i.e. copying just that material used in the film, together with perhaps 5-s handles either side of the clip used). This would guard against a situation where you needed to make substantial changes in the film after delivery – for example, if there were a sale requiring a markedly different version.

If you have shot digitally, you should keep at least one copy of your rushes on a drive on DLT tape. You may also find there is a market for your footage – for example, on stock footage sites, or to use in future films on similar subjects.

Master copies

You should have your own master copies of the final delivered film, together (in an age of cheap drives) with a digitised full-resolution version of the finished graded and mixed film. (This will save you a lot of time if you need to clip particular scenes from the film at a later date – for example, for the EPK or DVD.)

Music

Keep copies of the full tracks of all music used, particularly composed music.

Effects

Keep copies of any visual effects files – these would be time-consuming to remake for any reason, and you will need them to reconstruct your film from an EDL (see below).

EDL

You should keep an EDL (edit decision list) of the final film – and/or project file, depending on your editing software. The advantage of an EDL is that it is easily transferable between software packages.

Audio

Keep an OMF file of the final edit audio (with 'handles' as above), and an audio file of the final mix, with separated stereo NDME (narration, dialogue, music and effects) tracks. Again this could save substantial post-production time in making cut-down versions of the film at a later date.

Paperwork

Keep a copy of all your delivery paperwork and all original contracts. Ideally, make a pdf copy of delivery paperwork for easy future reference. You are bound to need to refer to it at some point.

Press materials

Make sure you have copies of all materials created for press and publicity (including the EPK – it's helpful to have a digital copy of this in order to circulate easily) and production stills.

Exercise

Download a copy of a PasC (Programme as completed) form for any broadcaster. Work through it, using as a case study any short film you have made, and list the materials you would need to provide in order to fill it in completely and deliver the film.

Note

[1] Cartier Bresson and Arnold, along with other photographers from Magnum Photo agency worked on *The Misfits*, which starred Marilyn Munroe and Clark Gable. See Toubiana, S. (2000) *The Misfits – Story of a Shoot*, London: Phaidon.

Bibliography

Theory

Adorno, T. (1991) *Notes to Literature Vol. 1.* ed. Rolf Tiedemann, trans. Shierry Weber Nicholson, New York: Columbia University Press

Aitken, I. (ed.) (1998) *The Documentary Film Movement: An Anthology,* Edinburgh: Edinburgh University Press

Aitken, I. (2005) *Encyclopaedia of the Documentary Film,* London: Routledge

Alter, N. (1996) The Political Im/perceptible in the Essay Film: Farocki's Images of the World and the Inscription of War, *New German Critique,* 68, pp. 165–92

Anderson, C. (2006) *The Long Tail: How endless choice is creating unlimited demand,* London: Random House

Arthur. P. (2003) Essay Questions: From Alain Resnais to Michael Moore, *Film Comment,* 39 (1), pp. 58–63

Armstrong, R. (2005) *Understanding Realism; Understanding the Moving Image,* London: BFI

Austin, T. (2007) *Watching the World: Screen Documentary and Audiences,* Manchester: Manchester University Press

Austin, T. and de Jong, W. (eds) (2008) *Rethinking Documentary: New Perspectives, New Practices,* Maidenhead: Open University Press

Aufderheide, P. (2007) *Documentary Film: A Very Short Introduction,* Oxford: Oxford University Press

Aufderheide, P. and Jaszi, P. (2004) *Untold Stories: Creative Consequences of the Right of Clearance Culture for Documentary Filmmakers,* Washington DC: Centre for Social Media, American University

Bainbridge, C. (2008) *The Cinema of Lars von Trier: Authenticity or Artifice,* London: Wallflower

Baltruschat, D. (2003) 'International film and TV co-production: a Canadian case study' in S. Cottle (ed.) *Media Organisations and Production,* pp. 181–207, London: Sage

Barnouw, E. (1974, 1983, 1993) *Documentary: A History of the Non-Fiction Film,* Oxford: Oxford University Press

Barsam, R.M. (1975) *Film Guide to Triumph of the Will,* Bloomington: Indiana University Press

Barsam, R.M. (1992) *Nonfiction Film: A Critical History,* Bloomington: Indiana University Press

Barta, T. (1998) *Screening the Past: Film and the Representation of History,* London: Praeger

Barthes, R. (1995) *The Semiotic Challenge,* Los Angeles: University of California Press

Basu, P. (2008) Reframing Ethnographic Film, in T. Austin and W. de Jong, *Rethinking Documentary: New perspectives, new practices,* Maidenhead: Open University Press

Bazin, André (2009) *What is Cinema?* (Timothy Barnard, trans.) Montreal: Caboose

Beacham, J. (1992) 'The value of theory/practice degrees', *Journal of Media Practice* 1 (2), pp. 85–97

Beattie, K. (2004) *Documentary Screens: Non-fiction Film and Television,* New York: Palgrave Macmillan

Beattie, K. (2008) *Documentary Display: Re-Viewing Nonfiction Film and Video,* London: Wallflower

Benson, T.W. and Anderson, C. (1989) *Reality Fictions: The Films of Frederick Wiseman,* Carbondale: Southern Illinois University

Biressi, A. and Nunn, H. (2004) *Reality TV: realism and revelation,* London: Wallflower

Blair, H. (2001) 'You're only as good as your last job': the labour process and the labour market in the British film industry', Work, Employment, Society, 17 (1), pp. 149–69

Blair, H., Grey, S. and Randle, K. (2001), 'Working in Film: an analysis of the nature of employment in a project-based industry', *Personnel Review,* 30 (2)

Boon, T. (2007) *Films of Fact: A History of Science in Documentary Films,* London: Palgrave

Bordwell, D. (1972) Dziga Vertov – An Introduction, *Film Comment,* Spring, pp. 38–42

Bordwell, D., Staiger, J. and Thompson, K. (1988) *Classic Hollywood Cinema,* Routledge: New York, London

Bottomore, S. (1988) 'Shots in the Dark – The Real Origins of Film Editing' in *Sight and Sound,* Summer, pp. 200–204

Bouse, D. (2000) *Wildlife Films,* Philadelphia: Philadelphia University Press

Bresson, R. (1977) *Notes On Cinematography,* New York: Urizon Books

Butler, A. (2002) *Women's Cinema: The Contested Screen,* London: Wallflower

Ten Brink, J. (ed.) (2007) *Building Bridges: The Cinema of Jean Rouch,* London: Wallflower

Bruzzi, S. (2000, 2006) *New Documentary: A Critical Introduction,* London: Routledge

Bruzzi, S. (2007) *Seven Up,* London: BFI

Burton, J. (1990) *The Social Documentary in Latin America,* Pittsburgh: University of Pittsburgh Press

Caplan, P. (2005) 'In search of the exotic: a discussion of the BBC2 series *Tribe*', *Anthropology Today,* 21 (2), pp. 3–7

Carroll, D. (1982) *The Subject in Question.* Chicago, IL: The University of Chicago Press

Caves, R. (2000) *Creative Industries: Contracts between Art and Commerce,* Cambridge, Mass: Harvard University Press

Chanan, M. (2007) *The Politics of Documentary,* London: BFI

Chanan, M. (2003) *Cuban Cinema,* Minneapolis: University of Minnesota Press

Chapman, J. (2007) *Documentary in Practice*, Cambridge: Polity Press

Chapman, J. (2009) *Issues in Contemporary Documentary*, Cambridge: Polity Press

Christopherson, S. and Storper, M. (1986) 'The city as studio; the world as backlot: The impact of vertical disintegration on the location of the motion picture industry', *Environment and Planning D: Society and Space*, 4, pp. 305–20

Christopherson, S. and Storper, M. (1989) 'The Effects of Flexible Specialization on Industrial Politics and the Labor Market: The Motion Picture Industry', *Industrial and Labor Relations Review*, 42 (3), pp. 331–47

Cianci, P.J. (2009) *Technology and Workflows for Multiple Channel Content Distribution*, London: Focal Press

Coe, J. (2004) *Like a Fiery Elephant: the story of B.S. Johnson*, London: Picador

Corner, J. (1996) *The Art of Record: A Critical introduction to Documentary*, Manchester: Manchester University Press

Corner, J. and Rosenthal, A. (eds) (2005) *New Challenges for Documentary*, Manchester: Manchester University Press

Cowie, P. (1990) *Coppola*, New York: Da Capo Press

Cronin, P (ed.) (2002) *Herzog on Herzog*, London: Faber & Faber

Curtis, D. (2006) *A History of Artists' Films and Video in Britain*, London, BFI

Danesi, M. (2002) *Understanding Media Semiotics*, New York: Arnold

de Jong, W. (2008) 'The idea that there is a truth you can discover is like chasing the rainbow: an interview with Ralph Lee', in Austin, T. and de Jong, W. (eds) *Rethinking Documentary: New Perspectives, New Practices*, Maidenhead: Open University Press

Dewdney, A. and Ride, P. (2006) *The New Media Handbook*, Abingdon: Routledge

Deuze, M. (2007) *Media Work*, Cambridge: Polity Press

Dex, S., Willis, J., Paterson, R. and Sheppard, E. (2000) 'Freelance workers and contractual uncertainty: the effects of contractual changes in the television industry' in *Work, Employment and Society*, 14, pp. 283–305, Cambridge: Cambridge University Press

DCMS Department of Culture, Media and Sport (2001) Creative Industries Task Force, *Cultural Industries Mapping Document*, London

DCMS Department of Culture, Media and Sport (2004) *Creative Industries Toolkit*, www.dcms.gov.uk

Dewulf, S. and Baillie, C. (1999) *How to Foster Creativity*, London: Imperial College of Science, Technology and Medicine

Dickinson, M. (1999) *Rogue Reels: Oppositional Films in Britain 1945–1990*, London: BFI

DTI (2005) Economics paper no. 15 *Creativity, Design, Business Performance*, London

Dovey, J. (2000) *Freakshow: First Person Media and Factual TV*, London: Pluto Press

Einstein, A. (1996) *Relativity: The special and the general theory*, London: Crown Publications

Eitzen, D. (1995) 'When is a Documentary? Documentary as Mode of Reception', *Cinema Journal*, 35 (1)

Ekman, P. (1973) 'Cross-cultural studies in facial expressions' in P. Ekman (ed.) *Darwin and Facial Expression: A century of research in review*, New York: Academic Press

Ellis, J. and McLane, B.A. (2005) *A New History of Documentary Film*, London: Continuum

Ernst, M. (1948) *Beyond Painting*, trans. D. Tanning, New York: Wittenborn & Schultz

Fairservice, D. (2001) *Film Editing: history, theory and practice*, Manchester: Manchester University Press

Fallows, J. (1998) *Breaking the News: how the media undermine American democracy*, New York: Pantheon

Faulkner, L. and Anderson, A. (1987) 'Short-term projects and emergent careers: evidence from Hollywood', *American Journal of Sociology*, 92 (4), pp. 879–909

Feldman, C. and Cornfield, J. (1992) *Stories of the Spirit, Stories of the Heart*, New York: Thorsons

Fleck, R. (2002) *Warte Mal!* (Hey Wait!), in A.-S. Sidén *Warte Mal! Prostitution After the Velvet Revolution*, London: Hayward Gallery

Florida, R. (2002) *The Rise of the Creative Class and how it's Transforming Work Life, Community and Everyday Life*, New York: Basic Books

Foster, G.A. (1997) *Women Filmmakers of African and Asian Diaspora: Decolonizing the Gaze, Locating Subjectivity*, Carbondale: University of Southern Illinois Press

Geritz, K. (2006) *Brave Outsiders: The films of Kim Longinotto*, www.bampfa.berkeley.edu/filmseries/braveout (accessed 5 March 2010)

Godmilow, J. (1997) 'How real is the Reality in Documentary film? Interview with Shapiro', *History and Theory*, 36 (4)

Grant, B, and Sloniowski, J. (eds) (1998) *Documenting the Documentary: Close Readings of Documentary Film and Video*, Detroit: Wayne State University Press

Gregory, R.L. (1998) *Eye and Brain: The Psychology of Seeing*, Oxford: Oxford University Press

Grierson, J. (1966) *On Documentary*, London: Faber

Grierson, J. and Hardy, F. (eds) (1979) *Grierson on Documentary*, London: Faber & Faber

Grossman, A. and O'Brien, A. (eds) (2007) *Projecting Migration: Transcultural Documentary Practice*, London: Wallflower

Guynn, W. (1990) *A Cinema of Non-Fiction*, London: Associated University Press

Guerin, F. and Hallas, R. (eds) (2007) *The Image and the Witness; Trauma, Memory and Visual Culture*, London: Wallflower

Harper, S. (2000) *Women in British Cinema: Mad, Bad and Dangerous to Know*, London: Continuum

Haraway, D. (1991) *Simians, Cyborgs and Women: the Reinvention of Nature*, London: Free Association Books

Hartley, J. (2005) *Creative Industries*, Oxford: Blackwell Publishing

Heathcote, D. (1984, 1990) in L. Johnson and C. O'Neill (eds) *Collected Writings on Education and Drama*, Cheltenham: Stanley Thornes Publishers

Hesmondhalgh, D. (2002) *The Cultural Industries*, Sage: London

Hesmondhalgh, D. (2006) *Media Production*, Maidenhead: Open University Press

Hicks, J. (2007) *Dziga Vertov: Defining Documentary Film*, London: I.B. Taurus

Hobbard, J. (2003) 'Cultural Geographies in Practice: In the border-zone: Warte Mal! – a video installation', in *Cultural Geographies*, 10, pp. 112–19

Hogan, P.C. (2003) *The Mind and its Stories: Narrative Universals and Human Emotions*, Cambridge: Cambridge University Press

Hoskins, C., McFadyen, S. and Finn, A. (1997) *Global Television and Film – an introduction to the economics of the business*, Oxford: Oxford University Press

Howkins, J. (2001) *The Creative Economy: how people make money from ideas*, London: Allen Lane

Ivens, J. (1969) *The Camera and I*, New York: International Publishers; Manchester: Carcanet

Jacobs, L. (1971) *The Documentary Tradition: From Nanook to Woodstock*, New York: Hopkinson & Blake

Jenkins, H. (2006) *Convergence Culture: Where old and new media collide*, New York: NYU Press

Jenkins, R. (2002) *Pierre Bourdieu*, London: Routledge

Juhasz, A. and Lerner, J. (eds) 2006) *F is for Phony: Fake Documentary and Truth's Undoing*, Minneapolis: Minnesota University Press

Jung, G. (1997) *Man and his Symbols*, London: Laurel Press

Kelly, O. (1996) *Digital Creativities*, London: Calouste Gulbenkian Foundation

Kilborn, R. (2003) *Staging the Real: Factual TV programming in the age of Big Brother*, Manchester: Manchester University Press

Kilborn, R. and Izod, J. (1997) *Introduction to Television Documentary: Confronting Reality*, Manchester: Manchester University Press

Kearney, M.C. (2006) *Girls make Media*, London: Routledge

Knudsen, E. (2008) 'Transcendental realism in documentary' in W. de Jong and T.R. Austin (eds) *Rethinking Documentary*, London: Open University Press

Landesman, O. (2008) 'In and out of this world: digital video and the aesthetics of realism in the new hybrid documentary', in *Studies in Documentary Film*, 2 (1), pp. 33–45

Leadbeater, C. and Oakley, K. (1999) *The Independents: Britain's new cultural entrepreneurs*, London: Demos (also available as a PDF file from Demos (2007))

Leadbeater, C. (2000) *Living on Thin Air: the New Economy*, London: Penguin

Le Grice, M. (2001) *Experimental Film in the Digital Age*, London: BFI

Lemle, M. (1998) 'Zen and the Art of the Documentary', in M. Tobias (ed.) *In Search of Reality, the Art of Documentary Filmmaking*, Studio City, CA: Michael Wiese Productions

Leyda, J. (1964) *Film begets Film*, New York: Hill and Wang

Levin, G.R. (1971) *Documentary explorations: 15 Interviews with Film makers*, New York: Anchor Doubleday

Lindley, R. (2003) *Panorama: Fifty Years of Pride and Paranoia*, Petersfield: Politicos

Lipkin, S.N. (2002) *Real Emotional Logic: Film and Television Docudrama as Persuasive Practice*, Carbondale: Southern Illinois University Press

Loizos, P. (1993) *Innovation in Ethnographic Film: From Innocence to Self-Consciousness, 1955–1985*, Manchester: Manchester University Press

Lorenzen, M. and Frederiksen, L. (2005) 'The management of projects and product experimentation: lessons from the entertainment industries', *European Management Review*, 2, pp. 198–211

Macdonald, K. and Cousins, M. (1996) *Imagining Reality: The Faber Book of Documentary*, London: Faber

Macdonald, S. and Basu, P. (eds) (2007) *Exhibition Experiments*, Oxford: Blackwell

MacDonald, M. (1998) 'Publicizing the Personal: Women's Voices in British Television Documentaries, in C. Carter, G. Branston and S. Allen (eds) *News, Gender and Power*, London: Routledge

Macy, J. (1991) *The World as Lover, the World as Self*, Berkeley: Parallax Press

McEnteer, J. (2006) *Shooting the Truth: The Rise of American Political Documentaries*, Westport: Praeger

Mediatique (2005) *From the Cottage to the City: the Evolution of the UK Independent Production Sector* (www.mediatique.co.uk/reports.html)

Mediatique (2008) *All Grown Up: Cash, Creativity and the Independent Production Sector* (www.mediatique.co.uk/reports.html)

Meadows, M.S. (2003) *Pause and Effect: The art of interactive narrative*, Berkeley: Peachpit Press

Nash, M. (2005) 'Kutlug Ataman's experiments with truth', in *Kutlug Ataman: Perfect Strangers*, Sydney: Museum of Contemporary Art

Nichols, B. (1987) 'History, Myth and Narrative in Documentary', *Film Quarterly*, 41 (1)

Nichols, B. (1991) *Representing Reality: Issues and Concepts in Documentary*, Bloomington: Indiana University Press

Nichols, B. (1994) *Blurred Boundaries*. Bloomington: Indiana University Press

Nichols, B. (2001) *Maya Deren and the American Avant-garde*, Berkeley: University of California

Nichols, B. (2001) 'Documentary film and the modernist avant-garde' in *Critical Inquiry*, 27, Summer 2001, pp. 580–610

Nichols, B. (2001) *Introduction to Documentary*, Bloomington: Indiana University Press

Ong, W.J. (1982, 2002) *Orality and Literacy: the technologizing of the word*, New York: Routledge

Okri, B. (1995) *Birds of Heaven*, London: Weidenfeld & Nicholson

Paget, D. (1998) *No other Way to tell it: Dramadoc/Docudrama on Television*, Manchester: Manchester University Press

Pearce, G. and McLaughlin, C. (2007) *Truth or Dare: Art and Documentary*, Bristol: Intellect

Perkins, R. and Stollery, M. (2004) *British Film Editors: The heart of the story*, London: BFI

Porcello, T. (2004) 'Speaking of sound: language and the professionalization of sound-recording engineers', *Social Studies of Science*, 34 (5), pp. 733–58

Rabinowitz, P. (1993) 'Wreckage upon Wreckage: History, Documentary and the Ruins of Memory', *History and Theory*, 32 (2)

Rascaroli, L. (2009) *The Personal Camera: Subjective Cinema and the Essay Film*, London: Wallflower

Renov, M. (1993) *Theorising Documentary*, New York: Routledge

Reynaud, B. (2003) 'Dancing with Myself, Drifting with my Camera: the emotional Vagabonds of China's New Documentary', *Senses of Cinema*, September

Richie, D. (2003) *Doing Oral History: a practical guide*, Oxford: OUP

Rieser, M. and Zapp, A. (eds) (2002) *New Screen Media: Cinema/Art/Narrative*, London: Routledge

Rifkin, J. (2000) *The Age of Access: the new culture of hyper capitalism, where all of life is a paid-for experience*, New York: Tarcher/Putnam Books

Robinson, K. (2002) *Out of our Minds: learning to be creative*, Florida: Capstone

Roscoe, J. and Hight, G. (2001) *Faking it: mock-documentary and the subversion of factuality*, Manchester: Manchester University Press

Rosenthal, A. and Corner, J. (eds) (2005) *New Challenges for Documentary*, Manchester: Manchester University Press

Rotha, P. (1952) *The Documentary Film*, London: Faber & Faber

Rotha, P. (1963) *Documentary Film: The Use of the Film Medium to Interpret Creatively and in Social Terms the Life of the People as it Exists in Reality*, New York: Hastings House

Rothman, W. (1997) *Documentary Film Classics*, New York: Cambridge University Press

Rouch, J. (2003) *Cine-Ethnography*, Minneapolis: University of Minnesota

Russell, P. (2007) *100 British Documentaries*, London: BFI

Saunders, D. (2007) *Direct Cinema*, London: Wallflower

Schrader, P. (1972) *Transcendental Style in Film: Bresson, Ozu, Dreyer*, Los Angeles: University of California Press

Seife de, E. (2007) *This is Spinal Tap*, London: Wallflower

Sherman, S.R. (1998) *Documenting Ourselves: Film, Video and Culture*, Lexington: University of Kentucky Press

Shub, E. (1972) *Cinema is My Life*, Moscow: Isskustvo

Silverstone, R. (1985) *Framing Science: the making of a BBC documentary*, London: BFI

Simpson, J. (1988) *Touching the Void*, London: Macmillan

Skillset (2008) Creative Industries Workforce Survey (accessible online on skillset.org.uk)

Skillset (2009) Creative Industries Employment Census (accessable online on skillset.org.uk)

Storper, M. (1989) 'The transition to flexible specialisation in the US film industry: external economies, the division of labour, and the crossing of industrial divides', *Cambridge Journal of Economics*, 13, pp. 273–305

Swan, P. (1989) *The British Documentary Film Movement, 1926–1946*, Cambridge, Cambridge University Press

Tate (2006) *Making History: Art and Documentary in Britain from 1929 to Now*, Liverpool: Tate

Trinh, T.M. (1992) *Framer Framed*, New York: Routledge

Tobing Rony, F. (1996) *The Third Eye: Race, Cinema and Ethnographic Spectacle*, Durham: Duke University Press

Todorov, T. (1977) *Poetics of Prose*, Ithaca, NY: New York University Press

Totaro, D. 'Film on the Internet', *Offscreen*, 11 (1) (31 January 2007); available at http://www.offscreen.com/index.php/phile/essays/film_on_the_internet/

Truffaut, F. (1985) *Hitchcock*. New York: Simon & Schuster

Ursell, G. (2000) 'Television production, issues of exploitation, commodification and subjectivity in the UK Television markets, in *Media, Culture and Society*, 22, pp. 805–25

Vaughan, D. (1999) *For Documentary: 12 Essays*, Berkeley: University of California Press

Vertov, D. (1984, 1992) *Kino-Eye: The Writings of Dziga Vertov*, ed. A. Michelson, London: Pluto Press

Vicente, A. (2008) 'Documentary viewing platforms', in W. de Jong and T. Austin (eds) *Rethinking Documentary. New Perspectives, New Practices*, Maidenhead: Open University Press, pp. 271–7

Waldman, D. and Walker, J. (eds) (1999) *Feminism and Documentary*, Minneapolis, University of Minnesota Press

Ward, P. (2005) *Documentary: The Margins of Reality*, London: Wallflower

Warren, C. (ed.) (1996) *Beyond Document: Essays on Non-Fiction Film*, London: New England University Press

Williams, L. (1995) 'Mirrors without Memories: Truth, History and the New Documentary', *Film Quarterly*, 46 (3)

Wilsher, J.C. and Grey, I. (2007) *Drama Documentary*, Writers' Guild of Great Britain

Winston, B. (1995) *Claiming the Real: The Documentary Film Revisited*, London: BFI

Winston, B. (2000) *Lies, Damn Lies, and Documentaries*, London: BFI

Wyver, J. (2007) *Vision on: Film, Television and the Arts in Britain*, London: Wallflower

Yinghi Chu (2007) *Chinese Documentaries*, London: Routledge

Youngblood, G. (1970) Expanded Cinema; available at http://www.ubu.com/historical/youngblood/expanded_cinema.pdf

Practice

The following books can be read in addition to relevant chapters in this book.

Abra, J. (1997) *The Motives for Creative Work*, Cresskill, New Jersey: Hampton Press

Alton, J. (1995) *Painting with Light*, Los Angeles: University of California Press

Angelini, Sergio (2007) *The Researcher's Guide*, London: Wallflower Press

Artis, A. (2007) *The Shut up and Shoot Documentary Guide: A Down and Dirty DV Production*, Oxford: Focal Press

Baker, M. (2005) *Documentary In The Digital Age*, London: Focal Press

Barbash, I. and Taylor, L. (1997) *Cross Cultural Film-making: A Handbook for Making Documentary and Ethnographic Films and Videos*, Berkeley: University of California Press

Belbin, M. (2002) *Team roles at work*, Oxford: Butterworth-Heinemann

Bernard, Curran, S. (2007) *Documentary Storytelling: Making Stronger and More Dramatic Nonfiction Films*, London: Focal Press

Bernard, Curran, S. (2004) *Documentary Storytelling for Video and Filmmakers*, Oxford: Focal Press

Bernard, Curran, S. and Rabin, K. (2008) *Archival Storytelling: A Filmmaker's Guide to Finding, Using, and Licensing Third-Party Visuals and Music*, Oxford: Focal Press

Block, B. (2007) *The Visual Story, Creating the Visual Structure of Film*, Oxford: Focal Press

Bowkett, S. (2005) *100 Ideas for Teaching Creativity*, London: Continuum

Brown, B. (2002) Cinematography: Theory and Practice, London: Focal Press

Cameron, J. (1992) *The Artist's Way: a course in discovering and recovering your creative self*, New York: Tarcher/Putnam

Chapman, J. (2000) *The British at War: Cinema, State and Propaganda 1939–1945*, London: I.B. Taurus

Chion, M. (1994) *Audio-Vision: Sound on screen*, New York: Columbia University Press

Chion, M. (2009) *Film: A sound art*, New York: Columbia University Press

Cunningham, M. (2005) *The Art of Documentary*, Berkeley: New Riders

Dancyger, K. (2006) *The Technique of Film and Video Editing*, Oxford: Elsevier

Emm, A. (2002) *Researching for Television and Radio*, London: Routledge

Evans, R. (2010) *Stand-Out Shorts: Shooting and Sharing Your Films Online*, London: Focal Press

Figgis, M. (2007) *Digital Filmmaking*, New York: Faber and Faber

Gawlinski, M. (2003) *Interactive Television Production*, Oxford: Focal Press

Gibbs, T. (2007) *The Fundamentals of Sonic Art and Sound Design*, Lausanne: AVA Publishing

Harrington, R. and Weiser, M (2008) *Producing Video Podcasts: A Guide for Media Professionals*, Oxford: Focal Press

Hewitt, J. and Vasquez, G. (2010) *Documentary Film-making: A Contemporary Field Guide*, Oxford: Oxford University Press

Hilman, C. (2006) *Creating Short Films for the Web*, Berkeley: New Riders

Holman, T. (2002) *Sound for Film and Television*, 2nd edn, Boston: Focal Press

Johnson, C. (2005) *Crafting Short Screenplays that Connect*, Burlington, MA: Elsevier/Focal Press

Kellison, C. (2005) *Producing for TV and Video: A Real-World Approach*, Oxford: Focal Press

Kellison, C. (2008) *Producing for TV and New Media: A Real-World Approach for Producers*, Oxford: Focal Press

Kriwaczek, P. (1997) *Documentaries for the Small Screen*, Oxford: Focal Press

Lees, N. (2010) *Greenlit: developing Factual/Reality TV Ideas from Concept to Pitch*, Basingstoke: Macmillan

LoBrutto, V. (1994) *Sound-on-Film: Interviews with creators of film sound*, Westport: Praeger

McKernan, L. (2007) *Moving Image Knowledge and Access: the BUFVC Handbook*, London: Wallflower

Prince, S.R. (2009) 'Principles of sound design', in *Movies and Meaning: An introduction to film*, 5th edn, Boston and London: Allyn & Bacon

Rabiger, M. (2009) *Directing the Documentary*, 5th edn, London: Focal Press/Elsevier

Rabiger, M. (1997) Directing: Film Techniques and Aesthetics London: Focal Press

Raymond, A. and Raymond, S. (1973) 'An American family', *American Cinematographer* (May 1973), 54 (5), p. 590

Reisz, K. and Miller, G. (1953, 1996) *The Technique of Film Editing*, Oxford: Focal Press

Rice, J. and McKernan, B. (2002) *Creating Digital Content*, Maidenhead: McGraw-Hill

Richie, D. (2003) *Doing Oral History; a practical guide*, Oxford: Oxford University Press

Rose, J. (2008) *Producing Great Sound for Film and Video*, 3rd edn, Boston: Focal Press

Rossi, F, (2005) *Trailer Mechanics: A Guide to Making Your Documentary Fundraising Trailer*, New York: MagaFilms

Ruoff, J. (1993) 'Conventions of sound in documentary', *Cinema Journal*, 32 (3), pp. 24–40

Schneider, N.J. (1989) *Handbuch Filmmusik. Vol. 2 Musik im dokumentarischen Film*, Munich: Verlag Ölschläger

Sonnenschein, D. (2001) *Sound Design: The expressive power of music, voice and sound effects in cinema*, Studio City, CA: Michael Wiese Productions

Sternberg, R. (1999) *Handbook of Creativity*, Cambridge: Cambridge University Press

Stradling, L. (2010) *Production Management for TV and Film*, Basingstoke: Macmillan

Toubiana, S., (2000) *The Misfits – Story of a Shoot*, London: Phaidon Press

Vineyard, J. (2000) *Setting up your shots: Great camera moves every filmmaker should know*, Michael Wiese

Ward, P., Bermingham, A. and Wherry, C. (2000) *Multi-skilling for Television Production*, Oxford: Focal Press

Warshawski, M. (2003) *Shaking the Money Tree: How to Get Grants and Donations for Film and Television*, New York: Michael Wiese Productions

Williams, A. (1980) 'Is sound recording like a language?' *Yale French Studies*, 60, pp. 51–66

Journals and magazines

Studies in Documentary Film
Creative Industries Journal
Journal of Creative Work
Broadcast
Dox
Screen International
Filmwaves

Useful websites

Every effort has been made to ensure that website addresses are current. All those listed here were accessed in November 2010, but it is possible that some may have changed since then.

4docs	http://www.4docs.org.uk/
Age of Stupid	http://www.spannerfilms.net
Amazon	http://www.amazon.com
Ameibo	http://www.ameibo.com
American Society of Cinematographers	www.ascmag.com
Artist's moving image, exhibition, distribution and publication	www.lux.org.uk
Atom Films	http://www.atom.com
Babelgum	http://www.babelgum.com
BBC	www.bbc.co.uk/filmnetwork
BBC Motion Gallery	http://www.bbcmotiongallery.com
Billboard	http://www.billboard.biz/bbbiz/ content_display/magazine/upfront/ e3i12fe2557a9382597671a522cc1cc901d
Brightcove	http://www.brightcove.com
British Film Institute, catalogue of historical documentaries	www.bfi.org.uk/filmdownloads www.britshorts.com
Brockett, Dan	http://www.kenstone.net/fcp_homepage/ location_sound.html
Canon USA	http://www.usa.canon.com/dlc/controller?act= GetArticleAct&articleID=2667
Catalogue and information on interactive documentary	www.interactivedocumentary.net
Comprehensive movie database	www.imdb.com
Content Republic	http://www.contentrepublic.com
Createspace	http://www.createspace.com
Creative Commons Licenses	http://creativecommons.org/about/licenses/ meet-the-licenses
Danish Documentary	http://www.danishdocumentary.com
Digital video cameras	http://en.wikipedia.org/wiki/ Digital_cinematography_cameras
Doc Space	http://www.docspace.org.uk
Dogma 2001: The New Rules for Internet Cinema	http://www.neocinema.com
DPA: high-quality Danish microphones (This website provides an excellent introduction to the professional use of microphones on location and in the studio.)	http://www.dpamicrophones.com/en/ Microphone-University.aspx
D-Word	http://www.d-word.com

Errol Morris	http://www.errolmorris.com
The EASA Media Anthropology Network is developing an annotated bibliography	http://www.philbu.net/media-anthropology/bibliography
European Documentary Network, co-producers, funding and education	www.edn.dk
Film Studies for Free	http://filmstudiesforfree.blogspot.com
Focal International (the trade association for Archive Libraries)	http://www.focalint.org/
Focal lengths	http://en.wikipedia.org/wiki/Focal_length
Francis Ford Coppola interview	http://www.youtube.com/watch?v=-wK9tHKVN80&feature=player_embedded#!
From Zero	http://fromzero.tv/eng.html
Funding information	www.britfilms.com/resources/fundinginformation
General cinematography blog	http://cinematography.com
Google Scholar enables you to search specifically for scholarly literature	www.scholar.google.com
Guide to Britain's film and TV history	www.screenonline.org.uk
IMDB	http://www.imdb.com
IndieFlix	http://www.indieflix.com
IndieGoGo	http://www.indiegogo.com/
Interactive Narratives	http://www.interactivenarratives.org/
Institute for Contemporary Art	www.ica.org.uk
International Documentary Networking Site	www.reelisor.com
iStock Photo	http://www.istockphoto.com/index.php
iTunes movie trailers	www.apple.com/trailers
Jaman	http://www.jaman.com
Joris Ivens	www.ivens.nl
Journal of the World Forum for Acoustic Ecology	http://interact.uoregon.edu/MediaLit/WFAE/journal/index.html
Kickstarter	http://www.kickstarter.com/
Massify	http://www.massify.com/
MediaChannel is a global network of more than 900 media-issues groups. It also provides links for the latest news on media industries, communication policy, technology and media arts.	http://www.mediachannel.org
Media Storm	http://www.mediastorm.org
Nature Footage	http://www.naturefootage.com
Net Flix	http://www.netflix.com
News e-bulletin for film industry	www.screendaily.com

Nichols, Bill: *Documentary and the Coming of Sound* discusses the transition from silent documentaries to sound documentaries.	http://filmsound.org/film-sound-history/BN
One Day Films	http://www.onedayfilms.com
One Line Film	http://www.onlinefilm.org/-/
Online magazine about contemporary documentaries and Filmmaking.	www.yidff.jp/docbox/docbox-e
Open Archive	http://www.archive.org/details/opensource_movies
Open Source Cinema	http://www.opensourcecinema.org
Overview of documentary film festivals	www.documentaryfilms.net/festivals
Sean McAllister	www.dazzlefilms.co.uk
Short documentary, production info and archive	http://www.seanmcallister.com
Short films sales agent	www.channel4.com/fourdocs
Surround sound	http://www.schoeps.de
To Shoot an Elephant	http://toshootanelephant.com/
Transmedia Generation	http://henryjenkins.org/2010/03/transmedia_generation.html
Tribe-funding/crowd-funding sources	http://www.biracy.com/
Tube Mogul	http://www.tubemogul.com
	www.ukscreen.com/screen
	www.vertigomagazine.co.uk
Vimeo	http://www.vimeo.com/
Watching and uploading short documentaries	www.mishorts.com
Website by and for documentary filmmakers with info on events, tips, jobs, festivals etc.	www.dfgdocs.com
Wikipedia	http://en.wikipedia.org/wiki/Books_published_per_country_per_year
Wikipedia	http://en.wikipedia.org/wiki/Itunes/
Without A Box	https://www.withoutabox.com/
YouTube	http://www.youtube.com/

Documentary filmmaking

An historical overview

Wilma de Jong

The selected overview here tends to be Anglo-Saxon and Eurocentric. Country-specific documentaries you can google and you will find information on specific documentary websites, Wikipedia or the Internet Movie Database (IMDb). For ethnographic documentaries you can go to the website of the Royal Anthropological Institute which offers a database and the possibility for interlibrary loans.

For an in-depth overview of the genre, see *Encyclopedia of Documentary Film* by I. Aitken (2005).

The following website offers a personalised but quite extensive overview: http://edendale.type-pad.com/weblog/2009/04/who-are-the-most-important-documentary-directors.html

1877

Edward Muybridge develops sequential photographs of horses in motion. He invents the zoopraxiscope, which made it possible to project and 'speed up' the photographs.

1883

Etienne Jules Marey develops chronophotography, the photography of people in movement.

1895

'It's life itself!' a member of the audience cried out when Auguste and Louis Lumière showed their films during the world's first public film screening on 28 December 1895 in the basement lounge of the Grand Café on the Boulevard des Capucines in Paris. The Lumière brothers' first films were:

- *The arrival of the train at the station*
- *Workers leaving the factory*
- *Feeding the baby*

Louis and Auguste Lumière

1895

A Senegalese woman is filmed by Félix-Louis Regnault during the Paris Exposition Ethnographique de l'Afrique Occidentale. This act started the use of the camera in ethnographic research.

1919

Russian filmmaker Dziga Vertov publishes his manifesto (*Kinoks-Revolution Manifesto*) in which he calls for a cinema that documents real life that reports 'truth'.

Dziga Vertov

1920s

Experimental filmmakers in Europe create impressionistic, poetic documentary forms. Experimentation with different editing techniques such as 'montage', associative narrative styles and more poetic visuals. The so-called 'city' films are well-known examples:

- *Berlin: A Symphony of a Great City (Berlin, die Symphonie der Grosstadt)* (1927, Walther Ruttmann)
- *Rien que les heures* (1926, Alberto Cavalcanti).

1922

Nanook of The North by Robert Flaherty is often considered to be the first feature-length documentary and one of the first ethnographic documentaries. It features many of the characteristics of future documentaries such as third-person narration but a subjective tone of voice and, as subject, indigenous 'others'.

- *Nanook of the North* (1922)
- *Moana* (1926)
- *Man of Aran* (1934)

Nanook

1922–25

Kino Pravda ('Film Truth'), news reportages by Dziga Vertov which develop into newsreels.

1925

Battleship Potemkin, Sergei Eisenstein.

1926

John Grierson (1898–1972) reviews *Moana* by Robert Flaherty for the *New York Sun* (February 8, 1926). He coins the term '**documentary**' in this article.

Other notable films of 1926 are:

Mechanics of the Brain (V.I. Pudovkin)
A Sixth of the World (Dziga Vertov)
Stride, Soviet (Dziga Vertov)
Melody of the World (Germany, Walter Ruttmann)
Menilmontant (France, Dimitri Kirsanoff)

1927

The Fall of the Romanov Dynasty (Esfir Shub)

The first 'compilation' documentary, based on archive footage from a variety of sources. Shub created a politically critical film which set up a new strand of documentary filmmaking – compilation documentaries. One could argue also that there was a tradition of female editors in this period, such as Heleen van Dongen (Joris Ivens) and Ruby Grierson, sister of John Grierson.

Esfir Shub

The Great Road (Esfir Shub)
The Bridge (Netherlands, Joris Ivens)

1928

The Russia of Nicholas II and Leo Tolstoy (Esfir Shub)
La Tour (The Eiffel Tower, France, René Clair)
La Zone (France, Georges Lacombe)

1928

John Grierson joins the British Empire Marketing Board (EMB) and sets up the EMB Film Unit. In the EMB, and subsequently within the film unit of the British General Post Office, Grierson produces a series of documentaries with different filmmakers, including Basil Wright, Humphrey Jennings, Alberto Cavalcanti, Edgar Anstey, Sir Arthur Elton, Stuart Legg and Harry Watt.

John Grierson

- *The Drifters* (1929)
- *Granton Trawler* (1934)

John Grierson

Humphrey Jennings

- *London Can Take It* (1940)
- *Fires Were Started* (1943)
- *Diary for Timothy* (1945)

Basil Wright

- *The Song of Ceylon* (1935)
- *Night Mail* (1936) (produced by Grierson; directed by Basil Wright)

1929

Dziga Vertov films *Man With The Movie Camera*.

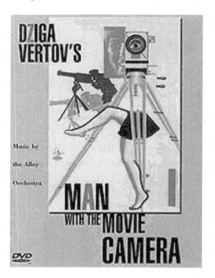

The film follows life in Moscow on one day from dawn till dusk. Vertov's aim is 'life caught unaware'. He is not just recording reality, however. Vertov attempts to highlight certain aspects and draw attention to the camera, the 'cinematic eye' or 'kino-glaz', which 'sees' more and differently from the human eye. Other notable films in this genre include:

- *Kino Pravda* (1922)
- *Kino Eye* (*Kino-glaz*) (1924)
- *Forward, Soviet!* (*Shagai, sovet!*) (1926)
- *Rain* (1929) (Netherlands, Joris Ivens)
- *Turksib* (Victor Turin, 1929)
- *Enthusiasm* (1931)
- *Three Songs About Lenin* (1934)

1930–37

The Workers' Film and Photo League is formed in the USA (Nykino in 1934, and Frontier Films in 1937) with the aim of making independent politically and socially progressive documentaries. Members include Joris Ivens, Paul Strand, Ralph Steiner, Leo Hurwitz and Willard Van Dyke.

1933

- *Land without Bread* (Luis Buñuel)

Pare Lorenz

Second half of the 1930s

The United States government produces a series of films as part of a public relations campaign on the New Deal. The following documentaries are produced as part of this publicity campaign.

- *The Plow That Broke the Plains* (1934, Pare Lorenz)
- *Native Land* (1942, Paul Strand)
- *The City* (1939, Willard Van Dyke)
- *The River* (1939, Willard Van Dyke)
- *Power and the Land* (1940, Joris Ivens)

Leni Riefenstahl

1935

Leni Riefenstahl, a German documentary filmmaker, makes *Triumph of The Will* about the annual Nazi Party rally of 1934. She is commissioned by Adolph Hitler and sets up a production with 13 cameras. The film is considered to be technically and cinematically sophisticated for its time and a well-known propaganda film for the Nazi Party.

- *Triumph of the Will* (*Triumph des Willens*) (1934)
- *Olympiad* (1936–38)
- *The Wonderful Horrible Life of Leni Riefenstahl*

Also in 1935, the newsreel series *March of Time* is developed by Roy Edward Larsen, an executive of Time–Life–Fortune, Inc. The *March of Time* series mixes re-enactments, location footage, and narration. The series runs until 1951 and is shown between feature films in the cinema.

- Covering 1935–40
- Covering 1940–48:
  Dawn of the Eye: Eyes of the World, 1919–1945
  Four Hours a Year: The Making of 'The March of Time'

1942–45

Documentary/propaganda series *Why We Fight*. Hollywood film director Frank Capra enlists in the US Army Signal Corps and leads this US-government-funded project to gather support for the war. Other filmmakers involved are Robert Flaherty, John and Walter Huston, Carl William Wyler, Carl Foreman, James Hilton, Lloyd Nolan and George Stevens.

- *Prelude to War* (1942)
- *The World at War* (1942)
- *The Nazis Strike* (1943)
- *Divide and Conquer* (1943)
- *The Battle of Britain* (1943)
- *The Battle of Russia* (1944)
- *The Battle of China* (1944)
- *War comes to America* (1945)
- *Appointment in Tokyo* (1945)

1950–60s

Emergence of Direct Cinema (USA), Cinéma Vérité (France) and Free Cinema (Canada and UK). Technological developments such as lightweight cameras with synchronised sound gave rise to a new form of documentary filmmaking.

For an overview of this documentary film tradition, see *Cinéma Vérité: Defining the Moment* (Peter Wintonick, 1999).

American tradition

According to the 'Ten commandments' of Direct Cinema by Drew Associates, published in the early 1960s (McDonald and Cousins, 1996: 250):

Robert Drew

- Thou shall not rehearse.
- Thou shall not interview.
- Thou shall not use commentary.
- Thou shall not use film lights.
- Thou shall not use stage events.
- Thou shall not dissolve.

British tradition

Free Cinema – exemplified by Karl Reisz and Lindsey Anderson (*We are the Lambeth Boys*, UK, 1959)

Technical characteristics of the observational documentary include:

– Long shots, long takes, natural light, sync sound, no direct address and absence of overt expression
– Hand-held camera
– Absence of voice-over
– Absence of re-enactment
– Editing that emphasises 'real time' and spatial realism
– Emphasis on loose causality
– Immediacy and intimacy
– No special effects
– Against the glossy 'professional' aesthetics of Hollywood cinema.

1955

Night and Fog (*Nuit et Brouillard*) (France, Alain Resnais)

1958

The Candid Eye, funded by The National Film Board of Canada: 13 half-hour documentaries, many of which represent a cinéma vérité, or direct cinema approach.

Richard Leacock

1960

Drew Associates produces *Primary*, covering John F. Kennedy and Hubert Humphrey in the Wisconsin Democratic presidential primary.

- *Letters from Vietnam* (1965)

Also in 1960, Jean Rouch, French ethnographic filmmaker, films *Chronique d'un Eté* (*Chronicle of a Summer*) about 'les parisiens' as a kind of tribe, involving his specific approach within the cinéma vérité tradition.

Jean Rouch

Russian-French tradition

- Jean Rouch: 'I'm one of the people responsible for this phrase (cinéma vérité) and it's really a homage to Dziga Vertov.'
- Dziga Vertov on documentary: 'Life caught unawares (or unrehearsed) (*Man with a Movie Camera*, Russia,1929)
- Jean Rouch, agent provocateur: '. . . to show people without masks, without make-up, to catch them through the eye of the camera in a moment when they are not acting, to read their thoughts, laid bare by the camera'. (Winston,1999:168)

1962

Lonely Boy by Wolf Koenig, a Canadian documentary filmmaker, on singer Paul Anka, and one of the first music concert films.

Lonely Boy

1963

Abraham Zapruder accidentally films the assassination of President John F. Kennedy with an 8 mm Bell & Howell home movie camera on 22 November.

1964

7 Up (UK, Paul Almond, Michael Apted)

Part of the *World in Action* series, the films follow a group of children growing up and as adults.

In *Point of Order*, filmmaker Emile de Antonio challenges the cinéma vérité tradition: 'Cinéma vérité is first of all a lie, secondly a childish presumption about the nature of film. . . . Only people without feelings or convictions could even think of making cinéma vérité. I happen to have strong feelings and some dreams and my prejudice is under and in everything I do.' As he uses footage from a variety of sources to make his 'leftist' point, his films are considered as compilation films. De Antonio films include:

- *Point of Order* (1964)
- *Rush to Judgment* (1967) . . . aka *The Plot to Kill JFK: Rush to Judgment*
- *In the Year of the Pig* (1968)
- *America is Hard to See* (1970)
- *Millhouse* (1971)
- *McCarthy: Death of a Witch Hunter* (1975) . . . aka *A Film of the Era of Senator Joseph R. McCarthy*
- *Underground* (1976)

1965

The War Game (Peter Watkins, UK)

1967

- *Don't Look Back*, D.A. Pennebaker on folk singer Bob Dylan.

Other Pennebaker films include:

- *Monterey Pop* (1967)
- *The War Room* (1993)
- *Moon Over Broadway* (1997)

Bob Dylan and D.A. Pennebaker

Also in 1967, *Titicut Follies* by Frederick Wiseman, prolific American filmmaker, whose observational approach on American institutions, schools and organisations provides a sometimes revealing inside view. Other Wiseman films include:

- *High School* (1968)
- *Hospital* (1970)
- *Welfare* (1975)

Frederick Wiseman

- *Meat* (1976)
- *Near Death* (1989)
- *Domestic Violence* (2001)

1968

Salesman by brothers Albert and David Maysles (with Charlotte Zwerin). Other Maysles brothers films include:

- *Gimme Shelter* (1970)
- *Grey Gardens* (1975)

Albert and David Maysles

1960s and 1970s

Filmmakers who engaged with the new social movements such as the civil rights, anti-war, women's and gay rights movements leave behind the more distanced observational approach of cinéma vérité filmmakers for a more politically engaged and activist approach. Above all, they provide subjective and minority points of view of the world.

Radical independent film collectives emerge, both in the UK and the USA.

- London Filmmakers Co. op.
- London Women's Film Group
- Sankofa
- Retake

1970s

The late 60s and 70s see the rise of the first-person or autobiographical documentaries due to the successful introduction of camcorders and an increase in popularity of a more subjective approach in documentary filmmaking. Examples of this genre include:

- *Daughters Rite* (USA,1979, Michelle Citron)
- *Sherman's March* (1986, Ross McElwee)
- *Tongues Untied* (1989, Marlon Riggs)
- *Intimate Stranger* (1991, Alan Berliner)
- *Silverlake Life* (1993, Tom Joslin, Peter Friedman)
- *Time Indefinite* (1993, Ross McElwee)
- *Dialogues with Madwomen* (1993, Irving Saraf and Allie Light)
- *Complaints of a Dutiful Daughter* (1994, Deborah Hoffman)
- *Healthy Baby Girl* (1995, Judith Helfand)
- *Halving the Bones* (1995, Ruth Ozeki Lounsbury)
- *I for India* (2005, Sandhya Suri)
- *51 Birch Street* (USA, 2005, Doug Block)
- *My Architect* (USA, 2005, Daniel Kahn)
- *The Gleaners and I* (France, 2000, Agnes Varda)
- *The Beaches of Agnes* (France, 2009, Agnes Varda)

1970

The Sorrow and the Pity (Le Chagrin et la Pitié) by French documentary filmmaker Marcel Ophuls

1971

The Act of Seeing with One's Own Eyes by Stan Brakhage, experimental documentary filmmaker and video artist

1973

An American Family, 12-part series broadcast by PBS (Alan and Susan Raymond). This series is considered to be the precursor of what is soon to be described as 'reality TV'. It follows the daily life of the Loud family.

1980

The Life and Times of Rosie the Riveter (USA, Connie Field)

1983

Reassemblage, Trinh Minh-ha, whose other works include:

- *Surname Viet Given Name Nam* (1989)

1983 also saw the release of *Sunless* (*Sans Soleil*) by Chris Marker, France. Other significant works include:

- *Lettre de Sibérie* (1957)
- *La Jetée* (1962)
- *A Grin Without a Cat* (1977)
- *Tokyo Days* (1988)
- *Berlin 1990* (1990)
- *The Last Bolshevik* (1992)
- *Le 20 heures dans les camps* (1993)
- *One Day in the Life of Andrei Arsenevich* (2000)
- *Immemory* (2009)

Chris Marker

Harun Farocki (Germany), *Ein Bild* (*An Image*). Other Farocki films include:

- *Die Bewerbung* (*Interview*) (1996) USA
- *Stilleben* (*Still Life*) (1997) USA
- *Ich glaubte Gefangene zu sehen* (2000) (*I Thought I Was Seeing Convicts*)
- *Die Schöpfer der Einkaufswelten* (2001) (*The Creators of Shopping Worlds*)
- *Erkennen und Verfolgen* (2003) (*War at a Distance*)
- *Nicht ohne Risiko* (2004) (*Nothing Ventured*) USA
- *Aufschub* (*Respite*) (2007)
- *Übertragung* (*Transmission*) (2008)
- *Zum Vergleich* (2009) (*By Comparison* – Europe, *In Comparison* – Canada)

1984

Far from Poland by Jill Godmilow. Her films also include:

* *What Farocki Taught* (1998)

1984 also saw the release of *This is Spinal Tap*, a 'mockumentary' by Rob Steiner about a fictional heavy metal band. This was the real start of a specific strand of documentary filmmaking – mock documentaries. Others in this genre include:

* *How to Irritate People* (1968) 'guide' by John Cleese, featuring Graham Chapman, Michael Palin and Connie Booth
* *Take the Money and Run* (USA, 1969, Woody Allen)
* *All You Need Is Cash* (aka *The Rutles*) (UK, 1979, Eric Idle and Gary Weis)
* *Zelig* (USA, 1983, Woody Allen)
* *Man Bites Dog* (Belgium, 1992, Rémy Belvaux)
* *Bob Roberts* (USA, 1992, Tim Robberts)
* *The Day Today* (UK, 1994, Chris Morris and Armando Iannucci)
* *Forgotten Silver* (New Zealand, 1995, Costa Botes and Peter Jackson)
* *Brass Eye* (UK, 1997, Chris Morris)
* *Best in Show* (UK/USA, 2000, Christopher Guest)
* *Mike Bassett: England Manager* (UK, 2001, Steve Barron)
* *Confetti* (France, 2002, Debbie Isitt)
* *First on the Moon* (Russia, 2005, Aleksey Fedorchenko)
* *Chalk* (2006, Mike Akel)
* *Borat: Cultural Learnings of America for Make Benefit Glorious Nation of Kazakhstan* (USA/UK, 2006, Sasha Baron Cohen)
* *Gamers: The Movie* (USA, 2006, Chris Folino)
* *Behind the Mask: The Rise of Leslie Vernon* (USA, 2006, Scott Glosserman)
* *Believe* (USA, 2007, Loki Mulholland)
* *Farce of the Penguins* (USA, 2007, Bob Saget)
* *Brüno* (USA/UK, 2009, Sasha Baron Cohen)
* *The Far Left* (UK, 2009, Adam Nicholas)
* *Welcome to Gentle Waters* (2010, Brent Kado and Jessica Hardy)

1985

Shoah (*Annihilation*) by Claude Lanzmann, France

1986

Handsworth Songs by John Akomfrah (UK), one of the founders of the Black Audio Collective. Among his other films are:

* *Testament* (1988)
* *Who Needs a Heart* (1991)
* *Seven Songs for Malcolm X* (1993)
* *Call of Mist* (1998)
* *Speak Like a Child* (1998)
* *Riot* (1999)

1988

The Thin Blue Line (Errol Morris, USA). Other documentaries by Errol Morris include:

- *The Dark Wind* (1991)
- *A Brief History of Time* (1991)
- *Fast, Cheap and Out of Control* (1997)
- *Mr. Death: The Rise and Fall of Fred A. Leuchter, Jr.* (1999)
- *The Fog of War* (2003)
- *Standard Operating Procedure* (2008)

1989

Looking for Langston, by Isaac Julien, filmmaker and installation artist, and one of the founders of the Sankofa Film and Video Collective. Other Isaac Julien films are:

- *Who Killed Colin Roach?* (1983)
- *Young Soul Rebels* (1991)
- *Black and White in Colour* (1992)
- *The Attendant* (1992)
- *The Darker Side of Black* (1993)
- *Frantz Fanon: Black Skin, White Mask* (1996)
- *Three* (1999)
- *The Long Road to Mazatlan* (1999)
- *Paradise Omeros* (2002)
- *BaadAsssss Cinema* (2002)
- *Baltimore* (2003)
- *Derek* (2008)

Isaac Julien

1990

The Civil War (Ken Burns, USA)
Paris is Burning (Jennie Livingstone, Canada)

1991

American Dream (Barbara Kopple, USA)

1991

Amateur filmmaker George Holliday captures how Los Angeles police arrest and beat Rodney King. The footage became important evidence in the subsequent trial.

1992

Manufacturing Consent (USA) by Mark Achbar and Peter Wintonick. Achbar also directed *The Corporation* (USA, 2003) together with Jennifer Abbott and writer Joel Bakan.

Mark Achbar, Jennifer Abbott, Joel Bakan

1994

Hoop Dreams (Steve James, USA)

1996

When We Were Kings (Leon Gast, USA)

1999

Buena Vista Social Club (Wim Wenders, USA)

2000

Dark Days (Mark Singer, USA)

2002

Etre et Avoir (Nicolas Philibert, France)
Feltham Sings (Roger Graef, Brian Hill and Simon Armitage)

2003

Touching the Void (Kevin Macdonald, UK). Macdonald's other films include:

- *The Making of an Englishman* (1995)
- *One Day in September* (2000)
- *Humphrey Jennings* (2000)
- *A Brief History of Errol Morris* (2000), interview with Errol Morris
- *Being Mick* (2001)
- *My Enemy's Enemy* (2007)
- *The Eagle of the Ninth* (2010)

Also notable in 2003 was *Capturing the Friedmans* (Andrew Jarecki, USA)

2004

SuperSize Me (Morgan Spurlock, USA)
Born into Brothels (Zana Briski, Ross Kaufman, USA)
Darwin's Nightmare (Hubert Sauper, France)
Control Room (Jehane Noujaim, USA)

2005

Grizzly Man (Werner Herzog, USA)

Other Herzog documentaries include:

- *Land of Silence and Darkness* (1971)
- *Echoes From a Somber Empire* (1990)
- *Bells from the Deep* (1995)
- *Little Dieter Needs to Fly* (1997)
- *My Best Fiend* (1999)
- *Wheel of Time* (2003)
- *The White Diamond* (2004)
- *Encounters at the End of the World* (2007)

Selected contemporary documentary filmmakers

Nick Broomfield

British documentary filmmaker who tends to make 'performative documentaries'. He works with small crews and records sounds himself while interviewing his subjects or commenting on the production process. Recently he has moved into docudrama, what he describes as 'Direct Cinema' as he works with non-actors who play themselves or related roles (*Battle for Haditha* (2007), *Ghosts* (2006)). Other Nick Broomfield documentaries include:

- *Proud to be British* (1973)
- *Juvenile Liaison* (1975)
- *Soldier Girls* (1981)
- *Chicken Ranch* (1983)
- *Driving me Crazy* (1988)
- *The Leader, His Driver and the Driver's Wife* (1991)
- *Too White For Me* (1992)
- *Aileen Wuornos: The Selling of a Serial Killer* (1992)
- *Tracking Down Maggie* (1994)
- *Heidi Fleiss: Hollywood Madam* (1995)
- *Kurt and Courtney* (1998)
- *Biggie & Tupac* (2002)
- *Aileen: Life and Death of a Serial Killer* (2003)
- *His Big White Self* (2006)
- *A Time Comes* (2009)

Kim Longinotto

Contemporary hybrid observational filmmaker who includes interviews in her films. Many of her films feature women, highlighting the discrimination, abuse or oppression they face in different cultures. Her documentaries include:

- *Pride of Place* (1976)
- *Theatre Girls* (1978)
- *Underage* (1982)
- *Eat the Kimono* (1989)
- *Hidden Faces* (1990)
- *The Good Wife of Tokyo* (1992)
- *Dream Girls* (1994)
- *Shinjuku Boys* (1995)
- *Rock Wives* (1996)
- *Divorce Iranian Style* (1998)
- *Gaea Girls* (2000)
- *Runaway* (2001)
- *The Day I Will Never Forget* (2002)
- *Sisters in Law* (2005)
- *Hold Me Tight, Let Me Go* (2007)
- *Rough Aunties* (2008)
- *Pink Saris* (2010)

Molly Dineen

Self-shooting documentary filmmaker who interacts with her subjects and is well known for her ability to make close contact with her subjects. Though often presented as a performative documentary filmmaker, she is never on screen; we only hear her voice. She could therefore be better described as a participatory filmmaker. Her documentaries include:

- *The Ark* (4 TV episodes, 1993)
    - *Tooth and Claw* (1993)
    - *The Political Animals* (1993)
    - *Natural Selection* (1993)
    - *Survival of the Fittest* (1993)
- *In the Company of Men* (3 TV episodes, 1995)
    - *The Brotherhood* (1995)
    - *The Novice* (1995)
    - *The Commander* (1995)
- *Geri* (1999)

- *The Lord's Tale* (2002)
- *The Lie of the Land* (2007)

Brian Hill

Documentary filmmaker known for his bold and brave documentaries, who is not scared to take a distinct approach and point of view on the topic he is filming. He recently also moved into drama. His films include:

- *Falling Apart* (2002)
- *Bella and the Boys* (2004)
- *The True Voice of Murder* (2006)
- *The True Voice of Rape* (2006)
- *The True Voice of Prostitution* (2006)

Brian Hill's documentaries include:

- *Cutting Edge – The Club* (1994) (TV episode)
- *Drinking for England* (1998)
- *Robbie Williams: Nobody Someday* (2002)
- *Feltham Sings* (2002)
- *Songbirds* (2005)
- *Cutting Edge – The Bigamist Bride: My Five Husbands* (2009) (TV episode)
- *Climate of Change* (2010)

Marc Isaacs

Self-shooting director who addresses a wide range of social issues through intimate and personal stories of his main characters. His documentaries include:

- *Lift* (2001)
- *Calais: The Last Border* (2003)
- *Someday My Prince Will Come* (2005)
- *All White in Barking* (2007)

Daisy Asquith

Self-shooting director known for her intimate portraits. She once made the comment challenging the 'boy' documentary filmmakers and their technical 'toys': 'If the camera does not fit in my handbag I won't use it.' Her films include:

- *Fifteen* (2003)
- *Whatever: A Teenage Musical* (2004) (TV)
- *Cutting Edge – The House Clearers* (2005)
- *My New Home 2005–10* (TV)
- *The Oldest People in the World* (2007) (TV)
- *Clowns* (2008)
- *Kimberley: Young Mum 10 Years On* (2009) (TV)
- *Liz Smith's Summer Cruise* (2009) (TV)
- *My Weird and Wonderful Family* (2010) (TV)

Michael Moore

Political and campaigning filmmaker who is always present in his films, asking the questions many Americans may ask themselves about some significant social issues in their society. His films include

- *Roger & Me* (1989)
- *Pets or Meat: The Return to Flint* (1992) (TV)
- *Bowling for Columbine* (2002)
- *Fahrenheit 9/11* (2004) 'Palme d'Or' in Cannes
- *Sicko* (2007)
- *Captain Mike Across America* (2007)
- *Slacker Uprising* (2008)
- *Capitalism: A Love Story* (2009)

Index

Made in the USA
Las Vegas, NV
26 August 2021